The United States

and Civilization

. . . so must I nedes confesse and graunt that many thinges be in the Utopian weale publique, whiche in our cities I maye rather wishe for, then hope after.—THOMAS MORE

The
United States
and Civilization

John U. Nef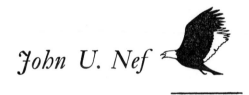

Second Edition

Revised and Enlarged

The University of Chicago Press

Chicago and London

Library of Congress Catalog Card Number: 67-28465

THE UNIVERSITY OF CHICAGO PRESS, CHICAGO & LONDON

The University of Toronto Press, Toronto 5, Canada

To Robert Maynard Hutchins

Preface to the Second Edition

It is more than twenty-five years since I released this book for publication in November, 1941, a few weeks before the United States entered the Second World War. Conscious though I was of my inadequate preparation for treating so vast a subject as the relation of this country to the major forces underlying a conflict from which many Americans had thought we could stand aloof, I felt I must speak.

What compelled me was the conviction that the future of the United States had become ineluctably entwined with the future of the entire world. In an age of increasing specialization, not least in my calling of historical scholarship, there seemed to exist an overwhelming need to discover something of the essence of the whole human being and of his relation to another essence equally elusive: the whole of history.

The French have a saying to sustain the bold in scholarship: "Il vaut mieux dire des bêtises que de ne rien dire!" " 'Tis better to make some blunders than to make the mistake of saying nothing!" That reflection encouraged me, between 1938 and 1941, to put aside some of my historical researches in order to write *The United States and Civilization*.

The book has been out of print for years. It is an honor to be invited by The University of Chicago Press to prepare a second edition. Doing so has been, in a way, as bold a venture as carrying out the original design. It is doubtful whether there was ever a quarter century of such rapid change in the human condition as the quarter century since 1942. How then can one make over a book intended as an appeal to mankind in the early forties so that it becomes an appeal to a new generation of multiplying mankind on the threshold of the seventies?

The logical answer to that problem might seem a new book.

But I find it as impossible for the same man to write two books on the same subject as for the same body to be in two places at one time. What I am now releasing is not the book I should have written if I had started on this assignment from scratch in the sixties. The fact that I wrote the essay long ago conditions my efforts extensively to revise it and in places to write afresh. While there are new ideas in it, what has resulted is, in many ways, the same old book!

How has it been mended?

The essay divides into three parts. Part Two (Ends of Civilization), which treats of human values, remains essentially as in the first edition. Nor does this seem inappropriate in view of the thesis which underlies the whole essay, that there are fundamental values independent of time and common to humanity.

Part One (Civilization at the Crossroads) treats briefly those historical developments, especially in western Europe, which led toward civilization and then toward a questioning of basic values underlying civilization. For two reasons it seemed necessary to do this part over rather extensively. First, because the conditions of crisis, which confront the United States and other countries, have been changed by the fantastically rapid changes in the human condition during the last twenty-five years. We are again at a crossroads, but it is another crossroads farther on the way. Second, because as an historian I have in the interval of a quarter century learned a bit more than I once knew about the history which brought civilization to a crossroads. Several of my sketches for a history of civilization, which were in manuscript in 1941–42, have been extensively developed and have now been published as books. Other aspects of that history, which I then ignored, have begun to take form in my mind.

Here are examples of new knowledge I have acquired, examples important for the argument of the essay as a whole and particularly Part One. Since writing the book I have learned that the word "civilization" had a definite and rather precise meaning when it was introduced in print two centuries ago (see pages 35–37). It has since acquired a different meaning. In the first edition the word is used in both senses, and so the meaning I attach to it was left ambiguous. As the original meaning of the word corresponds to the new view of historical evolution on which I have come to wager since the first edition was printed (a view which is hardly shared by most of my contemporaries[1]), "civilization" is now used with its original meaning throughout.

The new view of historical evolution, which I have come by as a consequence of my researches since 1941, has led me to drop out several sections of the old book. As they appear in the second edition, much of chapter 2, all of chapter 3, and section IV of chapter 4 are replacements. These have been substituted for different sections which appeared in the first edition, sections which represented my best judgment at the time but which I now regard as obsolete.

Part Three (Means of Approach) treats of possible reforms which might help humanity in general, and the United States in particular, to move constructively in the direction of those ends of civilization discussed in Part Two. The approaches which seem most hopeful today are in some important respects different from those which seemed most hopeful in 1941. Insofar as possible, I have tried to emend the first edition in the light of what has been happening since the end of the Second World War, and in the light of new experiences which life has brought me during the last three years. I hope both a more contemporary and a less imperfect exposition of possible reforms is presented than can be found in the version that has been long out of print.

In setting about to mend *The United States and Civilization* I have been fortified by the impression the essay created when

[1] See below, chap. 4 (IV).

it came out among seven friends, the first five of whom are no longer alive: Artur Schnabel, Alfeo Faggi, Waldemar Gurian, Kurt Wolff, William R. Castle, Jacques Maritain, and the Honorable James H. Douglas (whose advice in the last stage of preparing a text for publication has made this new edition less imperfect than it would have been). Out of most different national origins, upbringings, temperaments, professional careers, and religious persuasions, they all believed in this book and were glad it had been written. Having now reached an age and a domestic condition which happily relieve me from worldly ambition, I feel free to say, in all humility, that I hope their belief is not altogether without foundation.

What most of all has given me the temerity to try again, has been my companionship with my wife, Evelyn Stefansson Nef, whom I met just three years ago.

Among other less important things she has helped me with the revision. Proof correcting has been simplified by Mrs. R. Armour, my most efficient secretary in Chicago, whose admirable services have been at my disposal for more than twenty years. During the past year I have been assisted here in Washington by Mrs. Deborah Hollenbeck Trzyna, whose fresh outlook and extraordinary intellectual resourcefulness, energy, and enthusiasm have been the more meaningful for this book because she is a responsible member of the generation born and educated since the first edition was written.

JOHN NEF

Washington, D.C.
September 1, 1967

Preface to the First Edition

Some students at a neighboring college recently invited me to speak to them. Uncertain as to what kind of subject would be appropriate for the occasion, I appealed for advice, through a friend, to one of their professors whom I had met. This was the substance of his reply: In company with many other members of the "lost generation," I obviously felt, he said, that much was wrong with the kind of education we had had and with the civilization of which we found ourselves a part. Two world wars within three decades had done nothing to dispel our doubts. He suggested that I explain what is wrong, why it is wrong, and what can be done about it!

Those are the questions with which my essay is concerned. I need scarcely say that it makes no pretense at supplying either comprehensive or sufficient answers! I release it for publication with many misgivings, which arise from a deep sense of my inadequate endowment and training. But my essay is not the product of a hasty impulse. It was written before the professor asked me his questions. The argument and structure of Part One took form in my mind at least as early as 1934. I have made use of notes that I began collecting, in odd moments, in 1919 and 1920, when I spent my Junior and Senior years at Harvard following the Armistice. Such inadequate qualifications as I have for my task are a love of art (which I owe to my mother, my father, and my wife) and a study that I have been making of industrial history in relation to the history of civilization since the Renaissance. The present book is in the nature of an epilogue to that study—far the greater part of which remains to be completed, though I have in manuscript sketches for the whole of it. Epilogues should not be printed in advance of the work they conclude, and my excuse for publishing this one is the uncertainty of the times and the apparent relevancy to the issues that confront the United States today of the lessons which history has taught me. They are issues that need to be faced without delay. If, as I scarcely dare to hope, my essay should find a few readers and encourage them to face these issues, its purpose would be attained.

My historical work has kept me rather continually occupied during the past twenty years, so that I have had little opportunity to turn aside from it. Although I published articles on subjects treated in this book as early as 1939, it would not have appeared as soon as it has if Emery T. Filbey had not done me the honor of asking me to lecture under the auspices of the Walgreen Foundation in the spring of 1941.

My essay might never have been written at all but for the generous and constant encouragement I have received from the distinguished American to whom it is dedicated. Thanks to him, it is at the University of Chicago alone that the important problems with which I have attempted to deal have been seriously and continually raised during the last decade. The essay itself has benefited in many ways, as will be apparent, from his written works and from his speeches. It has been greatly improved, in ways that will be less apparent, by the frequent advice and help that he has given me at various stages of composition. I need hardly add that, like the other friends who have kindly assisted me, he is in no way responsible for the conclusions or the nature of the argument.

My wife has helped me in all manner of ways. My book treats, from a somewhat different point of view, several subjects she has dealt with in a book which she had in hand long before I began this one, and which should soon be published.[1] Suffice it to say that I am indebted to her, not she to me, for the resemblances.

[1] A part of that book was published after her death (Elinor Castle Nef, *Letters and Notes, Volume One,* ed. John Nef [Los Angeles: privately printed, 1953]). Material for the rest of her book, in typescript and manuscript, is in the archives of the University of Chicago and can provide a basis for an additional volume or volumes.

Professor Frank H. Knight has read through the whole essay, either in typescript or in proof, with a care for my interests that I would describe as Christian were I not afraid of offending him. It will be understood that he is in no way implicated in the result by the fact that his criticisms and suggestions have helped me to improve the work considerably. Professor Yves R. Simon has done much for Part Two. Professor Quincy Wright and Mr. James Dingwall, both of whom kindly read through an earlier version of the book, when it was in the form of lectures, made several useful suggestions.

I have derived help and encouragement from a number of friends and scholars who have not read the book. My obligations to Professor R. H. Tawney and Professor Jacques Maritain will be obvious. Both of them have gone out of their way to help me. Others whom I should like to thank also are Professor E. A. Duddy, Professor A. L. Dunham, Dr. Earl Harlan, Miss Stella Lange, the late Professor Marcel Moye of the University of Montpellier, Professor Robert E. Park, Dr. Artur Schnabel, Mr. Harrington Shortall, and the Rev. Von Ogden Vogt. Parts of several chapters have appeared, in a somewhat different form, in the *Review of Politics*, and I am under special obligations to its editor, Dr. Waldemar Gurian. Parts of two chapters were published in 1939 in the *General Magazine and Historical Chronicle* and the *University of Chicago Magazine*.

I am very grateful to the Walgreen Foundation for putting at my disposal the resources necessary to see the book through the press. My relations with the foundation were made especially pleasant by the thoughtfulness of its secretary, Professor William T. Hutchinson. The staff of The University of Chicago Press have provided me with technical assistance in connection with the typescript and proofs which only a person who has published books elsewhere can adequately appreciate. I am indebted to Mrs. Margaret DeVinney for her careful typing, and to Dean Robert Redfield and Miss Diane Greeter for putting her services at my disposal.

November 19, 1941

Contents

Contents

Part Three

Means of Approach

1 Introduction

History can teach what has been. It cannot teach what ought to be. It cannot even settle what is possible.

For a conception of what ought to be our ancestors turned, not to history, but to philosophy. According to traditions which derive from the ancient Greeks (Plato and Aristotle foremost among them), and also, I believe, from the ancient Chinese, the purpose of philosophy is to understand the true, the good, and the beautiful, insofar as a knowledge of them is accessible to human genius.

These philosophical traditions were adopted in the light of revelation by Christian, Indian, and Muslim philosophers during the two thousand years which followed the times of Buddha and later of Christ, down through the fifteenth century. During more recent times, beginning in Europe and America with the rise of the modern sciences in the late sixteenth and seventeenth centuries, and especially after Hume, Kant, Jefferson, and Tocqueville (who died in 1859), the conviction that truth could be defined in philosophical terms lost its hold on the minds of the intelligentsia. In the realms of virtue and of beauty, the existence of guiding moral and aesthetic principles was questioned and increasingly denied.

During these more recent times, the material conditions of life on this planet have been transformed. The spread of industrial civilization to Asia, Latin America, and Africa, the astounding multiplication of economic output and of population, the mechanization and automation of work, the application of new sources of energy culminating during the past twenty-five years in resort to power produced by nuclear fission and in journeys to outer space, were frequently considered as justifying the abandonment of firm principles. It came to be assumed that, not only does the manner of seeking to achieve the good and the beautiful change, as had always been recognized by great philosophers, but also the nature of the good and the beautiful. Insofar as the existence of the true was acknowledged, it was treated more and more, at least since the times of Auguste Comte, as the preserve of the sciences, to be proved or disproved by scientific demonstration.

Many among the modern intelligentsia appear to believe that the prevailing confusion concerning the goals of life is not only inevitable but healthy. They may be right. Certainly it is in the interest of individual liberty to respect their convictions. But in respecting these, should it not be recognized that the denial of the existence of truth, as the greatest ancient philosophers conceived of truth, is itself a *belief*, not a scientifically proved proposition? Should not the same liberty of speech therefore be accorded those who *believe* in the existence of truth?

This book puts forward, as an hypothesis, the proposition that truth exists, although it is beyond the power of any individual, or any collectivity, to possess it. If this hypothesis be accepted for the sake of discussing the goals of civilization, then the most important task of those who share it and who are dedicated to philosophy, to letters, or to the arts is to contribute to truth, to virtue, and to beauty, in those realms in which the sciences supply at the best inadequate and at the worst misleading answers.

The adoption of such a position need not involve the rejection of the rich mines of fresh knowledge unearthed by modern research, and refined by modern thought into new and often illuminating theories. If there should be fixed principles beyond all that transpires in the material universe, it should indeed be recognized that, with recent material changes, the *means* of discovering truth, of serving virtue, and of creating beauty have been profoundly modified. The sciences have the great task of guiding humanity in finding the most promising ways of rendering these principles more concrete and of discovering better means of serving them.

In one of his later papers T. S. Eliot wrote: "Of revealed religions, and of philosophical systems, we must believe that one is right and the others wrong. But wisdom is . . . the same for all men everywhere."[1] The need has never been so great as it is now to heal the divisions among mankind, to unite humanity by common hopes. To declare, as Eliot did, that wisdom is the same for all is to emphasize our common humanity. It is on behalf of all men and women that this book is written. It attempts to explore the ground of philosophical renewal, in terms that are intelligible to any serious person concerned with the future of mankind, in the hope that by doing so others may be encouraged to till that ground.

A faith in the universality of wisdom is meaningless unless it is accompanied by humility, by recognition that no man has or can have access in any final sense to wisdom. Those who are dedicated to the search for it are wary of categorical assertions. They never seek to implement their visions by force or by exercising power. They seek only to persuade, and hope to reach those who are already partially convinced. Like Socrates, they are forever asking questions, likely to provoke something approaching the right answers. Like Socrates, in critical moments of existence—as when the artist has to make decisions, the lover to choose, the believer to face the consequences of his belief—they are more uncertain of their uncertainty than those who deny the existence of beauty, virtue, and truth are certain of their certainty.

The transformation of the material world has been accompanied by revolutionary discoveries in the human as well as in the natural sciences. Recent anthropological, archeological, paleontological, sociological, psychological, historical, and economic discoveries are not alternatives to the search for wisdom. Nor is the search for wisdom a threat to advances in

[1] T. S. Eliot, *On Poetry and Poets* (London, 1957), p. 226.

knowledge. It should help to reveal, to the advantage of truth, not only the limitations of scholarship in all the sciences, natural as well as human, but the most noble uses to which new scientific discoveries can be put. Vast and rich resources have been made available, especially during the past two hundred years, concerning the economic, the political, the religious, the intellectual, and the cultural conditions of different individuals, different nations, and different societies—past as well as present. Philosophers can use new insights derived from these resources to present more concrete pictures of the nature of good ends than were possible for Plato, Confucius, Plotinus, Aquinas, ibn-Khaldun, Hume, or Kant, with their more meager knowledge in worlds without the material means which now exist for leading humanity toward unity.

What is lacking today in the study of history, and in social, economic, and humanistic studies generally, is a hierarchy of aesthetic, moral, and intellectual values. Such a hierarchy is no less important in the realm of scholarship than in the realms of architecture, music, literature, and the other arts.[2]

It is questionable whether the future progress of the physical, the biological, and the human sciences will lead of itself toward a hierarchy of civilizing values, such as emerged in Europe and America during the seventeenth and eighteenth centuries, partly out of men's religious origins, to provide foundations for the recent material progress which dazzles and astounds so many. Learned men have frequently assumed that, with the scientific advances they anticipate, the realm of speculation where intuition is the principal means of verification is bound continually to shrink. Doesn't this ignore a tendency, which many eminent scientists recognize, for scientific advances to raise new and hitherto unperceived problems as often as (or even more often than) they resolve old ones? Doesn't it ignore the discovery of relativity and indeterminacy in science? Doesn't it ignore also the imperative need persons

[2] See below, chap. 3 (IV).

have—especially those who exercise authority—to act on important issues which expert advice is never able precisely to cover? Are not the ways of faith and love indispensable in the search for that more comprehensive unity of human endeavor which the widening material universe is making possible? And are not faith and love governed by affirmations, unprovable scientifically, which derive their force from what Proust calls —speaking about works of art—"unexpected encounters with expressions of genius?"[3]

The limitations of the human sciences, as means of establishing the validity of constructive ideals, was demonstrated in an inquiry undertaken in 1949 by a number of social and biological scientists under the auspices of UNESCO. It was recognized that the doctrine of superior races, brought forward more than a century ago as an allegedly scientific proposition by Gobineau,[4] had much to do with the inhumanities we associate with the rise of the Nazis, the Second World War, and its sequels; with the liquidation in concentration camps of millions of men and women because they were supposed to belong to a particular non-Aryan race. It was hoped by some of the sponsors of the UNESCO inquiry that all scientists would unite in *proving* that all races *are* equal. Although a few of the participating scholars agreed on a rather innocuous statement tending to support such a proposition, several others expressed the view that it is no less *unscientific* to declare that all races are equal than to declare they are unequal.[5]

These scholarly experts said, in effect, that the humanistic and biological sciences, like the physical sciences,[6] cannot give

[3] Marcel Proust, Introduction to John Ruskin's *La Bible d'Amiens* (Paris, 1947), p. 92 n.

[4] *Essai sur l'inégalité des races humaines* (4 vols.; Paris, 1853–55).

[5] UNESCO, *The Race Concept* (Paris, 1952), pp. 11–16.

[6] For the limitations of the physical sciences in the search for truth, see Edwin Schrödinger, *Nature and the Greeks* (Cambridge, Eng., 1954), pp. 93–96, and the discussion of the matter in Nef, *Cultural Foundations of Industrial Civilization* (New York, 1961), pp. 65 ff.

Introduction

valid answers to all questions that are close to the heart and that are often of vital importance in the decisions reached by individuals. "I do not believe," wrote Professor Walter Landauer, one of the scientists who participated in the inquiry, "that ethical values can ever be directly derived from scientific data. . . . The declaration that 'all men are created equal' was a fine one and remains so, even though and in the best sense because it is untrue in the biological sphere."[7]

This suggests that if chained to science, ethics, like art, cannot fulfill the possibilities that it opens to humankind. Scientific exploration of behavior is often of great value. The discoveries of Freud, of Pavlov, and of the psychiatrists and psychologists who have followed, for example, have offered many people reassurances against terrors generated by religious dogma. But researches into behavior, like history, are incapable of teaching what ought to be. They cannot, by themselves, determine what is possible.

Insofar as the scientific spirit, with its sense of modesty and skepticism, helps men to be critical about knowledge and to recognize the limitations of all discoveries, including scientific ones, it becomes the servant of truth and faith. It is as servant, not as master, that the sciences can do most for mankind.

In the main as a result of achievements in the physical sciences and in their applications to technology, man is now confronted with greater dangers and blessed with greater opportunities than those which the human race has ever faced or enjoyed since considerable societies began to form many thousands of years ago. The way in which he responds to these dangers and opportunities depends not only upon further progress in the physical, the biological, and the human sciences, but upon the beliefs he holds. Men and women can hardly put forward what is best in them unless they acquire a greater faith than they have in the value of the human experience as they live it, unless they prefer life to death, goodness to evil,

7 UNESCO, *The Race Concept,* p. 19.

beauty to ugliness, love to hatred. Without rejecting the knowledge provided by scientific progress of every kind, humans
need to emancipate themselves from scientific determinism by
a new dedication to hopes, inspired by faith in the beautiful,
the good, and the true, that transcend scientific proof.

Nevertheless, it will be asked, what have these values, what
has wisdom, to do with the modern world? The answer is this:
Upon a vision of the ideal state, upon the vision of a fair realm
for mankind—conceived amid the skyscrapers, the noise of
turning machinery and of swiftly moving automobiles, railroad trains, and jet planes—depends the hope of the human
race to escape from slavery to computers, atomic energy, and
unscrupulous men whose credentials are the positions they hold
and the power they possess and exercise.

Part One

Civilization at the Crossroads

*L'amour de soi-même c'est
le contraire de l'amour.*

A. de Saint-Exupéry, CITADELLE

2 A New Breed of Mortals?

The extraordinary prosperity of the Western peoples in Europe and America at the beginning of the twentieth century, on the eve of the First World War, was reached after a series of efforts which began at about the time Leonardo da Vinci was born in 1452. In the twelfth and thirteenth centuries Europeans had generally agreed that the highest ideal of conduct was the renunciation of earthly pleasures, which found expression in the building of monasteries and the spread of religious orders. Men were disposed to subordinate actual life to certain absolute values, derived, as they believed, from God. Most of these values could be discovered by the human mind without revelation, insofar as men could rise above their human imperfections. It was never supposed that life in this world was actually being conducted in accordance with these values. Men saw evil all about them much more clearly than many see it today even when it stares them in the face. They had not, as many moderns have, other names to call it by.

Evil, for them, was explained by original sin. Its existence in no way led men to question the values themselves. By honoring these values, by groping after them here on earth, men felt they were working, however imperfectly, toward the Kingdom of God. The words which the priests and monks repeated, the plain chant in which so many participated in every Christian community from one end of Europe to the other, the orderly statues and the richly designed and colored windows of the recently built abbeys and cathedrals where people gathered—all reminded them of their common end. They were reminded, too, that in the end the wicked would be punished and the good rewarded. As an earnest of that belief, they possessed, through the Church, the knowledge that Christ had appeared on earth, a part of God in the image of a man.

Believing as men did in eternal life as the ultimate happiness, the goal of existence, they found it natural to work for the good of the individual through the good of each of the many communities into which the Christian world was divided. Artisans labored in common on common monuments. They seldom signed their work as individual artists. Philosophers almost never referred in writing by name to their contemporaries.

The twelfth and the thirteenth were centuries of rapidly growing population and remarkable material progress.[1] Hundreds of thousands of peasants were gaining freedom from serfdom, along with a higher standard of living. Townsmen were growing richer and much more numerous. There were many new openings for the amassing of considerable fortunes in trade, in finance, and even in industry.

The long and brilliant age of Romanesque and of the greatest Gothic architecture, when the area of cultivation and pasturage was extended in every direction into wooded, hilly, and even mountainous country, came to an end before the Black Death of 1348–50. The old conception of unity, derived from the subordination of actual life to the absolute values for which the Church stood, however inadequately, lost its force during the fourteenth century. This conception, whose origins go back to Roman times, had provided the turbulent continent of Europe with a measure of peace and order during the thirteenth century. This conception did not disappear in the fourteenth and fifteenth centuries, but its protagonists grew more dogmatic in their teaching and writing. As stated in its increasingly dogmatic form, the conception proved inadequate as a civilizing force. Its decay coincided with a period of religious, social, and economic disorder. The population of many countries stopped increasing. England, for example, apparently had fewer inhabitants in the fifteenth century than in the

[1] Cf. Nef, "L'art religieux et le progrès économique au 12e et 13e siècles," *Association pour l'histoire de la Civilisation* (Toulouse, 1952–53), pp. 23–29.

early fourteenth.[2] The volume of food and of industrial produce turned out each year in Europe as a whole seems to have
grown slowly, if at all, between about 1321, when Dante died,
and about 1452, when Leonardo da Vinci was born.

As the older conception of the ends of existence ossified,
a fresh conception began to form in a few men's minds. Its
beginnings can be traced back to the later fifteenth and the
early sixteenth centuries. This was a period of turmoil, bitterness, and bewilderment in the midst of material progress, not
unlike that which confronted the Western peoples again in the
twentieth century. The new conception of the Renaissance
gave a greater importance to the physical world, and to the
human being as an end in himself, than the Gothic conception
had done. It tended to make man the center of the universe.
As conceived by the greatest Italians of the Renaissance, the
highest goal of earthly existence for man consisted in the
embellishment of life by art. As conceived by the early Protestant theologians who were born in the midst of the new
Renaissance prosperity, the highest religious task was for man,
as an individual, to shoulder his moral obligations and strive
toward the Christian virtues.

The thought and art of the Renaissance were created by the
light of a vision of men and women, not as they usually are
in their daily lives, but as humans in the finest flights of their
imagination, with their love of perfection, would like to have
them. It was as if Italian artists were guided by a glimpse of
the mysterious distant land which Baudelaire was later to
evoke in the refrain to his "L'Invitation au Voyage":

> There, there is nothing else but grace and measure
> Richness, quietness, and pleasure.[3]

In the times of Botticelli, Raphael, and Carpaccio, the very
great majority of the people were concerned, as they have

[2] John Cox Russell, *British Medieval Population* (Albuquerque, N.M.,
1948), p. 235 and *passim*.

[3] As translated by Richard Wilbur.

always been, first and foremost with gaining their bread. But the goal toward which the industrial laborer, like the artist or the poet, was directed in his work was primarily quality, in the aesthetic sense, rather than quantity. The craftsman got far less in material things, in physical comforts of all kinds, than the workman in a mine or factory today, but he took part far more often than the modern laborer in work that was varied and absorbing. Its products were generally enduring. They did not disappear as quickly from the scene of the labor as do pieces of coal hewed by the machine which a modern miner sets in motion or the parts of an automobile or airplane on the assembly line after a factory worker has tightened a bolt with his wrench.

1. *The Industrial Expansion of the Renaissance*[4]

In contrast to the fourteenth and early fifteenth, the late fifteenth and early sixteenth centuries were a period of prosperity in most districts of Continental Europe. The Middle Ages drew to a close in the midst of great movements of discovery, colonization, and economic progress.

Between 1450 and 1530 the annual output of silver probably increased at least fivefold in central Europe.[5] There and in other Continental countries the production of copper, tin, iron, salt, and cloth grew almost as rapidly as that of silver. Printing was introduced in scores of towns in Germany, Italy, France, and the Low Countries. A number of products—such as paper, soap, glass, and gunpowder—for which the demand had been slight were manufactured for the first time in considerable quantities. All over the Continent the palaces of merchants, and the town halls and municipal law courts representing a flourishing mercantile society, were rising in pro-

[4] Cf. Nef, *The Conquest of the Material World* (Chicago, 1964), chap. 2.

[5] For the calculations on which this statement is based, see my note on "Silver Production in Central Europe, 1450–1618," *Journal of Political Economy*, XLIX, No. 4 (1941), 586.

fusion. Kings and princes, lay and ecclesiastical, were building castles mainly outside the old towns. Many of these castles were placed to dominate bourgs and villages.

One effect of the growth of trade and industry was to pull industrial enterprise away from the old towns. In some districts, particularly in Flanders and Brabant, the textile industries were spilling over beyond the ancient walls within which they had been largely confined. The cloth workers and merchants were transforming many villages into populous settlements, with streets shooting out in all directions—from a central square—"like the rays of a great star."[6]

Elsewhere, particularly in central Europe, thousands of miners and metallurgical workers were forming equally populous centers in the hills, the high valleys, and the mountains. Great horse-driven engines pumped up water from depths of several hundred feet to drain the pits. In at least one case some of the horses were driven to their stations down into the earth along a ramp, which wound about the main shaft like a screw.[7]

These economic changes were symptoms of the great new movement among the Western peoples, which was also reflected in the art and thought of the Renaissance and the religious ideas of the Reformation. The modern movement has been expansive to a degree without parallel in the whole of history, and eventually the emphasis on order and beauty in the products of craftsmanship, for which the Renaissance stood, gave way before the expansive tendencies. The search for new continents and a new celestial world, the development of contrapuntal music and new ways of creating a sense of distance in painting with perspective and color, the use of gunpowder to drive projectiles, the creation of credit money —Oswald Spengler has described these and many other of the expansive characteristics of the Western peoples in his cele-

[6] In Pirenne's picturesque language (Henri Pirenne, *Histoire de Belgique* [3d ed.; Brussels, 1923], III, 236).

[7] Nef, *The Conquest of the Material World*, p. 36.

brated book.[8] It is not necessary to accept his main thesis[9]—that now the only future for Western civilization, and a short one at that, is in military despotism—in order to recognize essential truths in the description.

On the economic side, the expansion has taken various forms. The method devised for getting horses into the earth to pump water out of mines was a sort of symbol pointing the way to those ingenious ramps for parking automobiles, typical of the industrial civilization toward which the Renaissance miners and technical experts were inadvertently working. After about 1780–1815 the Western peoples set out to multiply indefinitely, and at an ever increasing rate of growth, the volume of ores and minerals, metal and cloth, and durable goods of every kind produced each year. At the same time, and as a means of increasing the volume, they increased the size and scale of industrial units with the help of more and more powerful machinery, both by combining various industrial processes and by assembling workpeople engaged on the same product in larger and larger establishments. By the twentieth century, in every part of the world, these expansive objectives began to take possession of the societies that had been formed over the millennia.

The industrial expansion of the Renaissance had several modern characteristics, but it did not lead directly to the industrialism of modern times. It was not of long duration. It had spread from the south and east of Europe, from Italy, the eastern Alps, and the Carpathians, toward the north and west. It generally petered out first in the countries where it had first started. It came to a close in Hungary in the twenties of the sixteenth century, with the Turkish invasions, before it had begun to wane in Saxony and southern Germany. It culminated there in the thirties and forties, somewhat earlier than

8 *Der Untergang des Abendlandes* (2 vols.; Munich, 1918, 1922).

9 See below, chap. 4 (IV).

in Franche-Comté and the Spanish Netherlands, where it lasted almost until the first sack of Antwerp in 1576.

Eventually the rapid growth in output was followed in many parts of continental Europe by a long period of industrial stagnation and even of retrogression. The volume of production actually fell in Spain, and above all in the states of central Europe, at the end of the sixteenth century and during the first half of the seventeenth. At the close of the Thirty Years' War, in 1648, the output of silver in central Europe was probably little greater than at the close of the Hussite wars of the early fifteenth century, before the industrial expansion of the Renaissance had begun. In Italy there was no notable economic growth from about 1620 until the end of the eighteenth century.[10]

Despotism is not a medieval but a modern ideal of government, as Professor McIlwain has told us.[11] Unlike the constitutional monarch of more recent times, the king or prince in the twelfth and thirteenth centuries had no superior in civil government, but his actual authority did not extend beyond distinct limits defined by tradition and custom. The lack of a generally admitted right to tax the nation's wealth imposed one of the limits. The duties owed by the prince to God and to the Church imposed another, and one of some importance in an age when most Europeans believed in the Christian God. The local authority of feudal nobles, great churchmen, ecclesiastical foundations, municipalities, and even little mining communities imposed other limits.

In the age of Machiavelli (1469–1527) the despotic principle of government gained strength on the Continent. The bounds set up by medieval constitutionalism gave way as the whole religious, intellectual, and political structure of the Gothic Age lost its hold on the Western peoples. The same

[10] Nef, *The Conquest of the Material World*, p. 116.

[11] C. H. McIlwain, "The Historian's Part in a Changing World," *American Historical Review*, XLII (1937), pp. 219, 233.

countries—Italy, Germany, and Spain—took the lead in fostering despotism that were destined to revive it in our time. The sovereign authority in Italy and Germany was then split up among many princes and other governors, lay and ecclesiastical. During the late fifteenth and early sixteenth centuries, the princes were making the first great bid in Western history for the establishment of unlimited authority. As a part of their effort to control all phases of the lives of their peoples, they set about to regulate industry and to participate in industrial enterprise. They had much success. More and more, large-scale industry was brought under the control of political bureaucracies, able to curb the independence of the private merchants with industrial interests and other investors and, if necessary, to dispossess them, even though they were guilty of no crime other than that of exercising economic power.[12]

There was a conflict between this rise of despotic government and the aspirations of Renaissance people for a fuller life here on earth for the individual. At a time when the ideal of renunciation to the divine will was beginning to lose its hold over men, princes and their advisers were asking for a new kind of renunciation. They were asking the individual to accept the dominion of civil authority independently of the divine will, to accept the lordship of a man over men. In the early sixteenth century that conception of civil authority seemed about to triumph among the Western peoples everywhere in Europe. Americans were brought up to think of the modern age as an age of liberty. But it was under the auspices of growing authority and not of liberty that the modern age was ushered in.

In a famous generalization, Jean Bodin, the greatest political thinker of the late sixteenth century, laid it down that peoples living in a relatively cold climate—in the north or in mountainous country—were naturally inclined toward popular govern-

12 Nef, *The Conquest of the Material World*, pp. 52–57, 101–10.

ment, or at least toward elective monarchy.[13] The challenge to absolutism which came after the Reformation came especially in the countries of northern Europe. These countries had participated least in the industrial expansion of the late fifteenth and early sixteenth centuries. The challenge came in the late sixteenth and seventeenth centuries. It came at a time when the torch of commercial and industrial leadership passed from southern Germany, Italy, and Spain to the United Provinces, Sweden, France, and above all to Great Britain. In regions where the climate is chilly and the problem of wringing a living from the soil challenging, the Europeans set about to secure comforts and ease never enjoyed by the inhabitants of those parts of the earth where nature is kinder to man.

II. *The Human Factor in the Birth of Industrialism*

The modern stage on which the human comedy is acted is unlike any encountered by students of history or of archeology. Never before has the planet been nearly so thickly peopled. In spite of the persistence of misery in many countries, never have humans everywhere had at their disposal such vast quantities of goods and services. Never have they been so relieved from physical labor by power-driven machines and automata. Never have they communicated and travelled so fast in defiance of both time and space. Never have they been able to fill their leisure and even their work with impersonal diversions pumped—in the form of speeches, plays, interviews, parades, music, advertisements, information and misinformation—into homes, factories, offices, and swiftly moving conveyances. Never have men and women had the prospect of

---

[13] *Les six livres de la République* (Paris, 1583), Book V, chap. 1 (esp. p. 694). Of course Bodin recognized that geographical conditions were only one of a number of factors that determined the inclinations and manners of a people. He recognized that their natural inclinations, as derived from geographical conditions, might be greatly changed, if not completely transformed, by other circumstances.

Civilization at the Crossroads

living so long, of multiplying so fast, or of dying in such large numbers.

As the conditions with which all people must now cope differ so greatly from those of past ages, an historian is prompted to ask three fundamental questions, impossible though it may be to answer them. To what extent have changes in values been at the roots of this new world in which we live? To what extent are such changes a result of individual choices made by men and women with a measure of free will? Has the coming of industrialism all over the planet during the twentieth century rendered obsolete older conceptions of right and wrong, beautiful and ugly, true and false? For Picasso, a critic has recently suggested, "the fundamental categories are no longer the true or the false, the beautiful or the ugly, the given or the created—they are the high and the low, the noble and the vile."[14] Is this a real change of categories or only a change of names for the objectives that have always engaged great artists?

Looking back into history across centuries and millennia, the most persistent and inconsistently consistent element seems to be the human being. He is portrayed by artists beginning at least as far back as the ancient Egyptians, the Myceneans, the ancient Greeks. Some of the most moving works convey, as startlingly as does any meeting with beauty today, the presence of their bodies and their faces. We recognize something of ourselves in these persons whose lives have been prolonged into millennia by artists.

Writing of a golden cup fashioned thousands of years ago by "a nameless Mycenean artist," my wife speaks of "communication from the deep past by an unknown person, whom I suddenly 'knew' because of the emotional response he had

[14] Dor de la Souchère, *Picasso Antibes* (Paris, 1962). This is a small brochure in which the pages are not numbered. It is not to be confused with the same author's *Picasso Antibes* (Paris, 1960), a large work on the same subject of Picasso's contributions to the museum in Antibes.

20

evoked." We feel "the thin strong cord of human sameness that connects us with all our ancestors of whatever age."[15]

The bodies and faces of Europeans, painted by Titian, Rubens, Velásquez, and Rembrandt, or later by Ingres, Corot, Renoir, and Derain, resemble the figures presented by Phidias or by a nameless artist on that Grecian urn that inspired one of Keats's most moving poems. Maillol and Lehmbruck have given us women whom we see as first cousins to the incredibly beautiful Peplos Kore, the creation perhaps of a sculptor named Phaidimos about 530 B.C., in a statue which is now one of the glories of the Acropolis Museum in Athens.

So, in considering how the unique conditions of our time have come about, this perpetual man or woman provides the basic reference to which we can relate all our researches. While it may perhaps be plausible that history has changed man, man is certainly responsible for history, and in making history he has sometimes had to change himself more than history has changed him.

The origins of industrialism seem to be related to every aspect of human evolution in the Europe of its birth. With its rise and triumph, the history of Europe has been increasingly intertwined with the histories of other parts of the world. There, too, cultural, intellectual, religious, political, institutional, and social history appear to be inextricably mingled with economic history as factors in creating the unique and single world of industrialism which confronts us in this second half of the twentieth century.[16]

[15] Evelyn S. Nef, Introduction to "The Great Explorers Series," in Rhys Carpenter, *Beyond the Pillars of Heracles* (New York, 1966), p. xv.

[16] Cf. Nef, *La Naissance de la civilisation industrielle et le monde contemporain* (Paris, 1954); *Cultural Foundations of Industrial Civilization* (Cambridge, 1958); *The Conquest of the Material World*, Pt. III. I hope to bring all these and other studies of mine together in a single history of the coming of civilization and industrialism.

The birth of this world historically must be traced back, not as has been the practice among economic historians since Arnold Toynbee, the elder, to the reign of George III (1760–1820) in Great Britain, but at least to the sixteenth century. About the year 1540 it became certain that the earlier efforts of Erasmus, Luther, Zwingli, Calvin, and others to reform the ancient Christian worship would end not in union but rather in division over religious beliefs and practices. For more than a millennium preceding the Reformation, as already suggested, these beliefs and practices had been related, often closely, always at least remotely, to most concerns of Europeans. They had been related to all artists and to all art, including the literary art. Beauty and faith were inseparable.

The hundred years which followed 1540 were marked in some European countries—Great Britain, Sweden, Holland, Denmark, and parts of Germany—by fundamental changes in ecclesiastical government. As a result of confiscations by political rulers in those countries, the proportion of all landed property, mineral deposits, and other forms of wealth owned by religious foundations was very greatly reduced. The changes in ownership facilitated the progress of novel forms of industrial enterprise and the spread of more efficient machinery.[17]

These confiscations were made at about the time when streams of missionaries—in the beginning mainly Roman Catholic—set out in the wake of explorers to push their way overseas in company with traders and other lay emigrants to all the continents and many of the islands of this planet. In faraway Japan, between 1545 and 1590, something like half a million out of what are estimated to have been some twenty million natives were converted at least temporarily to the Christian faith, as that was presented by the great Jesuit priest, Francis Xavier. This penetration of Asia, unlike the earlier European emigrations of the thirteenth century, led to con-

---

[17] Cf. Nef, *The Conquest of the Material World*, pp. 230–32.

tinuous and ever more extensive commercial relations between Europe and the Far East. During the seventeenth century, other colonizers from Europe, especially to North America, were mainly members of the multiplying Protestant churches. They went in search of freedom to worship according to their consciences, as well as to seek new means of livelihood. They staked out political and cultural, as well as economic, claims destined in some cases, above all in the Americas, to bring into being at least one of the most powerful and wealthy nations of all time.

Thus during the sixteenth and early seventeenth centuries European ways of living and of worshipping, and examples of European (or at least of European-inspired) beauty, made their way in one form or another to the ends of the earth. European customs penetrated the lives of many people in the Near and Far East, Africa, and above all in the Americas.

The ways of living, of worshipping, of earning a living and of creating beauty, which the European colonizers carried with them, were changing during the hundred years following 1540. Some of these changes had a direct importance for the eventual triumph of industrialism. These have been the subject of economic history, as it came to be defined and studied under the influence of both Marxian and non-Marxian economics.[18] Other changes had an indirect importance, because they contributed to the rise of civilization, in the sense in which our eighteenth-century ancestors introduced that word.[19] These other changes were not economic according to the categories and presuppositions of most modern economists. The changes were intellectual and cultural. They were responsible in no small measure for the civilization in which industrialism was cradled and nourished. Without them industrialism might have been stillborn in the West, as it seems to have been in eleventh-century China.

Let us consider in order the two kinds of changes that com-

[18] See below, chap. 4 (IV).   [19] See below, p. 36.

bined to produce the unprecedented conditions of existence in which humanity finds itself today.

III. *An Early "Industrial Revolution"*

There have been two industrial revolutions in England, not one.[20] The first is still not given anything like the place in history to which its importance entitles it. It occurred during the hundred years that followed the dissolution of the monasteries in 1536 and 1539, and especially between about 1575 and 1620, in the times of Spenser, Hooker, Shakespeare, Bacon, and Donne. In the century between the Reformation and the English civil war, the output of coal in England increased some tenfold; the output of such products as salt, iron and steel, lead, ships, and glass, from fivefold to tenfold. Many new or virtually new industries were introduced, such as the manufacture of copper and brass, paper, sugar, soap, alum for dyeing, and tobacco pipes for the multiplying smokers.

The expansion of output in Great Britain, together with the development of industrial technology, changed the economic map of Europe. For rapidity in rates of growth in *volume* of production there had been nothing quite like it anywhere on the Continent, even in the late fifteenth and early sixteenth centuries. There was to be nothing quite like it again in any country until well on in the eighteenth century. On the eve of the English civil war, which broke out between 1640 and 1642, England, with hardly a tenth of the population of western Europe, had come to produce at least three or four times as much coal as all the other European states combined. She built more ships than any country except Holland. Rel-

[20] Cf. R. H. Tawney, *The Agrarian Problem in the Sixteenth Century* (London, 1912), p. 403; Thorstein Veblen, *Imperial Germany and the Industrial Revolution* (New York, 1918), pp. 89–95; A. P. Wadsworth and J. de L. Mann, *The Cotton Trade Industry and Industrial Lancashire* (Manchester, 1931), p. 11; Nef, *The Rise of the British Coal Industry* (London, [new printing] 1966), Pt. II; Nef, *The Conquest of the Material World*, chaps. 3, 4, 6.

ative to her population, she produced a larger volume of iron, steel, copper, and brass, of finished metal commodities, and of building material—such as bricks and lime—than any Continental country.

In the making of beautiful wares such as fine paper and books, lace, silks, and tapestries, and works of art modeled in glass, metal, clay, and stone, or etched and engraved for restrained multiplication by the newly invented printing presses, Continental nations, Holland and France in particular, retained and increased the advantage they had always had over the English. An economy of delight was evolving in Continental Europe. It derived from the industrial expansion of the Renaissance. But it extended to wider circles of society and of commodities; it became more humane and eventually less despotic and far more gentle in the manners which it nourished and which nourished it.

It provided civilizing elements which the coal economy lacked. In fact, the more disagreeable aspects of that economy shocked Continentals. Foreigners who visited London during the reign of Charles I (1625–42) were astonished by the coal smoke belching from tens of thousands of domestic hearths and kitchen fires and from hundreds of furnaces, kilns, and ovens in small factories and workshops. To them the city with its breweries, its soap and starch houses, its brick kilns, sugar refineries, and glass manufactures, seemed hardly fit for human habitation. There were plenty of Londoners who agreed with them. In 1627 a complaint was brought "full cry" to the privy council that an alum house near the Tower caused great annoyance to the inhabitants within a mile compass. The "loathesome vapour" from the factory was said to poison the very fish in the Thames, and an appeal was made to the college of physicians to pronounce the vapor damaging to the health of the citizens.[21] But in spite of many protests of this kind[22]

21 *Calendar of State Papers, Domestic* (1627–28), pp. 269–70.
22 Cf. Nef, *Rise of the British Coal Industry*, I, 157.

the factories grew in number. London had taken her place in Charles I's reign as the leading industrial city of the world.

Unlike the earlier industrial expansion of the Renaissance, that in England under Elizabeth and the first two Stuarts pointed the way toward the dominance of large-scale enterprise controlled by private capitalists. The attempts of the English crown to regulate industry and to participate in it, to make mercantile subsidiary to political interests, after the fashion of most Continental princes and kings, were undermined in the seventeenth century. The struggles which culminated in the English civil war and the revolution of 1688 established the rights of the private merchants and landlords to freedom from the arbitrary exercise of royal authority.[23] These struggles did more. They put political authority increasingly at the disposal of economic interests. Thus the English industrial expansion in early modern times helped to create a new conception of the ends of man in which the quantity—the volume—of commodities produced each year became the test of economic and indeed of all progress.

Coal mines had hitherto been little exploited on this planet, save possibly for a short time in Roman Britain and certainly and much more importantly in parts of China during the Sung dynasty from the late tenth to the early twelfth century. During that period the Chinese initiated new kinds of technological progress, anticipatory of much later developments in Europe. They invented the blast furnace for smelting iron ore; they reduced mineral coal to coke; they used mineral fuel extensively in many manufactures, including the manufacture of iron from its ores. All this happened some five hundred years before comparable strides in industrial technology were taken in Europe.

These inventions in China bred something resembling the

---

[23] Nef, *Industry and Government in France and England, 1540–1640* (Ithaca, 1957), esp. pp. 149–52; Nef, *The Conquest of the Material World*, p. 336.

early industrial revolution of Elizabethan and early Stuart Britain. But, in contrast, the progress of the Chinese in mining and metallurgy came to an abrupt end; they lost interest in their resources of coal and iron ore. There is no evidence that the Europeans learned how to exploit these resources from the Chinese. The direct technical contributions of China to Western economic progress were mainly in the arts; Chinese influence was important in the evolution of the economy of commodity and delight beginning with the development of printing in late fifteenth-century Europe. By that time the economic stir caused in China by the exploitation of the coal mines under the Sung had long been over. The early Chinese industrial revolution was petering out even before Marco Polo made his trip to Asia at the end of the thirteenth century.

From the mid-sixteenth to the late eighteenth century, many European mining and manufacturing districts became busy and warm with ingenious practical inventions. But the Chinese remained in a backwater in precisely those areas of industrial technology. The technological progress made in Europe and America in that later period was based, not on the Chinese, but on the much later English industrial revolution of Elizabethan and Stuart times. Instead of abating, as the coal economy in China under the Sung had abated, the preliminary technological progress associated with coal mining in the West was followed by the astounding spurt in production and in population which many twentieth-century Americans have come to take for granted.[24] This spurt in rates of economic growth began in the seventeen-eighties, on the eve of the French Revolution, first in Great Britain.[25] Thence it soon spread to all Europe and America. A hundred years afterward, at the end of the nineteenth century, the West was producing

[24] Cf. Nef, "Civilization, Industrial Society, and Love" (Occasional Paper, Center for the Study of Democratic Institutions, 1961), pp. 4–5.

[25] See Nef, *Western Civilization since the Renaissance* (originally published in 1950 as *War and Human Progress*) (New York, 1963), pp. 290–92.

Civilization at the Crossroads

an abundance of material goods and services such as had never seen the light of this world before. Yet around 1900, China, despite its large population of perhaps three hundred million people, was the most backward of societies in mining and metallurgy. At that time a well-informed observer of the Chinese economy had this to say: "China, notwithstanding its abundant supply of ores and coal, and the many applications it has received from foreign promoters for the privilege of exploiting and working them, is behind every other civilized country in mining and metallurgy. She has no native experts, and no scientific knowledge, and has made absolutely no progress in respect to these matters for the last five hundred years."[26]

In short, all knowledge of the considerable success achieved long before in the exploitation of this very supply of ores and coal had disappeared, even among the Chinese themselves. It was left for an American pupil of the Committee on Social Thought at the University of Chicago, Robert Hartwell, to reveal within the last decade the extent of this curiously modern seeming episode in distant Chinese history.[27]

IV. *The Fresh Hope in Humanity*

One is impelled to ask why the early industrial revolution of the Sung era had no sequel similar to that of the early industrial revolution in the West. The question suggests that a coal economy, combined with a notable increase in the output of iron and many manufactured products, even in a highly sophisticated society like that of eleventh-century China (then as populous as all Europe in the seventeenth century), was

[26] James H. Wilson, *China: A Study of its Civilization and Possibilities* (3rd ed.; New York, 1901), p. 43.

[27] Robert Hartwell, "Revolution in the Chinese Iron and Coal Industries during the Northern Sung, 960–1126 A.D.," *Journal of Asian Studies*, XXI (1962), 153–62; "Markets, Technology, and the Structure of Enterprise in the Development of the Eleventh Century Chinese Iron and Steel Industry," *Journal of Economic History*, XXVI (1966), 29–58.

insufficient to bring about the triumph of industrialism. Other developments beside the early industrial revolution are needed to account for the situation confronting humanity in the twentieth century. The Marxian interpretation of history, and other economic interpretations by anti-Marxists, have served mainly to conceal these conditions.[28] If the Europeans before the French Revolution had not made innovations,[29] other than economic, the coal economy of early Great Britain might have been buried in an oblivion comparable to that which long hid from historians the still earlier coal economy of China.

Mention has been made of the common humanity that artists reveal in individuals of the most diverse societies. In Chinese art we also find "the thin strong cord of human sameness" that connects us with other men and women of the distant past. We are linked with the Chinese as we are with the Greeks and Egyptians. We should not underestimate the possibilities for creative innovations which this common humanity offers. They are perhaps as inexhaustible as has been sometimes dreamed.

Men and women, through the societies of which they are part, have an enormous range of choice in the way they employ their human resources. At the very time, in the late sixteenth and seventeenth centuries, when Englishmen and Scots began to turn to coal for fuel, and to seek after technical inventions which would reduce the expense of mining and moving it, along with other inventions which would facilitate its use in manufactures, individual Europeans were beginning to achieve with their minds results of a kind that had remained unknown in their fullness to earlier societies. The era of the early industrial revolution was also the era of the scientific revolution. That revolution was not, as some have supposed,

28 See below, chap. 4 (IV).

29 Some of these innovations are discussed in other books of mine, for example, *Cultural Foundations of Industrial Civilization*, chap. 1 (I), and *La Naissance de la civilisation industrielle et le monde contemporain*, chaps. 1, 3, 5, 6, 7, 8.

rooted mainly in the new economy of quantity promoted by the rise of the British coal industry. It was pan-European. It was largely an independent, as well as a novel, manifestation of human genius.[30]

In the long run, that progress of the modern sciences which began in the minds of Europeans in the late sixteenth and seventeenth centuries was a factor of greater consequence for the conquest of the material world than the introduction of a coal economy. Substantial applications of new scientific knowledge to cheapen labor costs in industry, in transport, and in communications, hardly began before the eighteenth century even in Europe where the scientific revolution occurred. The symbiosis between the pure and the applied sciences, which has now changed the nature and purpose of manual labor and transformed the conditions of living throughout the world, was prefigured in the spurt in rates of economic growth at the end of the eighteenth and during the nineteenth century.[31] Technological invention, based on applied science, was increasingly responsible for that growth, after it had begun. During the past hundred and especially during the past twenty-five years, world population and the world output of goods and services have multiplied to such a point, as the result of applied science, that it appears to some we may soon have on earth standing room only.

It is not infrequently supposed that the outlook of scientists toward the use of new scientific knowledge for practical purposes has always been much the same; that a failure on the part of early scientists to appreciate the applicability of their discoveries to revolutionary technological inventions was responsible for the relatively slow progress of the applied sciences until the late eighteenth and nineteenth centuries. This seems to have been only part of the explanation. A knowledge of the possibilities for astounding practical results, inherent in the

[30] See Nef, *The Conquest of the Material World*, chap. 7, esp. pp. 318–28.
[31] See Nef, *Western Civilization since the Renaissance*, pp. 290–93.

new sciences, was abroad in Europe long before the eighteenth century. Scientists like Gilbert, Galileo, and Harvey, and philosophers like Bacon and Descartes, became aware of the fresh powers that were conferred on man by these newly discovered intellectual tools. They recognized the opportunities thus opened to him to conquer nature and, in so doing, to reduce physical labor and prolong the span of life. Some scientifically minded individuals in the seventeenth century foresaw as a consequence of the new knowledge the railroad, the submarine, the airplane, the possibility of journeying to the moon and other planets—even, it appears, the feasibility of wiping life off the face of the earth.

But they feared these consequences because of their consciousness of the evil inherent in human nature. This fear made scientists reluctant to tell all they knew, lest they should endow the human race with means of self-destruction. During the period of the scientific revolution, great scientists, such as Boyle and Newton, sought in a variety of ways to hinder the indiscriminate use of the new knowledge to which they had access.[32] At the beginning of the scientific revolution, at the juncture of the sixteenth and seventeenth centuries, there is said to have been a clear intimation of what men might do with the new sciences. Many on both sides of the English Channel then believed that the cold war of that age, the ideological confrontation of Catholics and Protestants, could produce a general showdown. Some Catholics declared themselves partisans of the extermination of all heretics, at a time when a large part of the European population had become heretical.[33]

In Great Britain a mathematician of genius, with much practical experience in coal mining and salt manufacturing, John Napier, inventor of logarithms, thought he had discov-

[32] *Ibid.*, pp. 196–98.

[33] Cf. Nef, *Cultural Foundations of Industrial Civilization*, p. 92, and see below, pp. 414–15.

ered a means of human extermination. He claimed knowledge of a weapon, which he offered to Queen Elizabeth shortly after the attempt of the Spanish Armada on Great Britain.[34] According to a manuscript that he apparently wrote in 1596, where the actual mechanics of his weapon are not even touched on, his new "engine" was capable of clearing a large area, five miles in circumference, of every living thing or of destroying an entire battle fleet by sea "att one shott," if all the vessels should be concentrated "within the appointed bounds."[35]

Long after the death in 1617 of this extraordinary man, a member of the family, Mark Napier, put together the first serious biography, which was presented to William IV in 1834 in the form of memoirs (including some unpublished manuscripts of John's). In the interval of two centuries there had been several abortive attempts at biography by members of the family, and two collections of John's papers, writings, and personal belongings had been destroyed by fire.

According to Mark, John Napier kept all the scientific and technological knowledge necessary to the unleashing of his weapon tightly compressed within his mind. He refused to divulge any of it when prodded to do so on his deathbed. He is reported to have said that: "For the ruin and overthrow of man, there were too many devices already framed, which if he could make to be fewer, he would with all his might endeavour to do; and that therefore seeing the malice and rancour rooted in the heart of mankind will not suffer them to diminish, by any new conceit of his the number of them should never be increased."[36]

This fear of evil restrained scientists from telling all they knew about their basic discoveries, from treating these discoveries as they came to be treated in the nineteenth century:

[34] Cf. Nef, *Western Civilization since the Renaissance*, pp. 121–24.

[35] Mark Napier, *Memoirs of John Napier of Merchiston* (Edinburgh, 1834), pp. 247–48.

[36] *Ibid.*, p. 246.

as the common property of the learned world to be put freely at the disposal of technological invention.[37] In all probability the changes in men's consciences were a factor of considerable importance in producing a symbiosis between the pure and the applied sciences and, consequently, in the rapid conquest of the material world during the nineteenth and twentieth centuries.

When did the change occur and what brought it about? What led scientists and philosophers to suppose "the malice and rancour rooted in the heart of mankind" might no longer be the threat to humanity they once had seemed?

The conditions that produced among the Western peoples a new confidence in man and his future were as novel as the scientific revolution and as alien to the Chinese and other peoples as the new sciences themselves. This confidence in the possible improvement of the human race, which some early Americans like Jefferson shared to the hilt, did not come all at once and it has not lasted. But its existence as a brief episode in history, together with the conditions which nourished it, laid foundations for the fantastically rapid material conquests which have been realized during the last hundred years, first in Europe and North America and now in other parts of the world.

The confidence is inseparable from civilization as the eighteenth century understood that word. It was not identified primarily with the new technological developments in the exploitation of coal and iron ore or with the budding economy of quantity to which these inventions contributed. As has been suggested, that economy had its origins especially in Elizabethan and early Stuart Britain. The direction taken during those times by European industrial development *generally*, particularly under French and Dutch leadership, was in the direction less of quantity than of quality.[38] Between the late

[37] This matter is discussed more fully in Nef, *Western Civilization since the Renaissance*, pp. 121–25, 194–99.

[38] See above, p. 25.

33

sixteenth and the late eighteenth century the Europeans dedicated themselves, more extensively than any peoples before them, to beauty in all forms, from craftsmanship in the fashioning of useful commodities to painting, literature, architecture, and musical composition.[39] This dedication spread to Great Britain and Sweden, to Russia, Hungary, and the Balkans. It spread to North America during the same period, when the Europeans absorbed artistic ideas from their contacts with the East, particularly in the decorative arts from relations with Japan and China.

An economy of delight and commodity was no new thing. The ancient Greeks and the Chinese, among other peoples, had cultivated such an economy, and both Greek example and Chinese experience had an influence upon Baroque art and artistry. But, in extending an economy of delight and commodity more widely into the domestic life, not only of the nobility and of rich merchants, but of many families in more modest circumstances, especially in Holland, the Europeans, both in Europe and in North America, added something that was new. This was a hope in the steadily increasing perfectibility of the human being. Men whose ideas had great influence through their books, from Montesquieu to Gibbon, Hume, and Guizot, felt that out of conditions of working and thinking and living, which men were achieving in Europe, a new and better breed of mortals, capable of guiding politics, was coming to exist. With the spread of these conditions to other parts of the earth, such Europeans foresaw the evolution everywhere, for the first time in history, of a civilized humanity.

Their optimism concerning the future flowered in the Enlightenment, whose origins need to be traced back at least into

[39] Cf. Nef, *Cultural Foundations of Industrial Civilization*, esp. pp. 128–38. I have recently developed the subject further in lectures at the University of Chicago for the Committee on Social Thought, entitled "Beauty in the Conquest of the Material World."

the early seventeenth century.[40] Much has been made in recent times, the mid-twentieth century, of the role played by individualism and liberty in the triumph of industrialism. The role of laissez faire economies in enabling both sides of a transaction to feel the satisfaction of gaining was no doubt important. But what nearly all exponents of free enterprise and a free society have failed to recognize is the historical importance of the belief, which persisted in Europe and the United States through most of the nineteenth century, that mankind was becoming more worthy of individualism and liberty than it had ever been before. There was a growing sense of *noblesse oblige*, by no means confined to the nobility. Contemporary exponents of free enterprise and a free society also miss the historical evidence that during the seventeenth and eighteenth centuries, when the new individualism and the new liberty first flowered, the progress of both was related to the dedication to beauty in craftsmanship of every kind from artisanry in the making of useful commodities to painting, literature, architecture, and music, all serving primarily to delight and inspire.

The spread of beauty was accompanied by the spread of commerce, gentle manners, and a hope in the practical value of high ideals that some of the great and influential men of the eighteenth century believed to be novel. In these respects all Europe was becoming, to use an expression employed at the end of the eighteenth century by Edmund Burke, a single great republic. Nor was there any basic obstacle, as Gibbon saw it, writing on the eve of the French Revolution, to the eventual spread of these civilized conditions everywhere. His idea was not that the West would impose its ways on the East and on other parts of the world, but that other peoples would adopt civilization, because they would want it, because it was recognizably good.

What was "civilization"? It is now supposed that the word

[40] Nef, *Cultural Foundations of Industrial Civilization*, pp. 145–51.

first appeared in print in a work of the Marquis de Mirabeau published in 1757, *L'Ami des Hommes ou traité de la population*.[41] The word is also found in the title of another of his works, which never got into print, but where it seems particularly appropriate, *L'Amy des Femmes ou Traité de la Civilisation*.[42]

Whether or not Mirabeau coined the word, civilization for him clearly referred to conditions which he and some others supposed had raised the Europeans to a higher and more humane level of temporal purpose than had been reached before on this planet. These are his words: *"The civilization of a people is to be found in the softening of manners, in growing urbanity, in politer relations and in the spreading of knowledge in such ways that decency and seemliness are practiced until they transcend specific and detailed laws. . . .* Civilization does nothing for a society unless it is able to give form and substance to virtue. The concept of humanity is conceived in the bosom of societies out of these ingredients."[43]

Civilization, then, appeared to some of our eighteenth-century ancestors as an unprecedented way of life opening to all mankind. This meaning is altogether different from that usually given the word today, a meaning that has evolved since archeologists revealed earlier societies, and dubbed them civilizations. The word retained its original meaning for most European writers at least through the times of Walter Scott, who used it in this sense in his *Tales of a Grandfather*, written between 1828 and 1831, shortly before his death. So did the great French statesman Guizot (1787–1874), who also wrote history for his grandchildren. For these writers civilization was a new achievement. Virtue had always existed, of course, even in so-

[41] Lucien Febvre, *Civilisation, le mot et l'idée* (Publications du Centre international de Synthèse; Paris, 1930), pp. 8 ff.; E. Benveniste, "Civilisation: Contribution à l'histoire du mot," in *Eventail de l'histoire vivante (hommage à Lucien Febvre)* (Paris, 1953), p. 48.

[42] Archives Nationales (Paris), M. 780, No. 3.

[43] *Ibid.* (Mirabeau's italics; my translation).

cieties without civilization. But they thought that it was not until modern times that virtue had been given a form and substance that promised it an ascendancy over evil in the affairs of nations.

The confidence in the future implied by the word was in all probability one of the roots of the speeding up in rates of economic and population growth which began in Great Britain at the juncture of the eighteenth and nineteenth centuries,[44] and which has spread since throughout the world. Industrialism has begun to conquer Russia and even China. It is knocking at the door of the tribal societies of Africa, a continent which is now thought to have been the habitat of the first human beings.

The question of man's origins had been reopened among the Europeans at the time the word "civilization" apparently originated. It became increasingly difficult to accept literally the testimony of the Bible. So, not unnaturally, the belief in original sin diminished. In place of that came the idea of evolution, which contributed for a time to the growing belief that human improvement was possible.

As hope in man's capacity to improve waxed, the increasingly numerous scientific community, which had become international in spirit, ceased to fear the consequences of disseminating the fruits of their individual researches. It became a duty to publish. As time went on there was also an increasing tendency among some scientists to work together with others—a tendency that has led now to research by teams. Secrecy, therefore, has become increasingly impracticable.

The momentum with which the new knowledge spread, generated in the beginning by the growing faith in the perfectibility of mankind and in the eventual enthronement of virtue, continued after this optimism concerning the moral capacities of men and women waned. Research into human origins since the mid-nineteenth century was accompanied throughout the

[44] Nef, *Western Civilization since the Renaissance,* pp. 290 ff.

world by a growing stress upon man's animality, upon nationalism, and upon racism. With the coming of world wars and the extermination of the Jews sponsored by the Nazis, the view that Erasmus had expressed long before the Enlightenment, that wars showed man to be the most ferocious of all the beasts, came again into ascendancy.

How did this waning of confidence in the potentiality of men and women for virtue come about? This is the subject of the next two chapters. Has the industrialism, which was nurtured by civilization, rendered obsolete the values associated with civilization as Mirabeau and other thinkers of the eighteenth century understood the word—values derived in no small measure from the art, the philosophical thought, and the religious beliefs, of ancient societies? That is the subject of the four chapters that form Part Two.

3   The Crisis in the Pursuit of Beauty

The phenomenal rise in rates of economic growth, which began in Great Britain in the seventeen-eighties, has continued ever since, with only a brief slackening in the wake of the First World War of 1914–18 and in the wake of the great depression of 1929–33. In the beginning a phenomenon of western Europe and America, it has become a part of world history.

The factors behind it have been many and complex. Here is not the place to try to synthesize them.[1] The concern of this chapter is with the crisis in artistic values which has accompanied the accelerated rates of growth in production and in people, especially during the past hundred years.

A notion has become widespread, not least in the United States, that material progress, as measured so often by economists in terms of rates of economic growth, is a major cause for progress in the arts. This view is closely allied to the supposition that "culture" can be bought, that what is mainly needed is millions to provide for cultural centers and more millions to subsidize the performing arts.

In the light of historical evidence, to what extent are such assumptions defensible?

Insofar as they have support from scholarship, they are based on what is often called the science of economics (or political economy). The principles of economics, as they are usually presented, are derived almost altogether from material conditions that have come into existence during the past hundred and fifty years, since the leap in rates of growth began. It is by no means self-evident that such principles of economics are a help more than a hindrance to an understanding of the

[1] I shall attempt to do so in the history upon which I have been working all my adult life and which I hope to complete in the years ahead.

forces at work in the historical evolution which laid foundations for the modern world. It is highly questionable whether more rapid material progress (as we conceive of material progress today), than actually occurred during the seventeenth and eighteenth centuries, would have been healthy for European art and craftsmanship. A rapid increase in productivity might have interfered in those times with another kind of progress: the spread of commodity and delight and the flowering of the arts. Greater scope was provided then than now for the artist and the artist-craftsman in connection with all kinds of industrial endeavor, including the fashioning of men-of-war and every kind of weapon. The claims of beauty and of elegance took time and pains to fulfill. So they may be represented as having interfered with economic growth. For the sake of art and craftsmanship, the Europeans devoted their skill and energy mainly to other objects than the maximizing of scarce means in the service of *quantity* production. They were maximizing scarce means mainly for the sake of *quality*, which makes different kinds of demands on ingenuity.

At the same time that the claims of beauty and of elegance interfered with production, they imposed brakes on destruction. They limited the extent of warfare.[2] As we have seen, the rise of civilization, which accompanied the spread of an economy of commodity and delight, helped to provide men with novel assurances concerning the future of human nature. These assurances seem to have contributed to the speeding up in rates of economic growth during the nineteenth century.

Since the American and French revolutions, the claims of utility and efficiency, of multiplication for its own sake, have obtained an increasing preponderance. The elements of expansion, always present among the Europeans since medieval times and increasingly prevalent since the advent of a coal-burning economy in Elizabethan and Stuart Britain, have

[2] See Nef, *Western Civilization since the Renaissance* (New York, 1963), esp. pp. 125–33 and chap. 14.

tended to get out of the control of the artistic disciplines which have nourished beauty. Let us illustrate by considering briefly, in turn, the course taken by the principal arts with the rise and triumph of industrialism during the past one hundred fifty years.

1. *Architecture and the Decline of Craftsmanship*[3]

The builder needs to serve at least three distinct objectives. One is firm structure. He cannot disregard the requirements of structural science, if for no other reason than because his building may fall apart. Another objective is utility. The building has to serve the domestic, the economic, the social, the political, or the religious purposes for which it is intended. The third objective may be called "delight," following the seventeenth-century English author of the *Elements of Architecture*, Sir Henry Wotton (a minor poet and diplomat as well as an architect), who in turn followed Vitruvius. This means that a building, both within and without and also in its position with respect to other buildings and to the community as a whole, should be a work of art.[4]

Ever since the Napoleonic wars, rapid industrial growth has increasingly complicated the problem of creating an enduring civilization and an architecture such as might express it and provide surroundings in which individuals could fulfill their needs for order, tranquility, and delight. With the continual changes in structural materials, in occupations, in economic and social, religious and cultural, demands, in means of transport, it is hardly astonishing that no coherent conceptions of new architectural styles should have evolved to replace what Geoffrey Scott called *The Architecture of Humanism*. All

[3] Cf. my sketch of the history of architecture, "Architecture and Western Civilization," in *Review of Politics*, VIII, No. 2 (1946), 192–222, and the authorities cited in that article.

[4] Geoffrey Scott, *The Architecture of Humanism: A Study in the History of Taste* (2d ed.; New York, 1924).

over Europe, between the mid-fifteenth and the late eighteenth centuries, the styles which concerned Scott in his book—the Classical, the Baroque, and the Rococo—were superimposed upon the Romanesque, the Gothic, and the flamboyant Gothic. An essential unity was maintained both with the additions to older communities and with the new villages and towns built in America as well as in Europe. Ships and town bridges fitted into these unified artistic conceptions. Consequently, in the late eighteenth century, a measure of harmony in styles persisted in Europe and wherever the Europeans colonized. The harmony extended to the utensils and to the furniture and decorations in domestic use.

During the nineteenth century such harmony was increasingly lost. For a long time the absence of any generally accepted discipline for the art of architecture combined with the unprecedented insistence of claims irrelevant to delight (in connection with structural science and with comfort and convenience) to produce alongside many individually handsome buildings some of the most wretched improvisations imaginable, such as often appeared in frontier settlements in the Americas. Seen as a whole, most contemporary towns are less attractive to the eye than those few medieval and early modern towns which remain today essentially as they were in the mid-eighteenth century.

Perhaps the most disorganizing factor in recent architectural history has been the increasingly insistent need to provide for larger numbers of people and for the urbanization of almost the entire population, as agricultural pursuits have come to occupy an ever diminishing proportion of the ever more numerous inhabitants. Long ago attempts were made to meet these needs by expanding the areas of cities and by building houses with extra stories. A kind of logic led further into the air, and skyscrapers began to be built in the United States more than a hundred years ago. In Europe there was a tremendous resistance to them. Laws were enacted in all the great European cities against structures of more than six or seven stories. So it was left to the United States to experiment with very high buildings. It seemed to some critics that these only added to the ugliness of towns. But before the end of the nineteenth century, and still more during the twentieth, architects, beginning with Louis Sullivan, found openings for a new and in many ways a unifying and beautiful style.

The response to the skyscraper of one of the most original minds of recent times, Henri Bergson, is of much interest in its bearing on the openings that exist for new beginnings, for fresh unprecedented adventures, such as might help men to surmount by a new delight the problems industrialism has brought. More than fifty years ago, in 1913, Bergson reported to a Franco-American audience in Paris his impressions of his first visit to the United States.

I seem to remember having read or been told that no house can make an agreeable impression on the eyes if it is more than two stories tall. The spectacle that confronts us in our large [European] towns seems rather to support that theory. It is perhaps impossible to produce an effect agreeable to the eye with four, five or six stories. . . .

I asked myself why this should be so. It occurred to me that two stories is the maximum height needed for a single family; . . . with four, five and six stories we have, therefore, the feeling that several abodes have been piled on top of one another. . . . The unity without which there can be no work of art is wanting.

But if you once multiply the stories to a point where we are no longer tempted to count, we have in our range of vision a collectivity; the impression we get is that made on us from afar by a crowd in which no individual stands out, and which constitutes a mass—single and indivisible. Unity reappears, or at least becomes possible, and, if the architect knows how to make the most of his opportunities, the building can once more become a work of art. . . .

I offer this explanation for what it is worth. Whether it is good or bad, the fact is certain that I have returned from New York with the conviction that it is easier for a house of twenty-five stories than for one of five to avoid ugliness.[5]

---

[5] "Les premières impressions des Etats-Unis d'Henri Bergson," *France-Amérique* (4th trimestre, 1965), p. 129 (my translation).

During the early twentieth century Bergson's conviction was being put into practice by Frank Lloyd Wright. He followed the principle that the demands of art required buildings that are either very low or very high, buildings perfectly suited to landscape. As a principle it reaches back more than five thousand years to ancient Egypt. Wright's early houses in the Middle West were always built close to the ground, in a new style which he invented to conform to the flat carpets of land around Chicago. Later he conceived of an entire city of overwhelmingly tall buildings. He never had the opportunity to construct such a city. But one of the most inventive and influential artists of the industrial era was exploring, to the advantage of delight, those very possibilities recognized by Bergson.

The idea Bergson expressed eventually impressed his fellow Europeans. After the Second World War the effective opposition of city governments in Europe to the construction of taller buildings broke down.

A number of eminent architects have come since Sullivan and Wright, among them Le Corbusier, and Gropius, and Mies van der Rohe. Along with some others they have worked out something that approaches a new architecture of delight. Yet we now know how far short of creating the happy conditions for which they have all hoped are the new cities, like New York and Chicago, Marseilles and Paris, with their crowding, their endless streets and boulevards clogged with multiplying motor cars slowed down from a hundred to four miles an hour or brought to a halt and then speeded up again. Notwithstanding a few stunning buildings, big cities seem to many increasingly uninhabitable.

"I am in anguish," a leading architect of Strasbourg is reported recently to have said. "It isn't that I lack orders. I have more than I can fill. But for some years, I am increasingly haunted by a strange feeling of isolation, of solitude in technical, social, moral, and intellectual matters. What are we building? I ask myself. Every day when I pass a group of my own constructions, I feel frustrated. All that I so recently attempted in the cause of humanism is already obsolete. I know only too well that the inhabitants of my buildings are not happy."[6]

The more a few outstanding architects and city planners have striven, with partial success, to create beauty out of new opportunities, the more modern technology—with its growing mechanization and automation—has thrown obstacles in their way. One of these obstacles is the decline, among persons who labor, of artistic craftsmanship.

In the Baroque period, with the spread of new kinds of artisanry, craftsmen were everywhere available to help artists. This was true in the fashioning of musical instruments, some of which, such as spinets and harpsichords, were often built in collaboration with great masters (with Rubens for example), whose pictures became part of the instruments. It was true, above all, in the building industries. Craftsmen of many kinds were available to carry out with artistic comprehension the intentions of architects, to furnish and embellish with statues and ornaments the houses and bridges and fountains and ships, including men-of-war.

Great Britain was weak, compared with France, Italy, and the Low Countries, in the visual arts in the time of Shakespeare. Sir Henry Wotton (1568–1639) repeatedly refers to the crudeness of English building. Yet during the seventeenth and eighteenth centuries, English-born architects assimilated a great diversity of foreign influences to advantage. From Inigo Jones (1573–1652) through Wren up to Gibbs and as far as William Kent (ca. 1686–1748) and the eighteenth-century Palladians, the best buildings are very good works of architecture. The English during those times were drawn to the developing economy of delight and commodity, until they rivaled the Continentals in artistic craftsmanship. This served the architect well. Until the uprooting which began at the

---

[6] *Le Figaro*, April 3, 1967, p. 5.

juncture of the eighteenth and nineteenth centuries, with the speeding up of economic growth, architects in England, as everywhere in Europe, and in America to some extent, had at their disposal ground-staffs of silversmiths, cabinetmakers, plasterers, pargeters (who raised ornamental figures), iron-work designers, carvers, turners, as well as skilled masons and carpenters, capable of carrying out artistic intentions.

Ever since the eighteenth century, the applications of steam, oil, hydroelectric, and now atomic power, combined with the seemingly inevitable mechanization and automation of all kinds of work (in the cause of profits, wages, productivity, and defense against passing enemies), at first gradually displaced and eventually almost eliminated the craftsman. The great architects of our time can no longer draw, as their predecessors could, upon a variety of skilled workers who have been trained as artisans. The population of western European origin, now spread over much of the globe, has increased from not much more than a hundred million in 1750 to nearly a billion today. But there are far fewer craftsmen now than there were then.

The claims of utility and sanitation, in connection with construction, have further complicated the problems of those architects and city planners who would like to serve the requirements of delight. Modern central heating and plumbing—comforting in themselves—have often led architects, who are not aesthetically resourceful in the presence of new demands, to alter their approach to building. And when architects more dedicated to beauty persist in adhering firmly to artistic standards regardless of the consequences for utility, their clients are likely to protest. Mies van der Rohe's first twenty-six-story apartment buildings in Chicago were criticized mainly on the ground that they did not provide adequately for garbage disposal!

Since the nineteenth century central heating and plumbing have been followed by air-conditioning. Oil and gas have superseded coal-burning furnaces. Refrigeration, radio, and television sets have introduced further discordant complications for architects. The demands for barracks-like space for storing materials and commodities, en route to consumers, in unprecedented quantities, and for accommodating small armies of clerks, salesmen and saleswomen, followed and sometimes supplanted by computers, have pushed the builders of large structures to conform to the requirements of mechanized haulage and mechanized elevation, and of easy selling and calculating, not infrequently at the expense of beauty.

Beauty is not created by collectivities but by individuals. To be successful financially, economic and political planning, as they are almost invariably practiced in our time, are the affairs of collectivities. They sometimes level creative human differences after the manner of a steam roller preparing a newly laid roadbed for heavy traffic. When, late in life, Henry James, great artist that he was, paid a visit to his native United States, he remarked that the landscape seemed to have been made for the railroad tracks rather than the railroad tracks for the landscape, as in Europe. Now, sixty years later, all over Europe as well as in America, not only railroads but throughways are beginning to absorb the landscape. While sensibility to beauty and longing for delight persist in individuals, the difficulties in the way of their fulfillment have grown with the multiplication of people, of production, and of speed.

II. *The Spread of Sound and Fury*

None of the other arts has escaped difficulties similar to those which the growing dominance of quantitative goals have placed in the way of architectural delight.

"Music is that which unifies." Those are the words of Seuma-tsen, written about two thousand years ago. This historian has been called the Chinese Herodotus. According to Stravinsky (who quoted the words in his *Poétique Musicale*[7]), the

[7] Igor Stravinsky, *Poétique Musicale sous forme de six leçons* (Cambridge, Mass., 1942), p. 94.

system of composition which originated in Europe and provided the framework for "the musical constructions which are of the greatest interest" was hardly maintained after the mid-nineteenth century.[8] By that time the fantastically rapid economic growth we now take for granted had begun to invade many parts of the world. In Europe after 1848 growth became most rapid in Germany. It helped to undermine artistic discipline in music as in architecture. The framework of composition of which Stravinsky speaks hardly lasted at its greatest beyond Beethoven and Schubert, who died in 1827 and 1828. It was hardly prolonged beyond Berlioz (1803–69) and Schumann (1810–56).

"Music that unifies," like that of Bach, can never be, in its spirit, the monopoly of any particular section of the human race. It would hardly have occurred to eighteenth-century composers, and seldom to their contemporaries who participated as players or as audience, to treat the compositions of their age as manifestations of nationalism, although the greatest musicians were all born in central Europe. They were expressing themselves in an idiom which derived from, and was being nurtured by, musical experiences lived in every part of Europe, at a time when some Europeans felt themselves to be part of a new and universal civilization open to all the world. The men whom many discriminating judges consider the greatest composers of all time—Bach, Handel, Haydn, Mozart, Beethoven, and Schubert—were not making German music: they were simply making *music*.

The German annexation of music as their special preserve came during the second half of the nineteenth century, when the German Reich was formed and began to conquer territory. Stravinsky tells us how Wagner (who was born in 1813) unleashed what Stravinsky calls musical decadence. Wagner died in 1883. Stravinsky remarks that he had to be a man of tremendous power to break away from essential musical form

---

[8] *Ibid.*, p. 27.

with sufficient energy to convince three generations of the value of his compositions and to conquer the musical stage, with the result that more than fifty years later, in the mid-twentieth century, "we are still buried beneath the trash and clatter of musical drama."[9]

These words remind me of an occasion twenty years ago when Artur Schnabel took me in Chicago to a performance of *Parsifal*. As the curtain descended on the overwhelming musical fireworks of the last act in that Civic Opera House, which had replaced Louis Sullivan's more civilized Auditorium, Schnabel stretched out his arms toward the disappearing stage and muttered in my ear: "Hollywood has not surpassed it."

What happened during the last quarter of the nineteenth century, when Wagner and Brahms dominated music, has been explained by an English critic whose witty judgments brightened early twentieth-century criticism, the late W. J. Turner.

No musician or critic would deny that [they] were composers of genius, but few to-day would regard them as among the supremely great masters of their art and it is likely they will be for ever linked together as examples of genius divorced from virtue, using the word virtue in a non-moral, strictly artistic, sense. . . . As Wagner's music is almost wholly external, so Brahms' is almost wholly internal; neither is related to that third reality which is represented by nature and man. The absence of this direct relation [to a higher order than the self] is what I mean by the absence of virtue. The highly gifted musical sensibility which comprises the genius of Brahms and of Wagner is allowed to function for its own sake subjectively, without being brought into discipline with any sensibility or life outside its own.[10]

Without examining further for the moment whether Turner's words *do* raise a *moral* issue, one can perhaps agree with Stravinsky that the works of Wagner represented a break

---

[9] Stravinsky, *Poétique Musicale*, p. 31.

[10] "The Last of the Classics," review of Wm. Murdock's *Brahms*, published in *The New Statesman* in the 1930's.

from an established order in music, to which Beethoven, for all his innovations, had adhered. One can perhaps agree that the universalism which the eighteenth century expressed in its music, and its musical drama, as created by Rameau, Handel, Gluck, Haydn, and Mozart, grew out of a joyful and almost unconscious adherence by the composers to that established order. Was not this order an integral part of a rich culture which unified, because of its dedication to *beauty* as a goal beyond the self?

However one may choose to answer, there can be no doubt that the place of music in society, and its influences on society, changed profoundly in the direction of self-expression and nationalism under the leadership of Wagner. The tendencies toward self-expression were carried farther by another German, whose foremost achievement in the ears and eyes of his countrymen was that "he retained for Germany the supremacy of music which had culminated in Wagner. [Richard Strauss] became, as Bülow called him, 'Richard II.' As for making music do what it is not, as an art, intended to do, Strauss carried on what Wagner had started. This became plain six years after Wagner's death, when in 1889 Strauss, then 25, conducted the premiere of his *Don Juan*."[11] That tone poem was the first of six of his works which, as Mrs. Tuchman writes, "created a new form—or, as the critics said, a new 'formlessness.'" In adopting the theme set forth by Nicholas Lenau, author of the poem on which the score is based, "Strauss committed himself fully to the business of making music perform a non-musical function: making it describe characters, emotions, events and philosophies, which is essentially the function of literature."[12] Mozart had set *Don Giovanni* and *Zauberflöte* to music with the help of librettos. Strauss tried to make *his music* tell the story of Don Juan. Much later he

[11] Barbara Tuchman, *The Proud Tower* (New York, 1962), pp. 291, 296–97.

[12] *Ibid.*, p. 296.

took what seems an almost perverse glee in spelling his own name—Richard Strauss—in the notes of one of his compositions. Here is a different conception of music's function, bound to produce different kinds of results.

While the Germans were foremost in asserting a musical nationalism at the juncture of the nineteenth and twentieth centuries, the emotions then let loose in Germany were part of a widespread nationalistic trend. There was now Russian music, French music, Italian music, English music, American music (meaning for a time the jazz identified with American Negroes), Spanish music, Latin-American music, Finnish music. This nationalism was extended beyond the Western world. Groups made a fetish of African music, Indian music, or the music of Bali. Chinese music and Japanese music were proclaimed as stars in the banners of the countries that produced them.

Before the world war of 1914–18, music had ceased to be, in the main, the unifying element in society it had been in the comparatively stable economic and social world of the eighteenth century, with its rising cosmopolitan "civilization." Nationalism and a literary intent, alien to the *art* of music, came into prominence with the mounting rates of economic growth. Cosmopolitan civilization suffered.

There were other reasons for this besides the break with the musical system of the greatest composers and the usurpation by music of non-musical functions. One was the application of economic values to works of music, which paralleled and was related to their application to works of architecture. According to the principles of economic growth, measured statistically and carried over into the realm of culture, it would appear that the greater the quantity of music reaching human ears, the greater should be the civilizing effects. And it is obvious that, first with the multiplication of instruments and orchestras (in which, too, the Germans were often leaders), and later with the spread of gramophone records, music pumped into public places, and music received at home by radio and television (in which the United States was the innovator), the numbers reached have increased much more rapidly even than has the population.

Music can have very different effects through the ways it is interpreted by performers and the ways it is received by listeners. In both respects changes have occurred which have added to the din, the confusion, and the division brought about by what Stravinsky dubbed the decadence of the compositions. While scores can be *read* to advantage, the effects of music, unlike those of literature and of the visual arts, depend (even more than those of plays) on performance. So composers of music must confide their wares to interpreters.

Since Beethoven's time, the conditions under which music is performed have enormously altered. Works of the greatest classical composers are now given prominence on programs. They are broadcast almost every day and night. So it is easy to assume that the opportunities to appreciate very great music have increased. In a sense this is perfectly true. The wide diffusion of music is in itself a good thing. But we must not imagine that the experience with works of Handel, Haydn, or Mozart, as these are received in homes and public places by mechanical means, is of the same order as the experience of playing them and listening to them at the time they were composed. Then, which is to say during the eighteenth century, the majority of those Europeans who heard music knew enough about it to participate. Today such participation is much rarer.

Moreover, with the increase in the number of instruments, and the replacement of the craft-built instruments of earlier times by manufactured instruments, the old works came to be interpreted on a scale and in a manner which was often inappropriate to their genius. Impresarios, those new musical middlemen, orchestra conductors, who have assumed a dictatorship in matters of performance unknown before, and labor unions, which have not infrequently prohibited adequate rehearsals, have often warped the sound of older music until their composers, if by some magic they were resurrected, would hardly recognize their compositions.

Take for example a most moving and beautiful work of Bach, *The Passion according to Saint Matthew*. It was first performed in Bach's lifetime by a group of thirty-four musicians in all—including the soloists and the chorus.[13] Since Bach was rediscovered by Felix Mendelssohn, performances of the Saint Matthew Passion have been swelled to proportions for which the music was never intended. The score has come to be executed by trained teams, combined for the occasion. These teams number hundreds, sometimes nearly a thousand men and women.

Vincent d'Indy (1851–1931), a composer and musician of considerable sensibility, conducted in Paris in 1925 the first performance I heard of this work. As nearly as I can recall there were hardly a hundred participants including the orchestra, all assembled on a relatively small stage. I was transported by the beauties Bach's music was allowed to reveal. Some ten years later I heard the work a second time as mounted in Orchestra Hall in Chicago by Frederick Stock. He had an immense orchestra and hundreds of singers—a force of perhaps eight hundred in all. By comparison with d'Indy, Stock's Bach seemed a bedlam, with sounds that split the ears.

Christ's suffering for us all, as revealed by Bach, is sufficient and can be almost infinitely moving. To magnify the sound, as modern performances often do, is to lose the beauty of the music. This can encourage a sadistic reaction in those who accept the interpretation. The intensity of the sound forces them to attend. But it is mainly with their blood that they listen.

We should not forget that Hitler and his followers are said to have declared on behalf of the Nazis, "We think with our blood." Nor should we forget that today bloodshed and violence have become staples of photojournalism and of moving

[13] See Stravinsky, *Poétique Musicale*, p. 88.

picture and television performance. The very quantity and frequency of these portrayals, visual as well as auditory, tend to dull our sensitivity and our comprehension. Shocking sights and sounds lose their ability to hurt us.

Stravinsky discusses, in his Harvard lectures, thickened interpretations of the most beautiful music, such as Stock gave to Bach. "Such a misunderstanding of the obligations of the interpreter, such pride in numbers, such lust after the multiple," he writes, "betray a total want of musical education. . . . The more you increase the number of points of emission [of sounds], the more confusing is the reception."[14] It is not confusion but simplicity and clarity which unite. So thickening can destroy the central function of music as defined by Seu-ma-tsen.

Yet we should not neglect the creative possibilities to which music in recent times has lent itself. They contain the promise of a possible future for delight in music, as do innovations by great artists for a possible future delight in architecture. According to Stravinsky, the problem for today's composers, and no doubt for contemporary interpreters of music also, is to find the strength to liberate themselves from confusion, emotion, and nationalism under a motto of Verdi's, "To go back would be to progress!"[15]

Insofar as the presentation of music is concerned, some progress of that kind has been made during the past fifty years, since the First World War. Among interpreters Artur Schnabel set a fine example, in his playing of piano works, by confining his programs entirely to compositions which, as he once said, "I have discovered that I can never succeed in playing as well as they should be played." The quality of programs has much improved since he began to set an uncompromising

[14] *Ibid.*, pp. 88–89.

[15] *Ibid.*, p. 31 ("Torniamo all'antico e sarà un progresso!").

standard. Along with better programs has gone a serious movement to perform the works of early composers, as far back as Byrd and even Machaut, as nearly as possible the way their creators intended. There is even an attempt to build old instruments by hand, so that the actual means at the disposal of the interpreters will be no less appropriate to the music than they were in the ages when the works were composed.

It is not enough of course to revive the beauty of the past, through a renewed approach to perfection in the performance of old works of genius. If music is to resume its unifying and civilizing role, it can be only through the creation of new music which is part of our time, different from, but no less unifying than, eighteenth-century music. Here the experiments of Stravinsky himself, of Schoenberg and his school, perhaps of Hindemith and Prokofiev and Copland, too, have led to immense changes in the nature of musical efforts, since audiences were drowned or drugged by the sounds of Wagner and Strauss and their followers. The humanization of industrialism, and the pursuit of the civilization toward which eighteenth-century Europeans were reaching, may depend to a greater extent upon the success of this movement toward order, restraint, and delight in music, and other arts, than upon the efforts to maintain high rates of economic growth.

III. *From the Moving to the Shocking*

In *Racine and Shakespeare*, which was published in 1825, Stendhal observed that the audience for works of literature had been changing. He foresaw that, for a time, persons would continue to assemble in the theatre as witnesses and participants in drama and comedy. But, he suggested, the great demand for stories would come in the future from an ever increasing number of people who would want to read at their own time and pace in the seclusion of their homes. Eventually in the mid-twentieth century people *have* taken to their sitting rooms and even to their beds to hear radio and watch television.

In Stendhal's age the novel was a comparatively recent form, if we consider the entire history of literature running as far back as Homer. It had been yielding remarkable results since the seventeenth century—in Spain with Cervantes, in France with Madame de Lafayette, Marivaux, and Voltaire, and above all in Great Britain with Defoe and Swift, Fielding, Smollett, Sterne, and Richardson. Then in Great Britain, at the outset of the nineteenth century, in Stendhal's time, came the works of Walter Scott and Jane Austen, with their noble motives, and, in the case of the young woman, with her exquisite sensibility, embedded in ethical standards which no other centuries more than the seventeenth in France and the eighteenth in Europe as a whole bequeathed to writers. In the United States novels permeated with humane values were beginning to find a market with Hawthorne and a much smaller one with Melville.

Stendhal foresaw a great future for the novel. His foresight has been justified by what has followed both in connection with the full length novel and with the short story, a form in which a young German of the Napoleonic era, Heinrich von Kleist (1777–1811), excelled. It is amazing how so much work of extraordinary talent and of genius could be squeezed out of the novel form. This suggests that, as is true in a sense of all great art forms, this one is inexhaustible. There was hardly any diminution of the genius either in Great Britain itself, from Thackeray and Dickens, Trollope and Meredith, down to Joyce and Virginia Woolf, or in France from Balzac and Flaubert down through Anatole France and Proust and Bernanos. The greatest achievements in the novel, perhaps, originated in Russia, with Turgenev and Dostoevsky and Tolstoy.

Looking back on the nineteenth century, as one now can from a considerable distance in this year 1967, it seems as if, for a long time, the novel steered clear of the divisive tendencies which appeared in musical compositions and in architecture. Some of the novelists—Balzac and Dostoevsky and Proust foremost among them—were incomparable creators of living individuals. Their characters have, sometimes at least, for the serious reader, an existence more real almost than that of persons he knows. The greatest of these modern writers have been so concerned with the deeper and more universal sides of experience, with the issues of good and evil which approach a common meaning for humans everywhere, that we find in the works themselves nothing substantial to swell the pride of particular nations or groups or classes. There is much to unite, little to divide.

Yet, when we carry history on through the mid-twentieth century, the impression recedes that literature has resisted the major tendencies that have infected architecture and music. In no domain of art perhaps has talent, and even genius, been so swamped by quantity.

A half-century ago Geoffrey Scott suggested that the book possessed enormous prestige when it was very scarce. This prestige was maintained, and the influence of the good writer enormously enhanced, with the rise and spread of printing. Books, with their ideas and their charm, provided the artist with what is, in a way, his most intimate means of communication. When both writer and reader speak the same tongue, there need be no intermediary between them, such as an interpreter provides, and no distracting barrier such as is injected by the presence of others at a lecture. So, until the nineteenth century, books had indirect effects on history that surprise us today. They possessed for a time a power to move almost greater than had verbal communication among the Greeks of the fifth century B.C.

The multiplication of printed matter, facilitated by the manufacture of cheap paper, which has tended to replace the paper made from rags, deprived the book of much of its prestige. One price has been to put a premium on the shocking and the obscene, to encourage writers to go to almost any lengths to capture readers. The temptation is the greater because publishers have been more and more interested not in the intrinsic value of a book but in its selling potential,[16] and the selling potential of the sensational, especially when publicized persons are the subject, has come to be highly rated.

Other developments have made it seem increasingly advantageous to shock in order to obtain readers. During the nineteenth century there had been for a time an increase in the idealists who felt humans were being delivered by progress from sin and evil, as Kant had believed and as later John Stuart Mill and Herbert Spencer, in the early phase of his thought, had hoped.[17] Then, in the decades preceding the First World War, sin and evil were rediscovered with enthusiasm, in most cases without benefit of the redemption of which faith in Christ has sometimes earlier inspired the hope. It has been recently suggested by Irving Kristol that three prominent figures in European letters occupy a place apart: Machiavelli, the Marquis de Sade, and Nietzsche.[18] Others object to the virtues Christ personifies only on the ground that they cannot be achieved, whereas these three deny that they are virtues. They "repudiated the Christian values themselves." During the interval between Machiavelli, the early sixteenth century, and Sade (whose works were not much read, even surreptitiously, until the nineteenth), letters and all the arts played their noblest and most civilizing role. Then, toward the end of the nineteenth century, that "absence of virtue," upon which W. J. Turner commented in connection with music, surged into the realm of literature.

From Sade and Nietzsche, the contemporary German theater derived the peculiar bent it has exhibited since the late nineteenth century. Tragedy became its staple. As Mrs. Tuch-

---

16 See below, pp. 224–25, 275.

17 Cf. Nef, *Western Civilization since the Renaissance*, pp. 383–85.

18 Irving Kristol, "Machiavelli and the Profanation of Politics," in *The Logic of Personal Knowledge*, Essays Presented to Michael Polanyi (London, 1961).

man writes, these German tragedies "were not so much cura-
tive, like Ibsen's, nor compassionate, like Chekhov's, but
obsessively focused on mankind's cruelty to man, on his bent
toward self-destruction, and on death. Death by murder, suicide, or some more esoteric form resolved nearly all German
drama of the nineties and early 1900's."[19] The ennobling character of tragedy, as presented most movingly by Racine, was
almost altogether lost.

Evil can be as contagious as virtue. To the fast multiplication of people and things, the mechanization and automation,
the hurry and the crowding which art has had increasingly
to absorb or contend with during the last hundred and fifty
years, has been added the peculiar fascination of doing wrong
as an end in itself, at a time when the word "wrong" has lost its
meaning and gratuitous acts of violence have acquired prestige.

Every people is now beset by these excesses. What is the
consequence?

The true artist cannot allow any excesses that bestir themselves in his inner life to determine the work that he does, or
even to color that work beyond the legitimate requirements
that are determined by the discipline of his art. Valéry is
reported to have said that an artist can be judged by the character of his refusals. The world of excesses, which has accompanied the very rapid triumph of industrialism, has made the
right refusals increasingly difficult.

It is even more remarkable, therefore, that in literature, as
well as in music and in architecture, there should have been in
recent times serious and partly successful efforts to surmount,

[19] Tuchman, *The Proud Tower*, p. 321. Professor Joseph O. Baylen of
the Institute for Advanced Study writes me: "I believe that Barbara Tuchman
has based *The Proud Tower* (1962) on your thesis in the last chapters of
War and Human Progress (1950)." However that may be, I am glad to have
confirmation for the story that book of mine tells from so accomplished a
writer. As the reader can recognize I have made much use of her book in this
chapter.

in the interest of beauty, the pervasive trends toward decadence. Of these efforts, Valéry is one example and Eliot another.

Eliot's restraint, his effort to resist evil, are evident in his work at all periods of his life. What strikes one in his poetry and criticism, as in the architecture of Wright and in the music of Stravinsky, is the attempt to keep the new material which the industrialized world has brought with it under the control of principles of art. Moreover, Eliot's rehabilitation, in his later criticism, of Milton, Tennyson, and Kipling, is in major part dictated by his sense of the value of principles which these poets exemplify and which helped him to provide a framework for his own verse, full as it is of imaginative innovations. A similar sense of the value of principles is manifested by Stravinsky in his predilection for the music of Bach, of Haydn, and of Mozart. So Eliot's work and Stravinsky's show that, even in the contemporary world, artists *can* successfully resist the divisive trends, powerful though these are.

What made art in the seventeenth and eighteenth centuries in the main a force in the building of civilization was "the presence of virtue," using that phrase in the sense W. J. Turner used it in considering its absence in the music of Wagner and Brahms. What has made for decadence in art in recent times is "the absence of virtue." The power which some artists have shown to surmount such tendencies is likely to seem to those who have absorbed the arguments of dialectical materialism, or the Spenglerian scheme of historical cycles,[20] almost a miracle.

If one had to reduce to a single phrase all the unfavorable conditions which confront the search for beauty in our times one could say perhaps that there is too much of everything. In her valuable discussion of recent German music, Mrs.

[20] Cf. below, pp. 98 ff.

Tuchman quotes Romain Rolland. He cannot be regarded as a confirmed anti-German, for he was under a cloud in France during the war of 1914–18 for his neutral position. *"There is too much music in Germany,"* Rolland wrote in italics shortly before the outbreak of that war. And he added: "This is not a paradox. There is no worse misfortune for art than a super-abundance of it."[21]

Goethe once said, in a much less affluent Germany, "In der Beschränkung zeigt sich der Meister." There is no such thing as beauty unlimited. The suggestion recently made by a biologist, that the progress of his science would produce a thousand Beethovens,[22] is calculated to turn the stomach of the discriminating. Among the greatest achievements of the civilization that the Europeans built up with the help of art, were the limits they were able to maintain in all domains. The incredible speed of change which has marked the past hundred and fifty years has made it increasingly difficult to maintain limits that are necessary to beauty.

It is disquieting to realize that among those Americans who have set, since the War of Secession, the most valiant example in the art of literature, several have found their principal nourishment abroad, in the Europe whence their ancestors came. This was partly true of Stephen Crane and still more of Edith Wharton. It was almost altogether true of James and Eliot, both of whom (and in the case of Eliot from a rather early age) chose to become citizens of Great Britain.

Contrary to what is still frequently taught by economic historians, Great Britain hurried into industrialism less rapidly and less violently than most countries.[23] There the process of industrialization began earlier than elsewhere, so that the shock of still more rapid change, when it came after about 1780, was somewhat mitigated. Mounting rapidly after the seventeen-

---

[21] Tuchman, *The Proud Tower*, p. 301.

[22] Cf. below, pp. 83–84, 236–37.

[23] Nef, *The Conquest of the Material World* (Chicago, 1964), p. 143.

eighties the rates of economic growth tended to slow down in Great Britain during the second half of the nineteenth century. The pace of industrialization became slow compared with that which then developed in most other countries, particularly Germany and the United States. In Great Britain literature could be created in relative peace, and absorbed by a reading public more quietly and at a more leisurely pace than in most other countries. So, since the mid-nineteenth century, literature remained a more intimate art in Great Britain than in the Americas or in central Europe.

iv. *Painting and the Tradition of Universalism*

Until at least the world war of 1939–45, there was, among the Western nations, a more striking exception even than Great Britain to the dizzy speed of industrialization which now besets the world generally. That exception was France. If James and Eliot chose to make their home in England rather than in France, it was partly because as writers, the English language was much closer to them than the French. But for the arts generally, and above all for painting, France, more than any country, provided a mecca for artists from all over the world, especially after its defeat by Germany in 1870–71. Stravinsky had already removed to Paris (which was to remain his home until the Second World War) when in 1913 Pierre Monteux, the orchestra conductor, gave the *Sacre du Printemps* its first performance.

By that time painters of exceptional gifts from all over the world had begun to find themselves especially in France. Van Gogh came from Holland; Mary Cassatt from the United States; Picasso from Spain; Modigliani from Italy; Fougita from Japan; Pascin from Bulgaria. In 1911, Chagall, an unknown young man from Russia, had settled into a modest studio in La Ruche, an apartmental haven provided in Paris for young and promising but impecunious artists. Called back to Russia in 1914 by his love for Bella, he finally returned in 1922–23 to the France he was never to desert. So the visual arts in France remained cosmopolitan.

Of all the arts, painting is the one which Westerners have made most their own, the art which has had the most influence, in itself and through its influence on other arts as well as on all pictorial expression, in bringing beauty into Western experience more closely than into that of other societies. Beginning as far back as the early nineteenth century, the pre-eminence of the French in the art of painting was foreshadowed in the work of Ingres, Delacroix, and Gericault, and of the slightly younger Corot and Courbet. Then, with the generation born in the eighteen-forties, with Manet and Monet, Degas, Renoir, Pissarro, Sisley, and Cézanne, French leadership began to be unrivaled. The supremacy of the French asylum in the visual arts was reaffirmed by the generations born in the eighteen-sixties, -seventies, and -eighties, perhaps by no one more than the young Seurat, who died at thirty, after having created "Un Dimanche d'Eté à l'Ile de la Grande Jatte." It has been spoken of as "one of those great pictures in which every generation finds the meaning best suited to it. . . . [It] remains the latest and the last of the *poesie* with which, after Giorgione's example, painters have endowed us."[24]

Many other extraordinarily gifted artists since 1886 have been helped by the French scene to provide beauty: Rousseau (the customs collector), Maillol (the great sculptor), Matisse, Rouault, Derain, Segonzac, Braque. Not to mention masters who, like Picasso and Chagall, are identified in everyone's mind with that legendary France of which the Swiss, Jean-Jacques Rousseau, had a Hungarian character say, in a little known play, that so far as the independent mind and heart are concerned France is "the common fatherland of the human race."[25] What drew great artists there was the persistence of

[24] John Russell, *Seurat* (New York, 1965), pp. 156, 160.

[25] Jean Boorsch, "Jean-Jacques Rousseau, Playwright," in *The American Society Legion of Honor Magazine* XXXVII, No. 1 (1966), 15.

the European universalism of the eighteenth century. The fruits of this movement in painting have now penetrated the entire world, for the language of pictorial art does not need translation.

In recent painting the fundamental importance of tradition and restraint appears perhaps most impressively in Derain. In 1920 André Salmon wrote of him with the highest respect as the "regulator"[26] among those artists, then still young, who were being fiercely maligned and who are now so widely recognized. Derain, more than the others, represented the traditional function Frenchmen had performed in art since the seventeenth century of stressing those principles of form and order which have provided scope in music, architecture, ballet, and literature, as well as in painting, for a long line of artistic creators.

Derain's career as a painter may be compared to Valéry's as a poet, of whom it used to be said, half in derision, half in admiration: "Comme il produit peu!" Derain waged an intense struggle within himself to keep his extraordinary gifts in leash, as a means of achieving the order and depth which are beyond technique and which so much twentieth-century artistic effort lacks. As a young man he destroyed many of his pictures, at a time when he could already have sold them to advantage. Unlike most of his contemporaries he stopped painting during his seven years of service as a soldier, when conditions did not permit his life to revolve around his art. According to Elie Faure, the distinguished historian, Derain did not even sketch during the war from 1914 to 1918. "But the war helped him to make discoveries in painting because it helped him to make discoveries in himself."[27] In the same essay Faure describes Derain's concern with a synthesis of all great painting. "Unlike his contemporaries," Faure wrote of him, "he does not fear to undergo and even to confess the influence

26 André Salmon, *L'Art vivant* (Paris, 1920), pp. 75–84.

27 Elie Faure, *Derain* (Paris, 1924; my translation).

that the masters, including the recent masters, have had upon his sensibility." He feared his own facility to the point of almost wishing he could tie his hands behind his back to avoid the smooth results he could so easily obtain. His restraint helped him to concentrate his powers on those few magnificent realizations which he managed to bring off in his most mature periods from 1910 to 1914, and still more from 1919, when he was demobilized, to 1926. That last date, curiously, seems to have put a term to some of the most serious efforts in the creative art of the twentieth century.

The history of painting during the hundred years from 1840 to 1940 may serve as a demonstration of the value of making haste slowly. While the population of the Western world increased some five- or six-fold during those hundred years, the population of France hardly increased at all. And we now know with statistical precision, through the recently published results of an inquiry conducted by T. J. Markovith, that as late as the Second Empire and even the Third Republic, the individual craftsman, working alone or with a few apprentices, was the dominant force in French industry. Even the French building industries and public works were still in the artisanal stage, with a preponderance of manual labor, as late as 1870. In manufacturing down to 1900 the major form of organization in France was still domestic work, labor which was often creative in the home or small shop, frequently an annex of the home. *Travail à domicile* had been responsible for four-fifths of the industrial output of France at the end of the *ancien régime*, between 1780 and 1790. During the second half of the nineteenth century it was still responsible for almost two-thirds of the industrial output.[28]

In a talk in 1963 in Washington, at a conference of the Center for Human Understanding, Marc Chagall asked, "Why have we become so anxious?" He confided to his audience his

[28] T. J. Markovith, "Les secteurs dominants de l'industrie française," in *Analyse et Prévision* (Paris), I, No. 3 (1966), 161–76, esp. 163–64.

fears about contemporary visual art, his own included. These were fears that painting has for long been invaded by forces of decadence similar to those we have touched upon in architecture, in music, and in literature. ". . . Little by little," he said,

our world seems to be a smaller world on which we small ones swarm, clinging to the smallest elements in our nature, until we submerge ourselves in the tiny pieces of nature, even in the atom.

Doesn't this so-called scientific gift of nature, by emptying the soul, limit the source of poetry? Doesn't it deprive man of even the physical opportunities for calm and quiet? And doesn't this deprive him of any sense of moral direction connected with his life and his creative work? . . .

While I pretend to no philosophical calling, I cannot fail to feel what today is strangling art and culture and sometimes life itself.[29]

Chagall's concern over the dangers to art is the more impressive, coming as it does from a contemporary who has managed to retain in his works, during the last sixty years, an element of delight, of joy, derived from color and fancy yet not abstract, which is different from Renoir but in an equally naïve way hardly less happy. Chagall has done this in the teeth of world wars, of poverty, of the communism from which he fled, and in the teeth of exile when he escaped from the Nazi invasion of France, to live in New York from 1941 to 1947.

There has been in recent times much rather foolish discussion as to whether "God is dead." If He exists He cannot die. Isn't this also true of beauty? In Chagall's own work, and in that of other contemporary artists, evidence is to be found that the visual arts exist. In Chagall's case an artist has turned, with remarkable success, in his seventies, to a renewal of the art of stained glass windows, which had died as a craft in Europe in the middle of the sixteenth century.

In the realm of visual ornamentation, as in the realm of architecture, there are promising efforts to make use of oppor-

29 See Nef (ed.), *Bridges of Human Understanding* (New York, 1964), pp. 117–19.

tunities for novel kinds of artistic achievement, which the triumph of industrialism and of the modern sciences has rendered possible. Man's outlook on motion has been changed by the acceptance of Einstein's theory of relativity and Heisenberg's theory of indeterminacy. Artists are showing that they can create works of beauty by objects in motion, just as architects are showing they can create works of beauty by skyscrapers. "Modern works [of kinetic sculpture]," writes Peter Selz, "are distinguished from all the automata of the past and the computers of the present in that their action attempts to be indeterminate."[30]

Invention in the arts may be only beginning. It is conceivable that humans could build a civilized world in the future with the help of art, as the Europeans set out to build a civilized world in the seventeenth and eighteenth centuries with its help. While this would be a different art from any art of the past, certain principles concerning form and order would have to be an inspiration not only for the artists but for society —and society now can be hardly anything less than world society. A resurgence of the great artistic principles out of which beauty has always been created, principles which help the artist to fall in love with his assignment, is indispensable. These principles were demonstrated tentatively in the early years of this century, by Wright in architecture, by Stravinsky in music, by Eliot in literature, by Derain in painting.

"Is there not a foundation for art," Chagall proceeds in his essay,

other than that offered by the decorative art which exists only to please, or by the art of experience, and by that pitiless art whose purpose is to shock us?
In connection with Art I have often spoken of the color which is Love. . . . It is childish to repeat the truth, which has been

[30] Peter Selz, *Directions in Kinetic Sculpture* (Berkeley, Calif., 1966).

known so long: In all its aspects the world can be saved only by love. . . .[31]

The values upon which industrialism was reared were different from those it has tended to foster. Yet, in spite of unfavorable conditions generated by rapid economic growth and mechanization, and by an economist's approach to creative work on the part of dealers in public relations, the principles basic to beauty have reappeared in new artistic forms. If, as seems more than probable, beauty is essential to civilization, the reaffirmation of these principles by artists in the times ahead may be of fundamental importance to the welfare of the human race.

In the future open to them, humans cannot have everything. They have to choose. The price of wanting too much may be to lose all. The price of choosing beauty, of discovering and fostering love which can nourish it, is a renewal of discipline and delight in quality, capable of making beauty a force in history such as it has never been before.

[31] *Bridges of Human Understanding,* p. 120.

4 The Moral and Intellectual Crisis

In the realm of the good and the true, tendencies similar to those in the realm of the beautiful are visible historically. Foundations for the spread and practical application of the modern sciences, and for the enthronement of the free market and the multiplication of production, were laid through a respect for moral and intellectual principles which the triumph of industrialism in recent times has tended to undermine. The increasing disposition to measure all progress in terms of rates of economic growth has contributed, not only to a crisis in the realm of art, but to a moral and intellectual crisis.

Desires for wealth as driving forces in the actions of individuals are nothing new. In the eighteenth century, when the control of bargaining and measuring was by no means as efficacious as it has since become, these desires were not inconsistent with a sense that all Europe could be a single republic of the spirit. When mitigated by restraints in the interest of honesty and generosity, the pursuit of gain contributed to the coming of civilization. What is novel, and what is associated with the rise of economics as a learned discipline, especially after the mid-nineteenth century, after the times of Adam Smith and J. S. Mill in Great Britain, Sismondi and Ernest Renan on the Continent, is the disposition to equate all values with material values. Wealth measured quantitatively in terms of money has been made by economic philosophers—Marxian and anti-Marxian alike—an end in itself, the end for which society exists.

Yet neither moral nor intellectual qualities, any more than the qualities that flower in beauty, can be brought into a satisfactory relationship with what the late Professor Pigou called "the measuring-rod of money."[1] To measure either morality

[1] A. C. Pigou, *The Economics of Welfare* (London, 1921), p. 11.

or intelligence in terms of the money they command currently in the market place is to destroy their meaning. The disposition among economists and others to extend the principles of economics to cover all aspects of human life involves a denial of the independent existence of man's mind and spirit. It was an axiom among the wisest philosophers of antiquity that happiness and righteousness in the individual were achieved when a proper harmony was maintained between what Plato called the three attributes of the soul—reason, passion or spirit, and desire or appetite. Harmony could be obtained only when the rational principle ruled both passion and appetite, and the spirit became the ally of reason rather than the slave of desire.

The multiplication of colleges, universities, and research centers during the past century has been accompanied by an increasing disharmony in this ancient philosophical sense. It is almost as if learning had come to regard it as proper for desire to govern both the spirit and the mind. It is almost as if what the wise men of the past regarded as the order necessary to human happiness had been stood on its head. Almost the only curbs on the appetite which learning now regards as important are those which contribute to man's physical well-being and material wealth, without reference to his mind and spirit. Thus the satisfaction of men's desires has come to be sanctioned as a contribution to the welfare ultimately not of the soul but of the body. The disharmony between the various attributes of the soul seems to be at the root of our distress. How has this disharmony been produced? What is the significance of the moral and intellectual crisis for those who are concerned with the future of civilization, and in particular with the future welfare of the United States?

1. *The Collapse of Standards*

We are faced with the breakdown of established beliefs and traditions concerning faith, ethics, and politics. The standards which have fallen have a long history. They can be traced back easily to early Christian and to ancient Greek society, as well as to the Middle Ages. As Western society seems to have grown up mainly after the tenth century, these beliefs and traditions, confirmed and amplified in the Gothic age, form an integral part of our heritage. It is not easy to determine when they began to give way. In a sense they were undermined before the Reformation. They were pieced together again in new forms in modern times. Their virtual obliteration is a recent phenomenon. It has taken place since the turn of the twentieth century.

There is a disposition—now rather less strong, no doubt, than a few decades ago—to blame our plight on the hypocrisy of our Victorian ancestors. That offers a comfortable means of evading responsibility, one of the cardinal points in the strategy of the older generations. Laying the blame on the nineteenth century has also the sounder excuse of being justified, at least to some extent.

"Oh triste dix-neuvième siècle!" Stendhal was fond of repeating in one of the incomparable novels with which he ornamented the years that followed the fall of Napoleon. Stendhal wrote in the midst of what he considered revolutionary developments, comprising not only economic but social, political, intellectual, and cultural transformations. Since Stendhal's times, since the mid-nineteenth century, such revolutionary transformations became part of the experience of all Western nations and eventually of all countries of the world; and after the eighteen-forties the pace of change was far more rapid in countries other than France or even Great Britain. But, in the initial stages of the rising rates of economic growth that had begun at the juncture of the eighteenth and nineteenth centuries, France as well as Great Britain seemed to be in the vanguard (from about 1815 to about 1848) of what Frenchmen and later Englishmen christened the "industrial revolution."[2] Combining more than any French writer of his times

[2] Nef, "The Industrial Revolution Reconsidered," *Journal of Economic History*, III, No. 1 (1943), 2–3.

the old classical tradition, that was dying, with the new romantic tradition, that was being born, Stendhal felt acutely the disappearance of the powers of reason, order, sweetness, and finesse, which had been cultivated with so many pains and such considerable success in the France of Louis XIV. Like Delacroix, the great painter who was his younger contemporary, Stendhal saw with deep misgivings these qualities swallowed up in a middle-class world. Money, machinery, and natural science were becoming the arbiters of man's destiny. Form was disappearing. The change was more shocking in France than in England, not because the actual increase in the volume of output was as rapid or the progress of large-scale industry in private hands as striking, but because France was less prepared than England for the change. The change in France was also more shocking because scientific knowledge and material improvement were somewhat less congenial as objectives to Frenchmen than to Englishmen, notwithstanding the remarkable originality of some French scientists and technicians. France has produced a number of inventive geniuses, but, until very recently, it has been other countries that have exploited their ideas. Pasteur's development of the germ theory of disease did not enable the French to reduce their death rate as effectively as other great Western peoples. De Gaulle's proposals for a mechanized army, rejected by the French military leaders, were perfected by the Germans who conquered his country.

In the century of Louis XIV, who died in 1715, France had made few adjustments to the new commercial spirit and to scientific thought, comparable to those made by England under the Stuarts. She was less well prepared than England to harness the new forces effectively for economic progress. Unlike Germany, France had neither the natural resources nor the traditions to make an efficient use of the new forces for European conquest. The attempt of the French to do so under Napoleon had no sequel.

It is natural to think of the nineteenth century as a century of economics and natural science. Yet for all the prestige that attached to economic and scientific thought, the methods of inquiry associated with them were not at once allowed to determine the character of other learned disciplines. During the greater part of the century, the attacks on Christianity and the older humanism did not succeed in destroying their autonomous influence in the family, in the churches, in the schools, colleges, and universities. For a time there was a reconciliation of, or at least a balance between, Christianity and humanism and the materialism bred of the new industrialism. However much thinkers like Renan questioned the foundations of Christianity as revealed in the Scriptures, they accepted the code of ethics contained in the New Testament as the only sound basis for conduct. Even Mill spoke, in his essay "On Liberty," of the survival of Christianity in the Roman Empire as an example of the triumph of truth in the face of persecution.[3] While scientific inquiry was beginning to undermine theology, it was seldom suggested that the principles of justice and compassion associated with the teaching of Catholic and Protestant churches alike were subject to doubt. The humanism of early modern times had freed man to some extent from his dependence upon constant community worship. In its English form it had freed him from the necessity of adhering to the universal Catholic church. But it had placed upon him, as an individual, the responsibility for maintaining the virtues for which Christ had been crucified. That responsibility had been accepted by Christian learning and incorporated into it. The traditions of Christian learning provided the Western peoples in the nineteenth century with a common bond which took the place of the common bond provided by theology in the thirteenth century. In Christian learning the Western nations found a unifying system of culture which partly offset the

[3] Cf. Nef, "On the Future of American Civilization," *Review of Politics,* II, No. 3 (1940), 261.

tendencies toward division bred of nationalism and economic individualism.

Christian humanism had flowered long before the nineteenth century. It was an expression of the Renaissance, which provided man with a renewed sense of his dignity, at the same time that it provided him with a new conception of government, which, if allowed to assert itself without restraint, was capable of crushing that dignity. Milton has been called the "last and greatest English representative" of Christian humanism.[4] But the values associated with it were not lost with Milton's death in 1674, for they had entered into the discipline of the churches and even more into that of the schools and universities. As John Morley once said, "the substitution of the Book for the Church was the essence of the Protestant Revolt." The reading of the Bible, made accessible everywhere with the spread of printing, was enjoined in the grammar schools and was practiced as a regular part of daily family life. What was especially significant, it was read aloud and was for many children the only book and for nearly all the most important. With this discipline of careful reading there was combined, especially among the Puritans, a tremendous sense of human responsibility for the good life, a responsibility expressed so movingly in *Paradise Lost*.[5] For generation after generation the English-speaking peoples absorbed the Christian ethics, in a pure form, in their early and impressionable years.

The persistence of the moral and intellectual values of Christian humanism, the acceptance by English thought of the responsibility of the individual for the maintenance of Christian justice, are brought out strikingly in the eighteenth century in the novels of Richardson and again in the nineteenth century in those of Trollope. The great enthusiasm for both

[4] *Times Literary Supplement*, January 18, 1941.

[5] Cf. Foster Watson, *The English Grammar Schools to 1660: Their Curriculum and Practice* (Cambridge, 1908), pp. 60–61, 114–15, and chap. 3 generally.

these writers in their time suggests that there was widespread admiration for the values they upheld. It is no accident that in our time, when Christian humanism has lost its strength, Milton, Richardson, and Trollope are all less read and less admired than some of their contemporaries who were not, as they were, first and foremost moralists.

During the late eighteenth and most of the nineteenth centuries, much was done to strengthen the practice of the Christian virtues, especially in the English-speaking countries. Partly, perhaps, as a result of material improvement, physical cruelty and—at least in Great Britain—crimes of violence were diminishing. The reformers of the industrial revolution were great humanitarians. They laid their emphasis on the duty of leaders to be charitable, and to diminish the suffering—above all the physical suffering—which men and women either passively or actively imposed on their fellows and which nature imposes, in varying degrees, on all people. It seemed for a time that, if improvement were left to the individual conscience, good could be counted on to triumph over evil. It seemed that the pursuit of private interests in economic transactions could be counted on to promote the general welfare for centuries to come.

"There must have been a catch in it somewhere; it all seemed to be working so well, yet it ended badly." In those words one of the most impassioned writers of our times, the late R. H. Tawney, summed up the nineteenth century. Why did that century end badly? What was the catch? Surely there was nothing wrong with feeding the poor, with reducing physical cruelty and suffering of every kind, with trying to outlaw war. All these were excellent things, the signs of a society in most ways more humane and enlightened than any other in history. The efforts of the humanitarians cannot be dismissed simply as manifestations of Victorian hypocrisy.

Much of the trouble lay in the growing disposition among the reformers to mistake means for ends. Woman suffrage, the spread of contraceptives, shorter working hours, for example, came eventually to be regarded as good in themselves rather than as providing men with opportunities to reach toward the highest standards of conduct and intelligence. The most generous men and women of the Victorian Age were devoting their lives, with their altruism and their love of mankind, to means. Few generous and intelligent persons were left to look out for ends. The opportunities offered by the improved material conditions were gradually forgotten. Progress in sanitation, heating, bathing, and refrigeration became ultimate objectives.

The case of a liberal and successful American professor in one of our leading universities is suggestive of what became a prevalent attitude. In his early years in the profession, he and his wife had campaigned for woman suffrage, for prohibition, for the eight-hour day, and for world peace. In 1920, when he was hardly on the threshold of what we now regard as middle life, he bemoaned to his colleagues and students that all these objectives had been won. That was, he admitted, a good thing in itself. But it had deprived him of the need of striving for human betterment. Since all the elements that had been lacking for human happiness had now been provided, with the ending of the great war waged to make the world "safe for democracy," there was, the professor explained, nothing more in life for him and his wife to strive after. Such a profession of satisfaction hardly helped him to hand on to the young a torch that would encourage them to labor for human betterment, although the lighting of such a torch was once regarded as the most important function of a great teacher. This professor's students concluded, not unnaturally, that there was no need for them to devote their lives to anything beyond making money or seeking promotion.

The humanitarian movements of the nineteenth century were accompanied by the gradual withdrawal of the training in responsibility and generosity that had done so much to produce the great reforming spirit of the age. The Christian morality and the Christian humanism that had emerged from the Reformation and the Renaissance were the expression in a new form of ancient principles which had piloted the Western peoples throughout their constructive history, however much the actual conduct of mortal men and women fell short of those principles. In their zeal for humanitarianism and gentleness many generous people began, not unnaturally, to distrust the authority and the methods of the principal institutions which had hitherto nourished virtue and had insisted upon the duty of men to fulfill moral obligations to their fellows. These institutions were the church, the family, and the school, with its emphasis upon classical training and upon the discipline of the mind without reference to material ends. As controlled by men and women somewhat less than perfect—priests and clerics, fathers and mothers, teachers and professors—these institutions exercised a tyranny sometimes physical, more often mental, over those confided to their charge. This led many distinguished men to believe that they should free the people from the obligation to serve these institutions. This was to be done, not by abolishing the institutions, but by changing their character. In the past they had been expected to arouse in their members a sense of responsibility, to inculcate in the young good moral and intellectual habits. Henceforth these functions were to give way before the demand for self-development. Family ties were to be loosened. As sharp distinctions between good and evil were no longer recognized, as it was taken for granted that children would find what was best for them if left to themselves, the young were to become the guides of their parents. Women were not only to be treated by men as equals; henceforth there was to be little differentiation between the spheres of activity of men and women. Women were no longer to be tied down to their homes. If women made a bad job of home management, so much the worse for the home. "To hell with the home," became the half-serious

77

slogan of advanced women, some of whom felt a great affection not only for humanity but for their own children. The schools were to turn to so-called "practical" studies. In extreme cases, attempts were made to have the studies conform to the wishes of the children, whatever these happened to be. Needless to say, little had been done to train the children in good mental and moral habits. It was felt to be enough if they had been trained, like dogs and other domestic animals, to take care of themselves physically. That was, perhaps, not the most efficacious way to prepare them to choose wisely how to train themselves in matters of intelligence and morality.

With some notable exceptions, the United States was tributary to Europe in its cultural life and in the development of its thought, especially during the early decades of the nineteenth century. This did not mean that the traditions of Christian humanism were less powerful or influential in the young republic than in the older European nations. In some ways those traditions were more effective than on the continent of Europe or even in early Victorian England. Theology, moral philosophy, and political economy in America may have been almost completely sterile insofar as original creative thought was concerned—but imitators and followers can hold beliefs with a greater intensity and much more dogmatically than the creators themselves.

The United States of the present has something in common with that of the early nineteenth century. There was then a similar spendthrift attitude toward the economic resources with which the people were blessed, a similar desire for physical change and movement, a similar distaste and even distrust of art and thought (when either was pursued with what Veblen might call "intemperate enthusiasm"), a similar pressure on citizens to conform in their manners and their morals to the ways of living of their neighbors. But there were then general standards in manners and morals.

In their manners and their moral outlook, the Americans of

the early nineteenth century were poles apart from those who now occupy this continent. In the United States a century ago, the people believed fervently in Christianity and in Christian ethics. On all such matters Tocqueville was the shrewdest of observers. He found the Christian faith more generally and more devoutly held by the members of the Catholic and Protestant churches in America than by churchgoers in those Latin countries where the state still countenanced only one form of worship. Nowhere in Europe, he found, was conjugal fidelity so respected. Nowhere was the family as a unit regarded as so sacred. Nowhere were the children brought up in as strict a code of Christian morals. In the schools and colleges great attention was paid to the fundamentals of spelling, arithmetic, and grammar, and to the study of Greek and Latin. The leading writers of classical antiquity and of western Europe were treated with no less respect than abroad and in the case of the theologians and moralists with no less reverence. As Van Wyck Brooks has shown, an intelligent renewal of an interest in classical and European culture at Harvard College helped prepare the soil for that "flowering of New England" which gave the United States its first important literary movement.

If, in spite of much bigotry and misunderstanding, Christian faith and schooling were once taken even more seriously in the United States than in Europe, the reaction against both was no less violent when it came. After the Civil War, and especially after the great growth of industry in the 1870's and 1880's, the leaders in American thought and education began to look upon the old conceptions of the family, the church, and the school, not as common bonds but as chains which they had outgrown. The decline of religious belief, the weakening of the sense of family responsibility, the abandonment of schooling in the disciplines of writing and careful reading, have gone on more rapidly during the twentieth century in the United States than in Europe. The emancipation of women from their obligations as sisters, wives, and mothers, the emancipation of most men and women from religious obligations, seemed to progressive-minded Americans to offer a highroad to the freedom of opportunity and the freedom of enterprise which they regarded as essential to progress. At the same time professors of education and university presidents began to advocate the substitution of practical studies for careful drill in the fundamentals of speaking and writing and for the reading of serious books, old as well as contemporary. Elementary schools were founded in which twenty-five-minute lessons in mathematics and English composition were interspersed with twenty-five-minute lessons in cooking, sewing, clay modeling, typesetting, geography, singing, gymnastics, and social relations. If the boys and girls still read any enduring works of literature in their childhood, they did it under the influence of parents whom the neighbors regarded as eccentric, because the task imposed interfered with playtime in the company of normal, healthy children. If the Bible was still read to them, they could not always expect a response from their playmates. "Have you read the Bible?" one of my friends in 1939 asked an excitable seven-year-old boy, to the astonishment of his very well-educated and widely read father, a publisher who has lived with books all his life. "What's that?" the child fired back.

The great increase in the number and the change in the character of immigrants after the Civil War facilitated the collapse of the old standards inherent in Christian morality, learning, and family loyalty. The primary objective of the later immigrants was economic improvement. Unlike many of the early settlers, they did not come to America because of the opportunities for freedom to worship as they chose.

Anyone who has had the experience of teaching in an American university, and who has tried to speak of justice, goodness, or truth, will realize that these words have lost almost all meaning, not only for the students, graduate as well as undergraduate, but also for many members of the faculty. Americans still defend the right of the individual to say whatever he may please. It is only with difficulty that they can be brought to extend this principle of free speech to cover the case of men who claim the right to judge what other men say in terms of its contribution to justice or goodness or beauty. It is easy enough to rule out what is said or done on the ground that it is unscientific or inexpedient, but it is nothing less than revolutionary to rule out what is said or done on the ground that it is unjust or evil or ugly in its implications. The case of a writer on social questions who was being considered for an honor in an American university is instructive. In support of his candidacy it was urged that he had devised some new methods of statistical calculation in relation to social conditions. When one of the committee brought forward the information that he had been recently detained on suspicion that he was a secret agent of a foreign government, his supporter was heard to murmur, "What's that against him?" If it had been possible to show that the man's methods of statistical calculation were being used to further the objectives of another government, the same question might have been asked, provided the government was not communist.

II. *Rise of the Human Sciences*

The new attitude toward firm standards in thought and art is a product to a large degree of the view that, in affairs of the mind, scientific experiment and observation offer the only reliable paths to certainty. There are several kinds of rational process, and the exclusive use of methods appropriate for dealing with matter and space leaves little room for beauty, virtue, or wisdom. As a result partly of the "unscientific" assumption that the methods employed in the physical and biological *laboratories* are exhaustive insofar as the reasoning mind is concerned, almost exclusive emphasis is laid upon the changeable and the fleeting. The existence of anything approaching permanent values is more and more denied. In the exploration of organic and inorganic matter, new theories are continually replacing old. As scientific methods have been extended to social and humanistic studies, the view has become very general in the social sciences and the humanities that today's knowledge exists mainly to be superseded by tomorrow's; that all constructions of the mind are merely scaffolds for scaffolds, that each generation writes a history, a politics, a sociology, or an economics almost entirely irrelevant for the next. In economic science the story of Alfred Marshall's gesture to one of his favorite pupils is suggestive of a viewpoint concerning the study of man in relation to man that was accepted literally, almost without question. He presented this pupil with a copy of his classic work, *The Principles of Economics,* the fruit of rather more than two decades of thought and labor on his own part and that of his gifted wife. On the flyleaf he inscribed the copy to his student, "in the hope that in due course you will render this treatise obsolete."[6]

The basic emphasis in the sciences is different from that in art or thought. Scientific investigations build on the works of previous scientists and often largely or entirely supersede them. The work of a great artist or a great philosopher is complete within itself. It is influenced profoundly by past art or thought, but as a creation it is independent of them. While it can influence and inspire future artists and philosophers, it cannot be improved on or done over again to advantage by another person, no matter how gifted. It has added something permanent to human riches. As Sainte-Beuve wrote:

Un vrai classique . . . c'est un auteur qui a enrichi l'esprit humain, qui en a réellement augmenté le trésor, qui lui a fait faire un pas de plus, qui a découvert quelque vérité morale non équivoque, ou ressaisi quelque passion éternelle dans ce coeur ou tout semblait connu et exploré; qui a rendu sa pensée, son observation ou son invention, sous une forme n'importe laquelle, mais large et grande, fine et sensée, saine et belle en soi; qui a parlé à tous dans un style à lui et qui se trouve aussi celui de tout le monde, dans un style

[6] J. M. Keynes, *Essays in Biography* (London, 1933), pp. 253–54.

nouveau sans néologisme, nouveau et antique, aisement contemporain de tous les âges. Un tel classique a pu être un moment révolu-
tionnaire, il a pu le paraître du moins, mais il ne l'est pas; il n'a fait
main basse d'abord autour de lui, il n'a renversé ce que le gênait
que pour rétablir bien vite l'équilibre au profit de l'ordre et du
beau.[7]

The ridiculous attempt made many years ago, and now happily forgotten, to finish Schubert's *Unfinished Symphony*
brings out a difference between the arts and the sciences. It is
frequently possible for a scientist to complete the unfinished
experiments of his predecessors. In the one case the material is
dominated by the human mind and spirit—in the other the
human mind is placed at the disposal of the material. When
the mind is mainly a free agent, as in art, it creates a work of
its own which appeals to the world because of qualities common to all men but which as a work is particular to its author
to a degree never quite true of even the most revolutionary
scientific theories of the twentieth century, even of those
which are altering the nature of the sciences.

An account was recently given me of an episode that
occurred when Heisenberg was visiting Cambridge University.[8] The discoverer of the principle of indeterminacy is a
gifted amateur pianist. One evening after dinner in hall with
the fellows of a college, he was persuaded to sit down at the

[7] "A true classic . . . is an author who has enriched the human mind and
spirit, who has really added to their treasure, who has led them to take another step, who has discovered an unequivocal moral truth, or captured some
eternal passion in the human heart where all seemed to be known and explored; who has conveyed his thought, his observation, or his invention in a
form which, whatever its nature, is broad and great, fine and subtle, sound
and beautiful in itself; who has spoken to all in a style of his own which
proves to be universal, new without new words, new and old, easily contemporary with every age. Such a classic may be revolutionary for a moment, may at least seem to be, but is not; it lays hands upon what lies about
it and overthrows what is in its way only to re-establish quickly the equi-
librium for the benefit of order and beauty" (C.-A. Sainte-Beuve, "Qu'est-ce
qu'un classique?" *Causeries du Lundi*, October 21, 1850). The translation of
this passage from Sainte-Beuve is mine.

[8] By Erich Heller.

instrument. He played the last sonata of Beethoven, Opus 111. He finished amid silence produced by the majesty of the music. "There, gentlemen," he remarked, "you have the difference between science and art. If I had never lived, another would have discovered the principle of indeterminacy. Given the evolution of science the discovery was inevitable. But if Beethoven had never lived, no one would have written that sonata."

It was Goethe who said, "Was ist das Allgemeine? Der einzelne Fall. Was ist das Besondere? Millionen Fälle!"[9] While he speaks as no one else could, the great genius in the realm of art or in the realm of thought speaks to everyone and for everyone as no scientist who is dependent on matter can ever hope to do.[10]

During this century the methods and outlook of the natural scientist have been extended in the American universities to cover all the activities of the mind. The scientists themselves are less responsible for this extension than the scholars who deal with the humanities and with social and economic relations. This led to scientific theories of aesthetics. Thus what has been called the physical process of "intellection," which belongs in the realm of psychology, has been extended to cover ontology, epistemology, and ethics, which are not subject to scientific analysis as is the physical structure of the brain. The old distinction between science and art, which was readily understood when Victor Hugo wrote his essay on Shakespeare a century ago, was almost entirely forgotten.

The extraordinary change in the outlook of scholars in these matters in the United States can be seen by comparing definitions in authoritative encyclopedias. Let us take, for example, the phrase "natural law." Natural law is indispensable to the whole conception of limited government, a conception of vital

---

9 "What is the universal? The unique. What is the particular? The everyday occurrence!" I am indebted for this quotation to the late Artur Schnabel. The translation is mine.

10 Cf. above, p. 81.

interest, as Professor McIlwain has shown, to anyone who wishes to preserve democracy.[11] In Western history the appeal to natural law has been a means of restraining tyrants, of preventing an arbitrary exercise of political power whether by a king or a representative assembly. In the *Century Dictionary*, prepared by American scholars of the 1880's, under the direction of the late Professor William Dwight Whitney of Yale University, the definition of natural law is this: "The expression of right reason or the dictate of religion, inhering in nature and man, and having ethically a binding force as a rule of civil conduct; the will of man's Maker."[12] Since at least the middle of the seventeenth century, the English phrase "natural law" has had another meaning—the scientific. The "laws of nature," in the sense of laws of matter or space, came into frequent use in England after the Restoration of 1660, especially among the ever widening circle of men and women who were influenced by the publications of the Royal Society and the experiments of its members. But the older meaning retained its importance throughout the eighteenth and nineteenth centuries. It is the meaning given for "natural law" and "law of nature" in the *Century Dictionary*, although the more modern meaning can be found under "law." In the fourteenth edition of the *Encyclopaedia Britannica*, published in 1929, the scientific definition alone is given. "Natural law, in science, means the formulation of some uniform characters or connection of things or events; but it is frequently used for the uniformity itself as it exists in natural phenomena. Any such uniformity may be called a natural law; for example, all laws formulated in physics and chemistry. On the other hand, the term 'law of nature' is sometimes restricted to irreducible or ultimate laws (like the law of gravitation), as distinguished from derivative laws (like Kepler's three laws of planetary motion)."

11 See below, pp. 367–71.

12 *Century Dictionary* (New York, 1895 ed.), V, 3942, 3944. There is, of course, a third meaning, which has had theological implications—the law of human life, to which all human beings are subject (cf. below, chap. 6).

It is not easy to see how this second definition can be used by free men as a bulwark against dictatorship, or for any moral or philosophical purpose. The contrast between the two definitions reveals the character of the changes that have swept over learning among the western European peoples and, above all, the Americans, during the twentieth century. As the methods of natural science came to be regarded as the only methods that the mind could appropriately employ in the higher learning, as all procedures of the mind that did not follow the scheme of the natural scientist were thrown into discredit, the belief that the mind is capable of creating durable values for the guidance of mankind was lost. That was what happened in the realm of learning between the times of Renan and Mill and those of Keynes and Dewey, with the spread of the ethical relativity (which Dewey did not fully share) that preceded the Second World War.

There is a widespread belief that the change was entirely for the good. It has been regarded as one of the most important elements in "progress." By this most people have in mind the tremendous material improvement that has added more than forty years to the normal life expectancy of a child at birth. The discredit thrown upon the relevancy for our present problems of the wisdom of great thinkers and artists of the past is supposed to have liberated men. They are supposed to have shaken off those ancient prejudices created by writers who tried conscientiously but unsuccessfully (for want of scientific methods) to be objective, to rise above their time, and to say something that would endure for all time, or at any rate as long as there were civilized men to read it.

Let us apply the pragmatic test to the recent progressive view of the methods that are appropriate to the study of man and to the study of his intellectual pursuits. Is it scientific to regard progressive education and modern social science as important causes for the material progress of the Western peoples, and the Americans in particular? The origins of that progress have to be traced back to the early nineteenth and eighteenth centuries. In the case of England they have to be traced back even further, to the early seventeenth and late sixteenth centuries. The fruits of machinery and large-scale enterprise were very striking all over the world during the last half of the nineteenth century. But it was not until the very end of it that the new patronizing attitude toward ancient knowledge, toward the great thought and art of the past, began to have an important influence on scholarship and on the curriculum of the schools and colleges.

We have therefore to admit that there was a great deal of material progress and a very substantial fall in the death rate before the advent of modern social science, which is largely divorced from reason and dependent almost exclusively upon the methods of the natural scientists. The Victorian age, with what we were brought up to regard as its hypocritical prejudices and its stifling exercise of authority in intellectual and moral matters, does not seem to have made impossible the material progress on which we now feed.

The happy conditions which have done so much to create a high standard of living in the United States were not brought about by the exclusion of reason and of moral judgments from social and humanistic studies. It would be more justifiable to attribute the wide acceptance of the new learning to a happy freedom from difficulties and responsibilities that twentieth-century Americans received as their endowment than to attribute the happy freedom to the new learning. The fall in the death rate among the Western peoples and the rise in the standard of living may with justice be attributed in the main to scientific and technological progress. They cannot with justice be attributed to the almost complete eclipse of faith, reason, and art as unifying elements in civilization.

Insofar as the actual production of wealth is concerned, even the most enthusiastic admirers of the economists or the political scientists would probably agree that the roles played by these scholars have been secondary to those played by the *natural* scientist and the *mechanical* engineer. Pasteur's contribution to the health of mankind was probably greater than that of all the economists who ever lived. His contribution to the wealth of mankind is easier to establish than that of Alfred Marshall—though not, perhaps, than that of Adam Smith. During the twentieth century the greatest contributions of social planning to health and physical comfort have been made not in the production but in the distribution of wealth. They have been the work less of scholars or university professors than of medical men and of social reformers like Jane Addams and Justice Brandeis. They have been the work, in short, either of persons trained in the natural sciences or of persons whose primary guide in life was not science but ethics. The important social reformers have been able writers rather than "social engineers," for no one would deny that the prose of Jane Addams or Justice Brandeis, while not of as high a quality as that of Jane Austen or Francis Bacon, is respectable, agreeable, and at times delightful.

The scientific approach to social studies bore valuable fruit, especially on the side of method, as long as the ethical and literary standards of society generally were high. These standards were essential to the maintenance of a high level of scholarship in the social sciences—but the social scientists, who were increasingly anxious to be scientific, did little to cultivate them or to emphasize their importance. As the principles of ethical conduct, along with the teachings of Christianity, lost their influence in the universities, they also lost their influence in society. They were replaced by materialism, individual selfishness, and extreme nationalism. In some countries the social scientists were expected by the government to promote the power of the nation even at the expense of truth; in others they were left to seek their own advantage or that of the groups they found it advantageous to serve. In many places the result has been a decline in the standards of objectivity and accuracy upon which nineteenth-century scholarship prided itself. Nowhere was the decline more precipitous than in Germany, the first home of scientific history. This suggests that the social scientist cannot help to improve the relations between man and man, or to hinder these relations from deteriorating, simply by examining the facts with which he deals in a scientific spirit. Something more is needed.

It would be unfair to throw all the blame for the recent state of the entire world onto the shoulders of the social scientists! But it is evident that social science has not done very much to resist the currents of extreme nationalism and extreme materialism that have been sweeping civilization toward destruction. The weakness of social science before these powerful currents was partly the result of its excessive dependence on the methods and objectives of natural science, divorced from the higher objectives of human existence, which are to live honorably, justly, graciously, and courageously, whether or not this contributes to greater material abundance or to greater personal influence and worldly prestige. A great deal is heard nowadays about the impact of this or that professor. The important questions, What is the nature of his impact? Is it good or bad? are almost never intelligently asked. Objectivity and accuracy cannot survive the strains of recent historical development unless there is a renewed emphasis on the good life as man's primary objective, an emphasis that we find in the greatest ancient philosophers and the greatest religious reformers.

It is not surprising that economic progress should have added to the prestige of the sciences. This would be no cause for regret if economic progress had not been accompanied by the almost complete eclipse of the prestige and authority that were once attached to faith, reason, and virtue. There is nothing to show that the denial of the independent controlling power of the mind in connection with social and humanistic studies has added substantially to our material wealth or that it has done much to bring about a distribution of wealth that has contributed to economic welfare.

A sound lesson to derive from recent history would be this. The economic experience of the hundred years from 1815 to 1914, great though the years were in material achievement, has not lifted man above the guidance of past knowledge and wisdom. Those hundred years, historically speaking, were an age of quite abnormal tranquillity and peace between the great nations of the earth. The signs suggest that we have again entered a period of strain and strife. Parts of the world have seethed with people and wealth before. For all the material comfort that industrialism has generated, it has not succeeded in creating a new kind of human being, so superior in moral and intellectual qualities to the human beings of the past that he can get along without moral and intellectual training. It is by no means clear that our intelligence and our morality are above those of earlier peoples, though our knowledge of natural science and our command of mechanical technique are obviously superior. We shall need more rather than less guidance from ancient saints and wise men if we are to survive the storms that have now appeared and that the generation born about 1900 was brought up to suppose would never return. To imagine that American industrialism is basically different in its effects from European industrialism, to imagine that the fundamental characteristics of human beings of the same stock have been greatly altered for the better by crossing the Atlantic Ocean, are errors. Such daydreaming creates illusions that the people of the United States cannot afford in the dangerous times ahead.

III. *Economic Welfare and General Welfare*

There is today a growing recognition in the United States that the world is confronted with a serious crisis, from which America cannot stand aloof. The majority of the persons who are concerned about the crisis think of it almost exclusively in terms of a cold war that we must win, with or without friends across the sea to help. The deeper problems facing civilization, of which the world wars were partly a reflection, are seldom even dimly perceived.

On the rare occasions when those deeper problems are considered, it is taken for granted that the way to meet them is by mechanical invention and economic planning. It is taken for granted, as it has been for some decades, that all we have to do is to improve the material welfare of the people. We are to look to natural sciences, to technology, to business administration, to economics, or to economic politics to save us. That is just what we have been doing for the last hundred years. That is just what we have been doing ever since the phenomenal material progress of the nineteenth century began to spread and men began to distrust economic individualism and to doubt whether material welfare could be counted on to take care of itself. Different medicines have been tried to improve our welfare, but all of them have been directed toward curing the physical ailments of the patient. The medicines have been administered by doctors of very different kinds. Some have been corrupt, some stupid, some skilful, many interested primarily in their fees and their fame, but others interested genuinely in the physical condition of the patient. They have disagreed on almost every conceivable matter save on the assumption that if they could only improve the patient's physical condition, his morale, his intelligence, his moral conduct, and his capacity to discriminate would improve automatically.

The intelligent physician knows that the mind and the spirit play a role of some importance in relation to physical health. He knows that if he is interested in making his clients into effective men and women he must work on their minds and spirits as well as their bodies to free them from concern about their bodies. The truly healthy person is free from worry and even from much thought about his body. Such a state of health cannot be achieved without the cultivation of a sturdy mind and buoyant spirit, for, after the flush of youth and young manhood, such a state of health is possible only when the spirit asserts itself independently of the body and when the mind is in command of both the spirit and the body.

Cannot American society derive a lesson from the knowledge of the intelligent physician? If the extraordinary reduction in the death rate from diseases such as tuberculosis, pneumonia, and typhoid fever, together with the virtual elimination of smallpox and bubonic plague, have not relieved the good physician from the need of nourishing the morale of his patients, is it likely that the great rise in the physical standard of living since the eighteenth century has relieved society from the need of nourishing the morality, the art, and the intelligence of its members? Sixty years or so ago it was common to believe that people were growing more just and truthful, more honorable and wise, in spite of themselves. It was common to believe that justice and truth, honor and wisdom, and even beauty, were natural by-products of the rapid growth in the national dividend. No doubt wealth does contribute to morality, and to intelligence, as both Plato and Aristotle pointed out some twenty-three hundred years ago. But neither Plato nor Aristotle made the mistake of thinking that morals were bound to improve and intelligence to increase simply because men and women grew richer. Goodness and wisdom cannot increase, even with the growth of wealth, unless they are cultivated for their own sake. The growing sense of disillusionment has been accentuated by the failure of our society during the past seventy years to cultivate effectively morality or intelligence. With the collapse of standards, men and women have been left with little to fall back on save science and wealth.

The material condition of society, like the physical health of the individual, is in a measure at the mercy of circumstances. That is no reason why men should not do what they intelligently can to promote the material wealth of society, just as they should do what they can to obey those laws without adherence to which, as science and medicine have shown, physical health is likely to be impaired. But if society devotes itself exclusively to matters of material wealth, the result may actually be damaging to wealth, just as a man who thinks of nothing but his health is likely to end up not only by becoming a useless citizen but by harming his health into the bargain. So the preoccupation with material improvement that has resulted during the past decades partly from the collapse of standards of morality and intelligence, has become a danger not only to man's morals and his intelligence, both good in themselves, but also to his physical standard of living. Men and women are no longer prepared to work as long, as seriously, or as carefully for material improvement as they once were. They expect technical tricks to relieve them from the necessity of hard labor. Materialism threatens to become its own worst enemy.

The doctrine that general welfare follows automatically from economic welfare has been widely taught in American colleges and universities, though it is not a doctrine to which all recent American economists have subscribed. It was held in an extreme form by the late T. N. Carver, in whose *Religion Worth Having* economic and general welfare are made practically identical. Few other scholars have gone as far as he did or have stated their position with his honorable bluntness. But most American scholars took a line which is, for practical purposes, the same as Carver's. One of them wrote, for example, "All forces . . . which impair . . . productive operations threaten the material and *therefore* the intellectual welfare of mankind."[13] If it is assumed that intellectual follows automatically from economic welfare, one is bound to concentrate all thought and action upon the improvement of economic welfare.

The view that increases in economic welfare necessarily

[13] N. S. B. Gras, *Business and Capitalism* (New York, 1939), p. vii (my italics).

contribute to general welfare is one which the wisest economic thinkers of recent times have seen to be false. Professor Pigou was at much pains to show that, even in a peaceful, stable, and progressive society, economic welfare is not only "a bad *index* of total welfare, but . . . an economic cause may affect non-economic welfare in ways that cancel its effect on economic welfare."[14] Non-economic welfare is likely to be modified, perhaps for the worse, both by the way in which real income is earned and by the way in which it is spent. What is at least equally important, non-economic causes—such as war or moral and intellectual instability—affect economic welfare profoundly. They may easily render a measure which, on purely economic reasoning, would promote economic welfare, harmful even to that. Professor Pigou concluded that it is safe to work for economic welfare without taking account of non-economic forces only "among nations with a stable general culture."[15] In view of the recent collapse in cultural standards and the world-wide political strife, it would require considerable optimism to think of industrial civilization today as exhibiting a group of nations with a stable general culture. Disharmony between nations, and even within nations between generations, threatens to become the chief characteristic of our times. If we believe that man's spirit and intelligence represent his highest claim to dignity, we should strive toward the establishment of high moral and intellectual standards whether they contribute to economic welfare or not. On Pigou's own showing, it is at least possible that we can do as much indirectly for economic welfare in that way as we can do for it directly through economics, business administration, economic politics, natural science, and technology. The two attacks on the problem are not alternatives. But, following the economists, we should attach a special value to the scarcer of the two, until the supply of it becomes adequate to our needs!

[14] Pigou, *The Economics of Welfare*, p. 12 (his italics).

[15] *Ibid.*, pp. 20–21 and chap. 1 generally.

Another economic thinker, whose influence upon the leading English economists was for a time hardly inferior to Pigou's, gives us a clearer view than he does of what is so sorely needed today to promote and even to maintain the welfare of the western European peoples both in Europe and the United States. As far as we know, the only things that can be said against the late Philip Wicksteed—and it must be admitted that they were damning things to say at one time—are that he was drawn to study economics by reading Henry George, that he was by inclination a moralist and by training a medievalist. But as the London School of Economics once put a seal of approval on his work, it had a certain respectability among orthodox American economists. "The enlightened student of political economy and of society," Wicksteed wrote on the eve of the First World War, before devastating blows had been struck at our stable general culture, "will take care to assume nothing as to the economic forces except the constant pressure which they bring to bear upon men's actions and their absolute moral and social indifference. . . . [He will] no more . . . take it as axiomatic that they work for social good than we should take it for granted that lightning will strike things that are better felled. . . ." How, then, are we to know what is socially good? Wicksteed leaves us in no doubt. "The prophet and the poet," he tells us, "may regenerate the world without the economist, but the economist cannot regenerate it without them."[16]

Since the Second World War, with the spread of general liberal arts courses in the American colleges, with the fresh interest that has been aroused in "great books" as a basis for education, and with the attachment of writers and other artists to many faculties, the oncoming generations are being exposed, to a degree that most of their elders were not, to the works of prophets and poets. Many are acquiring in their youth an en-

[16] Philip H. Wicksteed, *The Common Sense of Political Economy*, ed. Lionel Robbins (London, 1933), I, 191–92, 123–24.

thusiasm (lacking among most of their elders, who are now directing the governments, the businesses, and the graduate schools) for some of the values upon which, it has been suggested, civilization was based. The frustrating experience which has been confronting these young people, is that they find no place for their enthusiasm in the practical world that they all have to enter or even for the most part in the graduate training upon which an increasing proportion of them embark. Such zest for life as they have acquired finds little outlet in the world as it is now constructed. Their most noble beliefs, and their hopes for a creative existence, evaporate for want of replenishments. Disillusionments, cynicism, and distaste for the older generations replace these beliefs and hopes. They even threaten to produce a new kind of warfare within the United States, not a war between classes or races, but between generations!

The needs which the oncoming generations feel for a richer life than is provided by the world most of them enter will not be satisfied by the prevalent disposition among their elders to measure all progress in terms of mounting rates of economic growth. The doctrine that material improvement is all that is needed to promote the good life is not adequate to satisfy the wageworkers and salaried employees who now represent so large a portion of the growing populations in all countries and especially in the United States. Yet this doctrine is no less widespread among champions of higher wages and salaries than it is among those increasingly numerous economists who, partly because of the doctrine, are inclined to regard themselves, along with the experimental scientists, as the aristocrats of the contemporary intellectual world. One searches almost in vain through most books intended to contribute to the welfare of the workpeople, talented and altruistically conceived though some of these books are, for any ultimate objectives beyond bathrooms with plumbing, comfortable beds, adequate food, and proper dental and medical care. These are all very good things; it is certainly desirable to provide them for everyone. We are not suggesting that the economic welfare of the workers ought not to be considered or that they are always treated with conspicuous fairness by their employers. We are suggesting only that such a view of civilized values as we find in most books written on behalf of labor is essentially the same as that of the well-known psychologist whose researches led him to conclude that the "general goodness" of a community bears a close relation to the number of its dentists and the volume of its tobacco consumption. "All would be well," the writers of books which deal with the modern labor problem seem to say, "if only the government or some other agency would increase the quantity of bathtubs, refrigerators, television sets, marriage counselors, psychotherapists, and dentists in workers' quarters and thus raise them as near as possible to the cultural level of Pasadena or Evanston," the two places which, on the eve of the Second World War, according to Professor Thorndike's scores, possessed more "goodness of life for good people" than any others in the world.[17] Once the most influential professor of Teachers' College, Thorndike's influence in training teachers has by no means disappeared since his death. It has been amplified by the new mechanisms for spreading economic content: television, commercial advertising, and psychotherapy.

Such a conception of the ends of human life, by itself, could at best lead only to a great increase in the number of complacent middle-class people, without discrimination or a sense of their responsibility for the spiritual or even the material welfare of their neighbors. At worst it could produce a revolt among the active younger generation which is showing increasing signs of dissatisfaction with the society it has to enter. The pressing problems of our age will not be solved simply by enclosing the whole world in a large air-conditioned economy-class cabin—or, for that matter by enclosing it in a vast first-

[17] E. L. Thorndike, *Your City* (New York, 1939). I owe my knowledge of this book to my friend, the late Robert E. Park.

class cabin. In order to meet the future, men need the very values which have been disappearing in the moral and intellectual crisis of the last sixty years or so.

IV. *The Historical Unreality of the Cold War*

In place of these values, what have humans given themselves?

Economic growth fails to satisfy the incessant need men and women have to believe. Even if people claim there is nothing intangible worth believing, that is itself a belief, and it can be assertive to the point of becoming neurotic. Beliefs in evil or in error can be overwhelmingly strong. They can grievously damage the human condition. They could now lead to universal tragedy.

In a letter written to the Paris edition of the *New York Times* in 1965, the Spanish ambassador to France spoke of the ideological conflict that splits the world and divides all nations into two groups. If, as many assume, all countries and governments have to enroll on one side or the other of what has come often to be called the "cold war," it is in no small measure because of beliefs generated by recently formulated interpretations of history.

One is the cycle theory. According to that all extensive societies—for example, the classical, lasting from Homeric times to the fall of the ancient Roman Empire—have a time span as inexorably fixed as those slices of existence accorded individual men and women, who seldom last beyond a hundred years and, if they do, are no longer active agents in the human comedy. In its modern influential form, the cycle theory was originally sketched by Gobineau in his *Essai sur l'inégalité des races humaines*. That appeared in two parts in 1853 and 1855. The notion of a rigorously fixed term for great societies was given precision by Spengler's *Untergang des Abendlandes*, published at the end of the First World War, in 1918 and 1922.

The modern cycle theory has led people everywhere to believe all societies are doomed by nature in a relatively short time, which never much exceeds a thousand years, to decadence and death. Following Spengler's timetable (which Toynbee did not effectively alter) the unique modern industrialized society, which now penetrates the entire planet and extends even into outer space, is not the beginning but the end of a cycle. If an end is inevitable and imminent, people assume in the dark of this prospect that nothing effective can be done to transcend the ideological conflict. 156925

Powerful in bringing about this conflict are beliefs generated by the Marxist, and what, for want of a more descriptive phrase, may perhaps be called the anti-Marxist, interpretations of history. These interpretations do not despair of the salvation of present society in the same way that the cycle interpretation does. But they seek salvation in a victory of their side in the ideological conflict. Each summons all peoples to a showdown which can hardly be resolved except by force, instead of to constructive efforts to transcend the conflict and to build a civilization more comprehensive, more durable, and more united than the one which flowered in eighteenth- and early nineteenth-century Europe and North America, and helped make possible the conquest of the material world. Beliefs based on Marxianism or anti-Marxianism are not identical in their implications with beliefs derived from the cycle interpretation. But now that nations possess weapons capable of wiping human life off the earth they threaten to provide by total war all the evidence that is needed to support it!

The proponents of each of these beliefs assume they are founded on historical truth. But is the assumption valid?

Chapter 26 of *Das Kapital* opens with these words:

We have seen how money is changed into capital; how, through capital, surplus value is made, and from surplus value more capital. But the accumulation of capital presupposes surplus value; surplus value presupposes capitalistic production; capitalistic production presupposes the pre-existence of considerable masses of capital and of labour power in the hands of producers of commodities. The whole movement, therefore, seems to turn in a vicious circle, out of which we can get only by supposing a primitive accumulation (the "previous accumulation" of Adam Smith) preceding capitalistic accumulation; an accumulation not the result of the capitalistic mode of production but its starting point.

Marx's words bring out the predominant place which he and those all over the world who attempt to follow his thought give to production and capital as the vital elements in the coming of industrialism. Marx goes on to suggest that the *private* accumulation of all property—including of course capital which becomes with Marxists practically a synonym for property—was effected mainly by conquest, enslavement, robbery, and murder. In political economy, Marx wrote, primitive accumulation played a role which can be appropriately compared to the role of original sin in theology. Virtue with the Marxists becomes almost a monopoly of men employed for wages, who are summoned to break their chains. Redemption is therefore to be found in a class struggle to oust the private possessors of capital and to substitute the state as the alleged representative of virtuous workers. That struggle would provide the catharsis needed to provide a brilliant future for mankind.

Marxian doctrines concerning the origins of the industrialized world have had an astonishing influence on those opponents of Marx who have generated the beliefs that have served as fodder for the other side in the "ideological conflict." It is surprising that since the publication of *Das Kapital* economists who are anticommunist deal with economic history much as the Marxists do. For them too industrialism originated in capital accumulation and the growth of production, only they attribute a virtuous role in the main to capitalists and to competition. Their correct refusal to treat businessmen and capitalists generally as peculiarly corrupted by various forms of villainy or sin *has not led them to recognize the constructive parts played outside the market place by disinterested and novel searches for truth, beauty, and virtue in the evolution of industrialism, in man's triumph over matter.* The anti-Marxists mostly assume, like the Marxists, that the basic explanations of the present industrialized world are, for all important purposes, to be found strictly in economic factors.

These rival interpretations of the coming of industrialism have provided a great deal of the combustible matter which has come recently to inflame the violent propensities of men and to dictate the political policies and actions of those who govern. The present-day state of beliefs, derived from Marxist and anti-Marxist interpretations of history, reminds one of an apocryphal story. It circulated in the United States during the McCarthy era. A policeman arrests a man speaking to a crowd in a public square. As the man is being hoisted into a squad car, several of his audience protest to the policeman that he is making a mistake. "That man is not a communist," they say; "he is an anticommunist." The policeman dismisses the information as irrelevant. "I don't care what kind of communist he is," he hotly declares. "I'm against all communists!"

In championing one side or the other in the cold war, both the Marxist and the anti-Marxist philosophies have taken on a religious complexion. Each side claims a monopoly of virtue.

In a world where no one can hope to be perfect, the unreality of such assertions would be patent if the issues weren't so highly charged with emotions. Tawney, with his British socialist background, stressed the envy which entered into the outlook of the workers when they attacked the capitalist system. "They denounce, and rightly," he wrote a generation ago,

the injustice of capitalism; but they do not always realize that capitalism is maintained not only by capitalists but by those who, like some of themselves, would be capitalists if they could, and that these injustices survive, not merely because the rich exploit the poor, but because, in their hearts, too many of the poor admire the rich. They know and complain that they are tyrannized over by the power of money. But they do not yet see that what makes money the tyrant of society is largely their own reverence for it.[18]

On the other side, the anti-Marxists denounce, and rightly, the power wielded at the expense of free enterprise and all liberty by those who gain control of the state in the name of Karl Marx, and who increasingly betray the hopes and ideals of Marx himself.[19] The anticommunists become inflamed over the threat to freedom that is inherent in this seemingly uncontrolled exercise of power. But they do not recognize that the frenzy into which they sometimes work themselves deprives them of the very compassion and charity and objectivity which alone can temper the pursuit of power (from which no politics and no politicians are exempt) and produce that magnanimity, that self-restraint, in the exercise of authority which could provide a basis both for the relative peace and the relative freedom which are all that humans can hope to achieve on earth.

Having escaped three hundred years ago, by means of growing religious toleration, the religious confrontation that threatened our European ancestors at the end of the sixteenth century, a much more numerous humanity finds itself enrolled upon a larger stage and on a larger scale in a struggle, equally fanatical, derived from rival economic interpretations of history.[20] Insofar as historical truth is concerned, both interpretations rest on extremely shaky foundations. And the same can be said of the modern cycle theory of history, which is based on the assumption that human nature is incapable of improvement.

These interpretations of history provide incomplete impressions of the process that brought into being the unique, materially interdependent world of the twentieth century, with

18 R. H. Tawney, *Equality* (2d ed.; London, 1937), p. 248.

19 As Kostas Papaioannou has just effectively demonstrated in his *L'Idéologie froide* (The Hague, 1967).

20 See below, pp. 414–16.

which the human race has now to deal. Anti-Marxists and Marxists assume that the extraordinary conquest of the material world during the past hundred and fifty years has been brought about by capitalism or communism (or by a combination of both in the case of those Marxists who are most faithful intellectually to Marx himself). They fail to see to what an extent industrialism was nurtured by the civilization which many leaders of thought in the eighteenth and nineteenth centuries considered a novel achievement of the human race. The basis of eighteenth-century civilization was not, as has been suggested,[21] primarily economic. It was intellectual, cultural, and moral. It was not founded in evil, as the Marxists claim capitalism was and as the anti-Marxists claim communism was. On the contrary, civilization gave "form and content to virtue." Humans were finding, in connection with the new sciences, inventive powers of a kind that had never been exercised in the past. They thought they were finding in human nature a capacity to diminish the influence of evil to such a point that they could trust men to exploit fully the possibilities opened by the modern sciences. The dangers which ancient philosophers had seen in all efforts to realize sublime ideas in the temporal world seemed to be disappearing.

Neither the Marxist nor the anti-Marxist nor the cycle theories of history have done much that is positive to bring about the conquest of the material world. The process leading to industrialism was already underway before these historical philosophies were born. A passage in Chateaubriand's memoirs, written in 1841 when he was over seventy, suggests how inevitable that triumph had become before Marx or Gobineau began to publish.

If I compare "two globes of our earth," Chateaubriand wrote, "one at the beginning and the other at the end of my life, I no longer recognize what I see."[22] He is referring to

---

[21] See above, chaps. 2 and 3.

[22] Chateaubriand, *Mémoires d'outre tombe*, ed. Victor Giraud (Geneva, 1946), II, 404.

the fantastic rate of material change, which was bound, he believed, to continue and which was leading to the triumph over space and matter humans have now lived to witness.

Chateaubriand was no unwary optimist; he was far from ignorant of the part played in history by evil and the struggle for power. Yet he believed sufficiently in civilization, as the eighteenth-century minds had conceived of it, to foresee a "universal society" as a possible consequence of the conquest of the material world.

What will such a society be like? he asked. Will it be a society

in which there are no particular nations, which will not be French, or English, or German, or Spanish, or Portuguese, or Italian, or Russian, or Tartar, or Turkish, or Persian, or Indian, or Chinese, or American—which will be rather all those societies in one? What will be the result for its manners, its sciences, its arts, its poetry? How will the passions felt together, according to different peoples in different climates, be expressed? ...

What destiny will the stars, new for us, light up? Will their revelation be linked to some new phase of humanity?[23]

The triumph of industrialism, which Chateaubriand and others of his time foresaw, has been taking place before the eyes of all persons now alive. But we still await a universal society which could convert that triumph into the "new phase of humanity" which Chateaubriand envisaged as a possibility. It is sobering to realize how far we are from the fusion of peoples and nations which he thought might herald a fresh destiny for mankind.

Was this inevitable? The evidence is against inevitability. It suggests that men themselves have been responsible. Not least responsible have been those interpreters of history who have presented the fate of societies as no less inexorable than the fate of individual lives. Their historical philosophy leaves the human being *without an opportunity* to surmount his fate

[23] *Ibid.*, pp. 394, 406 (my translation).

by enriching the blood stream of the race, by merging his hopes as an individual with those of his brothers and sisters born and yet to be born. Not least responsible have been those other interpreters of history who have generated beliefs which split the world into camps and which (within those camps) encourage the growth of nationalism at the expense of universalism.

It is true that nationalism existed before the publications of Gobineau and Marx. Nor is national feeling, which is inevitable, necessarily dangerous to the human future. Creative nationalism, which nourishes diversity in the interest of unity, could become a constructive force for international understanding. But uncreative nationalism, which heats the embers of destruction engendered by the cold war, is a major obstacle to "universal society." It was given a fresh intensity and bitterness by despair over man as an instrument for good, bred partly by these interpretations of the past. They have infused themselves into the emotions of millions throughout the world who do not know their origins and have no direct acquaintance with the works of their authors. Whatever the national or religious or social persuasions of those who have adopted them, the beliefs have often become fanatical. They are working to set nation against nation, man against man, and man against himself.

The philosophies which were most influential when Chateaubriand was born in 1768—the philosophies of the Enlightenment—had been much less destructively nationalistic. The advent of Napoleon—a man whom Chateaubriand always opposed—did much to disappoint the hopes of the Enlightenment, but after Napoleon had gone, Chateaubriand (like his younger contemporary Tocqueville who died in 1859) did not regard those hopes as obsolete.

The notion of universal government reaching to the ends of the earth, and including non-Christian states on equal terms with Christian, had been put forward two centuries before

Chateaubriand's time, in a book called *Le nouveau cynée*, printed in 1623.[24] That notion has been periodically revived ever since, and if, as Chateaubriand thought, a universal society is possible, universal government—a world rule of law replacing force—would be a natural consequence.

Perhaps we could justify men's despair of achieving such unity, if the interpretations of history that have come to dominate beliefs since Chateaubriand's time were embedded in historical truth. But the actual historical processes that created the conditions of material progress which dazzled Chateaubriand were very different from those portrayed by the theorists whose views have influenced millions since his time. The material progress that he had witnessed, and that which he foresaw, could not have been achieved without the scientific revolution of the seventeenth century and, much later, the revolutionary applications of resulting scientific discoveries to the solution of practical problems. These applications were facilitated by new hope nourished among the Europeans and Americans by cultural progress which preceded the spurt in rates of growth in production at the end of the eighteenth century. The distinction Heisenberg drew between artistic and scientific genius[25] suggests that, once the intellectual processes leading to the achievements of the modern sciences had been set in motion, the scientific discoveries which have revolutionized the lives we lead had a kind of inevitability that *cannot be expected* in the sphere of art. These intellectual processes were already in motion in Chateaubriand's time, not only before the writings of Marx and Gobineau had an influence, but actually before they appeared. The material changes Chateaubriand foresaw were fruits not *only* of capital formation but of genius and compassion which transcend economics and economic interests.

[24] Cf. Nef, *Western Civilization since the Renaissance* (New York, 1963), pp. 142–44.

[25] See above, pp. 83–84.

The cold war is unreal because it is founded on an inadequate and essentially false view of the history that led man into the unique world where he now finds himself. The cold war stands in the way of that fulfillment of civilization to which the most generous minds of the Enlightenment looked forward.

It is puzzling why beliefs other than those which mainly nourished material progress should have made such astonishing headway during the late nineteenth and twentieth centuries. Everywhere there are still individuals, among them many of the greatest scientists, nurtured in the generous hopes which originated in the Renaissance, the Reformation, and the Enlightenment, who have been shocked by the spreading pessimism and cynicism. Why have they been often inarticulate and, when articulate, almost always ineffective?

Two recent developments in scholarship and the realm of public discourse have contributed to the dismaying success of those unreal interpretations of the past that have engaged our attention.

One is the growing specialization of the scholar, pushed so far that the fields of inquiry have been narrowed sometimes to the point of sterility. Specialization has made it increasingly difficult for any learned man to speak with authority outside his field and has diminished his influence even when he has been able to speak effectively. At the very time when an almost mystical value has been attached to the work and the lives of certain scientists—such as Einstein or Fermi—serious discussion in the realm of general ideas has all but disappeared, leaving that realm at the mercy of the cheap, the vulgar, and even the corrupt.

A second explanation for the present dominance of destructive and unreal beliefs is to be found in the growing currency given to abstractions as substitutes for concrete truths and for deeper and much simpler moral and aesthetic values. For this spread of the abstract, of the unreal, progress in many sciences is to no small extent responsible. Writing a generation ago concerning the origins of modern science, Whitehead had this to say: The whole system of organizing the pursuit of scientific truth, which has come to dominate modern learning in universities throughout the world, "is quite unbelievable." "This conception of the Universe," he proceeds, "is surely framed in terms of high abstractions, and the paradox only arises because we have mistaken our abstractions for concrete realities."[26]

As Whitehead went on to show, the two tendencies toward specialization and toward abstraction feed each other to the disadvantage of those concrete discussions of general problems that are lacking in the contemporary world of the mind. "Another great fact confronting the modern world," Whitehead wrote,

is the discovery of the method of training professionals, who specialize in particular regions of thought and thereby progressively add to the sum of knowledge within their respective limitations of subject. . . . Effective knowledge is professionalized knowledge, supported by a restricted acquaintance with useful subjects subservient to it.

This situation has its dangers. It produces minds in a groove. Now to be mentally in a groove is to live in contemplating a given set of abstractions. The groove prevents straying across country, and the abstraction abstracts from something to which no further attention is paid. But there is no groove of abstractions which is adequate for the comprehension of human life. . . . The remainder of life is treated superficially, with the imperfect categories of thought derived from one profession.[27]

This desertion of the concrete, this inadequate comprehension of human life, provided favorable conditions for the historical theories of the cycle historians, of the Marxists and the anti-Marxists. They annexed the realm of general discourse, which the specialists felt obliged to neglect, and framed their answers to the overwhelming questions, which the specialists

[26] A. N. Whitehead, *Science and the Modern World* (New York, 1926), pp. 80–82.

[27] *Ibid.*, pp. 175–76 (a passage called to my attention by Mary Swithinbank, of Cambridge, England).

avoided, in terms of high abstractions. These answers often seemed convincing to persons seeking for beliefs to replace their ancestors' religious convictions.

The abstractions they were offered were of kinds that appealed especially to the pessimistic and the cynical sides of human nature. Pessimism and cynicism led people to believe that man's capacities for peaceful construction could never become powerful enough to surmount his propensities for violence, evil, and irresponsible personal power. So the historical theories of recent times bear a heavy responsibility for the two total wars of the twentieth century. They threaten to precipitate a third which would, in all probability, be almost infinitely more destructive than the two some have witnessed.

Among the factors leading men to entertain these abstractions, so imperfectly founded in history, and even to embrace them with ardor as substitutes for religion, have been the prevalent notions that the scientific methods which had come to prevail in the nineteenth century, for handling data especially in the physical and biological sciences, could be utilized in dealing with all human relations and so with history. Gobineau considered his theories as strictly scientific. So did Spengler and Marx and Böhm-Bawerk. Human resources came to be treated as unchanging in their nature, much as matter, space, and time *had* been hitherto treated by modern scientists.

Sciences have begun to develop in new ways in the twentieth century. Sciences are beginning to take account, in the realm of matter, space, and time, of the relative, the indeterminate, and even the changing. Therefore a scientific approach to human behavior might now become helpful in guiding humankind toward the beautiful, the good, the true. But, in utilizing scientific methods in the domain of human thought and action, it must be recognized that any attempt to lay down laws that govern human behavior is likely to circumscribe men's potentialities. Such an attempt would work to block any "new phase of humanity." By such limited approaches to the human sciences, the conditions which govern the mind and heart would be frozen once and for all. Avenues for possible improvement in man's condition, through individual effort, would be blocked by signs reading "no entry."

The coming of civilization and industrialism depended on *new* commitments of the mind and heart. If scientific laws, based on what had happened to mankind before the Reformation, had governed the behavior of our ancestors from the late sixteenth to the mid-nineteenth centuries, the spread of gentle manners, firm devotion to moral values, the advent of an unprecedented economy of delight and commodity, the increasing freedom in France of small property owners (a subject which space has not permitted us to explore in these pages),[28] the practice of *limited* warfare, and even the rise of the modern sciences with their applications to certain kinds of technological progress making for greater productivity, speed of movement, and communication—all these novel developments would hardly have been possible.

A realistic view of man's past since the Reformation suggests that spiritual resources are deeper, more varied, and more inexhaustible than contemporary politics and scholarship admit. It is necessary to break through both. Renewals in *fresh* forms of *the search for perfection*, which is at the roots of the present industrialized world, alone can save humanity from the menace of total destruction.

The hopes for better human beings and more enlightened leadership are not dead. Elements for the fusion of mankind, which was part of Chateaubriand's vision, are still with us. In the third part of this book an attempt will be made to explore some of these hopeful possibilities. Before doing so it is necessary to consider whether the values on which civilization seems to have been built, have been supplanted now that industrialism has triumphed or whether they are essential to its fulfillment.[29]

28 A subject I hope to include in my general history (see above, p. 21 n.).

29 A preliminary version of this section was published in *Conflict Resolution and World Education,* ed. Stuart Mudd (The Hague: Dr. W. Junk Publishers, 1966).

Part Two

Ends of Civilization

> *The finest qualities of our nature, like the bloom on fruits, can be preserved only by the most delicate handling. Yet we do not treat ourselves nor one another thus tenderly.*
>
> *Thoreau,* WALDEN

5 Humanity

"I am seeking friends," says the little prince to the fox in Saint-Exupéry's fantasy. "Pray tell me what you mean by 'domesticate'?"

"It's something too often forgotten," says the fox. "It means 'to form binding ties.' . . . If you domesticate me, we shall need one another. . . . One only knows those one domesticates. . . . Men no longer have time to know anything. They buy everything ready made. . . . Since there are no dealers in friends, men have no friends. If you want a friend, *domesticate* me. . . . There's my secret. It's simple. One sees clearly only with the heart. The essential is invisible to the eye."[1]

Values guide the heart. They are fixed stars in whose light friends are made. Like friends, they can adapt themselves to every change and remain what they always were.

What conceptions are offered for a civilization of the future? Broadly there seem to be three—the totalitarian, the materialistic, and what may be called the humanistic. The first two are very much in evidence. Neither is worthy of the best in man. Both are partial. One glorifies the state, at the expense of all other values whatever, and ultimately this is likely to mean that it glorifies that state which is able to triumph by might over all others. The second glorifies material wealth. Both the state and material wealth are necessary to civilized welfare. Neither is properly an end in itself.

On the only ground that ought to count, on the ground of humanity, the materialistic is greatly superior to the totalitarian conception of civilization. That is because it aims, however one-sidedly, to serve man, while totalitarianism leads to

[1] A. de Saint-Exupéry, *Le Petit Prince*, in *Les Oeuvres complètes* (Paris, 1950), pp. 992–93, 996 (my translation).

the enslavement of man. But, in its present weakened form, a materialistic conception does not offer an adequate defense against totalitarianism. It is no longer at its best. Its chief grandeur consisted not in the opportunity it offered men to improve their economic welfare, important though that has been, but in the independence it allowed the mind, and in the sense of individual responsibility for the general welfare that it fostered. Its weakness today has come about partly because these qualities of reason and responsibility have been almost entirely submerged by selfishness. Too many men are now out exclusively to serve themselves or their groups rather than to serve man. Selfishness has always been, alas, the dominant motive behind the actions of most human beings. But the disposition in the world of the mind to make self-interest or group interest the final principle of judgment in all aspects of human affairs is more novel among the Western peoples. Matters of politics, culture, and even morality and religion are almost never judged according to whether they are true, or right, or beautiful; they are judged according to whether they will help "my" nation, "my" business, "my" trade union, "my" university or special subject, "my" racial group, "my" church, or "me." With the decline of reason and of the sense of responsibility to mankind, with the collapse of the cultural traditions of the West, the vulgarity inherent in a materialistic view of the end of life has come more and more into the foreground. The power of the materialistic conception of civilization has also been weakened because the economic and social, as well as the moral and intellectual, circumstances of the twentieth century have made it much more difficult than it was in the eighteenth and nineteenth centuries to satisfy men's economic ambitions. Men now expect to get much more with much less effort than their ancestors. What are needed today to meet the threat of totalitarianism are affirmations, based on deep thought and belief, and supported by enthusiastic, tireless action. What we have had are negations, and occasionally superficial appeals on behalf of ancient catchwords, such as "freedom," "liberty," "equality." Such words have lost their reality and hence their power to move us.

The third—the humanistic—conception of civilization might offer mankind a way of surmounting the catastrophe which threatens it. Such a conception might even offer hope for a world better than any in past history. Toward such a conception mankind can be said only to be groping. Attempts to move along the road indicated by such a conception are either misunderstood and misnamed or dismissed as utopian. That reproach—if it be a reproach—is justified. When one sets foot on this road, one is at once beset with a consciousness of one's unworthiness for the task of even sketching in roughest outline the way mankind ought to travel. One is reminded also of the words Thomas More is said to have spoken, in merriment, as he was about to mount the scaffold. Seeing that it had been hastily and flimsily built, he turned to the lieutenant from the Tower of London who had accompanied him. "I praye you, Maister Lieftenante," said he, "see me safe upp, and for my cominge downe let me shifte for myself."[2]

1. The Control of Appetite and Passion by the Intellect

Any suggestion that agreement should be sought concerning the ends of life arouses widespread misgiving. With the kind of education that has gained the ascendancy in the United States during the past half-century, the view has become deep rooted that democracy consists in leaving every person free to do whatever he likes. Now it is obvious that no person is actually free to do what he likes. His freedom is limited in almost every instant of his existence, if in no other ways than by his mental equipment, his physique, and his income, and even by the fact of his freedom, which forces upon him the obligation

[2] William Roper, "The Life of Sir Thomas More, Knight," in *The Utopia of Sir Thomas More*, ed. George Sampson (London, 1910), p. 271.

to decide between means, without reference to a few supreme ends. When a man chooses between means for their own sake, without any impersonal and firm ends to aim at, he is likely to be overwhelmed by the possible choices.

The view that man should be free to do whatever he pleases for the sake of doing what he pleases has been accompanied by another view—which seems to be in sharp opposition to it —that he is completely bound by material circumstances over which he has no control. This relieves him to some extent from the necessity of making an effort and thus contributes in a way at once paradoxical and treacherous to his sense of freedom. Like the modern conception of freedom, determinism helps to divest him of all responsibility to serve higher ends. Under the frequently unsuspected influence of these two views, which complement as well as contradict each other, the custodians of education in the United States have been led to the conclusion that the only possible roles for the individual mind, even among persons whose lives are ostensibly devoted to the higher learning, are two. The first is for the mind of each man to assert his own ego. This can be done in various ways. For example, it can be done by exercising the power of selection on such momentous questions as a choice between the various varieties of television sets, automobiles, washing machines, electric refrigerators, and cigarettes. Another role left to the individual mind has much greater value, especially if scholars realize that its results should never constitute the sum of knowledge. That role is to carry out investigations which will supply the world with additional knowledge and help to reveal the processes by which the lives of men and of societies are determined.

What is denied is the role of the trained, disinterested mind, impelled by a love for mankind, to help in determining the nature of the prejudices without which, as André Gide once suggested,[3] civilization is impossible. At a time when old values

[3] *Les Faux-monnayeurs* (Paris, 1925), p. 17.

and beliefs have broken down, the place for such a mind ought to be expanded. Instead it is being contracted until almost no room remains. The fostering of beliefs is left to untrained, undisciplined minds and to the charlatan. It is left partly to persons like the late Billy Sunday and Aimee Semple McPherson or to their more recent and rather less spectacular, but hardly less influential, successors. The motives of such persons are material gain and publicity. They appeal to these motives in their public. They appeal not to reason or to the spirit of domestication but to the emotions and the passions, divorced from every rational principle and made the slave of the appetites. The prejudices they produce are somewhat less inspiring than those which the wise men of the past have transmitted to society. While the "message" of a particular charlatan is soon forgotten, along with its author, there is no lack of charlatans to take his place and to dispense a new "message" of the same genus.

How can authority be fostered in matters of the mind without setting up a dictatorship? Such a question would hardly be raised if the mind were still generally regarded as independent. The question itself is a reflection of the mind's weakness, of its feeling of impotence in the modern world. The answer is that the establishment of authority, which arises not from the kind of position a man holds in politics, in business, or in the professions but from the simple power of the intellect itself, not swayed by the utterances of either political leaders or newspaper editors, or by facts when facts can offer no guidance, could provide a formidable barrier against dictatorship, if channels could be opened through which it might transmit its conclusions accurately and effectively, and thus influence the people who vote, the parents and teachers who train the young, the churchmen whose duty it is to look after men's souls, the business, political, and labor leaders who direct the economic life of the nation. Unless there is such a thing as trained authority within the country on moral, intellectual, and aesthetic questions, there is little to restrain unscrupulous people from making the central government the only arbiter on moral, intellectual, and even aesthetic questions. This has been done in Germany and in Russia. If dictatorship does not result from the lack of trained authority on these matters, then values will be at the mercy of the rich and prominent or of persons chosen by the rich and prominent for reasons unrelated to the intellect. This is already to a very considerable extent the situation in the United States.

Trained authority on moral, intellectual, and artistic questions cannot be obtained either by a process of voting or by leaving the guidance in the hands of businessmen, politicians, newspaper editors, and professors of current events. It can be obtained only by giving the wisest, the best-endowed, the best-trained, and the most disinterested philosophers, theologians, writers, and artists a prestige and power of leadership that our American civilization would now make it difficult for such persons to obtain even if they existed. So philosophers, theologians, writers, and artists should strive to establish for their ideas a place of authority. They cannot gain such a place by compromising their convictions, if these convictions are based on reason. They cannot gain it if they are moved by self-interest. They will have to gain it by the independence and the force of objective and impersonal thought, assisted by historical and scientific research and by the wisdom of ancient sages.

Now we hear a chorus of objections from our contemporaries. Who is to decide which minds are powerful and which minds are disinterested? What tests have we of truth? How can we become reasonably sure we are being guided by the heart in the service of the good?

In attempting to answer these legitimate questions, we must begin by invoking the guidance of the greatest minds of the past. By doing so we shall invoke the other of the twin bogies that stand in the way today of the cultivation of the intellect. These bogies are authority and the past. What justification, then, is there for seeking guidance in past thought? In what ways shall we seek it?

During the fourteenth and early fifteenth centuries Western civilization entered a period which resembles our own in certain respects. An age of great prosperity and phenomenal economic progress, which had probably begun in the eleventh century and had lasted through the thirteenth, drew to a close. The traditions and principles—the "prejudices"—that had bound the European peoples together in the Gothic age no longer served their purpose. As is the case today, one conception of the ends of life was breaking down, and no new one had been found upon which the Western peoples could agree. The decaying conception had solidified into a bigotry and a tyranny no less intense, and no more recognized by the intellectual bigots and tyrants, than the bigotry and tyranny that have grown up in our own time around various forms of totalitarianism.

Perhaps the greatest difference between the later Middle Ages and the twentieth century, in matters of the mind, is in the attitude of the institutions of learning toward the thought of the past. It is scarcely too much to say that at the end of the Middle Ages orthodox opinion in the Continental universities, as well as in the abbeys and priories, could see little virtue in an idea that had not been precisely stated by some great authority of the past. As late, even, as the early seventeenth century, when Kircher, the celebrated German physicist, expounded his views concerning the newly discovered sunspots to a provincial Jesuit professor, the man would not bother to look through the recently invented telescope as Kircher suggested he do. "It is useless, my son," he told the learned scientist, "I have read Aristotle through twice and have not found anything about spots on the sun in him. There are no spots on the sun. They arise either from the imperfections of your telescope or from the defects of your own eyes."[4]

[4] B. Hessen, "The Social and Economic Roots of Newton's 'Principia,'" in *Science at the Cross Roads* (London: Kniga, 1931 [?]), pp. 167–68.

The authority of Aristotle had become a tyranny. A great English poet, in celebrating the growing scientific enlightenment in which his countrymen were taking the lead, described the situation in these lines:

> The longest tyranny that ever sway'd,
> Was that wherein our ancestors betray'd
> Their free-born reason to the Stagyrite,
> And made his torch a universal light.
> So truth, while only one supply'd the state,
> Grew scarce, and dear, and yet sophisticate.[5]

If Dryden were here now he might conclude that the scientists, whose efforts he so greatly admired, had done their work too well. One extreme has given way to its opposite. The most persuasive and effective champion of the mean in the whole of history, Aristotle himself, has been the sufferer. If students now read Aristotle at all, they have learned from their teachers to dismiss his principles (including, no doubt, the one to the effect that murder, theft, and adultery are wrong altogether) as an example of the special values of the Greeks. The *Ethics* and the *Politics* are interesting to modern readers; but these readers seldom think of them even as rough guides to the solution of modern problems. Aristotle's remarks are regarded as no less irrelevant to the learning and the conduct of our progressive age than the telescope seemed to the science which interested Scholastic scholars. Who today would think of condemning an erring husband or wife for unfaithfulness by citing Aristotle?

In the realm of the intellect we have come to nourish, unwittingly, a tyranny hardly less complete than that exercised by Scholasticism at the close of the Middle Ages. The opinion of the pragmatists and some other social scientists that by testing all theories by facts we can escape from preconceptions, from all the idols of the tribe, is an illusion. The view that

[5] John Dryden, "Epistle II. to Dr. Charleton (1663)," in *The Miscellaneous Works of John Dryden* (London, 1767), II, 117.

the empirical methods of the natural scientist are sufficient for the study of social and intellectual problems is itself an idol of the tribe.[6] There is a great realm in which the intelligent mind finds it necessary to move, where the principles of conduct and of understanding cannot be determined by scientific experiments and objective tests. In this realm the only weapon is man's reason—his intuition and his powers of logical construction, as these are cultivated in the most intelligent beings by a long process of training and constant exercise, a continuous communion with the experiences of life and science, and also with those experiences as they have been distilled for us by the great minds of the past. The schools, universities, and churches of the later Middle Ages and early modern times made a grievous error when they allowed little room for experiment or even for observation. We are in danger today of falling into the equally serious error of allowing no room for the independent mind. It is not a want of science on which despotism has fed as much as a want of balance in matters of the intellect. There has been no lack of science in Germany during the past century. When the balance is overweighted, as it is today, on the side of natural science and the empirical methods of investigation derived from it, the freedom of the mind is no less threatened than when the balance is overweighted on the side of past authority, as it was at the end of the Middle Ages. It is the social scientists today who are playing the role of the followers of the Scholastics in early modern times. Today the champions of reason and past authority in matters of the intellect and the arts are no less the champions of human welfare than were the champions of natural science during the sixteenth, seventeenth, and eighteenth centuries.

This historical digression has put us in a position to answer the question which turned us into it. How are we to decide

[6] Cf. Frank H. Knight, "Social Science," *Ethics*, LI, No. 2 (1941), 127 ff.; Robert E. Park, "Social Contributions of Physics," *American Physics Teacher*, VII (1939), 327, 329.

which minds are powerful and which are disinterested? The answer is that the great works of the past—in philosophy, in literature, in history, and in the arts—provide us with standards in the light of which it is possible to estimate the achievements of our contemporaries. It is not that in matters of thought and art the wise men of the past were always right. It is not that conditions never alter in such a way as to make their statements on particular matters inapplicable to the present. We shall not advance the cause of the disinterested mind by repeating, parrot-like, the precepts of the greatest ancient philosophers or by copying slavishly the models of the greatest artists of the past. What it comes to is this: When we find ourselves in disagreement with the wise men of the past on moral, intellectual, and artistic issues, the burden of proof is on us. We must have really relevant new knowledge with which to refute their conclusions. We must be certain that they were wrong or that the differences between our times and theirs have made their statements obsolete. We must be sure we understand their position. It is common to say that they were prejudiced because of their want of scientific knowledge. It is necessary to recognize that the spread of scientific knowledge has brought with it new prejudices from which they were free. We must realize that they did not have our prejudices any more than we have theirs. Until their views are proved inapplicable, they should be treated as relevant to our problems rather than as mere curiosities and adornments of a world that has disappeared. Their strength rests in the fact that, while they worked in their time, their faith, their disinterestedness, their love of truth, enabled them to go beyond it. We cannot be sure that we share their strength. We should welcome all the light their works can provide.

The most original achievements in historical scholarship, an intelligent historian recently remarked, are made by proving, with the help of documents, what a wise and learned man's common sense or intuition tells him in advance must be so. The same thing is true to some extent even in the natural sciences, as is shown by the work of such great physicists as Lord Rutherford and Einstein. If we take away the role of intuition in learning, the study of past wisdom which nourishes it, and the training in orderly logical reasoning that alone can produce a disciplined mind able to convert its intuitions into enduring forms, documents and other data, by themselves, will not enable us to discover the truth. Still less will the data, by themselves, enable us to state the truths derived from social and humanistic studies in an intelligible and memorable way, worthy of the attention of men generally, now and in the future.

II. *The Threat to Firm Objective Values*

The existence of the values for which Christianity and humanism, at their best, have stood, is threatened, not only by armies, tanks, warships, warplanes, and nuclear weapons, but by the widespread denial among learned men of the existence of truth apart from verifiable experiments and observations of documents and of the physical world. By their denial of truth, the Western peoples have been preparing a gift for the powers of evil. The way has been paved for the triumph of error. It is as certain for society as a whole as it is for each individual that, without a continual striving toward what is right, society will become a prey to what is wrong. The way of truth, the way of beauty, the way of honor, is always the hard way. Did not one of the greatest of American teachers and philosophers, William James, tell us that the only successful method for overcoming a bad habit is never to permit one's self to indulge in it? Yet we have been schooled—if such an absence of teaching can be called schooling—to imagine that the good things of life will fall into our laps if we follow the line of least resistance, if we do what will bring the biggest immediate reward with the minimum of effort and particularly with the minimum of thought.

The task of defending civilization in the United States, the least insecure among the nations of the West by its size and its geographical position, would seem to require a renewed recognition of the existence of truth. In the difficult years ahead, Americans, if they are to retain the humanist tradition, will have to turn their backs on the casual habits of thought that the last two generations have acquired. One important step in the defense of civilization, and the one with which the universities and the schools, as well as the churches, should be primarily concerned, is to strengthen the moral fiber and the intelligence of our people. It is difficult to strengthen either if the only ends of life are material improvement and private advantage. Now it may be objected that, as one English liberal put it some forty years ago, "you can't eat moral values." While it is obvious that one cannot think or act without eating, what is apparently less obvious (though it is difficult to understand why) is that one cannot measure moral, intellectual, or artistic values in terms of wealth. Western civilization is suffering today (as the most distinguished of my colleagues once frequently pointed out) from a disproportionate emphasis upon material values, from a disposition to judge things that cannot yield an economic profit in material terms. Since there is no such thing as truth, since art is simply a matter of individual preference, regardless of whether the preference is based on intuitive gifts of judgment, we are inevitably thrown back on material standards for judging values of a higher order. A man's merit and his gifts are measured by the income he receives, the worldly position he occupies, and the publicity he manages to obtain. The value of a book is determined by its circulation, the value of a painting by its price, the value of an idea by its score in a Gallup poll. The important matters are not the ideas or the art but the way in which books and paintings can be exploited for the personal advantage of the author and his sponsors in a world of mass production and mass consumption.

Many say that the end of American civilization, the promise

of American life, is not material wealth, but equality of opportunity. Equality of opportunity is excellent—but is it not, after all, a means rather than an end? The question that is of moment for the future of civilization is—Equality of opportunity for what? In practice, the phrase frequently means equality of opportunity to get ahead in a material and worldly way, regardless of the methods employed or the consequences. Less frequently it means equality of opportunity for all to share in material goods. Or again, it means equality of opportunity to increase the material income of the nation. In the first case, the effects are mainly bad, even when ruthless methods of getting ahead have been camouflaged to appear harmless. "Do not be reconciled to dishonesty, indecency, and brutality because gentlemanly ways have been discovered of being dishonest, indecent, and brutal."[7] In the second case, the effects are good insofar as they contribute to the spirit of charity, bad insofar as they deny the obligation of man to think and to labor even for a small material reward. In the third case, the effects are mainly good, but insufficient.

Why do we say they are insufficient? While material improvement has contributed and can contribute to the highest ends of man, insofar as it becomes for the individual, for a class, or for a nation the end of life, there is nothing basically to differentiate men from animals. The object of animals is to live as long as they can and as comfortably as they can. Insofar as men exist to eat and sleep, to turn on the radio and go to the movies, there is nothing specifically human in their conduct.[8] Man's nature is not distinguished from the beast's mere-

[7] R. M. Hutchins, *No Friendly Voice* (Chicago, 1936), p. 4.

[8] It is not suggested that the better radio or television program could have been devised without intelligence or that the listeners and spectators never derive any ideas from the programs. The point is that the mere transmission of programs, even on the rare occasions when they are genuinely artistic, does not necessarily improve the population simply because it increases the size of the audience. It is participation that counts in forming taste, and a home audience is less likely to participate in a concert than a concert-going audience (cf. below, p. 251). Moreover, the time wasted listening aim-

ly by the fact that his intelligence has enabled him to command food, houses, conveniences, and diversions in larger quantities than tigers or birds of prey can do. Nor is man's nature distinguished from the beast's by the fact that his intelligence has enabled him to command murderous weapons to kill others of his kind and take territory from them by making war. There is nothing to distinguish human beings from other forms of life in either mere eating or mere fighting, though the one is always necessary and legitimate, if wisely indulged in, and the other may become so for purposes of defending the right if an objective, disinterested authority decides right is threatened.

It is significant that Sir William Bragg, one of the most eminent scientists of recent times, could regard the experimental achievements of the leading scientists as in some ways less noble, less excellent, than the lives of the noblest among them. In an address many years ago to the National Academy of Sciences, he put the philosophy and the conduct of Pasteur and Faraday on an even higher plane than their scientific discoveries. Their lives offer the world models of disinterestedness and goodness, of which it stands in greater need today than of new scientific knowledge. "The spirit in which knowledge is sought and the manner in which it is used are more important, more real than knowledge itself."[9]

What are the ends of man, if material progress is not an end but a means, and if armed might should be subordinate to the principles of justice and love? How can material progress and armed might best be ordered to contribute to the higher ends of man? Those are problems that American philosophy must

---

lessly to the great majority of programs, which are from the moral standpoint indifferent if not actually vicious, deprives the American people of a great amount of energy which they might otherwise use in strengthening their character—for example, by reading good books.

[9] "History in the Archives of the Royal Society," *Science*, LXXXIX, No. 2316 (1939), 452–53.

face if the United States is to help in preserving civilization rather than in contributing to its destruction.

III. *A Philosophical Justification of Humanism*

The ends of man, it may be suggested, are to be found in those attributes of his which are specifically human, which he does not share with the animals, and the cultivation of which gives him a place of special dignity on this planet. These attributes are common to the teachings of Christ and to the works of the greatest philosophers and artists, before as well as since the times of Christ. They consist in a refusal to accept the actual world of human beings, however improved by science, mechanics, and medicine, as worthy of the best in man. They consist in man's capacity to create with his mind a world of his own better than the world about him or to describe the weaknesses, the shortcomings, and the sufferings of the actual world in relation to the standards of the ideal world that the mind alone can create. They consist in bringing comfort to human beings through the heart and the mind independently of the body. Such attributes of man lose the qualities that give them dignity and force insofar as they are ordered to the material or the political life of man. Insofar as the material and political life of man is ordered to the higher ends of faith, moral philosophy, and art, it approaches that perfection of which man alone, unlike the animals, obtains glimpses. "We are all monsters, that is, a composition of man and beast," wrote Thomas Browne, "wherein we must endeavour to . . . have the Region of Man above that of Beast, and sense to sit but at the feet of reason."[10]

Such a view of the ends of man is to be found both in faith and in the humanism that goes back at least to Plato. "Human-ism is not the exclusive possession either of those who reject

[10] *Religio medici* (reprint of 1643 ed.; Oxford, 1909), p. 125.

some particular body of religious doctrine or of those who accept it," Tawney has said. "It is, or it can be, the possession of both. . . . Humanism is the antithesis not of theism or of Christianity . . . but of materialism."[11] Understood in this sense, humanism is the possession of all men and women, insofar as they are concerned with the mind and heart exercised for the disinterested benefit of qualities that are specifically human. It is the possession not only of those who belong to churches but of all who are striving, both as individuals and as members of society, for the values for which Christ lived and died.

What, it will be asked, is the justification for putting faith, virtue, beauty, and love in a higher category in the order of goods than material improvement, if they are the creation of the few and if the lives these few live always fall short of the perfection they seek with their minds and hearts? The answer is that while ideals must necessarily be conceived by the few independently of the many, there exists in nearly all men, to a greater or lesser degree, a need for moral, intellectual, and aesthetic standards, which cannot be satisfied by the multiplication through mass production of commodities and of entertainments.

As Robert Lowell suggests, "It is easier to be a good poet than a good man." Great works of religious thought and of moral philosophy serve as a pattern. They help to guide men toward the good in their everyday living. Great works of art help many men besides the artist toward a higher fulfillment than can be obtained from material comforts and entertainment. The contemplation of a great painting or a great building, the reading of a great book, the performance of a great work of music, enable a wide circle to participate to some extent in the experience of the artist. Even though the circle capable of benefiting directly from a work of art almost always represents a small minority of the population, the par-

11 *Equality* (3d ed.; London, 1938), p. 83. Cf. Jacques Maritain, *Humanisme intégral* (Paris, 1936).

ticipation of this minority, like the participation of churchmen and teachers capable of understanding the great works of religion and moral philosophy, serves as an example to a larger number. The people generally, insofar as they are impelled to reach upward toward perfection, obtain a sense of the importance of standards of conduct, knowledge, and art unrelated to private advantage. They obtain a sense of the importance of quality independent of quantity.

"The fading of ideals," wrote Whitehead, "is sad evidence of the defeat of human endeavour. . . . The drop from the divine wisdom, which was the goal of the ancients, to textbook knowledge of subjects, which is achieved by the moderns, marks an educational failure. . . . When ideals have sunk to the level of practice, the result is stagnation."[12]

It is an error to suppose that people benefit by having the theologian, the philosopher, or the artist stoop to meet them. It is only when people have to reach, have to exert themselves, that they benefit by faith, philosophy, or art. Civilized life, to be worth living and worth defending, must be a perpetual striving toward what is good. The "realizable ideals" which Americans have been told to work for are no ideals at all. To be valuable, the goal we set ourselves must remain beyond our grasp. An answer to those persons who object to the counsels of perfection contained in great works of moral philosophy or literature is to be found in one of the sermons of John Tillotson, archbishop of Canterbury from 1691 to 1694:

There is no manner of inconvenience in having a pattern propounded to us of so great perfection, as is above our reach to attain to; and there may be great advantages in it. The way to excel in any kind, is, *optima quaeque exempla ad imitandum proponere;* to propose the brightest and most perfect Examples to our imitation. No man can write after too perfect and good a copy; and tho' he can never reach the perfection of it, yet he is like to learn more, than by one less perfect. He that aims at the heavens, which

12 A. N. Whitehead, *The Aims of Education* (Mentor Books, 1949), p. 40.

yet he is sure to come short of, is like to shoot higher than he that aims at a mark within his reach.

Besides that, the excellency of the pattern, as it leaves room for continual improvement, so it kindles ambition, and makes men strain and contend to the utmost to do better. And, tho' he can never hope to equal the Example before him, yet he will endeavor to come as near it as he can. So that a perfect pattern is no hindrance, but an advantage rather, to our improvement in any kind.[13]

The philosophical justification for making faith, virtue, beauty, and love the primary ends of man is that they are indispensable if a nation is to reach the highest moral, intellectual, and cultural stature of which it is capable. Religious, moral, artistic, and compassionate objectives can also be justified as guides for civilized existence on the ground that they have greater powers of endurance than other objectives of men. Those Americans who think of civilization in terms of bathtubs, washing machines, electric refrigerators and air-conditioners, radios, automobiles, and television sets might meditate on the transient nature of these devices. Some men have the ambition, apparently peculiar to human beings, to leave their trace long after they are dead. Highly civilized societies have a similar ambition. No one who reads Pericles' funeral oration can suppose that, when he spoke with such moving faith in the example of Attica, he was speaking only for the people of his times. Societies of the past are remembered above all for their art, their philosophy, and their moral teaching. The exploits of great military captains are brought to us by great historians. The works of Homer, Aristotle, and Plato, and the magnificent Greek temples, had a powerful creative influence over men and women for centuries before modern archeologists dug up Roman baths and hypocausts and constructed their uncertain picture of classical central heating. We remember the achievements of the Gothic age mainly by the *Divine Comedy* of Dante, the *Summa* of St. Thomas Aquinas, the

[13] As quoted by Samuel Richardson in the concluding note to *The History of Sir Charles Grandison* (1753).

paintings of Giotto, and the wonderful cathedrals, the embodiment of a collective artistic effort which few other ages have rivaled.

The United States can hope to advance civilization only by working toward other ends from those which have gained the ascendancy and guided the actions of Americans during the last century, since we ceased to be a nation with a moving frontier. The United States can advance civilization only if virtue, wisdom, and beauty can secure places for themselves independent of material standards of value—only if they can make an impression of their own upon the life, the thought, the art, and the architecture in the new single world of which the United States is a part.

History suggests that societies disintegrate unless they have unifying beliefs. If we are to have a world society, or even a stable and enduring American society, it cannot be founded on administrative machinery or voting, though both good administration and popular suffrage are indispensable. Enthusiasm for ends does not interfere with improvements in the means. It spurs men on to make such improvements. The stuff of belief is old. It has not changed. What collapses is the form. In order again to find a form there will have to be an honest striving on the part of men to recapture the ancient values of faith, virtue, and beauty, which have been so freely discarded with the triumph of industrialism and partly, no doubt, as a consequence of the sweeping economic and social changes that have accompanied it. These ancient values are needed by all people. Their lives can derive meaning and direction from wise, independent minds. Such minds are not the private property of their possessors. They are among the glories of the human race.

6 Faith

A balanced view of the world, and of the place of human beings in it, is the chief mark of wisdom. It is the task of the philosopher, with infinite care and with supreme disinterestedness, to find a place for every aspect of human life and to arrange all aspects in a scheme where each is given a weight suitable to its importance for human welfare. The difficulties in the way of success in such a task may well seem insuperable. So pre-eminent a contemporary authority as Professor Gilson tells us that we need only three fingers to count the philosophers who have actually possessed the wisdom, the reasoning powers, and the detachment to approach perfection as metaphysicians. They are Plato, Aristotle, and St. Thomas Aquinas. "Their ambition was not to achieve philosophy once and for all, [which is not possible for any man] but to maintain it and to serve it in their own times, as we have to maintain it and to serve it in ours."[1]

In spite of the difficulties—or, to put it more truly, because of them—it is the proper task of civilized men to strive, according to the means each has at his disposal, toward a philosophical view of life, in the sense of a view that is at once just and balanced—balanced because it is just, just because it is balanced. Even though only a few men are capable of attaining to the dignity of philosophers, such men are the expression of a very high general level of thought in the country that breeds them. They speak for, as well as to, their fellow countrymen. The study of social and cultural history has not disproved the truth

[1] Etienne Gilson, *The Unity of Philosophical Experience* (New York, 1937), pp. 316–17; cf. Jacques Maritain, *Les Degrés du savoir* (Paris, 1932), pp. viii, xiv–xvii.

of Themistocles' answer to the Seriphian, as reported by Plato. The Seriphian was abusing Themistocles and saying he was famous, not for his own merits, but because he was an Athenian. "If you had been a native of my country or I of yours, neither of us would have been famous."[2] The most civilized nations have been those which have achieved, like the Athenians for a brief period in the fifth century B.C., an almost perfect harmony between all the goods of life. No nation which champions one side of life to the exclusion of others that history has shown to be important to civilized growth can hope to offer the peoples of the world the harmony which, if it were open to them and their eyes were open to it, they would embrace in preference to force. If we ever have, as some persons today hope we shall, a civilized world in which the various nations and races are in essential agreement, in which no single nation dominates the others by armed might, it will be only after all the nations have adopted a philosophical view of life that will bind them together closely enough to outweigh their individual economic, social, and political differences. While the history of Europe shows that a measure of common culture does not insure political agreement between independent states, it does not follow that unenlightened nationalism helps to prevent disagreement! Without agreement concerning the goals of human life, and the sympathy which such agreement would create among the peoples, it is doubtful whether any political treaties, no matter how ingenious, can endure. If the true goals should be found, every country of the world could make contributions toward them, determined by its special needs, subordinate to the general needs common to all nations.

With balance and reason such scarce commodities as they are today, their value for human welfare has become greater than at any time in the long history of the human race. No disinterested student of history, free from the modern idols of the tribe, would argue that the present American scene offers a

[2] *The Republic*, ed. Jowett (3d ed.; Oxford, 1888), i. 329E.

conspicuous example of balance in the philosophical sense. The extreme division of labor in economic life, the extreme division of thought in religion, in education, and above all in research, the almost exclusive use of scientific methods of inquiry in attempts to deal with subjects for which reason and art are primarily appropriate, the disposition to determine all values mainly in material terms—these are the most characteristic features of American life and activity today. All of them tend to make men narrow in their outlook, partial in their judgment, and violent in their expression, when the great need is for restraint, breadth of vision, and for the sense of humor which would nourish an all-embracing humanity.

The extent to which human beings in the United States have had their existence weighted in the direction of some specialty, at the expense of the cultivation of the mind and the heart, becomes still more apparent when we reflect upon the want of any binding ideas, in the philosophical sense, to hold the innumerable separate occupations and disciplines together, to show how all are related to the great common problems of human existence. The coming of industrial societies has brought the different parts of the world closer together with the fantastically rapid speed of the express train, the jet plane, and most recently, Telstar. At the same time, by both greatly complicating and overmechanizing the problem of getting a living, industrial civilization seems to have reduced the instinctive sympathy and understanding among men and women. The division of labor has tremendously increased, while the kind of labor actually required of the common run of men and women demands far less ingenuity. Almost every worker is a specialist, and the specialties which occupy the great majority give almost exclusive scope to the single gift for routine, mechanized labor, the form least stimulating to the faculties of the mind and least satisfying to the longings of the heart. Are not our inner lives more separate than those of our ancestors? Are we not more alone than they? Viewed superficially, the railroad, the automobile, the airplane, the telephone, and television have united us; in a day, most men can see more faces, hear more voices, than most peasants in the Middle Ages saw and heard during a lifetime. But what common ground for genuine understanding have a workman in a Ford factory, a western cowboy on a visit to the city, a laryngologist, a bank clerk, a business executive, a professor of philology, and a poet, who meet in the lounge of a distant airport? It is not mere travel, still less is it mere hearing, that creates understanding; it is participation in the same experiences, in similar thought, similar wit, and similar tasks, especially when these tasks call for the exercise of nimble discernment. In the eighteenth and early nineteenth centuries, European society all over this planet was bound together by the firm ties which such participation provides and strengthens. The remarkable increase in travel and in trade spread the consciousness of these similarities and helped to give the European peoples a deeper sense of unity than they have ever felt since. Extreme specialization undoes those ties that the performance of common and creative tasks tightens. If men are hungrier today for companionship than their distant ancestors, it is partly because the great majority have less.

The principal work that confronts the mind in the United States is that of restoring the balance that has been lost, by revealing to men and women all that they have in common, by reaffirming the value of faith, reason, art, and creative craftsmanship. By the performance of this work, learning and the arts can help to revive the sense of companionship that has largely disappeared in the modern impersonal, industrialized world. Advance along the winding and difficult way, with formidable barriers and deceptive bypaths, which alone can reveal the vision of our common humanity, has now become the promise of American life.[3]

[3] *The Promise of American Life* is of course the title of Herbert Croly's celebrated book, first published in 1909. For Croly, the promise consists

1. *Religion and Science*

The position of faith as the first of the ends of human existence toward which we are drawn in striving to bring out the best in man requires justification. Of all man's activities, are not religious observances the least balanced and scientific? If orthodox religion is partial and narrow, as scientific and liberal thought during the last hundred years has taught us to suppose, what business have we to invoke it or even to speak well of it, when our object is a balanced view of the world? Of all the learned disciplines that our ancestors inherited, none, some of us were led to suppose, has so warped the intelligent minds of past generations as theology.

The relation of men and of nature to their Maker is the principal subject matter of theology. Newman called it "the Science of God, or the truths we know about God put into a system."[4] If the rise of natural sciences has led to a weakening of Christian religious belief, this has been contrary to the wishes of many of the greatest scientists. As they developed in early modern times, especially in seventeenth-century England, natural sciences, with their increasing interest in observation and their new interest in experiment, were frequently regarded by the great scientists, though seldom by the Catholic church, and in the beginning not even by the fathers of the reformed churches, as an important ally of theology. By

---

mainly in better material conditions, but these were important because they would provide, his book seems to suggest, for the qualities Americans needed in order "to become better democrats"—the "qualities of high intelligence, humanity, magnanimity and humility. . . ." In formulating the promise anew in terms mainly of those very qualities, I have been influenced by witnessing the enormous changes in the conditions of American life, which were beginning when Croly wrote, and which he partly foresaw (see paperback edition of *The Promise of American Life* [New York, 1963], pp. 6–7, 99). His proposals for meeting them were increased economic planning and state interference. We have had plenty of both since 1909 (cf. below, pp. 334–36). The promise of American life now seems to call for different means of approach, as is suggested below in Part Three.

4 J. H. Cardinal Newman, *The Idea of a University* (London, 1899), p. 61.

wresting the secrets from matter and from the living bodies of animals and human beings, the scientists thought they would increase the wonder felt by men in the presence of the works of God. Observation and experiment were to be means of adding to "the truths we know about God."[5]

Such scientists failed to take account of the fundamental difference between the objectives of natural science and those of the Christian religion. The one aims to show what is, the other what ought to be. The one confines itself to the finite physical world; the other rises into the infinite world of the mind and spirit which transcends the matter visible through the most powerful microscopes and telescopes. Unless the objectives of natural science and religion are distinguished and reconciled, the emphasis on science is likely to breed disunity and confusion among the human family, harmful to faith and in the end to all the sciences.

Two developments in more recent times go a long way toward explaining why the hope of some of the early devout scientists that experiment and observation would strengthen religious belief has proved deceptive. As knowledge of bodily processes and of the composition of matter increased, both the body and the physical world were robbed to a considerable degree of their mysteries. This was not because, in actual fact, the power behind the behavior of the body and of matter was less mysterious after the scientists had probed further and further into them. Depths beyond depths and heights beyond heights always remained. But, as was natural, men came to be fascinated by the bodily and the material processes themselves to the exclusion of the power behind them.

Science has supplied the ordinary run of men and women with a vast number of new toys to occupy their leisure time in an age when the need for steady, continuous labor has diminished. When they become ill they learn from their physicians all about some new virus. While the physician does

[5] Cf. below, pp. 144–45.

not always understand it, it provides him with a convenient subject for talk beside the bed. The patient becomes absorbed in speculating on the way in which this virus develops and moves about within him. His body takes on the aspect of a battlefield, and he envisages with fascination, as a spectator, the reserve forces that he is able to throw against the enemy. When he recovers, the defeated virus provides a fertile topic of conversation. Conversation is an important need of a generation starved for it but left without the domestication necessary to make it. How many women's luncheons and tea parties have been saved from silence, if not from boredom, by one guest's talk about her peculiar form of allergy and another's description of her recent bout with diverticulitis!

Science and medicine have helped many people to think of their bodies and their lives almost altogether in physical terms. Love, birth, and death have become physiological matters—to be analyzed in the laboratory and presented to the public in museum exhibits or in ten-minute talks on television. They are no longer subjects for meditation in the church or the cloister or on some quiet countryside.

For the accuracy of the early supposition that scientific inquiry would renew the strength of religious faith, the extension of scientific methods beyond the realm of natural science, for which they were originally devised, has been even more serious than the diversion of the mind from the deeper problems of existence that we all have to meet. This extension was seldom brought about directly by the scientists. But eventually the new scientific methods, derived from the study of the natural sciences, came to be applied to the ancient science of theology itself. Since revealed theology rests ultimately on faith, the application of scientific criticism to the miracles of the gospel and to the history of the world as explained in the Old Testament, together with the application of scientific textual criticisms to the gospel, undermined faith itself. From the conclusion that there was no scientific proof of the truth of the New Testament, it was a natural step to the view that revealed theology was an impediment to knowledge. Theism remained. But the weakening of the faith in the divinity of Christ, possible under theism, made room for a far larger number of sects and forms of religious belief than the Reformation had admitted.

It is difficult to dispute the view of Bossuet concerning the effects of the Reformation on faith. "On énerve la religion quand on la change, et on lui ôte un certain poid, qui seul est capable de tenir les peuples."[6] The numerous religions which grew up with the triumph of natural science and industrialism in the nineteenth and early twentieth centuries have much less in common than Catholicism and the various branches of Protestantism had after the triumph of religious toleration in the north of Europe in the lifetime of Bossuet (1627–1704). The condition described by John Donne, in one of the most celebrated of his poems, has become a reality for the modern world in respect to religious belief.

> 'Tis all in peeces, all cohaerence gone;
> All just supply, and all Relation:
> Prince, Subject, Father, Sonne, are things forgot,
> For every man alone thinkes he hath got
> To be a Phoenix, and that then can bee
> None of that kinde, of which he is, but hee.[7]

During recent decades there has been, especially in the United States, a remarkable abandonment of articles of faith once regarded as essential to Christian belief among Protestant clergymen. An inquiry was made in Chicago and its environs in 1929 into the views of five hundred ministers in service and

[6] "One enervates religion by changing it, and takes from it a certain weight that alone is able to hold the peoples" ("On the death of Henriette-Marie de France, November 16, 1669," *Sermons choisis*, Vol. II [Lille, 1895]). Cf. W. K. Jordan, *The Development of Religious Toleration in England, 1640–1660* (London, 1940), II, 481–82, 487–88.

[7] "An Anatomie of the World. The first Anniversary" (1633), ll. 213–18 (*The Poems of John Donne*, ed. H. J. C. Grierson [Oxford, 1912], I, 237–38).

two hundred students in Protestant theological seminaries. They all answered the same questions covering the chief elements of Christian faith as historically defined. Only one-fourth of the students maintained "that Jesus was born of a virgin without a human father," as compared with nearly three-fourths of the ministers, most of whom belonged to an older generation. There was an even sharper drop from one generation to the next in the number who held that a belief in the virgin birth was necessary for the Christian. Of the ministers, 46 per cent, as compared with 3 per cent of the students, regarded it as essential.[8]

The decay of Christian dogma among the Protestants is partly a reflection of compromises induced by scientific inquiry. The clergymen's own beliefs were shaken, and they gave way to the illusion that they could fill half-empty churches by watering the stock of dogma to fit in with the discoveries of natural science, which changed the prevailing view of matter and physical processes from decade to decade, if not from year to year. They gave way to the illusion that this was the way to win over the professors and teachers alienated by the bigotry and harshness of American Fundamentalism and Puritanism. By hitching their cause to natural science the Protestant clergy were abandoning religion, which is concerned with the right and the eternal, for the actual and the fleeting. If religion is to adjust itself to each important new scientific discovery, there is no end to the changes that will be made and no limit to the number of sects that will be formed.

Persons who were not committed by their parents to any sect, and others who withdrew from the church in which they were brought up, reached the conclusion that men are better off without theology and even without any religious belief whatever. That was a logical result of the attempt to make

8 *Recent Social Trends in the United States* (New York, 1933), II, 1013. I am grateful to Fr. Cyril N. McKinnon for calling this reference to my attention.

religion scientific, in the natural scientist's sense. Such a conclusion became so prevalent that thousands of the most prominent members of the generation who occupy responsible positions in the United States were brought up by their parents and most of their teachers to regard all references to scripture, to theological matters, and even to God as evidences of a depravity in the human mind from which the enlightened twentieth century was happily to be delivered. Though perhaps somewhat extreme, the training of a scientist's daughter is nonetheless revealing of a common attitude toward religion in American education and society during the early years of the present century. This young woman had been continually exposed at home and school to the new doctrines derived from scientific knowledge by some of the pragmatists. She had always felt a distaste for mathematics. In her early twenties she lived in France. There she frequently saw references to Pascal in the writings of eminent men of the time. One day, out of curiosity, she bought the recently published third series of the massive Brunschvicg edition of Pascal's works and began to read the remarkable opening paragraphs of *Les Pensées*. There Pascal sets forth with great clarity and economy of words the difference between two kinds of reasoning—the mathematical, which can proceed logically only from principles artificially created by the trained mind and consequently difficult to comprehend, and the *esprit de finesse*. As Pascal explains, the nimbly discerning mind can, "at one bound," grasp by intuition something of the meaning of the infinitely complicated delicate relationships of the actual world in which human beings move. She could hardly believe that these subtle and illuminating distinctions had anything to do with mathematics, which she had always regarded as a singularly dry and meaningless subject, irrelevant to anything human. Pascal at once gave it meaning and explained why it had repelled her. She concluded that the French were right in claiming him as a genius.

Leading the life of continual social activity to which Americans of her class gave themselves up in the 1920's even in France, she found no time to pursue her reading beyond the first twelve pages. But several years afterward an illness gave her an opportunity to turn back to the writer who had made such a singularly favorable impression upon her. In the meantime she had acquired the small Massis edition, easier than the heavier Brunschvicg volumes to manage in bed. It opens with *Les Provinciales.* Imagine her astonishment, as she began to skim the pages, to find Pascal talking about theology and faith with the same assurance, the same clarity, discrimination, and balanced spirit which she had found in his discussion of the nature of reason. She was a woman of considerable intelligence. She had come to trust her own judgment in matters of art and thought. Here she was confronted with a mind which her experience, like all the most respected French authorities, told her was of the highest order. Her early life in the United States gave her the not erroneous impression that none of her American contemporaries could have distinguished between the mathematical and the far more human nimbly discerning mind nearly as effectively or convincingly as Pascal, or have shown with such skill as he why the best intelligence must employ both in order to approach truth. With the ascendancy of modern science, scientific methods had almost crowded out of existence these essential elements in the rational process, and threatened to make the word "reason" in the American academic world another name for experiment and the observation of measurable data and concrete documents. Recognizing the truth of Pascal's analysis, which differentiated nimble discernment from the proofs of the natural scientist no less than from those of the mathematician and the logician, she had no doubt that he was the intellectual superior of anyone she had met in the flesh. Was it possible that intelligence and faith could exist in the same being? Could it be that Pascal was right about theology and religion and that the persons who had brought her up were wrong? Was Pascal prejudiced or were they?

I do not know whether she ever answered these questions, for I lost touch with her. The answers are difficult for the members of her generation and for those of the one that follows, who are even less inclined than hers to believe in the divinity of Christ. If you have faith, then theology must be the most important subject in the whole realm of learning. If you have faith, and if you have also genius and the highest reasoning powers (as Pascal and Richard Hooker had, and, some centuries before them, Thomas Aquinas), then theology becomes, not only the most important, but the most all-embracing subject in the realm of learning. Its inquiries color every other subject, particularly philosophy. Once the initial step of belief in the divinity of Christ is made, there is unlimited scope within the properly restricted subject matter of Christian theology to reinforce faith by reason, to reinforce revealed by natural theology. As this young American woman observed, when Pascal wrote about matters of faith and Christianity, he wrote no more like a charlatan than when he distinguished between the mathematical and that more subtle kind of reasoning which he called nimble discernment (*esprit de finesse*).

What is needed in the twentieth century is the pursuit of good ends which will show mankind the essential unity of all branches of learning and all aspects of human existence. Nothing perhaps is designed to do this better than theology, though the danger that it will be abused by theologians is very great. It treats of the whole of existence, even as philosophy does. It has an advantage which philosophy lacks. It emphasizes man's dependence on a superior being who is infinitely good, above all human passions and weaknesses; it provides the heart with a vision of perfection amid the universality of worldly imperfection. It teaches hope in humility, and that is of particular value in an age when pride (if not downright boastfulness) has come to be popularly regarded as an essential part of a creditable career on earth. Theology covers much the same territory as philosophy; potentially it has far greater power to bind men together in sympathy for each other. As conceived by the greatest theologians, it not only strengthens faith—it exalts and fortifies the mind and the heart.

Some persons today admit that theology and religious belief are not, and have not been, as hostile to genuine scientific inquiry as was once assumed. We do not lack eminent scientific colleagues who speak on behalf of religion. They suggest that the discoveries of modern science are in no way incompatible with theism and even with Christianity. As is not surprising in the light of the religious views expressed by theological students, these scientists seldom discuss fundamental matters of Christian dogma, such as the divinity of Christ. It is not suggested that the scientist has, in fact, any special insight into such matters that is denied to other people. The question of the possibility of two natures, the one human and the other divine, existing in the same individual lies beyond the range of positive science. It is a philosophical question. The modern tendency to seek the guidance of natural scientists in a realm alien to their special training and knowledge is another manifestation of the prevalent disposition to assume that positive science is capable of solving all the problems of existence. But the pronouncements of scientists on religious matters, even when malapropos, also suggest that the scientists themselves are aware that science is not enough.

In spite of the views of scientists that the discoveries of modern sciences have not destroyed the grounds of Christian belief, in spite of the movement of the intelligence in France toward religious belief—as manifested years ago in men like Péguy, Du Bos, and Maritain—Americans now in middle life are always reminding each other of the practical difficulties that stand in the way of a renewal of faith. Whether we like it or not, whether it is desirable or not, whether it is scientific or not, we are told, Christian theology and religion are not going to resume the central place they held in Western history before the eighteenth and nineteenth centuries. That is possible. Without a renewal of belief in Christ, it is inevitable. Is it desirable? Looking at the matter purely from the point of view of life on this planet in the centuries before us, the eclipse of religious faith, if it should be complete, would not seem to provide a cause for rejoicing, as many men who deal with education in the United States often take for granted. They have not shown us anything that can replace it. By its very nature, natural science, dealing as it does with material evidence, cannot occupy the territory which properly belongs to theology. If faith should suffer an eclipse, that territory might conceivably remain vacant. In all probability it will be occupied by false gods. As we observed at the end of chapter 4, signs have not been lacking that the occupation has already gone far.

II. *Religion and the Study of Society*

The discoveries of historians, archeologists, sociologists, and anthropologists are frequently represented as obstacles in the way of the establishment of any common belief. These discoveries are represented as disproving the existence of such a thing as general truth. Early in the nineteenth century, students were provided in the colleges and universities with works like Sumner's *Folkways* and Westermarck's *History of Human Marriage*. These books were part of a liberal education. They were regarded by early sociologists as perfectly scientific, not least because they reached no conclusions and applied no moral or intellectual values to the conditions their authors discovered. Impartiality, in the sense of perfect neutrality on all moral and intellectual issues, was coming to be regarded as the final mark of scholarship in connection with the study of man. It was almost as if man's relations to man were placed by the scholar in the same category with the organic and inorganic matter of the biological and physical sciences. Indeed, Jacques Loeb was busy trying to demonstrate that human behavior might be analyzed into the same simple elements that he found in the behavior of the lower animals. It would be in accord with his general mechanistic philosophy to explain the manifestations of the human mind exclusively in terms of the structure and physiology of the brain. In the 1890's such mechanistic views as his revolutionized biological studies in the United States. They have had much influence on the work in every branch of modern scholarship.

The new attitude toward the study of man and his history contributed to the decline of religious faith. It even undermined the Christian ethics, which theists, deists, and agnostics, for the most part, had accepted as sound during the eighteenth and most of the nineteenth centuries. The study of human marriage revealed no uniformity in customs among human beings. Some primitive tribes were found to be monogamous, others polygamous, still other polyandrous, etc. The study of primitive peoples in the flesh, and the fresh information concerning ancient societies derived from newly found documents, inscriptions, and archeological remains, brought to light a host of different manners, customs, and religious beliefs. Of course Herodotus had written about this diversity more than twenty-three hundred years ago, but it was no longer common in the United States for university men to study Herodotus. So they took up archeology with all the enthusiasm of the mountaineer who thinks he is making a first ascent. University men in western Europe and even more in the United States concluded that man's salvation lay in acknowledging the relativity of all values. They not only claimed that neither truth nor virtue exists in an absolute sense—they denied that reason, whether mathematical or intuitional, can help men to edge closer to either truth or virtue. How was one to determine scientifically which system of marriage, which set of political institutions, which religion was the best? Justice, honor, and beauty cannot be made the subjects of quantitative analysis. What was not susceptible of measurement, or precise proof through observation and experiment, was not worth the attention of the social scientist. The deductive method, by itself, was regarded with increasing suspicion. Deductions from revealed theology became scientifically impossible. New students recruited to the new studies were taught to explore new tribes and peoples, to collect and classify more facts concerning them.

Most American social scientists and professors of philosophy take it for granted that religious beliefs, together with the moral and intellectual values that many Western poets, philosophers, and scholars once accepted, have now been rendered obsolete by research in the social sciences and the humanities. They seldom notice that their elders—including that dangerous saint, Thomas Aquinas—did not live or study in complete ignorance of the diversity of beliefs and values which are now regarded as so damaging to the existence of faith and moral or intellectual convictions of any kind. They generally forget that ancient sages did not regard such diversity as an insuperable barrier to a general philosophical synthesis and a consensus of religious belief.

Aristotle pointed out long ago that the subjects of investigation in ethics and political science "exhibit so great a diversity and uncertainty . . . [that] we must be content to indicate the truth roughly and in outline."[9] Shall we evade subjects simply because they are difficult? That would seem to be a poor reason. But it is not an uncommon one, particularly in an age when men have become accustomed to following the line of least resistance. One is reminded of the French economic historians who sent their students to study the French Revolution instead of the wars of religion because so many of the documents relating to the late sixteenth century are in a handwriting hard to decipher!

Once it is admitted that the disinterested mind has an independent part to play in dealing with social data, a role not directed or determined primarily by experiment or scientific observation but by reason, then it is inevitable that ethical

[9] *The Nicomachean Ethics* 1.1.

judgments concerning the value of different customs and traditions should be regarded not as a mere diversion in connection with the subject but as the most fundamental aspect of it. If, therefore, the mind is again given a place of its own in the higher learning, the approach to history, archeology, sociology, and anthropology will be very different from that hitherto regarded as alone appropriate.

When an ethical attitude toward the study of society is adopted, what impresses men is less the differences between the various religions than the fact that all advanced societies have had religion. This suggests that human nature is bound under all circumstances to be concerned with the power behind the material world that is revealed to it. As far as history is a guide, it suggests that even civilized men cannot exist without faith. Such a conclusion is startling for the numerous university men who assume that an absence of faith is an evidence of a superior education. Such a conclusion is bound to lead the intelligent to wonder whether we could free the heart from all prejudices. They might be inclined to agree with André Gide that "prejudices are the pillars of civilization."[10] They might conclude that it is the supreme duty of learning to try to guide mankind toward good prejudices. They will find nothing in the Constitution of the United States or in the thought of our great statesmen to support the proposition that all prejudices are of equal value.

If learning were to take this course, wise scholars would be bound to treat the diversity of religions among mankind as something more than a matter for curiosity. They would be impelled to raise the question: Which of all the religions known to history is the best for man? An inquiry into that matter could do nothing directly to restore faith. "Prejudice" can never serve as a sound basis for faith, which is a gift that reason has no power to offer. But the inquiry could do much to restore respect. It is conceivable that the growth of respect may make mankind more susceptible to faith.

10 *Les Faux-monnayeurs* (Paris, 1925), p. 17.

Unlike the study of comparative religions as mere curiosities, such an inquiry would almost certainly increase our admiration for Christ. Whether we consider religions from the standpoint of their doctrines or from the standpoint of their universality, Christianity can open the door at least as wide as Islam, Judaism, Confucianism, or Buddhism to the charity and self-restraint which are essential to the building of a world order. It is for people everywhere to nourish the love common to all these religions.

Even a person without the Christian faith can recognize that the counsel of Christ Himself concerning human conduct is the most sublime advice ever given to man and that it is intended for all.[11] He can recognize that the advice contained in the works of great writers before and since the time of Christ is in essential agreement with His advice. Men can recognize that the more closely they are able to follow Christ's precepts, the more they are able to put their trust in everything which, according to the gospel, He preached, the nearer they will attain to spiritual happiness, the easier it will be for them to suffer and ultimately to die when their time comes, and the more they will be inclined toward humility and love of their fellow men here on earth.

Man is born not to serve himself but "to love his neighbor." This was the counsel that the greatest surgeon of the sixteenth century prefixed to his treatise on surgery. Shall we say that this advice was simply a matter of Ambroise Paré's personal bias? Shall we say he was indulging in propaganda? Paré managed to cover his tracks so well that no historian (and few, if any, of his contemporaries) was able to determine for certain whether he was a Huguenot or a Catholic. He concealed his

---

[11] The late Professor Hocking, in fact, reached a similar conclusion in his comparisons between the principal contemporary religions in their bearing on a common faith. See W. E. Hocking, *Living Religions and a World Faith* (New York, 1940), pp. 228, 230, 232, 235–38, 240–41, 249, 268–69. For the matters on which he thinks Christianity needs to learn from other religions, see pp. 242–43, 254 ff.

religion for reasons of safety in an age of religious warfare. His admonition could not betray him, for it is no monopoly of Catholicism or Protestantism. It transcends both. It is older than Christianity,[12] but fundamentally Christian. In proportion as it serves to guide surgeons, doctors, and men in every walk of life, human existence is enriched.

By faith in Christ men are consoled for suffering and death. As Madame de Sévigné remarked in 1689: "Un retour à la volonté de Dieu, et à cette loi universelle ou nous sommes condamnés, remet la raison à sa place, et fait prendre patience."[13] This is not the advice of a mystic but of a lady supremely endowed with common sense, with *savoir faire*. The word "reason" is well chosen. The will of God is the most perfect insurance that man can hope to find against excess and insanity.

The ideas are prevalent in the United States today that we are born with a right to escape suffering and unhappiness, that the world owes us a living. Such ideas cause misery. They lead us to spend a large part of our lives trying to avoid suffering and trouble, or denying their existence. We spend our time trying to arrange life instead of living it, without ever reaching a satisfactory solution, because the problems presented by illness, death, and evil are not soluble, not at any rate by men.

Christianity makes untenable the prevalent idea that we are put here to indulge in a sort of perpetual good time. According to orthodox Christianity, men suffer not only for their own faults but for those of the human race, for which the Almighty bears no responsibility. Once this view is accepted, the reason and patience of which Madame de Sévigné spoke are always at man's disposal in the face of every difficult and terrible event. How often have we heard the men of what was once called the "lost generation" say, when confronted by the premature

12 Cf. Sigmund Freud, *Civilization and Its Discontents* (New York, 1930), p. 81.

13 "A return to God's will, and to the universal law that condemns us all, restores reason to its place and makes us patient" (*Lettres de Madame de Sévigné*, ed. M. Monmerqué, IX [Paris, 1862], 334).

death of a companion more virtuous than others who continue to live: "There is proof that God does not exist. If He did exist, how could He let men like Joe or Dave die in their youth like this?" They are deprived of that hope of which Milton spoke so movingly in his poem consoling a mother on the death of her infant daughter.

> O fairest flower no sooner blown but blasted,
>   Soft silken Primrose fading timesslie,
> Summers chief honour if thou hadst out-lasted
>   Bleak winters force that made thy blosome drie;
>
> .   .   .   .
>
> Then thou the mother of so sweet a child
>   Her false imagin'd loss cease to lament,
> And wisely learn to curb thy sorrows wild;
>   Think what a present thou to God hast sent,
>   And render him with patience what he lent;
>   This if thou do he will an off-spring give,
>   That till the worlds last-end shall make thy name to live.[14]

Here we find Milton using the same word, "patience," that Madame de Sévigné used. Next to conviction, which needs to be tempered by it, patience is, perhaps, the quality in which modern Americans are most deficient. Such a faith as Milton's, rugged and harsh, no less than the refined faith of Madame de Sévigné, calls us back to common sense. Is it not more in accord with reality than the doctrine of man's perfectibility in a godless world? As Tawney has said, ". . . In order to be at home in this world, it is not sufficient, unfortunately, to disbelieve in another."[15] Is such disbelief even the best preparation for improving this world? No less esteemed a modern thinker than Freud has suggested that the sense of guilt has been one of the great forces in the development of civilization.[16] With human nature what it is, this sense of guilt sometimes makes effec-

[14] "On the Death of a fair Infant dying of a Cough," *Poems, etc., upon Several Occasions* (London, 1673).

[15] *Equality* (3d ed.; London, 1938), p. 83.

[16] Freud, *Civilization and Its Discontents,* chap. 7, esp. pp. 108–9, 111, 121–22.

tive the admonition to love one's neighbor. Freud would almost certainly have rejected the use of his thesis on behalf of
the Christian religion; he traces the sense of guilt to the Oedi-
pus complex.[17] Yet it is difficult to deny that the Christian religion fostered this sense of guilt by its dogma of original sin,
by its emphasis on man's limitations, his imperfections.[18]

"All that a man hath will he give for his life." These are the
words of Satan in the Book of Job. They are also the words of
irreligion and materialism in the modern United States. Life
becomes so supreme a good, it is so much the only good of
which we have any scientific proof, some of the young men
and women of this country have come to say in recent years,
that anything and everything are worth sacrificing merely for
the sake of survival. Such is hardly the road to the true love of
life. Since life in this world must go for all, since the closest approach to earthly fulfillment is in the shared love for another,
happiness can come to those who, fortified by such fulfillment,
are able to reconcile themselves to death sufficiently to put it
out of their minds and to live fully and decently enough to surmount a personal sense of guilt. Such persons are prepared to
meet evil as well as death, for in the end there is only one
answer to the words of Satan if the test comes. That answer is
their rejection. To most men the test of their truth does not
come in so crucial a form. It comes, nevertheless, in a multitude
of minor forms, almost every day of their lives. For example,
men are forever being called on to give up what their conscience tells them is right, for the sake of personal advantages
of one sort and another. The measure of the power of man's
spirit and of the strength of the civilization that has bred him
consists in this: When the test presented by Satan comes, is he
able to make the right choice? Has he the courage to act in
accordance with it? Who can doubt that the Christian faith
has helped many to make the right choice and to act on it?

[17] *Ibid.*, pp. 103, 118.

[18] Cf. T. E. Hulme, *Speculations* (London, 1924), *passim.*

When we consider not only the words of Christ and their power but the history of Christianity, we are also led to the conclusion that its significance cannot be dismissed as a mere matter of the mores of a particular tribe, race, nation, or society. Christianity was born among the Jews in Palestine almost two thousand years ago. It established itself in the Roman Empire as part of the classical society in the Mediterranean area. Western civilization was the product of natural resources, races, and circumstances other than those which created Greco-Roman society. No Classical tradition grew in strength during the decline of the Roman Empire as the new Christian faith did. This was fed by several sources both philosophical and religious. After the fifth century, men ceased to read even commentaries upon the commentaries on the works of Aristotle and the other great writers of antiquity. But their faith deepened when economic life became more primitive, as they repeated the plain chant together and listened to the story of the gospel told them by the priests. Faith was hardly weakened by the break between the Western and the Eastern church. With the rise of Western society and the growing strength of the Papacy in the eleventh and twelfth centuries, the Christian gospel assumed a universality in the life of the European peoples, and also in that of the very different Eastern peoples of the Balkans and of Russia, that it never possessed among the Classical peoples into whose world it was introduced. Even if we take no account of the relation of Christianity to the ancient Hebrew religion, it is evident that the Christian faith has provided consolation to a medley of races, living under a great diversity of economic and political systems and belonging to an almost equally numerous diversity of cultures. An ethical study of general history from the sixteenth through the eighteenth centuries is capable of raising the question whether Christianity may not have been one force behind civilization.[19] Even scientists are faced with the problem whether the sense of reality, which in recent dec-

---

[19] Nef, *The Conquest of the Material World* (Chicago, 1964), pp. 364–66.

ades men have thought they were achieving through science, is in fact truer and more comprehensive than that embodied in the religious beliefs which have gone.[20] They are led to ask the same question that the young American woman asked when she became acquainted with Pascal. The study of society, if approached philosophically, can hardly enable these men to return with perfect confidence the answer that Pascal was more prejudiced than a modern atheist or positivist.

III. *Religion and Wealth*

Thus far we have limited our discussion of Christianity to the Founder's message. We have omitted all reference to the churches and to the ecclesiastical foundations that have made it their business to teach religious doctrines and to look after men's souls. Such a treatment of the subject may be said to resemble, not the play with Hamlet left out, but Hamlet with all the other players and all the scenery left out. When we are concerned with the ends of human existence, the words of Christ rightly seem far more important than their propagators. But as students of civilization, it is impossible to separate ecclesiastical history from Christian faith.

Nearly two centuries ago that busy clergyman, Dean Josiah Tucker, of whom it was said that religion was his trade and trade his religion, sought to reconcile the new doctrines of political economy with the teachings of the Anglican church. One of his efforts was an analysis of conditions favorable and unfavorable to material prosperity, as these were revealed by a comparison of France and Great Britain.[21] In the case of France he found arbitrary and despotic government[22] the first

[20] Edwin Schrödinger, *Nature and the Greeks* (Cambridge, 1954), pp. 93–96.

[21] Tucker, *A Brief Essay on the Advantages and Disadvantages Which Respectively Attend France and Great Britain with Regard to Trade* (2d ed.; London, 1750).

[22] For a historical inquiry into the relation between government and industrial development, see Nef, *Industry and Government in France and England, 1540–1640* (Ithaca, N.Y., 1957).

disadvantage to freedom of trade, which he and Adam Smith, among so many others, regarded as the primary objective of civilized existence. The second disadvantage was "the Romish Religion; which has added to its many other Absurdities, a Spirit of Cruelty and Persecution, so repugnant to the Scope and Tendency of the Gospel."[23]

During the last seventy years or so, few subjects in economic history have received as much attention from eminent scholars as this one of the influence of religion upon material progress. There is hardly an economic historian who has not touched on the matter since it was reopened, first in the 1890's by a chapter on "the canonist doctrine" in Sir William Ashley's *Introduction to Economic History and Theory*, and then in 1904 by Max Weber's far more celebrated and elaborate essay, which took a line different from Ashley's.[24] Brentano, Cunningham, Sombart, Troeltsch, Coulton, Tawney, Hauser, Sée, Fanfani, Groethuysen, Bieler, Delumeau, E. G. Léonard, and others in several countries, have made valuable contributions to the controversy. The main problems remain much the same as those suggested by Tucker. First, how far has Catholicism discouraged, and how far has the rise of Protestantism encouraged, the growth of the capitalist spirit and of large-scale enterprise in private hands? Second, how far has the Catholic church interfered with the increase in economic welfare; how far has the rise of Protestantism promoted it? The two questions are not quite different aspects of the same question, for it does not appear that under all circumstances increasing freedom for the private capitalist promotes economic welfare.[25] In spite of the intelligence of much of the reasoning that has been directed to the subject, many aspects remain unsettled. Facets have hardly been examined.[26]

[23] Tucker, *A Brief Essay on the Advantages and Disadvantages* . . . , p. 24.

[24] *The Protestant Ethic and the Spirit of Capitalism*, trans. Talcott Parsons (London, 1930).

[25] Cf. below, chap. 10, sec. II.

[26] The soundest, most balanced treatment of the part played by Protestant doctrine in the growth of private enterprise seems to me that of Tawney, in

There is a certain unreality in considering the reciprocal relations of religious and economic history, since both religious and economic factors obviously influence and are influenced by political, constitutional, and intellectual factors and also by geography and natural resources. The human mind has not yet managed to deal satisfactorily with the causal relationships of history as a whole, though a promising beginning has been made in the works of Spengler and Toynbee.[27] When religious and economic history are considered together, as has been the practice in connection with this controversy concerning religion and wealth, it becomes fairly clear that during much of western European history the existence of religious institutions, and especially of the Catholic church, has served as something of a restraint upon the accumulation of riches in the hands of private capitalists, upon the increase in the volume of production, and in particular upon the growth of large-scale privately owned enterprise. Does it follow that a strong Christian church always hampers the increase of what Professor Pigou called the national dividend?

We look back on the twelfth and thirteenth centuries as a great age for the Christian faith. Notwithstanding all the religious ardor, all the time and thought spent in developing the science of theology; notwithstanding the vast amount of labor which was devoted to the building and the maintenance of monasteries, churches, and cathedrals designed to glorify God and to teach the people the lessons of history as they were interpreted by Christians, the population grew rapidly, serfdom diminished, towns thrived, and the standard of living rose among most classes nearly everywhere in Europe. In every country economic welfare was considerably improved. Not

---

Religion and the Rise of Capitalism (2d ed., London, 1936), and also in his *Introduction to Thomas Wilson's Discourse upon Usury* (London, 1925), pp. 105–72.

[27] For reservations concerning the truth of their historical philosophy, see above, chap. 4 (IV).

until the eighteenth and early nineteenth centuries were all the European nations again bathed as frequently with comparable increases in prosperity. Whether economic progress would have been even more striking than it was without the Church or if the Reformation had come three or four centuries earlier than it did are questions that cannot be answered with assurance. The historian is unable to experiment with a past society by leaving out one of its elements as the chemist can so often do in his analyses. It is impossible to think of any side of European society in the Gothic age without the Church. When religion formed so integral a part of life, we may reasonably suppose that it helped infuse into the people the consolation and confidence that presumably had something to do with their material development. The passage of the year A.D. 1000, which tradition had set for the possible end of the world, is thought to have produced a fresh interest among the Western peoples in economic improvement. It did not prevent the strengthening of ecclesiastical institutions. The power and influence of the Papacy increased during and after the lifetime of Hildebrand (1020–85).

The ecclesiastical foundations, which controlled a considerable part of all the land in Europe, did little to hinder and a good deal to encourage the clearing and use of land for pasture and arable farming and for the mining, metallurgical, and salt-making industries. By its success in persuading rich men who had amassed their wealth in worldly careers to atone for their sins of greed by making large gifts or bequests for the glory of God, the Church dissipated many, if not most, of the large private fortunes which would have been available for investment in industry and trade. But in the Gothic age investments of capital in large blocks were much less essential to industrial progress than they became at the end of the Middle Ages. The great income of the Church was used in large part to command labor that produced no consumable commodities. But the hundreds of majestic buildings, which the Church alone was rich enough and powerful enough to undertake, provided work for the growing population, without interfering seriously with the labor and skill devoted to agrarian, commercial, and industrial pursuits which ministered to physical needs.[28] Even when we recognize that Catholic historians have greatly exaggerated the direct part which priests and monks took in manual labor, and the part which ecclesiastical foundations played in supplying capital for productive purposes, it is still difficult to show that all the construction which the Church financed held back economic progress from the time of Abelard to the times of St. Thomas and Dante. The medieval cathedrals, churches, and monasteries built in the twelfth and thirteenth centuries cost a sum equivalent to many billions of dollars,[29] in terms of modern American money, at a time when the yearly dividend of western Europe probably ran into hundreds of millions instead of hundreds of billions, as in the mid-twentieth century. Some modern economists take the view that there are circumstances which render a program of public works beneficial to economic welfare, even though the works themselves are of no use in the production or carriage of commodities. May not this have been the case in the late twelfth and thirteenth centuries? Work had to be found for the ever more numerous inhabitants. As a result of improvements in economic technique and management, it was not necessary to employ all of them in producing, transporting, and selling consumable goods in order to supply the people generally with a higher standard of living than that to which their ancestors had been accustomed before the Gothic age.[30]

At the end of the Middle Ages the conditions of economic

[28] Nef, *The Conquest of the Material World*, pp. 224–29.

[29] Cf. Henry Adams, *Mont-Saint-Michel and Chartres* (Boston, 1913), p. 94. (Allowance has been made for changes in the value of money since 1840, the date Adams took for his estimate.)

[30] This matter is considered in Nef, "L'Art religieux et le progrès économique aux 12e et 13e siècles," *Association pour l'histoire de la civilisation* (Toulouse, 1952–53), pp. 23–29.

progress had changed, together with the place of the Church in civilized life. Mining and metallurgy, for example, could be carried on effectively in the thirteenth century by small partnerships of manual workmen. In the late fifteenth and early sixteenth centuries these industries had come to require, in many cases, capital running into the modern equivalent of scores of thousands of dollars. The effective development of economically indispensable industries had come to require a freedom in the use of land and money seldom needed in the Gothic age. At the same time ecclesiastical foundations seem to have become, speaking generally, rather less enterprising in economic matters than they had once been. The strength, together with the prestige and influence, of the Papacy had declined.

Through its control over property and through the doctrines that it taught concerning science and economic and political life, the Church stood, at the end of the Middle Ages, in the way of the kind of economic development that led to the triumph of industrialism. Ecclesiastical foundations were not prepared to invest large sums in enterprises within their own lands. They were seldom willing to lease their lands on as favorable terms as lay landlords to persons who wanted to invest large sums. Land belonging to the Church, unlike land in private hands, was almost never for sale. So the ecclesiastical ownership of landed property interfered with its use for large industrially productive ventures of all kinds.

The dissolution of the monasteries and other ecclesiastical foundations in sixteenth-century England was accompanied and followed by the transfer of a vast amount of land, rich in minerals, from the Church to the Crown and to laymen. This transfer facilitated the exploitation of the coal mines[31] and the introduction of large, efficient plants for smelting iron ore.[32] As

[31] Nef, *The Rise of the British Coal Industry* (London, 1966), I, 133–56.

[32] The great development in Sussex of the blast furnace (then in its infancy in Europe) came directly after the dissolution of the monasteries in

an early "industrial revolution" was based in a measure on coal, and a later more famous one on the union of coal with iron, the Reformation played a part of some significance, through the confiscation of religious property, in promoting the progress of all the heavy industries.

In France ecclesiastical foundations retained until the French Revolution—for two and a half centuries longer than in England—almost as much landed property as they had held during the Middle Ages. We catch a glimpse of the attitude of monks toward the use of water-driven machinery and the development of heavy industry in connection with the famous abbey of La Grande Trappe. In 1351, a metallurgical work was mentioned near Laigle in what is now the Orne Department. Later the Trappist monks closed down this plant of theirs on the ground that the noise of the falling hammers at the forge and of the machine-driven pincers pulling out the metal wire interfered with their solitude.[33] Is it not safe to say that, on monastic estates, economic had frequently to give way to religious considerations when there was a conflict between the two?

A rather comprehensive survey was made of the iron manufacture in France in 1789.[34] This survey shows that in Church lands the furnaces for smelting iron ore were much smaller and less modern in equipment than most of those in lands belonging to laymen. In the departments of Côtes-du-Nord, Cher, Indre, Nièvre, Moselle, Haute Saône, and Saône-et-Loire, *only a negligible proportion* of the furnaces for which we have records were in Church lands. The average annual output per furnace in these departments was about 475 tons.[35] In the de-

---

1536 and 1539, and many of the new ironworks were erected on land, formerly the property of the Church, most of which had not been used for smelting iron ore, even on a small scale, before its confiscation (Ernest Straker, *Wealden Iron* [London, 1931], pp. 32, 49, 292).

[33] M. Leroux, *L'Industrie du fer dans le Perche* (Paris, 1916), pp. 106–7.

[34] H. and G. Bourgin, *L'Industrie sidérurgique en France* (Paris, 1920).

[35] I have worked out these and the other figures of production at the French furnaces from data in the book of the Bourgins. My figures are not

partments of Ardennes, Meuse, Haute-Marne, Côte-d'Or, Isère, and Savoie, something like a third or more of all the furnaces recorded were in lands still held by ecclesiastical foundations. The average annual output per furnace in these departments was 320 tons. There can be little doubt that it was the furnaces in Church lands which brought down the average. There are two departments—Isère and Ardennes—for which it is possible to separate the furnaces in Church lands from those in the lands of laymen. In Isère the former produced on the average about 180 tons a year, as against an average of about 320 tons for all the furnaces in this department. In Ardennes they produced about 75 tons, as against about 380 tons for all those in that department. The output of the French iron furnaces in territory held by the ecclesiastical foundations appears to have been much smaller in 1789 than that of the average furnace in England and Wales on the eve of the English civil war,[36] a hundred and fifty years before. While the greater scale of ironmaking in England cannot be explained exclusively or even mainly by the dissolution of the monasteries,[37] the confiscations of ecclesiastical property had something to do with the differences.

Apart from the influence exercised by the Church over the use of land, the expense of maintaining large armies of priests and monks, engaged mainly in devotional rather than in economically productive activities, imposed something of a handicap in early modern times upon the progress of large-scale industrial enterprise and the growth in the output of cheap commodities, made with the help of horse- and water-driven ma-

---

precise for several reasons. The survey does not include all the ironmaking enterprises; most of the statistics actually given are approximations; the exact weight of some of the units in which production was measured (e.g., the *quintal* and the *millier*) is not always clear.

[36] Nef, "Iron Production in England, 1540–1640," *Journal of Political Economy*, XLIV, No. 3 (1936), 401.

[37] For some of the other causes, see Nef, *La Naissance de la civilisation industrielle et le monde contemporain* (Paris, 1954), Pt. I.

chinery. The Church no longer played the leading part in financing building operations, as it had done in the Gothic age. Like the French nobility, the French clergy largely escaped the payment of direct taxes, which fell almost entirely on the untitled people. Like the nobility, the clergy was much less interested than the mercantile class in investing large sums in the heavy industries or in the sale and purchase of cheap conveniences. When the ecclesiastical foundations as institutions wanted ornaments, hangings, and furniture, they looked more for the beautiful and the lasting than for useful commodities, such as were in demand among the middle class everywhere and in England, to some extent, even among the best-paid manual workmen.[38] The use which the Church made of its immense income did not stimulate the demand for the products of heavy industry as much as the equivalent income in the hands of the mercantile and the laboring classes would have done. In 1676 Sir William Petty, one of the fathers of economic thought, passed on an exaggeration that we hear with a little surprise from this meticulous statistician. It serves, nevertheless, to bring out a point which is of concern in connection with economic welfare. "The Hollanders," he wrote, "observe that in France and Spain . . . the Churchmen are about one hundred for one, to what they use or need; the principal care of whom is to preserve Uniformity, and this they take to be a superfluous charge."[39] The maintenance of a far more numerous clergy and of far more costly religious institutions in France and most other Continental nations than in England, during the two hundred years following the Reformation, helps to account for the slower progress of capitalist enterprise and the slower expansion of the heavy industries.[40]

[38] The influence of royal absolutism was similar, as I attempted to show in my *Industry and Government in France and England, 1540–1640*, esp. chaps. 4 and 5.

[39] *The Economic Writings of Sir William Petty*, ed. by C. H. Hull (Cambridge, 1899), I, 263.

[40] Cf. Nef, *The Conquest of the Material World*, chap. 5.

In most discussions of religion and the rise of capitalism much less emphasis has been laid upon the influence on economic history of ecclesiastical institutions, with their wealth, than upon the influence of Christian dogma. By emphasizing a side of the problem which has not received as much attention as it would seem to deserve, we do not suggest that the doctrines and teachings of the churches have been unimportant for economic welfare. The bigoted opposition to scientific experiment and observation that was so prominent in late Scholastic thought at the end of the Middle Ages was encouraged by the Catholic church and in the beginning by the founders of the new Protestant sects as well, although the early Protestant writers broke with Scholastic thought at many points.[41] As Dr. James Conant has pointed out, the mine and factory have helped the laboratory just as the laboratory has helped the mine and factory. There has been in modern times a sort of symbiosis between scientific inquiry and technological improvements of every kind.[42] Over and over again each has stimulated and encouraged the other. Both have been indispensable to the rise of industrialism. The decidedly tepid enthusiasm of churchmen—and particularly Catholic churchmen —for both perhaps interfered with the introduction of labor-saving devices and other improvements in industry and transportation. Finally, while the doctrines of the Catholic church imposed restraints upon political power, they were generally unsympathetic to popular sovereignty. The authority of an absolute prince under God, which the Church endorsed in early modern times, was no more favorable to the freedom of private capital and to the unrestricted rights of private capital-

41 Cf. T. B. Macaulay, "Lord Bacon," *Essays* (London, 1866), II, 376.

42 J. B. Conant, "Lessons from the Past," *Industrial and Engineering Chemistry*, XXXI (1939), 1215–17. At the time of the scientific revolution, *ca.* 1580–1700, the use of scientific discoveries for technological purposes was restrained (Nef, *The Conquest of the Material World*, pp. 318 ff.). Later, a new hope in man's power to resist evil helped to bring about the symbiosis which impressed Conant (see above, pp. 30–37).

ists in their business operations than the authority of the Church itself.

In a variety of ways, the doctrines of Christianity, as expounded by churchmen, interfered with the accumulation of capital in private hands and with the unrestrained pursuit of profit by communicants. It was only by means of compromises, made invariably with reluctance, that the taking of moderate interest on loans could be brought into any sort of accord with the dogma of the Christian fathers. Priests and pastors were in no position to offer a wholehearted endorsement of the careers of men whose rise in the world was brought about principally by their skill and success in amassing fortunes, such as were needed for launching large private industrial and commercial enterprises. The extent to which private accumulation and freedom for private business enterprise promoted economic welfare is impossible to estimate, because those countries (of which Great Britain was the foremost) in which large-scale privately owned enterprise made the greatest headway were countries where, besides religion, other conditions—such as peace and easily accessible mineral resources—were favorable to quantitative progress. There were some ways in which the discipline of the Catholic church stimulated production. It encouraged diligence among owners of businesses, technical experts, and workers, and it accustomed the workers to accept without question orders given them by foremen and managers. Dean Tucker was of the opinion that French workmen were much more thrifty, obedient, and industrious than English workmen.[43]

There has been a disposition on the part of the religious authorities, at least since the twelfth century, to come to terms

[43] Tucker, *A Brief Essay on the Advantages and Disadvantages . . .*, pp. 36–37. Tucker called the "Want of subordination in the lower Class of people . . . the first and *capital* Disadvantage" of Great Britain with regard to trade, as compared to France. On this point his testimony is at variance with the more recent view of Max Weber, who thought that Protestantism encouraged diligence among the workers as well as the capitalists.

with the world on those issues where dogma has interfered with economic progress and even with the making of money.[44] The influence of capitalism upon the power of churches, upon religious thought, and upon the doctrines expounded by the clergy has been, in a sense, more striking than the influence of religion upon capitalism. The former influence is positive, the latter for the most part negative. Religion has tended to hold back industrialism. Industrialism has tended to change the nature and even the meaning of religion. In preparing for the change the Reformation was of much importance. Partly as a result of the Reformation a greater concern with conditions in this world (as distinguished from the next) was felt by Catholic leaders as well as by Protestant reformers.[45] Honest work of every kind was felt to be more important in the sight of God than it had been in the Middle Ages.

Though it was not the intention of their founders, the Protestant churches were in many ways better adapted than the Catholic church to make compromises with the mercantile conception of life, and to permit the private capitalist freedom in the pursuit of profit. Before the middle of the seventeenth century the Protestants generally, and the Puritans in particular, welcomed empirical scientific studies and even made reason subservient to empiricism. They began to see in new scientific discoveries an important means whereby men could glorify God. The Catholic atmosphere was somewhat less favorable than the Protestant to scientific inquiry, because the Catholics clung more to the view that experiment and observation, while desirable if pursued in moderation, were a source of vanity, contrary to the true Christian spirit, when they were regarded as more important than faith or even than reason.[46]

[44] Cf. Tawney's remarks in Weber, *The Protestant Ethic and the Spirit of Capitalism*, p. 8.

[45] Cf. Nef, *Cultural Foundations of Industrial Civilization* (New York, 1960), pp. 94–103.

[46] Cf. R. K. Merton, "Puritanism, Pietism, and Science," *Sociological Review*, XXVIII, No. 1 (1936), 1–20; B. Hessen, "The Social and Economic

By the beginning of the seventeenth century, if not considerably earlier, doctrines of popular sovereignty were treated
with greater favor by many of the Protestant sects than by
most Catholic writers. As Weber showed, Protestant doctrine,
especially in its Calvinist forms, encouraged the view that salvation for the layman lay less in renunciation and resignation,
as the priests taught, than in intense worldly activity. Such
activity came to be directed, particularly after the middle of
the seventeenth century, to the development of industrial,
commercial, and financial enterprises. In this way, as Tawney
expresses it, certain aspects of later Puritanism provided the
capitalist spirit with "a tonic which braced its energies and
fortified its already vigorous temper."[47] The pursuit of riches
for their own sake by men of business was given religious
support which had been lacking.

After the middle of the seventeenth century, if not before,
Protestant doctrine, especially in its Calvinist manifestations,
looked with less disfavor than Catholic doctrine on most kinds
of interest and on private accumulation in general.[48] Even
earlier, in the sixteenth century, when there was little to choose
between Protestant and Catholic teaching on economic questions, the reformed churches had at their disposal for the en-
forcement of dogma neither the strong sanctions nor the elaborate ecclesiastical organization that the Church of Rome re-

---

Roots of Newton's 'Principia,' " *Science at the Cross Roads* (London: Kniga,
1931 [?]), pp. 167–68; F. Engels, *Socialism, Utopian and Scientific* (Chicago,
1918), p. 25; G. N. Clark, *Science and Social Welfare in the Age of Newton*
(Oxford, 1937), pp. 79–84.

[47] Tawney, *Religion and the Rise of Capitalism*, pp. 226–27.

[48] Henri Hauser, "Les Idées économiques de Calvin," *Les Débuts du capita-
lisme* (Paris, 1927), pp. 78–79; cf. Tawney, *Introduction to Wilson's Discourse
upon Usury*, pp. 118–21. For a somewhat different view of the matter which
has not been widely accepted, see H. M. Robertson, *The Rise of Economic
Individualism* (Cambridge, 1933), pp. 120–29. See the reply to Robertson by
J. Brodrick, S.J., *The Economic Morals of the Jesuits* (London, 1934).

tained.[49] Even though the views of a few reformers were more orthodox on some points than those of the Catholics, it is by no means certain that they carried as much weight.[50] What mattered was not simply the nature of the doctrine but its effectiveness. So there were many ways in which the rise of Protestantism helped to release brakes that tended to hold back the progress of capitalism.

Yet it is easy to exaggerate both the influence of Protestantism in facilitating industrial progress and that of Catholicism in holding it back. The Protestant sects generally gained their chief strength in countries, like Holland and Great Britain, where the pressure on religion to adjust itself to new economic developments was much stronger, for many reasons that have little to do with religion, than in countries like France, Italy, and Spain, which remained Catholic. War, despotism, and a want of accessible mineral resources are among the important factors which hindered industrial, commercial, and scientific development on the Continent in the late sixteenth and seventeenth centuries.[51] The want of enthusiasm for natural science and for new labor-saving devices in industry was common among Protestants as well as Catholics in most countries of Continental Europe, while in England the enthusiasm can be explained only very partially as an indirect result of the Reformation. If economic progress in the Catholic countries had been more rapid at this time than it was, Catholic thought would undoubtedly have made greater concessions to economic progress.

History does not prove that a strong church organization and a numerous clergy, together with the widespread ecclesi-

[49] Cf. Weber, *The Protestant Ethic and the Spirit of Capitalism*, pp. 104–5; Tawney, *Religion and the Rise of Capitalism*, p. 97.

[50] Cf. Tawney, *Religion and the Rise of Capitalism*, p. xii.

[51] See Nef, *Western Civilization since the Renaissance*, Pt. I; *Industry and Government in France and England, 1540–1640*, chaps. 5 and 6; *La Naissance de la civilisation industrielle*, chap. 4.

astical ownership of property and the maintenance of economic doctrines that discourage materialism and the private accumulation of wealth for its own sake, are a handicap to economic welfare under all circumstances. The experience of the last four centuries of religious history is not necessarily the best guide for the future. The conditions of economic progress appear to be changing again, as they changed at the end of the Middle Ages. Is it not possible that the relation of Christianity to material welfare in the Gothic age is more relevant to the present turning point in Western history than the relation of Christianity to material welfare at another turning point in early modern times?[52]

The assumption that underlies some of the discussion of religion and capitalism since the time of Dean Tucker would seem odd to the early Christian fathers and to medieval churchmen. It has been widely taken for granted that churches justify their existence primarily by their contribution to economic welfare or even to the rise of capitalism. It was hardly for the benefit of rich men or even for the goal of material improvement that Christianity was founded. As a result of Western history during the last four centuries, an age like our own, which tends to value all things in terms of material wealth, often looks at religion from points of view that the wise men of the past would find some difficulty in recognizing as religious. These points of view may, perhaps, be divided into two types. There is, first, the disposition to regard religions of every kind as the enemies of economic progress and to turn away from the churches altogether on that account. There is, second, the disposition to try to reform religion. The object in this case is to make religion the ally of economic progress. The end of religious services becomes material improvement, and it is assumed that every increase in "economic

[52] Cf. below, chap. 10, sec. IV.

welfare," in Professor Pigou's sense, will bring about a corresponding increase in general welfare. Naturally, it is the sects which have already made the most compromises with wealth which lend themselves most readily to such a reform of religion.

Neither of these positions is likely to be of great help to mankind in the age that lies ahead. If materialism can become its own worst enemy, salvation hardly lies in making materialism the principle upon which one chooses or rejects a particular form of religious worship. Still less does salvation lie in making over religion for the sake of materialism.

Much of the life of mankind may properly be devoted to material improvement, but that is not the object of the religious life. We do not condemn the Christian faith in modern times simply by showing that economic welfare would have improved more than it has during the last four centuries if the Catholic church had been abolished in the age of the Renaissance or if it had never existed. That begs the question whether western Europe could have reached the state of civilization it achieved after the Middle Ages without Christianity, and whether such a state of civilization was a preparation for the rise of industrialism, as we suggested. It begs the question how far ethics derived from Christ, through the contribution they have made in modern times to constitutional government, to peace, stability, and honesty within the various nations of the West, may have helped to provide conditions that were a necessary foundation for economic progress since the Reformation.[53] It is not possible without an answer to these questions, and simply on the basis of a discussion of the reciprocal relations between religious and economic history, to say that the Western world would be as well off as it is today, even in a material sense, if the Christian churches had never existed.

In any case the justification, in a worldly sense, for an ecclesiastical polity and state lies not in making men rich but in

[53] Cf. Nef, *Cultural Foundations of Industrial Civilization,* chap. 4.

their contribution to the love, the virtue, the beauty, and the wisdom of mankind, to which material improvement is properly only a means. In a religious sense, the justification for an ecclesiastical polity and state lies primarily, not in the contribution they make to temporal perfection, even of a moral and intellectual character, but in the belief in a divine life which they cultivate, through grace, faith, and mystical experience.

It is possible to argue that a church devoted primarily to the increase of material wealth would be desirable. That is precisely what Carver once did in his *Religion Worth Having*. It is not possible to argue, as Carver was aware, that such a church would be Christian. It is difficult to argue, according to the meaning given the word in all previous societies of which we have record, that such a church would be religious. At the present turning point in history, it may even be doubted whether a church devoted to economic progress will actually do as much for material welfare as a church devoted to peace on earth.

iv. *Religion and Civilization*

Faith, a belief in eternal life, is the primary object of a Christian church. As students of civilization, we are concerned not with eternal life but with the contribution which Christianity has made, by nourishing faith, to *humanity*, to the general welfare of human beings here on earth.

From the worldly point of view, which cannot be the final test for religious believers, the greatest contribution of the Christian religion to the welfare of mankind is that it enlists on the side of the mind and spirit forces that are supernatural and all powerful. In all civilized societies the best in man has lifted him toward the supreme human values of honor, truth, love, goodness, wisdom, and beauty. The best in man has made him long for impersonal, disinterested agreement concerning the nature of these values. As their nature can never be settled by algebraic formulas or by the discoveries of natural science, they must always remain elusive. Eternal vigilance by persons who recognize their existence is the price that has to be paid if there is to be any approach to an understanding of them, or much action in fundamental accord with them. As set forth in the gospel and in the books of the greatest saints and theologians, the Christian religion puts the existence of these values beyond the realm of debate.[54]

Christianity can be, therefore, the ally of the good life. It can teach men and women that honesty and charity are right whether they lead to worldly recognition or not. Even if, in a world that is losing its balance and is also losing the meaning of words, the qualities of honesty and charity are called selfishness, they ought still to be cultivated. Why should it be assumed that there is, in our present irreligious world, any close connection between goodness and popularity? Were not the acts of the Savior the cause of his persecution and crucifixion? Did not the Jews protest when Pontius Pilate referred to Christ as their king? When we falter in our duty to honor and truth out of fear of any kind, nothing can sustain us so much as the belief that we are following, however humbly and inadequately, in Christ's footsteps. Nothing can sustain us so much as the belief that we are striving to act here on earth according to the light He has provided for us, and not out of any desire to advance ourselves according to the transient and fragile fashions of this world.

As St. François de Sales says in his benign way, devotion is a sort of sugar for the spirit. It takes some of the bitterness from the difficult acts of life—those which we make in response to duty rather than to self-interest. It infuses into such acts and into all the experiences of life an element of pleasure even when they are painful. "Elle sert de feu en hiver, et de rosée en été; elle sait abonder et souffrir pauvreté; elle rend également utile l'honneur et le mépris; elle reçoit le plaisir et la

---

[54] Cf. Nef, *The Conquest of the Material World*, pp. 360–62.

douleur avec un coeur presque toujours semblable, et nous remplit d'une suavité merveilleuse."⁵⁵ At a time when all over the world, and not least in the United States, people seem unwilling to assume responsibilities on behalf of humanity, when most people in their public and private relations think mainly in terms of what they can get in a worldly way and very little in terms of what they can give in effort and honesty and sweetness, there is a tremendous need for a renewal of the sense of obligation. Nothing helps men so much to assume obligations, to take a course that is difficult and unpopular, as the belief that an all-wise Being is looking on with approval when they turn away from the course that is easy or popular or likely to save their skins but that is unjust or unwise or cowardly, if not actually wicked.

Faith then can be the ally of reason as well as of virtue. Reason has fallen into discredit in recent decades, until even in supposedly learned circles the distinction between reason and opinion has ceased to have meaning. An eminent American astronomer tried to divide all learning into the scientific and the non-scientific. The first, he said, "is the public domain of positive knowledge," the second, "the private domain of personal convictions." "Each man," he added, "starts from scratch and acquires his own wisdom from his own experience."⁵⁶

These views ignore the power of the trained and richly endowed mind, in dealing with problems of morality, knowledge, or beauty, to form objective judgments in essential accord with those of wise men in past ages and to go beyond them. These views ignore the whole rich world of the mind

⁵⁵ "It serves for fire in winter and for dew in summer; it knows how to abound, and how to suffer poverty; it renders equally useful honour and distrust; it receives pleasure and pain with a heart almost always the same, and fills us with a marvelous sweetness" (*Introduction to the Devout Life*, trans. Allan Ross [London, 1937], p. 7). I have changed several words in the translation, in order better to fulfill the meaning, as I see it.

⁵⁶ Edwin Hubble, *The Nature of Science, and Other Lectures* (San Marino, Calif., 1954), pp. 6–7.

to which Pascal introduces us in the opening paragraphs of *Les Pensées*.[57] The avowal that there is a realm of human experience to which positive science is inapplicable is sound. But to call the sense of truth that some achieve in that realm "a private revelation," as Hubble did,[58] is to leave the true, the good, and the beautiful to the tender mercies of radio commentators, motion picture directors, newspaper reporters, and other professors of current events, by inadvertently giving their pronouncements and those of persons even less qualified to reason than they the same weight as those of a disinterested, richly endowed, and well-trained mind. For if it is claimed, as it frequently is, that everyone has a right to his *"personal convictions"* and that there is no test for their validity other than the prominence of their holder, what basis exists for *judgment* outside the sciences? Therefore, to speak of personal "convictions" and "private revelation" in this connection belittles a region which is, from the point of view of human happiness, not less important than the scientific. Proust has felicitously explained the nature of verification in this region of intangibles, when persons have unexpected meetings with the product of a great creative mind whose work confirms their own hidden convictions, their own revelation.[59]

Truth is in the intellect, according to Aquinas. According to the Christian theology generally accepted in Western history, there is a very simple explanation of the inability of the mind to reach perfectly true statements in this realm. Man attains his power of reasoning from God. By cultivating reason all his life he may in a few rare cases almost overcome his prejudices, his appetites, his faulty education, his material circumstances, and his limited experiences. He may approach wisdom. But he can never attain it, because perfect knowledge, like perfect goodness, is an attribute only of the Supreme

[57] See above, p. 141.

[58] Hubble, *The Nature of Science*, pp. 18–19.

[59] See above, p. 5.

Being. What a few wise men (among whom Plato, Aristotle, and Aquinas are the outstanding examples in philosophy) have managed to discover through reason about human life is almost flawless as far as it goes. It has never been and never can be exhaustive. But the opinion so widespread in the United States that, since men can never attain complete wisdom, each man should begin over again from scratch, without the help of the knowledge and wisdom that human beings have captured by reason in the past, is a serious danger to every kind of knowledge. If such an opinion prevails it is likely to reduce further and further the level of civilization.

Religious faith once provided reason with a shield. As the Christian faith has been weakened, as the churches have made compromises to meet material standards, this shield has grown rusty. The modern world has denied the existence of wisdom because it has seen in the work of the wisest men of the past flaws which they would be the first to recognize. No truly wise man, any more than Socrates, ever claimed that he had found wisdom. Religious faith offers an explanation for the flaws. At the same time, it shows how unimportant they are in comparison with the disaster involved in denying the existence of truth. For one does deny truth when it is claimed that every man is equally equipped to reason, regardless of his natural endowment, his circumstances, his training, his character, and his effort. While it was certainly not Hubble's intention, his words lend themselves to that interpretation.

Faith can be the ally of beauty as well as of truth. No work of art, whether it involves the alteration of matter, like a statue, or is abstract, like a musical composition, is possible without the exercise of the mind in ways that are largely irrelevant to the problems of the natural scientist but are closely related to the ways of faith.[60] At least since the time of Socrates, and consequently long before the advent of Christianity, philosophers have suggested that great poets and other great artists

[60] Cf. Jacques Maritain, *Art et scolastique* (3d ed.; Paris, 1935).

are divinely inspired. The natural scientist is concerned with unraveling the secrets of tangible conditions. When he uses matter, the true artist uses it in accordance with principles related to a lofty purpose evolved in his own mind with the help of the minds of fellow artists of the past as they have revealed their secrets in their works. Unlike the scientist and the technician, he is concerned with achieving a result that is unique.[61] In order to go beyond technique, the artist has to impose on his material, whether it be actual matter or sounds and ideas, a lofty conception derived from his mind and his spirit at the service of his mind. This conception is suggested by the actual world but transcends it. Whether the artist is a Christian or not, this conception takes him into a realm closely akin to that visited by the religious believer.[62] Like the true believer in the act of faith, the true artist in the act of art rises above the world as he sees it with the eyes and feels it with other senses. Thus true faith strengthens art by keeping alive belief in a world of the mind and more especially by making what the heart feels the principle which actually controls the materials the artist uses.[63]

As I am suggesting, the authority of the disinterested and cultivated mind alone can provide an adequate bulwark against totalitarianism in the age that lies ahead.[64] By identifying this barrier against the exercise of arbitrary power with the Supreme Being, who is wholly good, as Christianity has done, it is given a firmer foundation and the subjects have better protection from a tyrant. The ancient Greeks believed that jealous gods would punish civil tyrants and conquerors

[61] Cf. above, p. 84 n.

[62] Cf. Von Ogden Vogt, *Art and Religion* (New Haven, Conn., 1921), esp. chap. 3.

[63] Artur Schnabel, *Music and the Line of Most Resistance* (Princeton, N.J., 1942), pp. 79–80. Schnabel suggested that the spirit behind modern absolute music (cf. above, p. 48), for which we have no equivalent in the music of past civilizations, was not unrelated to the spirit of Christian love.

[64] See above, chap. 4; below, chap. 11.

when they usurped to themselves a power which does not properly belong to men. The Christian explanation of the fate that awaits such cruel men is far nobler. Their punishment comes not as vengeance—for God is not subject to human passions—but as the consequence of evil; it comes not because they have acted in place of God but because they have acted in a way that is completely alien to His nature. Evil makes it impossible to use as an instrument of creation a creature who insists upon alienating himself from the life of his Creator.[65] Thus, Christian belief in the limits of power, found hardly less infrequently among those who do not profess to be Christians as among those who do, acts as a restraint on tyranny and conquest. John Donne has explained the situation in a few lines.

> That thou mayest rightly obey power, her bounds know;
> Those past, her nature, and name is chang'd; to be
> Then humble to her is idolatrie.
> As streames are, Power is; those blest flowers that dwell
> At the rough streames calme head, thrive and do well,
> But having left their roots, and themselves given
> To the streames tyrannous rage, alas, are driven
> Through mills, and rockes, and woods, and at last, almost
> Consum'd in going, in the sea are lost:
> So perish Soules, which more chuse mens unjust
> Power from God claym'd, then God himselfe to trust.[66]

"Power from God claimed" as an instrument of *ecclesiastical* government has not lost its dangers, although since Donne's time the extent of ecclesiastical sanctions has tended to diminish all over the world. What has become in our time even more dangerous for the future of freedom, independence, and dignity is authority claimed, not from God, but from what is represented as the people's will. "The human image needs the support of a higher nature, and human freedom

[65] Cf. A. J. Toynbee, *A Study of History* (London, 1939), IV, 256–57.

[66] "Satyre III," ll. 100–110, *The Poems of John Donne*, I, 158.

reaches its definitive expression in a higher freedom, freedom in truth."[67]

In the Middle Ages, and to a much smaller extent in early modern times, Christianity provided an intellectual foundation for limitations upon political authority. Such authority passed mainly by inheritance. That differentiates it sharply from the modern governing power of dictators, which in many other respects resembles it. The earlier form of dictatorship in Western history goes under the name of "royal absolutism." There is some justification for calling the new form "democratic absolutism." Totalitarianism operates in the name of democracy. The people relinquish their individual wills to the will of a leader and have none left. As Tocqueville warned us more than a century ago, this new absolutism, if it came, was likely to be more arbitrary and more cruel than any Western society has known. If totalitarianism ever takes possession of the United States, we have been told, it is likely to masquerade as democracy. The most hopeful means of preventing this is to reaffirm the meaning of words, which is being lost, and at the same time endow the *disinterested* mind and heart with a worldly prestige they have always lacked. If faith can strengthen virtue as a limitation on both political and ecclesiastical authority, and thus invest the principles of liberty with a greater validity than attaches to mere opinion, faith could become the strongest ally of true democracy.

It is doubtful whether in the whole history of mankind the worldly case for a universal faith has ever been stronger than now.[68] The trouble with appeals to faith is, as it always has been, that faith is in the keeping of mortal men in the case of all religions, including the Christian religion. Unless there can be, as some in the eighteenth century hoped there could be, a new and better breed of mortals, appeals to faith will retain

---

[67] Nicholas Berdyaev, *Dostoievsky* (New York, 1934), p. 76.

[68] See also Hocking, *Living Religions and a World Faith*, p. 246.

Ends of Civilization

the hollow ring they now often have for those who are genuinely seeking virtue.

Again and again, the Christian churches have disappointed the hopes that one reasonably puts in the followers of Christ when one is familiar with the gospel. However we view church history, we are bound to admit that the millions of mortal men who have had charge in various capacities, exalted and humble, of the administration of ecclesiastical discipline, have fallen short frequently in their stewardship of the ideals expressed and the life lived by the Founder here on earth. They have sometimes made use of the Founder and His words as a sort of cloak behind which to commit the very sins which He condemned.

In any discussion of the relation of Christianity to civilization, account has to be taken of the shortcomings of the Catholic church and of the Protestant churches. The Catholic church, in particular, has left some scars on the pages of history that no impartial inquiry can overlook. The fact that wicked churchmen may be expiating their sins in the inferno which Dante painted does not permit us to ignore these sins in a worldly essay like this one. The question whether the Church has interfered with economic progress is of far less concern than the question whether it has, on many occasions, interfered with virtue, intelligence, and beauty, which are the ultimate values that justify wealth in civilized societies, and with the love which nourishes these values. Doubt on this point should make the most ardent believer hesitate, insofar as he has the temporal good of mankind at heart, to advocate a revival of the power exercised by the Church in medieval times.

A scholar who has been regarded as an opponent of the Catholic church is said to have remarked on one occasion that his position had been misunderstood. He was quite prepared to admit that, taken together, those who have professed the Catholic faith have been, from the temporal point of view, roughly 5 per cent better than the rest of the Western peoples. But, he added, "only five per cent better; no more than that." This scholar is known for a readiness to meet his critics half way. His interlocutor, another scholar who, unlike him, is regarded as friendly to the Catholic church, expressed the view that 5 per cent was much too liberal an allowance!

No doubt our eighteenth- and nineteenth-century ancestors, with their horror of the excesses of the Church, painted a one-sided picture of its iniquities. Some of our contemporaries even embellish that picture. It remains true that many of the acts of church bodies and of individual churchmen during the Middle Ages and also in modern times have stood in the way not only of scientific advance and material progress but also of art and humanistic inquiries of every kind. Church bodies also stood in the way of virtue. The Catholic church set itself up to judge, to excommunicate, and to burn thousands of persons who believed themselves to be the better Christians for disregarding certain details of Church ritual. This was bound to horrify the enlightened men of a later era. Whatever their faults (and they have been grave), these men helped to diminish physical cruelty, to establish toleration for persons who chose to worship God in their own way, and to lessen the fear of Hell, which has sometimes tormented young minds groping toward the good. The achievements of the great humanitarian movement of the eighteenth and nineteenth centuries should be husbanded today. The greatest saints, it may be suggested, are those who have insisted that an indifference about the ethics of this world is not the best preparation for life in the next. Mankind can be forgiven for not feeling indifferent to the fact that tens of thousands of persons protected by the cloth have exercised their power unintelligently and not a few wickedly.

The object of the Reformation was to remedy these evils. Mankind was to be relieved of its dependence on ecclesiastics for its religious knowledge. The object was to bring men into more direct and, it was hoped, closer communion with the gospel and through the gospel with Christ and with God. Insofar as the change was consistent with the maintenance of faith, there was much to recommend it. Benjamin Franklin would hardly be regarded as a good judge by a religious man. There is truth, nevertheless, in his words, "I think vital religion has always suffered when orthodoxy is more regarded than virtue."[69] When a practicing Christian becomes so enamored of orthodoxy that he refuses to recognize morality except among persons who go through the motions required by his church, he in effect rejects those impulses toward good which exist in men independently of Catholicism and even of Christianity and which are themselves gifts of God. The reforming sects were not altogether misguided when they set out to diminish the emphasis on form and ritual.

Yet, paradoxically, in a world peopled by hundreds of millions, institutions of a kind which often lend themselves to unintelligent orthodoxy, and even to violence and downright corruption, are apparently necessary to keep vital the knowledge of Christ and His teachings, the most powerful influence on behalf of compassion that humanity has ever been offered. As Richard Hooker pointed out, perhaps more tellingly than anyone else, the Reformation contained seeds which were ultimately to create grave religious weaknesses. Pursued to its logical conclusion, the rise of Protestantism, particularly in its Calvinist forms, left every man free to adopt his own individual interpretation of the truth. This made it relatively easy to alter dogma. It encouraged the disintegration of Protestantism into an ever larger number of sects, at the cost eventually of conviction about the importance of religious faith itself. Speaking of Henry VIII and the Reformation, a great English historian who was not insensible to the cruelties of religious persecution has written these words:

---

[69] As quoted by Conyers Read, "The English Elements in Benjamin Franklin," *Pennsylvania Magazine of History and Biography*, July, 1940, p. 321.

Then, now, and ever, it was and remains true, that in this great matter of religion, in which to be right is the first condition of being right in anything—not variety of opinion, but unity—not the equal license of the wise and the foolish to choose their belief—but an ordered harmony, where wisdom prescribes a law to ignorance, is the rule which reasonable men should most desire for themselves and for mankind.[70]

James Anthony Froude was not a Catholic but an Anglican who eventually broke with the high-church movement. In his historical writings he never laid himself open to the charge of prejudice in favor of the Catholic church.

When one comments upon the weaknesses and corruption of churches and ecclesiastical foundations, it is necessary to balance against these weaknesses and this corruption the preservation of the Christian faith itself, with its exaltation of the qualities of humility and love as opposed to the doctrines of force. The question of the worldly value of the Catholic church would not be settled against the Church even if it were possible to show that professing Catholics have been only 5 per cent better in their temporal lives than the members of the Protestant sects or of the Western peoples who have left the churches altogether and of those peoples who have never been Christian. The question would not be settled against the Church if it could be shown that they were no better. It could not be settled even by showing that they were worse. All such comparisons beg the question whether the non-Catholics everywhere in the world may not be better than they would otherwise be through their knowledge of Christ and the ethical traditions associated with Him, which the Church has done so much to preserve for nearly twenty centuries. Faith in Christ could never have been kept alive in the Roman Empire, and extended during the Dark Ages that followed, without a great Church organization. Few men who consider the Christian religion as we still have it today can feel

[70] J. A. Froude, *History of England from the Fall of Wolsey to the Defeat of the Spanish Armada* (London, 1870), III, 62.

as confident as some of our eighteenth- and nineteenth-century ancestors that the price was too high to pay. Unlike them, we have lived to see men tortured and extinguished, without even the honor of martyrdom often permitted by the Church to heretics. They have been tortured and extinguished for the sake only of worldly power. Without in any way condoning the Church for its treatment of heretics, we are forced to admit that the end for which the religious persecutions were carried on was less ghastly than the end of modern political persecutions. Churchmen at least *claimed* that by burning heretics they were saving a much larger number of the human race from the same fate after death.

Let us hope that such barbarism as theirs may never be the price that our descendants pay for a renewal of religious faith. But let us not feel sure, as men like Gibbon and Buckle did in the eighteenth and nineteenth centuries, that the Reformation, the victory for religious toleration, and the decline of Christianity provide us with perpetual insurance against the return of such barbarism. Let us not even feel sure that without the Church we should have escaped the barbarism of medieval and early modern times, which the thinkers of the eighteenth and nineteenth centuries so justly censured. Who knows whether, without the Church, medieval men might have been, for some far less worthy cause than Christianity, at least 5 per cent more cruel than they were?

Today the Protestant churches and the Church of Rome are faced with a more critical task than any that has confronted the custodians of the Christian faith since the Reformation. The Protestant churches, especially in America, have become more and more compromised, by their efforts to adjust themselves to the teachings of natural science and to the material standards of the modern world, at the very time when the Western peoples need more than ever non-material standards and a return to the principles for which Christ spoke through the gospel. The Catholic church has not by any means escaped such compromises. What is more serious, it has not, in the face of the terrible political crisis of our times, offered any really effective resistance to the growing power of the arbitrary state. One waits for great theologians, of the stature of a Bossuet, who will read devastating lessons directed against the monstrous efforts to stifle free opinion in the name of naziism, fascism, communism, and anticommunism. One awaits the implementation of the infinitely moving appeals of Popes John XXIII and Paul VI for peace on earth.

It is all very well to say that politics is of no concern to the Church. No Christian church which makes peace with anti-Christ on anti-Christian terms can remain a Christian church. Were the words "Render unto Caesar the things that are Caesar's" meant to cover the case in which Caesar claims powers which do not belong to him? If mankind today is to regain its soul, churchmen in high places need to show even greater courage than the most inspired among them have shown.

It often seems as if the actions of modern Catholics were based on the principle that the object of Christianity and religious beliefs is to maintain the Church, instead of on the principle that the purpose of the Church is to maintain faith and provide consolation for suffering men. If the churches are to reclaim a considerable proportion of the multitudes who have lost faith, they will have to provide leadership on a higher plane than has been revealed in past times.[71] They will have to show themselves to a credulous but little-believing people, in whom the sparks of virtue and love nevertheless exist, to be true children of Christ. It may well be that this is beyond the power of the churches as they are at present constructed and organized. Their very organization sometimes prevents them from acting on critical issues on behalf of Christ, whose message was directed to all mankind.

The peoples of the world are in need of religion. They are

[71] Cf. below, chap. 9, sec. III.

in need of religious unity, in an age full of fads and fake religions. But, if we are not altogether mistaken, they need neither materialism nor a compromise with political persecution in the guise of religion. Whether or how the great need for faith can be filled is something no man can foresee. It can be filled only if religion succeeds in rising above the human limitations of our time, and in convincing men everywhere who are groping toward the good that faith is at once true, divine, and eternal. Religion must lay emphasis more on substance than on form. It must welcome men into faith less as a means of saving their souls and more as a means of saving the well-being of suffering and ill-guided humanity. Religious leaders will have to be, as the early Christians were, on the side of the humble and disinterested rather than on the side of the politically strong and of those whose interest in religion is to gain salvation for themselves. A church must come forward in every country and transcending all countries, not primarily as a political power, but as a religious one, strong enough and courageous enough to re-create, after Christ's example, that spiritual freedom for which Christianity at its best has stood. It will have to reconsider, not only the world, but church organization and power itself, in relation to the words, "Many that are first shall be last; and the last first."

The United States was not born a Catholic country. It is not today a Catholic country. The future of Catholicism here depends upon its making concessions, as well as in asking others to make them. There would seem to be a need for a Reformation, not only of the reformed churches, but of the Catholic church as well. Is it to come from within or from without? Is it to come at all? We cannot bring it about by recognizing the need for it. Purification and unification are only to be obtained from some higher mountain than that which the human intellect enables man to ascend.

The advice of the Savior to His disciples, as reported by St. Luke, is not perhaps irrelevant in concluding these remarks on faith. May not the words, "he that is not against us is for us," be applied to religious organization, to the Church? What He required was not fidelity to the Church or even to His disciples. What He required was fidelity to Him. "He that is not with me is against me; and he that gathereth not with me scattereth."[72]

[72] Luke 9:50; 11:23. Cf. Hocking, *Living Religions and a World Faith*, pp. 231–32, 234–36, 253, 269, 281.

7 Virtue

Faith is a gift, independent of and superior to wealth. It is not an enemy to material well-being here on earth insofar as such well-being is consistent with the good life of the individual, of the state, and of humanity. Faith is an end in itself, insofar as it offers mankind the possibility of striving toward an ultimate society free from evil. It is a means, in the sense that when it is genuine and pure it is bound to help human beings toward the attainment of virtue, wisdom, and beauty—ultimate ends of man here on earth. Religion can provide a superhuman sanction for labor toward these ends.

Even if it comes about, the revival of faith as a civilizing force is bound to take time. It cannot solve our problems or restore reason to its proper place suddenly. For good or ill, neither the hope of a heaven nor the fear of a hell after death is very real in most of the Western countries today. With the doubt which exists among some honorable people, especially in the United States, concerning the capacity of men to cultivate the good life on earth by working directly for religion,[1] with the doubt which exists among others concerning the capacity of any church worthily to represent Christian virtues, it would be discouraging—and let us hope untrue—to claim that labor toward the good life cannot be carried on without faith. The road to faith may well be indirect. It is a comfort to believe that the highest worldly ends are in no way hostile to the teachings of Christ or Buddha or Confucius or Mohammed.

Three hundred and eighty years ago, when the Christian

[1] Cf. Frank H. Knight, "Religion and Ethics in Modern Civilization," *Journal of Liberal Religion,* III, No. 1 (1941), 4, 7.

religion was a matter of much more vital concern to men than it is now, the greatest English theologian wrote: "While riches be a thing which every man wisheth, no man of judgment esteems it better to be rich than to be wise, virtuous and religious." Richard Hooker's words suggest that even as profound a believer as he could regard wisdom and virtue as objects separate and distinct from religion, though complementary to it. No wise theologian has ever claimed that faith and revealed knowledge, by themselves, are adequate to meet all the problems of society or all those of the individuals who compose it. No wise theologian has claimed that faith makes reason, observation, and experiment unnecessary. Before the coming of Christ, the greatest Greeks did not regard it as futile to strive toward the objectives of virtue, wisdom, and beauty. The study of the nature of wisdom and virtue, the study of the conditions that are likely to make them less scarce commodities than they are today, is the province of moral philosophy. Philosophy could provide all men who devote themselves to the advancement and the transmission of knowledge with guideposts and a map, which would make possible the diffusion among mankind of the lofty, ideal conceptions of both knowledge and virtue.

Moral philosophy is properly concerned with the fullest happiness of the individual, of the state as a collection of individuals, and of humanity. Such happiness depends upon the establishment of the most perfect harmony possible between the needs of the body, the spirit, and the intelligence, with reason and its more humble companion, common sense, the master over both the body and the spirit. This is what Plato meant by happiness, and Aristotle was in agreement with him. The ideal state would be one in which the needs of all the citizens for material comfort and security from violence are satisfied in the ways most compatible with the happiness of the citizens, in this Platonic and Aristotelian sense. In our time the ideal state need not involve slavery, as it did with the

Greeks. It would be achieved by bringing the citizens into those occupations they were fitted to perform with the greatest happiness to themselves and to the community of which they form a part.

The word "happiness" should not be misunderstood. Like most words, it has no precise meaning for most people today. Contemporary Americans generally suppose that happiness means having a good time. Everyone, we are told, has his own way of having a good time. "One man's meat is another man's poison" is a generalization that applies not only to diet but to everything man has to do with.

Happiness has had a different meaning for philosophers, at any rate until very recently. In the Aristotelian sense, happiness is not a matter of individual whim. It consists not in seeking pleasure for its own sake but in gaining it from doing the right things or behaving in the right way, according to the accumulated wisdom of the human race. The concept of happiness, therefore, takes for granted the existence of certain absolute values; it takes for granted the existence of good moral, intellectual, and artistic habits. As everyone who understands words and who has read Aristotle's *Ethics* should know, the existence of good habits does not depend upon the establishment of fixed rules of conduct that will fit every situation. There are certain actions—such as murder, theft, and adultery —which Aristotle regarded as wrong altogether. The "happiness" which some modern psychologists might claim is obtained from committing such acts is counterfeit happiness. It is not happiness in the Aristotelian sense, which is based upon a moral code. But Aristotle saw that morality generally consists in the most appropriate response to a given situation, the action that is most perfectly in accord with virtue under the circumstances. Circumstances differ greatly. They are obviously not the same now as in Aristotle's time. This does not mean that a man is made "happy" at any time by doing what he pleases without regard to common principles. Since the rise of Christianity, happiness for Christians should relate to the practice of the Christian moral virtues—humility, liberality, chastity, gentleness, temperance, patience, and diligence. Some of these virtues do not differ fundamentally from the good habits set forth in the works of both Plato and Aristotle. For both Greek and Christian philosophers happiness consists in effort, not in the absence of effort. It does not consist in the effort to please someone for your own advantage; it consists in the effort to do right.

It will be obvious that, unlike the economic science of Adam Smith and most of his English followers through Alfred Marshall, moral philosophy does not concern itself exclusively or even primarily with material happiness. Unlike the newer economic science, moral philosophy does not take the wants of human beings, whether they are material or not, as given and then concern itself with the conditions which would enable men to satisfy their wants to the fullest possible extent regardless of the consequences for virtue, wisdom, and beauty.

History shows us that the nature of men's wants is continually changing. In Elizabethan England, for example, ale and beer were regarded as, after bread, the mainstays of nourishment. A passage in *Othello* suggests that the Elizabethans regarded the drinking powers of Englishmen as superior to those of other peoples. Iago shouts: "Some wine, ho!" and sings a drinking song. "'Fore Heaven, an excellent song," says Cassio, his lieutenant. "I learn'd it in England, where (indeed) they are most potent in potting; your Dane, your German, and your swag-belli'd Hollander . . . are nothing to your English . . . . He drinks you, with facility, your Dane dead drunk; he sweats not to overthrow your Almain; he gives your Hollander a vomit ere the next pottle can be fill'd."

The statistics which moderns favor show that this was no idle boast. According to Colin Clark, the Englishmen gainfully employed were, on the average, approximately three times as well off in units of real income already before the Second

World War as at the end of the seventeenth century.[2] At that time one of Clark's intellectual fathers, Gregory King, estimated that almost a sixth of the national income in England was spent on alcoholic drink in various forms, as compared with about a ninth in France and about a tenth in Holland. In England the expenditure per head on drink was about twice as great as in France and much greater than in Holland.[3] The beer and ale consumed per capita was at least four times what it is in modern England; perhaps nearly ten times what it is in the United States. In Shakespeare's day the real income of the English worker was probably somewhat less than in the late seventeenth century. But the per capita consumption of alcoholic drink was probably even greater.[4] The Elizabethans were not only capable of wonderful feats in drinking bouts; beer formed, after bread, the chief element in the diet of the common man. He consumed more in a day than the modern American ordinarily does in a week. For all that, the wits of the Elizabethans were not conspicuously inferior to ours.

Another comparison between the two periods also shows how wants change, though the physical benefit of the change in this case is less apparent than in the first. In the sixteenth century the European workman regarded religious worship as hardly less essential to his well-being than food and drink. When large industrial establishments were laid out for the manufacture of alum, metal, or salt, the owners—whether they were princes, nobles, or laymen—always built chapels for worship as part of the plant. They provided priests or pastors to conduct the services. Such wants as these are far less urgent among the modern workers. The industrial entrepreneur in

2 *The Conditions of Economic Progress* (London, 1940), p. 83.

3 Gregory King, *Natural and Political Observations and Conclusions upon the State and Condition of England* (1696) (bound with George Chalmers, *Estimate of the Comparative Strength of Great Britain* [London, 1804]), pp. 47, 64–65, 67. Cf. Colin Clark, *National Income and Outlay* (London, 1937), p. xvii.

4 Nef, *The Conquest of the Material World* (Chicago, 1964), pp. 197–98.

America who included religious facilities as part of his costs of production would be regarded as somewhat eccentric.

From the point of view of learning there are, broadly speaking, two possible attitudes toward changing human wants. It is possible to say that the changes are not the concern of learned men. Wants should be determined by private taste. The historian, the sociologist, or the anthropologist may collect data on the wants of different peoples at the same or different periods of history. They may compare them as a matter of scientific curiosity. They may discuss the effect of indulging them, insofar as the physical and the biological sciences seem to warrant tentative conclusions on that subject. If, for example, it can be shown that constant drinking shortens the average length of life, it follows that men in a society where drink is used as a food will have a shorter life-expectancy, *if other things are equal,* than men in a society where little beer or wine is drunk. That seems obvious enough. In the study of man, the application of scientific methods sometimes does little more than emphasize the obvious. But any judgment concerning the moral or aesthetic or even the social value of different wants for the individual or for society lies outside the province of the learned man. Such is the first position that can be taken in this matter of human happiness.

What other general attitude can the moral philosopher adopt? He can attempt to discover what is good for man and for mankind—morally, intellectually, and aesthetically. He can set about to decide tentatively, with reason as a guide and experience as its helpmate, what wants and what combinations of wants contribute most to the happiness of the individual, the nation, and humanity.

What could be the consequence of this second attitude toward wants? Like religion, moral philosophy is concerned with values. For the moral philosopher, happiness need not be left entirely to chance. If it were possible for wise men to agree to some extent on the order of goods in a world full of riches and people as never before, and brought into contact with one another to a greater extent than ever before, then something might be done to guide mankind, intelligently and disinterestedly, in the direction of their better desires. Something might be done to cultivate in them a love of the best things in life for themselves and their fellow men. By indicating, however imperfectly, the nature of the ideal, as moral philosophy should try to do, it might enable the world to fall less far short of the ideal than it would otherwise fall. It might light a beacon for the guidance of future generations, as Plato and Aristotle did some twenty-three hundred years ago.

One objection frequently raised today to the study of moral philosophy in this sense is that there is no possible way of distinguishing helpfully between good and evil. Yet perhaps human values have not been so completely lost that the ordinary man would consider five thousand dollars spent in the narcotics traffic as equally desirable with the five thousand dollars or so that were probably required to feed, clothe, and house Hogarth while he painted his famous pictures of "The Rake's Progress" and "Marriage à la Mode," depicting the consequences of earthly indulgence. The fact that people have been willing to pay for narcotics no less readily than for paintings which strive to drive home moral lessons does not prove that the choice between the two is a matter of indifference for society. It is true that the philosophical value of the same want is not necessarily the same in different places or at different periods in the same place. It should be possible, nevertheless, to work out tentatively the relative merits of different wants, in terms of moral, intellectual, and aesthetic values. It should also be possible to determine tentatively how far to give priority to such values as over against the purely material values of increasing the volume of production and consumption. It should also be possible to determine tentatively how the production and distribution of economic goods and services can be made to contribute to the higher values. All this should be more easily possible now than ever before, with the vast amount of data put at our disposal by the natural and the biological sciences, as well as by the humanities and social sciences.

The very fact that human wants change shows that these great philosophical questions of the relative moral, intellectual, and aesthetic value of different kinds of wants, judged in terms of human happiness, are a part of human experience. It shows that moral philosophy should not be divorced from life, that it should aim to guide wants in directions that will contribute to human happiness. In the ideally ordered society, all branches of learning and all departments of education would be allied with moral philosophy in this aim. The realm of moral philosophy will no more remain vacant, if wise and virtuous and disinterested men cease to cultivate it, than will the realm of theology. In the United States, and in the Western world generally at present, this territory which is of such great importance to mankind, this territory which might be of supreme importance for the future of civilization, is not being cultivated by the learned world at all effectively. It is denied that problems of value, in the moral, intellectual, and aesthetic sense, are proper subjects of impartial inquiry and study. Each person, it is said, is the best judge of his own wants. When there is a conflict between the desires of various persons, it can be resolved by a vote of the majority. That is the only way to avoid dictatorship.

Let us consider the consequences of such a position. Leaving aside any question of the morality of most persons (leaving aside the common assumption that all persons are equally intelligent or foolish, equally good or bad, unless they are put in asylums or locked up in jails), we are assuming that in the modern world everyone knows what he wants. We are assuming, further, that everyone is in fact free to choose without the intervention of any external interested influence.

It is enough to state these assumptions to see that they are unwarranted. No man, no matter how strong and wise he feels himself to be, is prepared to act on every issue that confronts him without advice or guidance. In view of the decrease in moral, intellectual, and aesthetic training, fewer persons have a genuine and decided preference one way or another today than a century or more ago. With the decrease in the knowledge most people possess of the way in which the commodities they eat and use are produced and prepared, they have no basis for judging even material values. So they seek advice. There is no lack of "experts" to supply them with it on special subjects, though a man does not always find the perfect agreement that would be reassuring if he takes the trouble to consult more than a single expert.

But where are we to seek guidance when it comes to a choice involving matters of morality, social justice, wisdom, or beauty? The natural place to turn is to a priest or pastor, if one belongs to a church, or to a professor or teacher, or to one's father or mother, brother or sister, or intimate friend. And increasingly with the development of psychiatry these have been supplanted by professional practitioners. Yet most of these persons have been trained in the modern doctrine (if it can be properly called a doctrine) that there is nothing approaching philosophical standards.

Disagreement on philosophical issues is now frequently regarded as beneficial to society. This is not the disagreement of reasoned argument, which contributes to knowledge because distinctions are made in the interest of greater truth, with the object of reaching better, deeper, and more comprehensive generalizations. This is disagreement for the sake of disagreement, disagreement for the sake of the ego. Americans take pleasure in saying that there are a great many sides to every question. That enables anyone to say and do just what he likes with a completely free conscience and with an almost completely empty mind. The lack of any firm judgments which people respect, in matters of morality, intelligence, or beauty, is not surprising when we remember that moral philosophy in the Socratic or Aristotelian sense—the field of human values—has been almost entirely abandoned by learning. We go to doctors and surgeons to find out how to keep well. We go to investment counselors to find out how to invest our money. We go to interior decorators to find out how to furnish our homes. When the advice we obtain from the three experts creates a serious moral or intellectual issue, as it often does, we have only our own principles to fall back upon—those of us who retain any. It rarely occurs to us that books written by wise men of the past might help us. When it does, we realize that we have wasted our lives without reading them for this purpose and that we cannot make up overnight for an ill-spent childhood and youth. There can be no index to wisdom, but we find ourselves in an age where indexes and other short cuts (useful as guides to information) are wrongly regarded as substitutes for culture. We have experts in every field except the supremely important one which encompasses all the others.

It is a mistake, nevertheless, to assume that the individual's predilections—his "own philosophy" as he is fond of calling them—are in fact determined without outside influences. We all take advice without knowing it, much as Molière's famous would-be gentleman talked prose without discovering what he was about until he hired a teacher to instruct him in the manners of polite society. In matters of morality, intelligence, and aesthetics, pressure is brought to bear on us from the time we are born. It is brought to bear on us by the mores of our schoolfellows and playmates, by the very lack of judgment concerning these great problems which we generally find in our parents and our friends, our teachers and the ministers in the churches we visit, if we happen to go to any. More interested pressure comes, as we grow older, from advertisers and from the businessmen they represent. These persons are eager to enlist us as consumers and, less frequently, as workers. Politicians seek our votes—sometimes for purposes that are lacking in the finer shades of ethics! The very fact that no one has referred us in early life to principles, or led us to saturate ourselves with books where they can be found, enables any person with sufficient money or publicity to give advice and to gain influence concerning current issues. Such advice is full of philosophical implications. In a society which recognizes no special competence except in the limited cases susceptible to scientific proof, such advice masquerades frequently as knowledge. Men use it "to make friends and influence people" on matters of morality, social justice, and aesthetics, not always with the best motives and almost never with the best thought.

Moral and even intellectual and aesthetic issues are often placed at the mercy of anyone who finds it advantageous to direct them for purposes of business, politics, or graft. In the universities the learned man, if he is also a good man, because of his very modesty is made to regard any "prejudice" he may have in favor of impersonal and durable standards as a private matter, if not an idiosyncrasy. He is allowed to try to guide his own life by these "prejudices," but if he speaks of them in public or adjusts his learned activities to them, his efforts are dismissed as "evangelical." A pastor tells him that he should not speak on behalf of virtue unless he joins the local church. If he joins it he must leave matters of morality to his pastor, who has usually ceased to have any firm judgments concerning them. If he happens to mention his "prejudices" to his colleagues and suggests that it might be worth while for others to act on them, he is told that he takes life too seriously.

Is it better for man to have matters of morality, intelligence, and beauty settled exclusively by the give-and-take of the market place and by the improvised daily relations between men and women—sometimes moral, sometimes amoral, and at least occasionally immoral—or is it better to have a few gifted men who devote their whole lives to these questions, who are passionately seeking to benefit mankind, with no hope of private gain beyond a competent salary, exercise an influence in the realm of moral philosophy? Some of those who take the first view have been saying that time will repair all the evils which seem to flow from it. They are like the specialists in higher learning who denounce honest efforts at value judgments on the ground that time is not ripe. Time is neutral. Unless wise men grasp its opportunities and work for good, evil will gain the day. On the whole, time worked in favor of morality and justice in the nineteenth century. This was largely because enthusiasm for civilization still influenced men to try to make it work that way. Now that standards have broken down, is there not danger that bad money will drive out good? In the natural sciences we rightly take it for granted that special gifts, training, and study, together with special enthusiasm for the subject, confer on a man a particular competence. Is it only on behalf of human welfare generally that the scholar is to be prohibited from showing enthusiasm and from exercising to the full the powers of his mind, tempered and fortified by his love for living? Is the nature of virtue to be left at the mercy of power?

Whatever answers the United States gives to these questions, it is hardly possible to claim that affirmative answers are the best means of protecting us from dictatorship. If there are no skilled and impartial judgments on matters of morality, intelligence, and beauty, the firmest bulwark of good democratic government will be removed. Masked by political, judicial, or economic authority, violence and corruption will be given rein. As Gilson has said, "The problem of philosophical unity is in itself an essentially philosophical problem, and unless philosophers tackle it, somebody else will solve it for them, and probably against them."[5]

1. Moral Philosophy and Science

Some persons may say, of course, that, notwithstanding his great reputation and notwithstanding what happened in June, 1940, M. Gilson was talking nonsense. It is one of the charms

[5] Etienne Gilson, *Medieval Universalism* (New York, 1937), p. 14.

of the "freedom" we enjoy in all affairs pertaining to the mind that every person, whether learned or not, is free to berate any learned man, living or dead, no matter how eminent, who makes a judgment independent of scientific data, without examining his case at all, let alone paying him the compliment of studying and reflecting upon it. If we are not to fall into this error of what Mr. Hutchins once called "freedom from thinking," it is incumbent upon us and upon M. Gilson to consider the case that is presented against him.

Modern learning has, it is said, at least two ways of determining whether wants are desirable, at least two ways of measuring values. One is the pragmatic test of seeing whether a set of propositions emanating from scholars works. In the minds of the pragmatic philosophers this meant asking the question, Do these propositions contribute to the welfare of the community? But, since that question is exceedingly difficult to answer and since it was coupled with the idea that the experience of communities, as distinct from the judgment of the trained mind, which cannot be simply a mirror of that experience, is the best judge of what will benefit them, the question asked by social scientists is generally a far simpler one. It is this: Does the public take up the propositions or does it reject them?

The other and closely allied method of determining values is to subject these propositions to scientific examination. This can be done by making experiments or by the application of some kind of objective tests.

Let us consider, first, the pragmatic test. It is perfectly true that in the long run ideas, to be effective, must influence a considerable number of persons. This does not mean that other ideas, which do not catch on, might not benefit the human race more than those which are successful. Still less does it mean that the ideas which benefit mankind most are those which are immediately popular. In the modern United States, the test of popularity, or "influence" as it is frequently called, is generally that what is right is what pays or what a majority supports. This assumes that the current public view of moral, intellectual, and aesthetic values is the best possible view. Now this is a proposition for which we have no scientific proof whatever. Unless moral philosophy is cultivated in relation to the whole of knowledge, unless the impartial, wise, carefully trained mind, impelled by a love for human life and a love of beauty, is encouraged to work according to the needs which it finds in this field, and to make such uses of special studies as are appropriate to its purpose, no evidence of value can be offered either for or against the proposition. Experience, as John Stuart Mill suggested, is against it. "No government, by a democracy or a *numerous* aristocracy," he wrote,

either in its political acts or in the opinions, qualities, and tone of mind which it fosters, ever did or could rise above mediocrity, except in so far as the sovereign Many have let themselves be guided . . . by the counsels and influence of a more highly gifted and instructed One or Few. The initiative in all wise or noble Things, comes and must come from individuals; generally at first from some one individual.[6]

It is just this lesson which the sovereign "Many" in the United States today have forgotten. Is it an undemocratic lesson? Mill, at any rate, has not been usually regarded as a champion of totalitarianism or of any form of despotism. In view of his judgment, it would be of help to those persons who are interested in getting at the truth, and who believe that human wants work out for the best if left to take their course, to offer their opinion as a hypothesis to the moral philosopher, if and when he appears.

Objections will be raised to such a course. The first is that moral philosophy cannot be scientific. "The true," writes John Dewey, "means the verified and means nothing else."[7] The

---

[6] *On Liberty* (New York, 1898), p. 119.

[7] *Reconstruction in Philosophy* (New York, 1920), p. 160. Cf. John Herman Randall, *Our Changing Civilization* (New York, 1929), p. 338.

second is that the propositions which scholars offer the public already have scientific validity. This leads us to the experiments and objective tests which are supposed to justify laissez faire in the realm of moral philosophy. The propositions have already been tested in the social laboratory or by one of the many new "techniques" (as they are called) which social scientists have been devising. It is the special virtue of several modern philosophies that, unlike the ancient philosophies which (to the great benefit of the human race) they have replaced, they rest not on opinion but on "science." The public and the economic and political leaders are not making a choice without guidance. They are offered a great number of packages. Many of these packages are stamped with a scientific trademark. The public is free to decide what weight to give to the various brands which bear it. If it is foolish enough to turn to one which bears no scientific trademark, the scientists are not to blame.

Now the answer to these objections is that both are true, and that both illustrate the need for treating moral philosophy, along with faith and art, as the principal objective of civilized humanity. Aristotle pointed out that ethics could never be an exact science. But what should determine the value of a science is not the degree of precision possible within it, but its importance for human welfare. We have attempted to show that methods derived from natural science for the investigation of human societies are insufficient for the solution of every problem that confronts the humanities and the social sciences.[8] Let us offer one further example of the misdirected use of scientific methods.

I recently listened to a discussion between two foreign and two American university men. All four were at once scholars and what is sometimes called by the rather inelegant name of "educators." The word always reminds one of those crackers that as children we were encouraged to eat. It is apparently

[8] See above, chap. 4, sec. II.

hoped that the "educators" will have a wholesome effect upon the students of the same material kind claimed for the crackers. The subject of this particular discussion was the training of students in the reading, writing, and speaking of foreign languages. One of the Americans referred to the economy of teaching people languages in long stretches early in childhood, if possible by putting them into situations where they have to carry on all their studies and even amusements in foreign tongues. The second American objected. One of the educational foundations, he said, had recently sponsored a scientific inquiry into the question of the best age for teaching languages. Research had shown that a person could generally learn better and with less expenditure of time and labor at fifty than at ten. To his surprise, the two foreign scholars, both of whom had been trained in the classical tradition, threw up their hands. In unison they exclaimed: "It simply isn't so!"

It is quite possible, of course, that for the purpose of acquiring a vocabulary in connection with some specialty the conclusions reached after this "scientific" research are correct. A child would have much less knowledge of the specialty than a person who had worked at it all his life. But if the man of fifty had learned the language as a child, he could have got up the vocabulary of his specialty at fifty in a small fraction of the time that would be required if he had not. The statement the learned American made on the basis of the scientific research is not only misleading but entirely unscientific. This illustrates the mistake of trying to apply so-called scientific methods to matters where the observation and, above all, the judgment of wise, experienced, and well-read men are better guides.

Even in matters where scientific investigations are appropriate, where they provide a fruitful way of adding to our knowledge, the results obtained are always extremely partial from the standpoint of a unified philosophy. As almost all wise scientists are ready to admit, scientific conclusions are morally, socially, and aesthetically neutral. So we cannot be sure that the stamp of approval which learning at present puts on a package of propositions, connected with the ordering of society, is actually scientifically valuable. Should we, on the basis of the research sponsored by the foundation just referred to, abandon all teaching of foreign languages until men and women reach upper middle life? Even with the increase in life-expectancy, can we assume it will be more useful for a man or woman to learn a language at fifty than at ten?

The view that moral philosophy is not a science in the sense that chemistry or physics is a science is a sound one. The attempt to make moral philosophy into this kind of science can end up only by confusing it with logic or psychology or some other branch of knowledge more closely related to the natural sciences. While the results of scientific, historical, and anthropological research can be of great importance to philosophy, philosophical inquiries themselves cannot be conducted primarily under the direction of methods appropriate to the study of the natural sciences. Moral philosophy cannot be partial, as any particular science must be, any more than it can be indifferent to problems of good and evil. It can never take anything for granted. It can never say, as some other disciplines so easily can, "other things being equal." In reaching their results, moral philosophers must strive to take into account all aspects of matter and of human beings as individuals, as members of an institution, of a community, of a nation, and of the world. They must attempt to command the essentials of all the learned disciplines. For such labor scientific method has to be a servant, not a master. What is required above all in philosophy, as in art, is genius, together with a long and disciplined training in the thought and culture of the race. The philosopher must have complete freedom, insofar as a human being can attain it, from every kind of partiality, save partiality for the good, the true, and the beautiful. The philosopher makes use of logic and of the results of scientific experiments and of the observation of measurable data when he finds them appropriate to his philosophical problems. He also uses intuition and the wisdom of the past. The more perfectly he can use all these instruments in their proper places, the better for his results. But the vital matter is that he should use them all as philosophy demands and not allow any to take the place of philosophy as a guiding principle governing the edifice that he builds. The very attitude of scientific sufficiency, which has come to pervade learning, takes away that breath of humanity indispensable to philosophy. The doctrine of the market place—"every man for himself"—should have no influence on philosophers. The attitude now widely regarded as a mark of the sound scientist—"I cultivate my own field without relation to the rest"—is no better than a somewhat sophisticated version of that doctrine. "Even for economic policy much more is involved than 'economic' freedom and progress," writes Frank Knight.[9] "Economic relations are inseparable from . . . other features of social culture (in the anthropologist's meaning). Especially in point are family relations and 'culture' in its other meaning of refinement—moral, intellectual, and aesthetic—that is *improving the general public sense of values.*"

Few men, it may be said, could possibly live in so rarefied a realm as that of moral philosophy as we have pictured it. This is true. It does not follow that its reclamation for learning would be of no benefit to mankind. It does not follow that even persons who have not the endowment to find themselves at home in it cannot do something, however small, to lead wise men to cultivate it in the future. A philosopher who succeeds in moving in that high realm cannot do so without taking into account the results of the scholarship to which so many tens of thousands of conscientious workers have contributed during the past two centuries. It is equally true that if scholars recognized the real meaning and high purpose of moral philosophy, it would make possible in many separate branches of knowledge, enriched by recent scholarship, the creation of works of

[9] In *Ethics,* LXXVI, No. 3 (1966), 177.

greater benefit to mankind than most of those which at present issue from American universities. Scholars would come gradually to understand that the moral and intellectual purpose and the artistic skill and meaning, behind a work destined for publication, are of the first importance. Thus they might be able to reorganize their study of man according to an intelligent, orderly, and philosophical plan.

Facts are necessary to a book; but a collection of facts is not a book. Any book worthy of the name has an inner necessity that develops in the mind of its author as he writes it and can develop only when he is gifted with reason, wit, and a sense of beauty. If a collection of facts were a book, there would be nothing to prevent the multiplication of masterpieces as rapidly as radio receiving sets or electric refrigerators. In fact there has been a tendency recently among intellectuals to compete in teams with these mass products by devoting their skilled energies to dictionaries, encyclopedias, and other voluminous compendia of knowledge on most of the innumerable subjects into which learning has proliferated. The works are very useful, but they are not direct contributions to moral philosophy. Still less to independent works of art.

Natural science today has little to fear from the revival of a genuine philosophy. The true moral philosopher will always welcome and make use of new scientific knowledge, just as the true scientist will always derive inspiration and help from the sound restatement of philosophical truths that is now so greatly needed. But neither the true philosopher nor the humbler scholars who wish to help him on his way will regard any of the sciences as substitutes for philosophy and theology, as do most of the writers of the hundreds of books and thousands of articles on philosophical and theological subjects that appear every year in the United States. The chief dangers today are not, as American university men seem to fear, that natural science and the scientific method will be stifled by philosophy, as in the later Middle Ages, or that philosophy will be solidified in a single system of what our contemporaries describe as "absolutes." The chief danger is that ethics in the ancient Aristotelian sense will die from lack of cultivation. For civilized man that would be, as an Englishman in Shakespeare's times might have said, a "sore alteration."

II. *Moral Philosophy and Wealth*

The true moral philosopher looks with favor upon the increase in material wealth, for individuals or for nations, only insofar as riches contribute to general happiness. In dealing with the relation of wealth to general happiness, as in all philosophical subjects, the philosopher has to establish himself in the high kingdom of generalization and remain there. Only there is it possible to make statements of truth that will endure. It is not for the philosopher, as a philosopher, to take a position on controversial and transient issues. Action has to be left to the statesman, the legislator, the judge, the administrator, and other men of affairs. The philosopher's task is to formulate and develop principles that can guide and fortify in each and all of his acts the public man seeking the good of his country and humanity. While these principles have no specific relation to a particular action—such as a senator's vote on a piece of civil rights legislation or a bill raising the income tax—they can infuse into public men (and likewise into scholars and teachers who deal with narrower subjects than philosophy) the spirit in which they should make each of their practical decisions. The philosopher can show them the ends toward which all their actions should be directed. With the present poverty of philosophy, the denial of the existence of truth, and the confusion over the nature of democracy, most public men in the United States have no guide but the pressures from their own lust for power or from opinions expressed by polling services and by organized petitions from constituents.

Such pressures are designed to affect the action of public

men in choosing between means. Shall interest rates be raised? Shall money be appropriated for new nuclear weapons? If the public officeholder knows his job he will be a far better judge of the technical matters that are of primary importance in a choice of means than the pressure groups and most of the organs of publicity that presume to tell him. If he believes in the good as such, he will have a guide beyond a search for power.

What the public man needs is guidance concerning ends. He can find it only in the wisdom of the past, kept alive by disinterested philosophers and thinkers of the present. Today the statesman who is seeking the good of the United States and of mankind will do far better to devote most of the time he now spends examining petitions or telegrams and scanning newspapers or magazines to Plato and Aristotle, Montesquieu and Montaigne, or even to Dante and Shakespeare. He can be sure that the motives of such sages and poets in guiding him are not suspect, that they are not seeking to drown him in information or misinformation. Their counsel will help him to rise above the heat of the moment. It will help to arouse in him the inner voice that is present to some degree in all sensitive persons and that is no person's private property. In these ways the public man will be helped to order his acts to a great purpose. He will have a firm basis for choosing between means.

In formulating principles for economic and political life, the moral philosopher's objects should be clear. They are to promote the production of wealth and to encourage its distribution in ways that will contribute to virtue, wisdom, and beauty. Philosophy alone can relate all human activities to these ultimate worldly ends. Each of them is independent of the other two but not in fundamental conflict with them. Philosophy must not starve one for the sake of the others, for happiness depends upon the cultivation of all three.

As happiness is the end sought by moral philosophy, power

and influence should be granted to individuals, parties, and institutions only if they are likely, according to the impartial views of wise men, to contribute to happiness. This does not mean that all men should be treated as equal in intelligence, knowledge, administrative capacity, or artistry. They are not so. Only a society lacking in intelligence will fail to recognize it. As Pascal wrote in his notes, "A mesure qu'on a plus d'esprit, on trouve qu'il y a plus d'hommes originaux. Les gens du commun ne trouvent pas de différence entre les hommes."[10] Will these remarks be attributed to their author's bias? Will it be said that Pascal was indulging in propaganda? The difficulty in the way of establishing such contentions would be considerable. By general acknowledgment Pascal was a wise as well as a noble man, one who possessed the very highest reasoning powers. There is not a shred of evidence that he hoped the notes which he jotted down in his seclusion at Port-Royal, where he went to await death, would bring him any sort of worldly advantage.

Insofar as possible, the body politic should be so constructed and the body economic so ordered that each individual will be given weight proportionate to his power to contribute to the happiness of the community. The moral philosopher should occupy a place apart. He should stand to gain in no way personally from the adoption of any of the measures he advocates. He is concerned with impartial inquiry, with ideas, and with values. From such a vantage point he is in a unique position to advise and to guide mankind.

What was done to some extent, especially in the English-speaking countries, from the seventeenth until the twentieth century was to give men an influence within states commensurate to their contribution to the general welfare of the community. The part played by Locke, Montesquieu, and es-

---

[10] "In proportion as one has intelligence, one discovers men of originality. It is common men who cannot discover any difference between men" (*Les Pensées,* ed. Adolphe Espiard [Paris, n.d.], I, 59; my translation).

pecially Adam Smith, together with their successors, in producing a state of mind among the people favorable to material progress and thus in shaping laws and political institutions in a manner likely to contribute to riches, health, and long life is not adequately appreciated. Our age has become obsessed with the view that a man's mind is a powerless victim of circumstances. It is well to remember that, as a shrewd Frenchman has put it, "there is no historical fatality except when one believes in such a thing." Our ancestors in the seventeenth and eighteenth centuries were far from thinking that the mind was incapable of independent action. One should allow for the conditions of their times, for the part played by the remarkable economic progress in Great Britain and Holland at the beginning of the seventeenth century in nourishing the philosophies of Hobbes, Descartes, and Bacon. After that has been done, it is still impossible to resist the conclusion that their works, together with those of many other writers and of many artists, among them Rubens and Callot, were positive factors in preparing for the modern industrialized world, with its exceedingly high material standards of living.[11] The influence of these men upon industrial technology and industrial growth was indirect and came mainly long after they were dead. They derived no personal advantage from the ideas they propagated. If they had felt, as Uncle Joe Cannon is said to have felt, that they need do nothing for posterity because posterity had done nothing for them! they would hardly have written or painted as they did.

Bacon's philosophy, like the much more subtle philosophy of some of his successors who were in essential agreement with him about health and wealth, was one-sided. It made man's material well-being the primary, and almost the exclusive, end

[11] This thesis is developed in two series of lectures I am giving for the Committee on Social Thought at the University of Chicago on the role of beauty and the role of thought in the conquest of the material world. The lectures form part of the volume on the coming of industrialism upon which I am at work.

of human existence. This led eventually to the popular view, so widespread in the United States, that economic and general welfare can be regarded for all practical purposes—and thought has now been largely lost in practical purposes—as identical.

In spite of its partiality, the philosophy of material improvement has been of great benefit to man. It grew up at a time when orthodox philosophies, derived from the classical and medieval schools, often raised singularly unintelligent opposition to advances in the natural sciences and to improvements in the material side of life. As a reaction against a philosophical outlook that was also partial, the "new philosophy" was pulling, however violently, in the right direction.[12] It was pulling the mind away from error, although as a doctrine it never contained anything like a perfect statement of truth. By focusing the attention of men on the opportunities for material improvement opened to them by new continents, abundant new natural resources, and freedom from the almost continual warfare that had been waged between the peoples of Europe, the new philosophy helped the Europeans, led by the British, to create a world far richer in the volume of commodities produced than any achieved by earlier civilizations.

For a number of generations, the one-sidedness of the "new philosophy" was offset, to a considerable extent, by the persistence of ancient humanistic traditions and by the continued influence of the teachings of Christ. Tradition and religion stressed the value of wisdom, virtue, and beauty. The one-sidedness of the "new philosophy" was also offset by the influence of other philosophers who did not share its prejudices. In spite of the enthusiasm which he expressed in one of his works for material improvement, Descartes' influence was thrown mainly on the side of elegance. He overstressed the independent power of the mind, particularly what Pascal called the mathematical side of the mind, and denied the speculative

[12] Cf. above, chap. 5, sec. I.

value of natural knowledge. While this led him into another kind of philosophical error from that of Bacon, an error such as hardly marred the thought of Plato, Aristotle, or Aquinas, Descartes' philosophy provided something of an antidote to the growing materialism inherent in the thought of Bacon and Hobbes. In the seventeenth century French society made the most of this antidote, at a time when Englishmen were more easily seduced than Frenchmen by the promises which natural science held out for material improvement. France used the Cartesian philosophy in the cause of beauty, balance, finish, and sweetness. At the same time France drew on the thought of the great Jansenist philosophers, Pascal and Nicole, who exalted the highest moral conduct as the primary end of existence. The proper position of natural science in the realm of learning was explained in these words by the greatest French philosopher of the late seventeenth century, Father Malebranche:

> Les hommes peuvent regarder l'astronomie, la chimie et presque toutes les autres sciences, comme des divertissements d'un honnête homme [he wrote in his *Search after Truth*], mais ils ne doivent pas se laisser suprendre par leur éclat ni les préférer à la science de l'homme. ... La plus belle, la plus agréable et la plus nécessaire de toute nos connaissances est sans doute la connaissance de nous-mêmes. De toutes les sciences humaines, la science de l'homme est la plus digne de l'homme.[13]

As built up in seventeenth-century France, civilization had a tremendous influence in Europe. Its influence was by no means negligible in England and even in America. It helped restrain the excesses in thought to which the "new philosophy" of the English naturally led. The values for which civilization stood

---

[13] "Astronomy, Chymistry, and most of the other Sciences may be looked on as proper Divertisements for a Gentleman. But Men should never be enamour'd with their Gayety, nor prefer them before the Science of Humane Nature. . . . The finest, the most delightful, and most necessary Knowledge, is undoubtedly that of Our Selves. Of all Humane Sciences, that concerning Man is the most worthy of Man" (T. Taylor, *Father Malebranche His . . . Search after Truth* [London, 1700], Preface).

were by no means neglected later in Victorian England. Newman, Ruskin, and Arnold, each in his own way, helped to
remind Englishmen that, although economic pursuits are, as
their younger contemporary, Alfred Marshall, defined them,
the "ordinary business of life," this does not justify learned
men in measuring civilization in terms of the volume of production or the quantity of real income, or in making economics, in Marshall's sense, independent of philosophy. Still
less does it justify learned men in making economics, in Marshall's sense, a substitute for philosophy. To do so is to identify
thought with the ordinary business of life when, to have any
substance, thought must be extraordinary. To do so, consequently, is to weaken thought and to make what is dressed up
to resemble it as transient and fleeting as changing economic
conditions. Against this destructive process, Thoreau as well
as Arnold and Ruskin did what they could. For example,
Thoreau wrote: "Even the *poor* student studies . . . only
political economy, while that economy of living which is
synonymous with philosophy is not even sincerely professed. . . ."[14]

During recent decades the defenses provided, both by the
ancient traditions and beliefs in which Western civilization
was reared and by philosophers who emphasized the importance of reason and virtue, have broken down. While France
and England have not lost altogether the general culture that
nourished European civilization since the early seventeenth
century, this culture has been weakened in both countries.
What is perhaps still more serious for the faith in man as a
rational being, striving toward the good, the true, and the
beautiful, the authority of French and English culture in the
Western world dwindled in the late nineteenth and early
twentieth centuries as the two countries lost their economic
and political ascendancy to Germany and the United States.

[14] Thoreau, *Walden* and *Civil Disobedience,* ed. Sherman Paul (Boston,
1960), p. 35.

In neither Germany nor the United States were the ancient Christian and humanist traditions and beliefs as deeply rooted in past experience of everyday life as in France and England. In neither was the emphasis on reason and virtue as ends of human existence as entrenched. Germany shared in and contributed to the European society, with its important classical ingredients, during the twelfth and thirteenth centuries. She borrowed copiously from Italian society at the time of the Renaissance and from French and English society in the seventeenth and eighteenth centuries. But in Germany the characteristics of classical society and Christian culture were eventually fused with a more ancient German tradition in which efficaciousness and force were dominant. That tradition came to subordinate all the other ingredients derived at home and imported from abroad. A doctrine of the master race became the instrument of national policy. For the time, at least, more moderate doctrines were denied the right to live. The cult that man exists for the state was embellished by the claim that the human race is divided into masters and slaves and that overlordship is the mission of the Germans.

Insofar as the United States can be said to have developed a characteristic philosophy, it is one which measures the happiness of the community in terms of the physical health, the length of life, and the quantity of material wealth of its citizens. "Culture" is proclaimed, but moral and aesthetic values are neglected because it is taken for granted that there can be no firm standards in connection with either. The intelligence is denied a role independent of scientific inquiry. Experiment, together with the examination of measurable data, controls the intelligence—not the intelligence, observation and experiment. As Dewey explains in one of his books, pragmatism is the logical development of the Baconian philosophy, purged of all the mystical and transcendental elements present in the European philosophies which followed Bacon. According to Dewey, Bacon's great achievement consisted in his denial of the value for philosophical truth of independent reason and literary art.[15]

The success and influence of the pragmatic philosophers were not caused mainly by any elements of leadership toward the good life which their doctrines contain—sincere believers though they were in goodness, when it could be obtained (as it could be in the nineteenth century) at no great cost. Their success was brought about, rather, by the fact that their views fitted into the conception of civilization that was coming to please Americans, particularly Americans of wealth and power. Some of these Americans were altruistically inclined— as is shown by their enormous gifts to medicine and education. But, as they would have been the first to admit, they were not thinkers, certainly not philosophers. They were not even scientists. Pragmatic philosophy came to mean—to a considerable extent in spite of the pragmatic philosophers, most of whom were disturbed by the tendencies they observed in recent American life—giving the public what it wants or what businessmen, publicity men, and politicians tell it that it wants. The pragmatists and their associates can hardly be regarded as a university sect willing to face martyrdom for their ideas. Those who think otherwise would do well to read the letters of Henry Castle, the brilliant young editor of the *Honolulu Advertiser,* who met a premature death in the North Sea at thirty-two. His early thought does not suggest that he would have become a pragmatist. But, like many of the pragmatists, he had studied philosophy in Germany in the eighties and was a close friend of George Mead, who later became a leader in pragmatism. In 1889, Castle tells us, Mead decided to start his career not in philosophy but in physiological psychology. In reaching this decision he was guided by the fact that "he has [here] a harmless territory in which he can work quietly without drawing down upon himself the anathema and excommu-

<hr>

[15] Dewey, *Reconstruction in Philosophy,* pp. 28 ff.

nication of all-potent evangelicism."[16] Such a choice was hardly the portent of a career destined to lead education in an unpopular direction. "What did any of us have," said another less famous pragmatist, "except a great deal of ambition to succeed?" Of course he was not fair to his distinguished and gifted associates, most of whom were disinterested searchers after truth. They actually derived little personal gain in money or even in position or fame from their labors. Except in educational circles the role they have played in American life has been hardly recognized. But they were swimming with the current, for all that. As the busy people rushing after money and worldly success had little or no respect for the mind, it was not likely that the persons whose work with their minds helped to justify the current would be noticed or treated with respect if they were. Pragmatic philosophy, in a corrupt form alien to the hopes of the best pragmatists, took possession of the country with no serious opposition. It became part of the everyday life of millions who had never heard of pragmatism. It offers another glorious American success story, fit to set beside the rise of poor boys to great riches as portrayed by Horatio Alger, except that in this case it was not the poor boys but their ungrateful companions who got most of the riches. The element of tragedy, to which American social scientists have closed their eyes, cannot be kept out of a true history of pragmatism.

The *partial* nature of Baconian philosophy, justifiable philosophically in the beginning as a reply to another philosophy no less partial, has been left in the United States without any effective philosophical force to balance it. When deprived of their function of striving to arrange the various goods of life in an order that will contribute to the general happiness of mankind, philosophical speculations lose their independence. Philosophy becomes the mere handmaiden, at best of science

[16] Henry Northrup Castle, *Letters* (London, privately printed, 1902), p. 579.

or of economics, at worst of publicity men and the seekers after political office. As a result partly of the emphasis on natural science and on the study of man in the "ordinary" and changing "business of life," the distinction between reason and opinion, so vital to cultural and scholarly life, has been largely lost. It is hardly more possible to draw a definite frontier between reason and opinion than between the economic and the non-economic aspects of life. That does not justify us in extending the economic to include the whole realm of existence; nor does it justify us in extending opinion to cover the whole realm of speculation, as social scientists have done under the influence of statements that "the true means the verified and means nothing else."

The special need for moral philosophy occasioned by the partial character of modern political economy is brought out strikingly by the words of one of its most intelligible exponents. They were written before the outbreak of the First World War, when economists still had much cause to be optimistic concerning the future of industrial society. According to Wicksteed:

Inventions and discoveries of every kind steadily tend to place mankind in fuller control of the powers of nature, and to give them larger means of accomplishing their desires. But this enlarged power has no direct or inevitable tendency to make those desires wise or worthy, or to correct the inequalities that have historically emerged between the powers possessed by different men to direct the resources of others toward the accomplishment of their own desires. The network of interchanges created and sustained by the economic forces is, morally, socially and esthetically, absolutely indifferent. . . . Economic forces never have been, never can be, and never should be left to themselves. . . .[17]

How are economic forces to be guided in the interest of general happiness? The task of the economist, as Wicksteed goes on to say, is to understand these forces better, in the hope

[17] Philip H. Wicksteed, *The Common Sense of Political Economy* (London, 1933), I, 395, 397.

that it may be more easily possible to control them. The task of the moral philosopher is to consider the nature of happiness; to consider how the constantly changing desires of men can be guided in directions that are morally, socially, and aesthetically beneficial to mankind. Moral philosophy is concerned, among other matters, with the choice of wants, economics with the means of attaining wants that are given. It should be a function of the moral philosopher to show society what wants are beneficial and thus to provide the economist with a basis for favoring those that are worth attaining. The future of economics depends upon the development of a moral philosophy, in the Platonic and Aristotelian sense, and upon the collaboration of economists and philosophers. The two subjects can be studied independently. But in their higher reaches, the one cannot be treated to advantage without reference to the other. Without moral philosophy the economist can to some extent show (and has shown) how to control economic forces—but only under its guidance might he learn how to control them for the benefit of humanity.

III. *Moral Philosophy and Civilization*

As the resources and conditions which invited the growth of a Baconian and partial philosophy of material improvement are ceasing to exist in the world of our time, the need for a renewal of a more comprehensive moral philosophy than any offered in the universities of the world today is compelling. It is doubtful whether there was ever in history a powerful country materially better and intellectually worse endowed than the United States today to make its philosophers kings. For a fraction of the money spent every year in subsidizing research in the social sciences, often valuable in a limited way for the data it provides, we could nourish genuine philosophers. There is no question that we could afford them. The trouble is that wealth cannot create them.

The conditions of our mores, our business life, and our politics are all hostile to their appearance. More than one hundred years ago Tocqueville noticed the special obstacles which confront the free mind in the United States and make it hardly less difficult for men to take an unpopular position on behalf of truth than in a totalitarian state. He wrote:

En Amérique la majorité trace un cercle formidable autour de la pensée. Au dedans de ces limites l'écrivain est libre, mais malheur à lui s'il ose en sortir! ... Avant de publier ces opinions, il croyait avoir des partisans; il lui semble qu'il n'en a plus, maintenant qu'il s'est découvert à tous; ceux qui le blâment s'expriment hautement, et ceux qui pensent comme lui, sans avoir son courage, se taisent et s'éloignent.

The majority says to him, in effect:

Vous êtes libres de ne point penser ainsi que moi; votre vie, vos biens, tout vous reste; mais, de ce jour, vous êtes un étranger parmi nous. ... Il cède, il plie enfin sous l'effort de chaque jour, et rentre dans le silence, comme s'il éprouvait des remords d'avoir dit vrai.[18]

The situation has changed little since the words were written. A man who tells an unpopular truth today finds himself no less an outcast than he did a century ago. Meanwhile the need for the independent mind has increased. There is today an overwhelming need for a balanced view of the world, such as can be secured only with the help of an accurate knowledge of past experience and a just sense of the present structure of

[18] "In America the majority raises very formidable barriers to the liberty of opinion. Within these barriers an author may write whatever he pleases, but he will repent it if he ever steps beyond them. . . . Before he published his opinions he imagined that he held them in common with many others; but no sooner has he declared them openly than he is loudly censured by his overbearing opponents, while those who think like him, without having the courage to speak, abandon him in silence. . . ." The majority says to him, "you are free to think differently from me, and to retain your life, your property and all that you possess; but if such be your determination you are henceforth an alien among us. . . . He yields at length, oppressed by the daily effort he has been making, and he subsides into silence as if he were tormented by remorse for having told the truth" (Alexis de Tocqueville, *De la démocratie en Amérique* [Paris, 1888], II, 154–55). I have changed slightly the standard English translation.

society in relation to the constitution of the ideal state. It is necessary to provide for all the needs of man that are legitimate in the sight of God and not simply for his desire to become wealthy and to exercise authority and dominion over his fellows. It is necessary to provide a place for all the races and all the nations on the globe and not to accord them especially good or especially bad treatment because they are Aryans, Negroes, or Jews, or because they are Argentines, Portuguese, or Chinese, but to see that they get recognition for the contribution they are making and can make to the common cause of mankind as this is determined not by might but by philosophy.

Moral philosophy might offer a corrective for those excesses in teaching, expression, and action into which the people of the United States have drifted and for which we were justly censured by foreigners. Moral philosophy might offer a comprehensive, balanced view of life, such as is especially difficult for a nation with large cities, many races, innumerable separate occupations, and separate branches of study to acquire. Moral philosophy exalts the place of the intellect in human affairs, at a time when Americans have denied that the mind has a role to play in civilized existence independent of either private interest or scientific experiment and observation. Moral philosophy calls attention to the fundamental importance of virtue at a time when it has become almost a creed to deny that there are any standards of morality. Moral philosophy, properly cultivated, becomes an ally of beauty, the third of the three great ends of civilized existence.

It may be said that in a world of many races and nations, each with its own special view of life, in a world of changing conditions and changing human wants, any definite scale of values, such as moral philosophy sets about to supply, is impossible.[19] The widely held opinion that there is something peculiar to our time in changing conditions, that the world has become dynamic whereas in the past it was static, is of course

[19] Cf. *ibid.*, Vol. III, Pt. III, chap. 18, for an answer to such a contention.

mistaken. It would be idle to deny that the social and economic changes of the last century have done much to undermine the traditional conceptions of morality among the Western peoples. But the disappearance of ethics is not a necessary part of change, as so many American university men have come to assume. Change is not new. Every society of which we have record has been in process of change. In the past, moral and intellectual standards have survived changes hardly less cataclysmic than those of the nineteenth and even the twentieth centuries. It is true that people's desires and wants are different from those of past peoples, but that has always been true of every society with which philosophers have had to deal. The things that mark off the world today from the worlds of earlier philosophers are not the elements of change. The differences are that the stage is a bigger one, involving a much larger territory and a much larger population, and that the machines and weapons in man's hands are vastly more powerful both in a productive and a destructive sense than they ever were in the past. The task of the moral philosopher is doubtless more complicated than it has ever been, but let us not imagine that his task was ever simple. The few approaches made in the past to a true philosophy have been made in the teeth of overwhelming difficulties. They have always involved a grasp of the essentials of many disciplines and occupations, in which the philosopher himself was not and could not be an expert or an actual worker, as the participants in special disciplines and special occupations must be. The few approaches that have been made to a true philosophy have always involved a reduction of the enormously complex to clarity, harmony, and unity. "Much more would be done if people believed less was impossible," wrote Malesherbes. This is especially true today. Moral philosophy has always involved, as it involves now, an attempt to influence the changing wants of man in the direction of human needs which have a greater permanence.

Let us distinguish further between wants and needs. Apart from the desires for food, warmth, and sleep, sex, comfort, entertainment, and display, satisfied in very different ways, there are the needs for faith, for love, for security (both against death and the evils of life), for justice, for good moral and intellectual habits, and for art. The satisfaction of human needs may not be necessary for life, but their satisfaction, at least in a measure, is indispensable for civilization. It is only when wants are tempered and guided by needs that they can be satisfied in ways that are distinctively human, that fortify the soul. Values that exist in connection with needs are eternal insofar as human beings are concerned. The recognition of them, still more the partial satisfaction of them, draw people together. They are not satisfied at the expense of other men and women to the same degree as wants. The fulfillment of wants, without regard to needs, is almost certain to breed envy. The fulfillment of needs is inclined to breed altruism. In short, what can help to keep wants within bounds, and so diminish the friction and enmity which their satisfaction causes, is to subordinate them to the need for faith, for virtue, and for beauty. Wants are inevitable. Many of them are indispensable. Without them, life cannot go on. The satisfaction of some is always harmful to mankind, the satisfaction of others is always helpful. But the satisfaction of the great majority of wants is now harmful and then helpful. With changing conditions and with different societies, it is desirable now to encourage the increase of certain wants, now to discourage their increase. That is notably the case in connection with the desire for material comfort and riches.

It is mainly accurate in one way and mainly false in another to say that absolute truth exists for the moral philosopher. His objective is always the same—human happiness in the highest sense, in the sense of the satisfaction of human needs. But the means of working toward human happiness vary.

The task of the moral philosopher is by impartial inquiry— and with the vast new supply of data now at his disposal—to help mankind to guide their changing wants in the direction of their far more permanent needs. Even a partial philosophy can help, if it is based purely on disinterested inquiry and if it exerts a pull in the right direction. There is a place for philosophers whose thought falls considerably short of the wisdom of Plato, Aristotle, or Aquinas. But it is indispensable that, as Aristotle might have said, the emphasis should not be laid on increasing the errors of emphasis that already exist. The modern exponents of the Baconian philosophy, the pragmatists in particular, for all their merits, were inclined to fall in with the current which, if our analysis is not completely wrong, is taking man farther and farther away from truth and happiness, away from those aspects of human life which need now to be nourished if civilization is to survive. Insofar as pragmatism seeks the happiness of the individual everywhere, its aim is sound and desirable. Its exponents have rendered a service to man by emphasizing the importance of happiness. The mistakes that are so widely made by the pragmatists, and even more by the logical positivists and most other present-day philosophers, are likely to defeat their own aims. The mistakes are these. They divorce happiness from principles of wisdom, virtue, and beauty, and deny that reason can be the guiding principle in the study of man's relation to man. They assume that their philosophy is universal rather than partial and—since they themselves tell us it is a philosophy of means, not of ends— that means can be encouraged to develop in our mechanized and crowded world without any direction. In its popular form, and even to a considerable extent in the writings of leading exponents, such as Dewey and Mead, pragmatism emphasized human wants and neglected needs. It emphasized the material side of life and neglected the spiritual and intellectual. It encouraged drifting at the expense of order and direction. Far from being the best philosophy for our times, as its exponents and followers have assumed, it is in many ways the worst.

To help mankind now and in the immediate future, the philosopher will have to emphasize needs rather than wants. He will have to emphasize the permanent rather than the fleeting. He will have to emphasize the spiritual rather than the material, unity rather than diversity, reason rather than experiment and observation for their own sake. A place for a moral philosophy which pulls in the necessary direction is required, not only for the welfare and the health of philosophers and writers, but for the welfare and health of man. Unless moral philosophers and writers cultivate the general welfare they will give us neither philosophy nor literature.

The Renaissance taught the Western peoples to exalt the value of man. After the religious wars this came to mean the fulfillment of all the good sides of man's instincts. During early modern times the two chief societies of Europe—the French and the English—came to emphasize different sides of man's aspirations. The French emphasized his aesthetic and intellectual, the English his material and moral, aspirations. There was enough interchange of ideas between the two countries so that the overemphasis of the one did something to offset that of the other, especially in the eighteenth century. In more recent times the balance has been weighted more and more exclusively on the side of man's material aspirations. Can the United States, as a relatively young and fresh nation, go beyond the attention our economists have focused on rates of economic growth and restore the balance that has been lost? Can we cultivate all the good sides of man's desires? Can we realize the dream of Renaissance humanism, which has never been fulfilled?

The answer to these questions lies to a considerable extent in the realm of moral philosophy. It depends upon the place which this wealthy nation is intellectually able to accord the subject and the influence which wisdom is allowed to have in the remaking of American society. We cannot answer these questions the right way unless we are prepared to recognize our faults and shortcomings. Self-criticism is generally a sign of strength. A recognition of weaknesses when and where they exist is an essential step toward wisdom. Let us hope that this great nation will recognize its weaknesses and rise above them.

8 Beauty

Never in the history of the world have so many people been writing books as in our time. What city dweller today would be likely to feel his pulse quicken if he were introduced to an "author"? Almost everyone, at any rate in learned circles, is an author. If anything gives a man distinction nowadays it is not that he has written a book or even many books. What distinguishes a man who moves about in colleges or universities or in society is that he has not written a book. The "man of letters" has been lost in an ocean of hastily improvised words.

Among modern Americans it is widely believed that anyone can write. Were we not told in our youth that every man or woman had it in him or her to compose a single great book—presumably an autobiography in one form or another? The disposition to act upon this assumption seems to be widespread. Recently a man of fifty, who had made a small fortune in business, presented himself to a learned colleague of mine. The man announced his intention of writing a doctor's thesis on an ambitious subject, for which few data could have been obtained. After warning him of the difficulties likely to be caused by the want of materials, my colleague asked to see a sample of the man's written work. "But I've never written anything," came the reply. "What, not even a theme or term paper in college?" "No, I can't remember that we were ever asked to write term papers at the college I attended." "What makes you think you can write, then?" "Anybody can learn to write," he replied, "and I can learn anything." The implication was that a person who had made a million dollars could hardly fail in a matter requiring so much less talent.

What we have today is a writing public. If there are to be

again "men of letters," there will have to be a reading public. Although the literacy tests are high, few find the time or the patience to read. So the very great majority of books are hardly read at all. The fact that they are bought proves little. If some of my learned colleagues in the graduate library school are right, a large portion of the books widely purchased have mainly what they elegantly call a "snob sale." The books find their way onto the living-room table, where visitors and guests will see them and, it is hoped, will regard their owner in a higher light than would otherwise be the case—but they find their way no farther.

Regret over the lack of a reading public is somewhat tempered when we consider the caliber of most contemporary books. They fall roughly into two large categories. There are, first, those written to sell. There are, second, those written to give the world new facts and ideas of a scientific nature.

There is no doubt that a fair number of the authors of books written for the market attain a high level of technical competence. This has been true notably of novels written in England during the last fifty years. Never have so many neatly constructed, polished novels been published before. Some are smooth and slick to the last degree. One trouble is that great works of art are neither smooth nor slick. They are authentic. Like most authentic things, they are often full of roughness. Like real emeralds, they have flaws. Few who battle genuinely and deeply with the problems of life—as the true artist must— can avoid flaws. Nothing that is merely smooth and pretty can inspire a deep and lasting affection. When Montaigne expressed his profound love for Paris, he could find no words better than these:

[Paris] a mon cueur dés mon enfance; et m'en est advenu comme des choses excellentes: plus j'ay veu depuis d'autres villes belles, plus la beauté de cette-cy peut et gaigne sur mon affection. Je l'ayme par elle mesme, et plus en son propre estre que rechargée

de pompe estrangiere, je l'ayme tendrement jusques à ses verrues et
à ses taches.[1]

It is much easier to learn to write in a style that is smooth
and slick than it is to say something important even in a style
that is crude and labored. The inner voice with a power to
move mountains cannot be acquired with the same ease as good
technique. The catch in the work of authors who write books
perfect in the technical sense is that they have nothing important to say. They have the foreign and acquired embellishments; they have little else. Their authors have no message to
give the world, no conviction about life they are bursting to
state. They are not writing because of any inner necessity.
They are writing for money, because they have a talent for
writing and find they can make a living more easily in this way
than in some other. While the arrangement of their plots and
the technical form of their paragraphs leave little to be desired,
their books have little warmth or depth. Their words and
images lack power and even beauty, such as is given only by a
sense of humanity, an inner elevation of spirit, and a distinction
of thought. Some of their books are amusing. A few are side-
splitting. But nearly all lack the quality of wit which comes
from an audacious imagination, creating comparisons at once
surprising and apt enough to lift both the writer and the reader
out of the actual world in which they live.[2] The force and the
dignity of words and phrases that characterized English literature in Milton's time, hardly less than in Shakespeare's, are no
longer popular.

Some years ago I overheard, between acts at the theater,

---

[1] *Essaies*, Bk. III, chap. 9: "That city has ever had my heart from my infancy; . . . the more beautiful cities I have seen since, the more the beauty of
this still wins with my affection. I love her for herself, and more in her own
native being, than in all the pomp of foreign and acquired embellishments.
I love her tenderly for herself [to the point of loving] her warts and blem-
ishes" (Cotton trans., ed. W. C. Hazlitt [London, 1902], IV, 97). I have
changed somewhat the last line of the translation.

[2] For the disappearance of "wit" in modern literature, see T. S. Eliot,
Homage to John Dryden (London, 1924), pp. 42–46.

the conversation of a young man accompanied by a woman of his own age, whom he was apparently taking out for the first time. Katharine Cornell was appearing in a little play called *No Time for Comedy*. At one point the play contained some unimpeachable sentiments, but it could hardly be regarded as an important work of art. The young man told his companion this was his idea of a good play. He would go to such a play any time rather than listen to Shakespeare. *Hamlet* was being given uncut in a neighboring theater. The young man explained that on no account would he waste an evening there. Frankly, Shakespeare bored him. "It's easy," he remarked, "to get too much of Shakespeare. I teach English literature at the junior college, you know."

He was not exactly the kind of teacher one would select if the object of teaching were to fire young people with a love of literature. Persons who see the absurdity laugh or shrug their shoulders. It does not occur to the large number of teachers, and the far larger number of laymen who feel as he does, to ask whether the fault is theirs. They assume that, without a cultural tradition, without serious training in literature, without a love of art, and without an intellectual effort, they are competent to pass judgment on any plays, books, paintings, or works of music. If Shakespeare bores them, they take it for granted the fault is his. They find the majority feel as they do, and the two traditions that most of them have learned are that everyone should be free to say anything he pleases and that the majority is always right.

Under these conditions, how can we feel confident that the public for whom writers now publish their works has the right judgment about present-day literature? Can we assume that there is any connection between the sale of a book and its value? Even in the seventeenth century, Milton was paid only a few pounds for *Paradise Lost*. Had it not been for the income he received from his father, who had made a fortune as a scrivener in London at the turn of the sixteenth and seventeenth centuries, Milton might never have found the time for writing poetry.

Not all books written in the modern world are expected to sell. The authors of those which fall into the second of the two broad categories we have mentioned aim at technical perfection of a different kind. Some are contented with little or no perfection of any kind. They generally hope to have their books reviewed favorably in a few learned magazines, which deal with a special field of scholarship. They write to fit into this groove. If they are successful, their book is purchased by the chief libraries. It is also purchased, but seldom read, by a few score scholars in the field. Writers of such books are able to bear the expense of preparing and publishing them, either because they have private means or because they are financed by rich universities or colleges, by business houses, or by the educational foundations established by wealthy men in the interest of knowledge and instruction.

The object of the best of these learned works is to present new explanations and information concerning the behavior of matter in the physical and the biological world, new explanations and information concerning the nature and history of man in his relations with other men. The rewards sought are scientific reputation, academic promotion, and various kinds of distinctions.

Many of these scholarly works contain much that is of value for mankind. It is no disparagement of them to suggest that, from the point of view of art or creative thought, most of these writings are useful mainly as materials. The subject matter of great works of literature, whether it is presented in the form of poetry or prose, is chosen not primarily because of its novelty but because of its importance. Neither art nor thought is ever achieved by letting one's materials do most of the work. A mountain of facts, even when they are carefully arranged in categories, has no power to speak to us. In one of his letters, written in 1760, Diderot, who was a champion of science and of industrial technology, refers to a long survey of French economic life that had been recently published in three bulky volumes by a Frenchman named Ange Goudar.[3] Of Goudar and his work Diderot writes, "Il a un monde de choses dont il ne sait rien faire; et le génie sait faire un monde de rien."[4] The words contain a lesson of which American scholarship is in need. No quantity of materials can take the place of genius, even in the study of society. While genius is partly determined by birth, even that very rare human being, a born genius, will be lost without opportunities for genius to grow.

The object of the artist and the thinker is less to say something for the first time than to say something that matters with greater power and meaning than ever before. It is easier to say something "original" on subjects that are small and insignificant than on subjects that are profound and of great consequence for human welfare. According to the criterion sometimes applied in the social sciences, a person who determines from old timetables how many car miles were probably covered by the Baltimore and Ohio Railroad in the year 1857 makes an "original contribution" to knowledge no less than a second person who says something fresh about the problem of meeting life. It is always easier (and safer) to say something entirely new about a subject that is of no concern to anyone than about another which has been of vital concern to everyone since the beginning of human experience.

When the scholar who has made his reputation by what are called "original contributions" to knowledge turns away from his specialty to write a textbook or some other kind of book for sale or publicity or both, he is generally guided by the agents of publishing houses, by magazine editors, and others

[3] *Les Intérêts de la France mal entendus* (3 vols.; Amsterdam, 1756).

[4] "He has a world of facts and doesn't know how to do anything with them; and genius knows how to make a world out of nothing" (*Œuvres complètes de Diderot*, ed. J. Assézat and M. Tourneux [Paris, 1876], XVIII, 480; my translation).

whose business is to make money. It is from such persons that the scholar finds out, either directly or indirectly, what the public wants. As he is not brought to his labor by a desire to supply the public with what it needs, as he makes a virtue of leaving questions of that kind to the give-and-take of the market place, he is generally no less anxious to supply the public with what he learns to think it wants than is the professional writer. In the not very numerous instances when the scholar has talent for writing, he is capable of achieving in his popular works a competence, a smoothness, and even a slickness little short of that exhibited by the best professionals. What he almost never succeeds in creating, any more than the professional of the present day, is a work of art. What he almost never succeeds in making, any more than the professional, is a contribution to thought. He is no more impelled to speak out by the deep inner necessity common to all great artists (and which is quite separate from the desire for worldly renown) than the professionals who, if successful, are handsomely paid for their labor. Very often he is told that the way to sell his wares is to "talk down" to his audience. He falls in readily with the suggestion, which generally coincides with his own views, derived from teaching. When he can talk down he is relieved from the necessity of probing his own materials deeply. Instead he dilutes the stock of information and ideas which he commands. It is not always a very large stock. He is likely to confuse this process of dilution with the clarification and simplification that are a part of art. His confusion and the results of it hardly contribute to the education of his audience or even of himself.

The results both of so-called scholarly writing and of the attempts by scholars to popularize their knowledge are sometimes unrelated and often harmful to art and creative thought. The net effect is to detract from the intelligence and the beauty of American society. Neither kind of work hits the mark that counts in forming a living culture. A certain American writer was recently spoken of with enthusiasm in a group of our so-called intelligentsia. His merit, it was said, was that he wrote in plain language that the common man could understand. He was not, it was said in his favor, "at all learned."

Now all great writers have put their thoughts in plain language, understandable to any person with a genuine education who has the time and inclination to make the effort of understanding them. But this result has never been obtained by weakening their thought or evading difficulties that arise as it develops. The slur on learning implied in the remarks about the American writer was not justified. It is a much greater achievement to put complex and learned thought into simple language than commonplace thought or no thought at all. Simple, plain language has no great merit unless it has valuable content.

In an age like our own, when technique is regarded as the principal kind of labor which calls for skill and training, when there is little recognition of the need for special competence and drill in connection with the higher play of the intellect, the difficulties of learning to paint or to compose music naturally seem much greater than the difficulties of learning to write. To the ordinary person, the technical problems of painting and composing appear far more complex and mysterious than those of writing. So in numbers neither the painters nor the musical composers can compare with the writers. Composers, and especially painters, are exceedingly numerous nonetheless.

The smoothness and slickness so characteristic of much recent writing are not so apparent in modern paintings and musical compositions, though they are apparent in many musical performances. The smoothness and slickness are there all the same. Balzac said of Raphael's famous "Spozalizio," or "Marriage of the Virgin," in Milan, "Ce n'est pas le comble de l'art, c'en est bonheur."[5] Few critics of painting would be

[5] *La Cousine Bette* (1847), Pt. I. "It is not the apex of art, but its happiness."

likely to disagree that in the purity and smoothness of his effects, Raphael was unequaled among the painters of the Renaissance. Is it not partly this characteristic of his works that makes them less profoundly moving for us than the greatest Rembrandts, Cézannes, and Giottos?[6] Pictures are painted today that might almost be mistaken for Raphael's were it not for their subjects. Few pictures are painted today that could be mistaken for Rembrandt's, Cézanne's, or Giotto's—except, of course, when a deft attempt is made to copy them. Few musical compositions even approach the almost perfect fusion of mind and heart indispensable to the permanent beauty achieved by Bach and Mozart.

The best-informed and most intelligent students of music and painting tell us that technical proficiency is the long suit of the most accomplished artists of recent years. Lacking convictions, most modern artists resort to tricks. At these they are often exceedingly skilful, and many of them get results on a canvas or in an orchestral work that are technically superb. Like the writers, the painters and composers are seldom drawn to their labor because they have something of overwhelming significance to communicate. It is true, of course, that the subject matter of music is far less literal than that of literature, even of poetry. The convictions of the musician, especially of a very great musician like Beethoven, Mozart, or Bach, are distilled into a medium that is highly abstract. It does not follow that the convictions of the musician are of no importance, that it is a matter of indifference whether or not he is drawn to his art by a tremendous inner necessity which comes from his mind and heart. A dedication to "virtue" is of no less importance in great music than in great writing. A sense of humanity, a deep belief and faith, as well as the highest order

[6] Balzac gave a higher place to Raphael's works in general than the best critics of the last half-century would do. His remark was made in comparing the "Marriage of the Virgin" to other paintings of Raphael's, which he considered greater. I share Balzac's view.

of intelligence in connection with artistic labor, are essential ingredients of all very great art. Without them no one is blessed with what the Greeks called "divine inspiration." Without them no one can rise above the smooth and talented. Technical competence is indispensable in all art. But it is no substitute for higher qualities, which have become more and more scarce in the painting and music of the Western peoples during the last hundred years.

In many artistic circles today it has come to be an accepted axiom, the French writer Raymond Cogniat tells us,[7] that painters should eliminate subject matter from their compositions. They should assert the purity of visual art, by avoiding those misunderstandings to which pictures with subjects lend themselves. Cogniat is troubled by this obiter dictum. He reminds us that Oscar Wilde once defined an artistic masterpiece as a work which lends itself to the largest possible number of misunderstandings! And Cogniat asks whether the contemporary insistence on the uselessness of subject matter has not impoverished the art of painting. If he is right, may not this insistence be a cause for that very weakening of the contemporary visual arts to which Chagall drew our attention?[8]

Not long ago, in 1950, Eliot provided, out of his experience as a poet, confirmation of the doubt Cogniat expresses and of Wilde's definition of a masterpiece. Eliot then presided over a seminar of the Committee on Social Thought devoted to his *Four Quartets*. Four students presented their interpretations of these poems. They offered half a dozen explanations of the meaning of a line in *East Coker*. As it seemed to them, the explanations conflicted; so they appealed to Eliot to settle the matter. What had he meant when he wrote the line? To their surprise, Eliot answered he thought he had meant all

[7] In a brochure, issued (Paris, 1966) in connection with a forthcoming new *Histoire de la France*, in many volumes.

[8] See above, p. 66.

those different things. He suggested that the power of verse consists in its *richness*, in its variety, of meaning.

If this be true, by eliminating subject matter from painting, the artist is deprived of one important source of the enrichment upon which the strength of a work of art rests.

The same is true of other arts and specifically of music. Music is indeed warped if the *notes* and *rhythms* are designed to tell a particular story, as, for example, in some of Richard Strauss' compositions[9] in which he has tried to leave no room for doubt. The greatest music is profoundly meaningful, in part because of the possible diversity of valid understandings in the listener! It is this very richness of the sounds that makes it virtually impossible to play the music as well as it ought to be played.[10] The incredible variety in a major work, for example of Mozart's, is what makes the music approach perfection to such a point that a close and deeply emotional friend of mine once remarked that it is Mozart who "invented perfection"—an exaggeration which contains enough truth to make us glad she said it.

The variety of human temperaments suggests that there are no restrictions to the forms which can be invented, and that if, as is often claimed in connection with art, everything has been said it is equally true that everything remains to be said. This would seem to be profoundly the case under the new conditions brought about during the last twenty-five years by the overwhelming revolution in economic, social, political, and cultural life. So, in recognizing the importance of tradition and of artists who make the right refusals, we should not restrict the fields of exploration open to them. Even if the rich misunderstandings created by new explorations should lead to quarrels, they would not be the quarrels that contribute to organized war! They are more likely to offer outlets alternative to such mass violence. And organized war[11] has now become the most dangerous disease which confronts humanity.

[9] See above, pp. 50–51.   [10] See above, p. 54.   [11] See below, chap. 12.

1. *Art and Moral Philosophy*

If our analysis of the condition of modern art contains an element of truth, it follows that literature, painting, and music are suffering from the same kind of weaknesses which have been causing the disintegration of religious faith and of ethics. Beauty should not be confused with faith, with virtue, or with knowledge. Each has a realm of its own that must be cultivated for itself. But all have this in common—they alone among the goods of life have the capacity to lift man completely out of himself, to help him escape from self-love. Just as faith is the ally of virtue, it is also the ally of beauty. Art has need of both faith and virtue. Moral philosophy and religion both have need of beauty. All three of them are expressions of the same combination of exaltation and intelligence. All three are supreme expressions of the human spirit. As long as one of them is alive there is always hope for a revival of the others.

If our analysis contains an element of truth, the future of art depends upon increasing recognition that its *main* purpose is to treat of the deeper meaning of human existence. Its object cannot be to add to the artist's income or his popularity in the open market. If art is to help mankind, true artistic inspiration and conviction should as never before rule the market for their own ends. These are not personal. They control the artist; they may lead him in ways that are against his private advantage and even his private wishes.

It is true, of course, that the inspiration of the artist must be met with comprehension and recognition by some of his contemporaries if his work is to survive, if it is to have an influence on others besides himself, and if he is to develop to the full his potential powers. But what is important is not that he should be in tune with current values. What is important is that at least a tiny public should be in tune with greatness, should be able to recognize it and to respond to it when it is presented to them. The relationship of the artist to the public has been well explained by one of the most dedicated modern musicians, Artur Schnabel. The artist's inspiration is no more the creation of the public, than a man's voice on some high mountain side is the creation of the rocks, crags, and peaks that rise about him. Yet the extent to which that inspiration is used depends, in a measure, like the use of the voice seeking an echo, upon the surroundings. If the echo comes, the mountaineer is encouraged to go on calling and to try out his voice in new ways. If he gets no response, he will relapse into silence sooner. So with the inspired artist. "The preservation and renewal of cultural creation," Schnabel wrote, ". . . depends upon a public demand, expressed by understanding and love."[12]

Faith and the study of moral philosophy, as it has come down to us from the greatest Greek philosophers, can be of assistance to art. Faith and virtue each help to create among the vast stretches of hills and valleys formed by human societies—among the population as a whole, rich and poor alike—the conditions that make possible an echo. If faith and virtue are to make an impression upon the future, both must be revived in new forms. The old forms of the thirteenth and eighteenth centuries no longer have a hold on mankind, but the principles contained in them are not dead. As long as civilizable societies exist, these ancient principles provide, however imperfectly, for the deepest human needs. Can those needs be met in the decades and centuries which lie immediately ahead, unless these ancient principles of religion and of ethics are cultivated in relation to the industrial world that has grown up during the past century and a half? Religion in its basic Christian form, as set forth in the New Testament, teaches us that the test of a man's mind and spirit, as of his moral conduct, cannot possibly be worldly success. No message is of greater importance for art today than this one. Religion also shows us that man's mind and spirit cannot be at the command merely

[12] Cf. Artur Schnabel, *Reflections on Music,* trans. César Saerchinger (Manchester, 1933), pp. 9–10.

of a worldly despot, that they belong in an independent realm subject to the dictation of no mere man. By showing the heights to which man's mind and spirit are capable of reaching, faith can help reveal to men their potential powers as artists. When some Greeks spoke of the great artist as "divinely inspired," they were recognizing that he derives his force from serving a higher purpose transcending the self. This does not mean that any great artist must avert his eyes from the commonplace and the ugly or that he himself is untouched by them. It means rather that *in his art* he reveals them for what they are.

Moral philosophy, in the best sense, exalts the intellect and emphasizes its importance as the controlling factor in the study of man. It demonstrates the autonomy and the value of the trained, independent mind, with its power to reason both geometrically and by intuition. Thought and art have much more in common than either has with technology or even with science. Both order their materials for ends determined by the mind. Artists and thinkers strive to create works that are unique—that are valuable as subjects of contemplation and reflection. Science is more concerned with existing conditions, and applied science with making use of scientific knowledge for practical purposes. Thought is indispensable to science, and intuitive genius (like that of the artist) is indispensable to the greatest scientific discoveries, just as correct knowledge of matter and of facts is indispensable to thought, but the emphasis is different in the work of the thinker and artist from that in the work of the scientist. Any attempt to deny the importance of the difference leads to the absorption and diminution of science and technology in favor of thought and art or to the absorption and diminution of thought and art in favor of science and technology. The great danger in our time is not the diminution of science and technology. It is the denial of the independence of thought and art. If it were possible to lay down hard and fast rules and laws governing art, as it is to lay down tentatively laws governing mechanics, then it would be possible to turn out works of art by mass production. It is precisely the fact that a work of art is not mechanical but is the product of man's independent mind and heart that gives it a permanence denied to products of the laboratory as well as to those of the factory. Some art today, together with social and humanistic study, suffers from an overemphasis on purely scientific and technical aspects. So the lessons which moral philosophy has to teach are of great importance to the future of art. What is needed is a combination of the indifference to sales, characteristic of the best research work done by scholars, with art as well as with science.

Moral philosophy is also of importance to art because it seeks to establish, tentatively at least, a hierarchy of values concerning knowledge and also concerning conduct. In the realm of the intellect, moral philosophy is concerned with distinctions of every kind at a time when men have forgotten that there are any important distinctions save those imposed by material necessity. The question of material necessity can be properly given only minor importance in art. So the success of art as well as of moral philosophy depends upon the establishment by impartial minds of the right intellectual values.

It is frequently supposed that art and virtue have nothing in common or even that they are opposed. In the period immediately preceding and following the First World War, the public came to regard artist colonies as hotbeds of moral laxity. Their view was not entirely without foundation. A good many persons who obtained temporary renown as artists did little by their personal conduct or their work to prove that it was false. In some quarters persons who aspired to become artists felt that they were establishing their artistic reputation almost as much through their irregular hours and their powers as drinkers as by the quality of the poetry they wrote or the pictures they painted.[13] Such is still the fashion.

13 Cf. Malcolm Cowley, *Exile's Return* (New York, 1934).

What has not been recognized is that these activities are no less irrelevant, and possibly even more harmful, to the pursuit of artistic objectives than the confusion of technique with art and the encroachment of science upon thought. All these aberrations were an evidence of the growing materialism which was bound to damage art by submerging it under material values with which it has little in common.

Insofar as moral philosophy can help to teach the artist just proportions in the conduct of life, insofar as it can help him to acquire good moral habits, it is bound to help him as an artist. It will help him to put his body at the service of his mind and heart, not to allow his mind and heart to become slaves of his body.

What is of far greater importance to the artist is the significance of moral philosophy, not for his personal conduct, but for the treatment of his materials. Recent art has suffered greatly, as Ramon Fernandez and later Eliot were first to point out, from the lack of any hierarchy of values. Quite independently of the artist's conduct of his own life, he can only be inspired to the intensity of conviction woefully lacking in recent art, by a consuming love of beauty, justice, and truth. If the existence of permanent values in connection with beauty, justice, and truth is denied, as it has come to be so largely in recent times, then a great source of artistic inspiration is removed. No one can look at the wonderful scenes carved on medieval abbeys, churches, and cathedrals without realizing that the artists who created them had a compelling sense of the difference between right and wrong conduct and that they could count on the audience who came to worship to share their "prejudices," as modern social scientists would call them. The artists had a compelling sense of the difference between justice and injustice, as these were conceived in the mind, with the help of faith, and not as they were laid down arbitrarily by a despotic ruler in order to increase his own power. In a more recent age, what gave such strength to the works of Balzac or Dostoevsky, was the deep sense of moral values felt by their authors, combined with the detachment with which as artists they could write. The standards of right and wrong are essentially the same in two writers of such completely different temperament and background as Balzac and Trollope. Their work is equally dependent upon the existence of these standards. It is of little or no significance that Balzac's personal habits as a writer were exceedingly irregular and excessive, while Trollope's were a model of methodical balance, annoying to persons who take for granted that art can thrive only on eccentricity of conduct. Balzac and Trollope were united in this—both were concerned in portraying, in different ways, the overwhelming value of goodness and the overwhelming iniquity of evil. On this vital question there is no room for two opinions in connection with art.

Unless the modern world can honor a sense of virtue independent of the self and combine orderly discipline with love for another, the future of beauty is not hopeful. Art without a sense of justice, without a belief in truth, is hardly more possible than art without beauty. Much criticism has been leveled at Keats's celebrated line identifying truth and beauty, and not without cause. It remains true that a society which denies either ultimately denies both.

ii. *Art and Wealth*

Some historians have been struck by the apparent association of exceptionally rich artistic achievements with periods of remarkable material advance. One of the most striking examples is the flowering of Greek culture during the short sixty years between the Battle of Marathon in 490 B.C. and the outbreak of the Peloponnesian War in 431 B.C. During those six decades there worked at Athens, a town hardly as populous as Sinclair Lewis' "Zenith," at least seven of the very greatest figures in the entire history of art and thought. If any competent judge since the Renaissance had been asked to name the hundred leading artists and thinkers of all time, he could hardly have omitted Aeschylus, Phidias, Sophocles, Herodotus, Euripides, Thucydides, or Socrates. All of them, except Aeschylus, were born between 500 and 470 B.C. All of them, except Aeschylus, who died probably in 456, were seen by most Athenians during the two decades 450–431. In those twenty years the Parthenon, the Erechtheum, and the Propylaea, with their monumental embellishments, were all going up on the Acropolis under the direction of Pericles (*ca.* 495–429), to form one of the most perfect groups of buildings ever conceived by man. There they remain after twenty-four centuries. It is sobering to realize that they might not survive a war fought with nuclear weapons.

The years between the Persian and the Peloponnesian wars were a time of prosperity for the Greek city-states and above all for Attica. The population was growing; new colonies were being founded overseas; the imports of grain and timber were mounting rapidly. Attica had almost as many inhabitants as she had before the Second World War of 1939–45. Her increasing wealth was swelled by vast supplies of silver won from the recently discovered mines of argentiferous lead ore in the mountain of Laurion. There some of the shafts went down three hundred feet, an uncommon depth in those days at which to make a livelihood. The slopes and valleys were full of men washing, breaking, and preparing the ore or separating the silver and lead. It is natural to assume that economic progress had something to do with the culture of the Athenians.

Similar associations between a rapid increase in the volume of production and wonderful artistic achievements are to be found in the Gothic age in France and Italy, in the Renaissance of the late fifteenth and early sixteenth centuries in Italy and southern Germany, and in the Elizabethan and Jacobean periods in England from about 1580 to 1640. The first of these periods gave us Albertus Magnus, Thomas Aquinas, Roger

Bacon, Giotto, Dante, and the greatest cathedrals. The second gave us Michelangelo, Leonardo, Giorgione, Titian, Dürer, and the architecture of humanism. The third gave us Shakespeare, Spenser, Donne, Milton, Hooker, Francis Bacon, and the most delightful English music. Like the Athenian period in Greek history, each of these ages of giants was an age in which population grew and with it the command of men over matter in agriculture and industry. In the time of Aquinas, in the time of Leonardo, in the time of Shakespeare, the merchant could look forward with confidence to a rapid growth in his traffic from decade to decade and almost from year to year. During the great reign of St. Louis (1226–70), the production of silver and copper in Europe may well have increased threefold or more. During the lifetime of Leonardo (1452–1519), the output of iron in Styria, a leading center of the industry, grew at least fourfold. During the lifetime of Francis Bacon (1561–1626), the coal imports of London mounted from less than ten to more than a hundred thousand tons a year.

A superficial historical observer might conclude that rapidly increasing industrial output is indispensable to great art or even that it leads inevitably to great art. If he were a natural scientist, he might conclude that there is a symbiosis between a remarkable increase in the volume of material production and the development of a very rich culture.

History hardly supports such theses. Greece was probably not conspicuously more prosperous when Plato died in 347 B.C. than on the eve of the Peloponnesian War, a few years before his birth. Neither he nor Aristotle (384–322), who was his junior by some forty years or so, apparently lived in what the economists would call a rapidly expanding economy.

It may be objected that Plato and Aristotle were the fruits of a creative movement that developed originally because of exceptionally prosperous conditions. But it would not be possible to show that the so-called classical period in French art coincided with a rapid increase in the national income, such as occurred in Greece in the fifth century B.C. It his been often said that France, more than any other Western country, is heir to the Greek cultural tradition. No period in French history—except, perhaps, the thirteenth century—had been as rich in artistic achievements as the seventeenth. Descartes and Pascal, Poussin and Georges de la Tour, Racine, Corneille, Molière, La Fontaine, Bossuet, Lulli, Couperin, and Mme de La Fayette all were born between 1594 and 1668. Couperin was the only one to survive Louis XIV, who died in 1715.

The seventeenth century was an age in which Frenchmen learned to write poetry, music, and prose, to paint, to build, and to decorate with reason, harmony, balance, grace, and finish unknown to their ancestors. But it was not an age in which the population of the French provinces, or the volume of their agrarian and industrial output, grew rapidly, as the agrarian and industrial output of England grew during the reigns of Elizabeth I and James I. There were only two periods of striking prosperity: the first two decades of the century, when France recovered from the religious wars, and the sixties and seventies, when Colbert directed the national economy. Both were followed by long periods of depression. While France had acquired some new territory, few of the French provinces were much more productive at the beginning of the eighteenth century than at the beginning of the seventeenth or even the beginning of the sixteenth. The last three decades of Louis XIV's reign were a time of serious economic depression. The output of several industrial products, such as coal and many varieties of cloth, was on the decline. Vauban, the famous fortress-builder, who Voltaire tells us was the only general who preferred the welfare of the state to his own, has painted a picture of the material distress at this time. It is hardly less gloomy than the one painted by the Scotsman, John Law, who came forward with an offer to put things right by reorganizing the national finances and developing credit. Law was a special pleader; so we might expect him to exaggerate. But the same exception cannot be taken to Vauban's description. Michelet's remark, that the reign of Louis XIV finished many things but began nothing, is nowhere really applicable except to some extent in the sphere of economic progress as that is measured by modern economists in terms of rates of growth in production.

Economic history before the eighteenth century, then, contributes further to the doubts, already expressed in these pages,[14] on the basis of more recent history, as to whether rates of economic growth provide a satisfactory measure of creative opportunities in connection with the arts. Economic progress, as so measured, may be of great importance to material welfare. Nor is it inevitable that such progress should become a handicap to the arts, provided the values that are indispensable to the creative life can establish themselves effectively alongside, and independently of, those which contribute to material affluence. But the values are not the same. A society governed by the values of economics is inhospitable to the values necessary to creative art. So it is a vital question whether a place can be found for both. May not the future of civilization partly depend upon an affirmative answer?

Until the appearance, at the beginning of the seventeenth century, of what John Donne called the "new philosophy" and more especially until the rise of "classical economics" with Adam Smith, it was taken for granted that philosophers and artists should be concerned in their labors with truth and beauty in relation to man's welfare as a whole. While it was no less true then than now that philosophers and artists had to be fed, clothed, and housed by the manual labor of other persons, it never occurred to anyone to measure their contribution to society in terms of the money they received for their products. Only in recent times, and especially in the United States, has it come to be sometimes assumed that economics is

---

[14] See above, chap. 3.

not simply the science of wealth but that the standards set up by economists are applicable to all aspects of life, including philosophy, art, and politics. So we get, occasionally, the novel doctrine that the work of the poet, the painter, and the musician can properly be judged by the extent that they stimulate the business administrator to arrange land, labor, and capital in such ways as to provide a larger output. Or, much more frequently, we get the hardly less novel doctrine that they can be judged by the extent that they provide work for ushers, bookbinders, publishers, art dealers, and motion-picture officials. Instead of being led by the artist, the artist's public (through the often unrepresentative agents who manage entertainment and art, and confuse the two to the great damage of art) has come to insist that the artist be led by persons whose purpose is almost exclusively the making or the spending of money.

A historian of civilization who considers the history of art in relation to wealth is in a position to reach certain tentative conclusions. The late Geoffrey Scott has explained the relationship very well. In *The Architecture of Humanism* he wrote, "Prosperity is a condition of great achievements [in architecture]; it is not their cause. . . . Rich and flourishing societies have not seldom grown up, and are growing up in our time, without [making architectural history]. . . . "[15] The same thing is true of art generally, as our short excursion into its history suggests. Circumstances which increase the command over nature possessed by any great society are generally favorable to art, insofar as they free men from the necessity of working to provide for the material side of life. Whether or not this freedom is used for purposes likely to lead to beauty depends on the maintenance of a proper balance between the desires of the body and the needs of the mind and spirit.

[15] Geoffrey Scott, *The Architecture of Humanism* (2d ed.; New York, 1924), p. 26.

Insofar as art is made a servant to the material wants of society, it ceases to be art.

It is fortifying to find that these conclusions, reached from a study of history, agree with the view of one of the wisest men who ever lived. "There seem to be two causes of the deterioration of the arts," Socrates tells Adeimantus in *The Republic*. "What are they?" he is asked. "Wealth," he says, "and poverty."[16]

III. *Art and Civilization*

Archdeacon Cunningham, one of the fathers of economic history, remarked that the Parthenon was sheer waste from the standpoint of the economist. While a large number of workers, craftsmen, and artists were once employed in its construction, this temple and all the other public works built on the initiative of Pericles were unproductive. Athenian treasure "was locked up in forms that are artistically superb, but economically worthless."[17] The same thing could be said of the Gothic cathedrals and of all edifices, which, unlike homes, factories, shops, and banks, are not lived in or used for purposes of production, commerce, or finance. Since the object of all genuine art must be to appeal to the mind and the heart, it follows that art (together with religion, philosophy, and knowledge generally insofar as it is disinterested) is bound to remain largely parasitic in Cunningham's sense.[18] If the concepts and the precepts of economics are extended to cover the creative labor of the artist, or its products, they enter a

[16] *The Republic* iv. 421 (Jowett trans.).

[17] W. Cunningham, *An Essay on Western Civilization in Its Economic Aspects* (Cambridge, 1898), pp. 119–21.

[18] I am aware that there are modern economists—notably Professor Frank Knight and his school—who do not expound the kind of economic doctrines reflected in Dr. Cunningham's remarks. His view of what is economically productive is widely accepted nonetheless, especially in popular thinking in the United States.

realm in which they have properly no place, and in which they are bound to do harm. What is essential to the artist is a world of his own. That does not mean that art should be divorced from life. It does not mean art for art's sake. It does mean art for the sake of man, not for the sake of those perfectly legitimate, but incomplete, sides of man's aspirations that he has in common with the animals. To the extent that truth, beauty, and justice permeate the animal side of man, he is always fortified. To the extent that the animal side of man dominates the human, he is always weakened.

If civilization is to survive, or if it is to be revived in the future, it is essential that the mind and the heart should lead, not follow. It is essential that art, and also religion and philosophy, should be independent of material ends. The ends of religion and philosophy can be materialistic only insofar as a better body contributes to a better mind and a more honorable spirit. What gave the Christian religion much of its force was the view that it is necessary to do right whether or not it pays. Honesty can never be made a matter of policy without a loss to honesty. If material reward comes with doing right, that is always a cause for rejoicing, but it is the duty of society to see to it that material reward conforms to right and not right to material reward.

Like virtue, beauty rests on the belief—frequently held in sophisticated societies—that it is possible for man, with his mind, or with his hands at the service of his mind, to create a world better and more beautiful than the actual world in which he lives. That need is present to a greater or lesser degree in all men. It does not disappear with the increase in material wealth. However rich human beings become in worldly goods, their experience here on earth will always remain incomplete, if not unhappy. Nothing is more depressing, and even tragic, in modern America than the efforts made by men and women to prolong their childhood and to drug themselves by television and other forms of entertainment into a denial of old age and suffering. The inevitable result is to unfit them for life, to unfit them to defend even the material civilization, for which they often express such enthusiasm. Pascal once wrote that it is the knowledge of his sufferings, of his unhappiness, that distinguishes man from the animals. That is why true art, even comedy, is always basically sad. When Count Almaviva asks Figaro, "Qui t'a donné une philosophie aussi gaie?" he answers, "L'habitude du malheur. Je me presse de rire de tout, de peur d'être obligé d'en pleurer."[19] It is the unsatisfied aspect of man's nature, the needs of his spirit, and not his capacity to produce more wealth with the help of science and technology that constitute his highest claim to dignity. The reason great poems and great novels are almost always sad, as well as beautiful, is because the human experience falls short of the vision of it granted to the poet and the novelist. If human experience does not fall short of a man's vision of it, he is not an artist. That is why men squeeze art out of a society when they succeed in making the artist conform to the wishes of men whose vision is limited to material ends. The utility of art, as distinguished from production, is that by helping us to rise above our fate it prepares us to meet it. While it is good to keep the body young as long as we can, this is only of great value if the heart also stays young. As Lord Sankey, the distinguished English judge, once suggested, what the Greeks meant when they said "whom the gods love die young," was that the good die young in mind and spirit whatever their age.

The partial opposition between the ends of art and the ends of production can be seen in striking relief in connection with architecture.[20] When he saw Monticello, a French marquis remarked that Jefferson was "the first American who had con-

---

[19] "Accustomed to Misfortunes, I laugh at every Event, lest on consideration I should find myself more disposed to cry" (*The Barber of Seville*, Act I, scene 2).

[20] See above, chap. 3 (I).

sulted the fine arts to know how he should shelter himself from the weather." Jefferson's example has not been widely followed, though the achievements of some American architects—notably the late Louis Sullivan—in solving, with the help of the fine arts, engineering problems raised by the skyscraper have been important. To be great, the architect, like all artists, has beyond a certain point to proceed according to principles of his own, which are not determined by economic ends or even by technical rules relating to the materials he uses or the problems of support. These principles can never be precisely stated, for they arise out of the inner necessity for the architect to solve particular problems as they present themselves. The problems are invariably new and individual, as in all the arts. What is indispensable is that, as the problems arise, the artist or architect should be free to solve them according to the demands of art rather than according to the demands of mechanics or comfort. If the requirements for heat and refrigeration, for gadgets and material conveniences of all kinds, or for large profits take precedence over the requirements of beauty in the construction of a building, architecture is bound to suffer. Similar conflicts present themselves in the other arts as a result of the attempts to commercialize them.

How can these conflicts be satisfactorily solved? They can be solved only by admitting that there has to be a distinction between economic ends and artistic ends and by providing, as many far less wealthy societies of the past have done, the means to enable art, philosophy, and religion to be cultivated for the good of man, rather than exclusively for the sake of those aspects of man's instincts which he shares with the animals. It is not suggested that there is anything wrong with these instincts or that they should be suppressed. But they should not be allowed to devour art, as they are tending to do at present. Instead, art should be given a place of its own, where it can sweeten and embellish life.

There is a widespread feeling in the United States that material progress is threatened by any activity which has not as its objective an increase in material wealth, by any activity which does not yield a return in money. It is questionable whether this materialistic attitude, by depriving the mind and the heart of that sustenance once supplied—however imperfectly—by religion and by the reading of good books, has not weakened the moral fiber of our people to a point where they are incapable of defending even the material civilization that our ancestors have built up. While we put a special store upon material things, we are more prodigal of them than any people of the past. We are ready to waste everything save time. Every waking moment must be filled, no matter how. Americans are submerged by hastily devised radio and television programs and motion pictures, by drives on behalf of good causes, by fund-raising dinners, by teas and cocktail parties. These provide them with a world of make-believe and artificial excitement, until many of them are so drugged with unreality that they are no more capable of a genuine human experience than a person saturated with morphine. For the trained intellect, time is the one thing that can be wasted fruitfully. The mind has sometimes to lie fallow if it is to achieve the full fertility of which it is capable.

The choice before us is not between the cultivation of art and the promotion of a higher material standard of life. The material sacrifice we shall have to make in order to cultivate genuine art is small. Art depends upon quality, not upon quantity. There is no danger that all men, or even a large minority, will become artists. Nor is there any danger that the artist, like the despot, will aim to dominate the world. The artistic success of the artist is never at someone else's expense.

All the costs required for endowing genuine art and allowing it to flourish, regardless of its capacity to please the dealers in art, would be more than covered by the enormous waste which takes place in the United States. The difficulty is that modern Americans are disposed to think with disapproval of everything that does not command a market and with approval of everything that does, even if to the uninitiated it seems to perform no useful function. Many Americans apparently see less waste in the action of a housewife, who throws a large part of the food she buys at the local retail store into an incinerator, than in the labors of an artist, who writes a work of creative literature that represents a contribution to human understanding but does not sell. I recently listened to a discussion among a number of learned economists dealing with waste. They brought up the fictitious case of a farmer who made his living, not by tilling the soil, but by hauling out automobiles which skidded into the ditch beside a road near his house. To improve business he kept the road muddy by watering it every night. Was this waste? The candidate for the doctor's degree in economics, who handled himself better than most other candidates I have known, was at a loss to explain why it was waste. If he and other American students of economics were less heavily committed than they are to the notion that value is related altogether to services for which the public will pay, they might feel tolerant toward the creative artist whose works do not happen to please the publisher or the dealer or to lend themselves readily to advertisement.

As Milton's experience suggests, great artists seldom prosper in their formative years by the sale of their works in the public market. The idea that it is easier now than in the past to train a large portion of the population in genuine artistic discernment is illusory. In many ways it is much more difficult. The encroachments of the methods of business and the ways of thought associated with business upon the administration, the teaching, and the research in colleges, universities, churches, and schools for art have left little or no place for the cultivation of artistic values. The multiplication of machines and conveniences has done more to dull than to sharpen the natural impulses of men to appreciate and to understand true works of art. The need for making commodities individually, with the hands, teaches good craftsmanship, an essential element in art. As this need has diminished, the understanding of craftsmanship has diminished. Even the widespread distribution of works of art, made possible by mechanical improvement, has contributed, in some ways, to the deterioration of delight. It has reduced, for example, the number of persons who participate in music and the attention which listeners pay to it. A century ago Eugène Delacroix, the distinguished French painter, suggested that the physical effort of going out to a concert and finding a seat among others who had made the same effort enhanced the charm and the meaning of great music. After hearing Beethoven's pastoral symphony in a large auditorium one Sunday afternoon, he noted in his diary that he would not have had so rich an experience if the orchestra had played for him in his studio while he reclined on his couch.[21] If he had lived to listen to the phonograph, or to radio concerts introduced by an advertiser of cigarettes and sandwiched between the hasty remarks of a news commentator and the hasty account of a prize fight, he would hardly have changed his mind.

As the work of musicians, painters, and writers has got into the hands of dealers and promoters, there would seem to be only one way to foster true art. It is to provide the few who have inherited a sense of the great artistic traditions of the past with the opportunity to build on these traditions and to cultivate the arts without debasing them. All great movements in human history have had small beginnings. They have been the work of a handful of indomitable men with firm convictions. That is true of art as well as of politics. It will be true in the future as it has been in the past.

IV. *The Future of Civilization*

If there is truth in our analysis of the relation of wealth to art and of art to civilization, it is the tendency we observe in modern Europe and America to deny the need of man for a

[21] *Journal de Eugène Delacroix*, ed. André Joubin (Paris, 1932), I, 275–76.

more perfect experience than physical life can give him that largely explains the meagerness of our recent artistic and cultural history, in spite of our tremendous wealth. The situation with respect to art is similar to that with respect to religion and to moral philosophy. Whether Americans like it or not, the United States is faced with a choice of ends. We can continue to regard it as the main objective of private and public life to make ourselves and the public rich in material goods. Or we can regard material wealth as a means, important for the contribution it makes to physical health and to the sense of well-being but valuable ultimately only insofar as, through the improvement of physical health and comfort, it contributes to the dignity of man—only insofar as it increases the esteem in which faith, righteousness, wisdom, and beauty are held by our people. If we follow the latter course we shall have to find an honorable place for genuine religious leaders, for true philosophers, and for true artists—if and when they appear. We shall have to make conditions more favorable to their appearance than they are at present. We shall have to accord them an influence in the life of the United States. This does not mean that they should be granted large material rewards. It does mean that the present disposition to judge every man by his income, by the administrative position he holds, or by the publicity he receives cannot prevail. In place of those standards, there will have to be a revival in a new form of the standards associated with the teachings of Christ and the greatest philosophers and artists of history.

Various objections can legitimately be raised to making faith, righteousness, wisdom, and beauty ends of civilization. It can be said, for example, that Americans prefer to go on with "their way of life," directing all their professional energies exclusively to the advance of their private fortunes, to the further progress of natural science, to an increase in physical comforts, to reaching for the moon. They prefer to go on devoting all their leisure time to entertainment, to dabbling in painting, music, and poetry, and to absorbing bits of information here and there, presented in forms which frequently resemble boxes of assorted cigars.

In his recollections, the Pennsylvania Quaker, Logan Pearsall Smith, Berenson's brother-in-law, wrote about a letter he received in 1921 from a person whom he calls "the wisest man I know." Having lived the life of an American *émigré* in Europe in the age of James and Wharton, Smith had been obliged by his need for an operation to return for a brief stay in the United States. He was concerned to find that America then accorded little place to "culture." His friend agreed that there was little room in the United States for the "mind," which, he said, "in our lips means, I suppose, the liberal or aristocratic life, the mind turned to pure reflection and pure expression and pure pleasure. But why," he added, "need all the tribes of men sacrifice at our altar?"[22]

The way in which the mind was defined betrays the weakness of the tradition in these men's hands. "One thing is certain," writes Roger Hinks, "great art is never a feat of escapist virtuosity."[23] With Smith and his friend, art and thought were divorced from life; they had become mere decorations, pleasant but unessential.[24] Their potentialities for good had been forgotten.

A similar attitude in relation to learning is widespread in the American universities. When I was an undergraduate at Harvard, I listened to a conversation between two graduate students preparing for the doctor's degree in philosophy. One expressed concern to the other. He was thinking seriously of abandoning his studies. "I can't see any earthly use for this subject," he said. The other student, who was somewhat older and who later became a prominent and influential "intellectual,"

[22] *Unforgotten Years* (Boston, 1939), pp. 283–84.

[23] *The Criterion*, XVIII, No. 70 (1938), 68.

[24] Cf. R. H. Tawney, *Equality* (3d ed.; London, 1938), pp. 77–82; Arthur Clutton-Brock, *The Ultimate Belief* (New York, 1916), pp. 102–3 and *passim*.

reassured him by telling him, "it hasn't any use." Once he had divested himself of the "prejudice" that learning should have a purpose, the younger student, like the older one, felt free to devote his life to it as a sort of pleasant game, demanding rather more skill and time than bridge, crossword puzzles, or even chess.

Both these students of philosophy and Smith's friend were under the influence of Francis Bacon and his successors, who see no use in any thought unless it contributes directly to physical health or to wealth.[25] If the "intellectual" had meant that the search for truth is an end in itself, he would have been in agreement with the greatest philosophers; but what he apparently meant, and what others hearing him would certainly assume that he meant, is that it is a matter of indifference to mankind whether philosophy is cultivated or not. As Tolstoy pointed out, art in modern times (like philosophy) has become more and more escapist and obscure, more and more a hothouse plant. So Smith and his friend assumed that art must be inevitably escapist and obscure, that for a wholesome democratic society it must remain parasitic.

Yet, even if we recognize that great art and philosophy must not be confused with feats of escapist virtuosity, even if we recognize that they are of benefit to mankind, the question remains, "Why need all the tribes of men sacrifice at the altar of the mind?" Our answer must be that there is no such obligation. We cannot force men to cultivate the mind and spirit. That is not what philosophers mean when they speak of permanent values. They mean that the mind and spirit exist and have a need for these values.

The American people have a right to choose their destiny. But they should know what they are doing. They should not imagine they are now cultivating the intellect. That is make-believe. They should frankly admit they are trying the ex-

[25] Cf. Nef, "L'Universalité française," *The French Review*, XXIX, No. 5 (1956), 383–88.

periment of starving the intellect by denying that it has needs
of its own independent of man's physical wants and desires.
While excellent things in themselves, scientific observations
and experiments do not by themselves, and without the help
of philosophy and art, insure the future of the mind. Still less
does the widespread dissemination of information by the newspaper and the radio contribute, by itself, to the intelligence
of the population. As long as the mind is treated as a sponge
it does not increase its powers. It is only by exertion directed
toward concrete objectives that the mind can increase its
powers.

No one has the authority, no one should have the authority,
to prevent the United States from attempting to build a society for the future in which there is no place for the trained,
independent, disinterested mind. But it is to be hoped that if
the attempt is made, it will be recognized that no society in
the past has discarded the intellect and retained even its material civilization for any great length of time. The Romans
tried it after the second century A.D., after the time of Juvenal,
Galen, and Lucian. There is now general agreement among
historians that material welfare in the empire began to decline
in Italy early in the third century and in most of the provinces
by the end of the third or the beginning of the fourth century. It does not follow, of course, that the disintegration of
the intellect was an important cause for the economic decline
of the empire. We cannot be certain that if the Romans had
cultivated the intellect classical civilization would have flowered anew. But the historical evidence, for what it is worth,
does not support the view that our present treatment of the
human mind and heart in the United States offers a highroad
to the progress which most Americans believe in almost as an
article of faith. Americans are fond of claiming that they have
a special willingness to experiment. They should recognize
that the experiment of discarding the intellect has been made
by earlier societies. It is the experiment of cultivating it after

the symptoms of disintegration have appeared that would be new.[26]

The United States has open to it the possibility of leading the peoples of the world—who have become so much more numerous and so much more interdependent than ever before —into the Promised Land. One price of making the attempt— and no doubt it is a high price—is to become a partner of these other peoples. To become a partner the United States needs to give up both its superiority complex and its inferiority complex and to cultivate among its citizens a world-mindedness which is rare today.

In recent decades American example in the realm of economic growth has had an enormous influence among other peoples. The economy of abundance, in which the leader is now the United States, with its cheaper methods of manufacturing, transport, and distribution, its packaged foods and bottled drinks, its smart ready-made women's clothing, its readers' digests and its films, seems to be now congenial to many countries. These and many other cheap conveniences— such as short cuts to education and time-fillers—have spread to the ends of the earth.

Many precedents exist for extensive American initiative. It can hardly be only cheap utilities and cheap methods of producing them which would interest the British Commonwealth, Europe, South and Central America, Africa, the Near and Far East. If the United States were to excel in philosophy and the arts, the country might help to provide the moral example, the prospects for a full life, after which elements of humanity in every land are hungering.

Since the mid-nineteenth century, for the first time in history, an economy of abundance (in the establishment of which European countries shared) has replaced in many parts of this

[26] Cf. A. J. Toynbee, *A Study of History* (London, 1939), IV, 38–39.

planet economies of scarcity which formerly prevailed everywhere, among large societies as well as among primitive peoples. This quantitative progress went hand in hand with serious and partly successful efforts to open doors to the underprivileged, doors not only to better health but to justice, which had always been shut in earlier societies. Serious and partly successful efforts were made to reform the laws, the courts, and the prisons, so as to diminish, even to abolish, special privileges for the rich and powerful, to provide equal economic, political, and educational opportunities for all. These achievements are immense. The United States has played a big part in each. It has been the leader in some.

The outstanding weaknesses have consisted in failures to cultivate, or even to maintain, the values attaching to civilization—as that had been created from the sixteenth through the eighteenth centuries—civilization which provided foundations for the triumph of industrialism. The high ideals, the tender manners, and the discrimination achieved among a numerous few in many countries have been watered down or have ceased to count as they once did in connection with political and cultural leadership. Craftsmanship and peasant ownership, which offered large numbers of people interesting and varied physical work, have largely disappeared. The cheap and vulgar, which were always plentiful, have in recent decades acquired a standing which they were denied by our ancestors through most of the nineteenth century. The cheap and vulgar, even the shady, possess sanctions they formerly lacked. Public relations firms have appeared as dealers in prestige. Espionage of divers kinds has become more pervasive than ever before, equipped as it is with new and more refined means of eavesdropping and of framing the innocent. Public and private spying and the assassination of character have acquired a *respectability* that was largely withheld from them during the nineteenth century and even during the eighteenth. In sum, the new plenty has been too often tarnished by the manner in which it is obtained and the manner in which it is distributed. The multiplication of wealth has not been used, to the extent which was hoped, "to give form and substance to virtue" and so to strengthen civilization.

It is not enough to offer the many a higher material standard of life. Those who are capable of it need opportunities to live *better* lives than their ancestors. Longer survival, even on terms of more affluent consumption, can become a great comfort, even for those who appreciate it, only if it serves as means toward the attainment of inspiring goals. Opportunities to excel in serving higher ends than those of the self could alone fulfill the needs of those who deserve to survive. A smaller proportion of the vastly increased Western population has this opportunity now than was the case during the eighteenth and nineteenth centuries. The riches of the mind and heart have not kept pace with the comforts offered the body.

If the United States is to serve civilization, if it is to provide leadership to which the best elements among all the peoples of the world can respond—whatever their color, whatever their national and political allegiances—the riches of the mind and heart will have to be cultivated as never before. The values with which Part Two of this book has been concerned suggest goals toward which the mind and heart can bend. The best elements in the United States need to serve these goals in company with the best elements in other nations, some of which have a better foundation for such dedication than we have.

If the United States is to help all peoples of the world find the way toward an enduring universal community, in which creative, local diversities are respected and encouraged, it will not be by cultivating either materialism or military despotism. Those are ancient conceptions. Where they lead ought to be obvious. Is it illogical to suggest that the hope for a new form of society, that the hope for civilization, lies in refusing to be bound by past experience and in cultivating the aims of life defined for us by faith, by moral philosophy, and by art, with the help of the enormous material wealth and leisure with which we are endowed? These aims alone can provide the guidance that is so sorely needed when mankind has lost its compasses and its rudders. The late Thorstein Veblen once suggested that the Western peoples are not naturally adapted, physically or spiritually, to the mechanized industry and the mechanical civilization which have now taken possession of them.[27] If he is right, it may be possible for us to turn away from our present ways of thinking and behaving more readily than we suppose. Struggle and labor, inspired by the drive and hope that are human, are what created civilization. It is only by making a superhuman effort to establish on a world stage a new and better form of society that the hopes of our European and American ancestors could be renewed and could provide a rallying ground for all the peoples of the earth.

A word of caution is necessary before turning, in the next and final part of this book, to possible means of working toward those ends with which this second part has been concerned. In considering the civilization in which eighteenth-century Europeans and Americans took pride, stress was laid on the importance of limits, of the right refusals, for the attainment of beauty. It may seem that the quest upon which we are now embarking does not take account of the restrictions which are imposed on all utopian aspirations by the limitations of human nature.

Men and women are not angels. It is necessary to recognize the prevalence of evil among them and to beware of the free rein again given to evil during the twentieth century. It is not only brutalities and cruelties of naziism, fascism, and communism which stare us in the face. We have only to go to the cinema, to look at the television screen, to read the stories and look at the photographs printed in many newspapers and in

[27] *The Instinct of Workmanship* (New York, 1914), esp. pp. 320–21.

innumerable magazines and books, to recognize the pervasive appeal of lust and violence as *selling* counters nearer home.

Such aberrations are so prominent that it has become almost unfashionable to regard them as deviations. Violence is no doubt inherent in our nature. Before the world wars of this century, Nietzsche said the German people found in war the opportunity they sought to commit suicide with a good conscience.[28] In this propensity toward self-destruction, the Germans were representative of an aspect of human nature. That makes it easy for some to conclude that the human being is basically a destroyer. Doesn't he like to hate? Doesn't he take pleasure in killing and in being killed, in taking his own life? many are inclined to ask. If the answers are affirmative, what hope is there in trying to build civilization, now that for the first time in history, as the result of the progress of the sciences, humans have the means of satisfying their inclinations for destruction—with ten tons of TNT available for each of the three billion inhabitants of the globe?

The questions one is bound to ask, in the present plight of humanity, are these: Are hatred and violence the greatest forces in human nature? Is it necessary to satisfy them by total nuclear slaughter?

There is certainly another yearning, another passion, besides hate basic to human nature. It is love. Perhaps loving is a form of madness, like hating. But unless love is defiled, its expression can never be cruel. It must be tender. Therefore the great hope for humanity in the nuclear age would seem to rest with choosing the right madness.

Love is not abstract. To be an effective force, it has to be tangible. When love is strong, we love individuals in particular, above all one particular individual. We love particular pursuits, above all one particular pursuit. The opportunities which might lead mankind back from the brink it is approach-

[28] Nef, *Western Civilization since the Renaissance* (New York, 1963), p. 409.

ing are the opportunities for constructive love. Loving another is not conducive to destroying the human race to which the loved one belongs. Loving one's work is not conducive to the destruction of the creative process of which humans alone possess the secret.

An awareness of the universality of imperfection is as necessary to love, and to the civilization love might nurse into existence, as the vision of perfection that inspires love. There is a great danger for civilization in the perfectionism which makes an unreal fetish of life without conflicts and sorrows and hard work. In the long book, *Citadelle*, which Saint-Exupéry had not finished when he set out on his last air mission in the Second World War, he wrote a passage which explains this danger and offers a way of meeting it.

Don't invent an empire where all is perfect. Good taste is the virtue of caretakers in museums. If you abolish bad taste, you'll have neither paintings nor dances, neither palaces nor gardens. In your desire to eschew dust and sweat and earthiness, in your fear of bad taste, you'll enthrone distaste. The emptiness of your perfection will deprive you of all that arouses enthusiasm for living.

Instead of inventing an empire where all is perfect, invent one where all is fervent.[29]

Fervor in the cause of love, fervor on behalf of faith, virtue, and beauty, fervor on behalf of the relative peace without which these ends cannot be served, could help humankind to build a Citadel.

[29] A. de Saint-Exupéry, *Les Oeuvres complètes* (Paris, 1950), p. 468.

Part Three

Means of Approach

> *The enemy of man is not germs, but man himself,*
> *his pride, his prejudices, his stupidity, his arrogance.*
> *No class is immune, no system holds a panacea. . . .*
> *Nothing can bring about a better world but our own*
> *desire for it.*
>
> Henry Miller, THE COLOSSUS OF MAROUSI

9 Education

The final end of civilization is to cultivate truth, virtue, and beauty of and for themselves—or, to put it more correctly, for the sake of man, who alone among the creatures of the earth has discovered them. When we say "of and for themselves," we mean that these objects of civilized existence belong to humanity, not to anyone as an individual. The measure of an individual's grasp on them is his capacity to rise out of himself, to think and act on behalf of one or another of these objectives, not for the sake of something else, not for the sake of worldly honors, but as an ultimate end. For human beings, the end is in the striving. No man or woman is capable of achieving the perfection embodied in each of these three goals. Labor toward these goals, unlike labor for the sake of amassing riches or fame, is not subject to diminishing returns, except in the sense that the flesh is always weak, so that men require rest to recuperate from their work. In the pursuit of such ends the rest itself is creative. One begins the ascent anew, not all over again from the valley, but from the point on the mountain where one stopped the day before. The higher one is able to ascend, the more wonderful the quest becomes. It is as if one were drawn upward by the sun, whose rays illuminate each day new features of a distant landscape.

Truth, virtue, and beauty are separate and distinct from each other. Each is an end in itself. The individual can seldom pursue them all with equal intensity. The good society must not lay predominant emphasis on any one at the expense of the others. But as ends for mankind they are never in conflict in the same way that the pursuit of worldly profit, or of sensuous enjoyment, can come into fundamental conflict with the search for truth, virtue, and beauty. The ideal state would be one in which the material aspects of life, together with the search for new scientific knowledge and improved technique, were so ordered as to provide for the cultivation of morality, intelligence, and beauty to the maximum degree possible, in the lives of the people generally, as well as in those of the prophets, philosophers, poets, and other artists who help to show the way.

In modern industrialized civilization, how can mankind be guided in the direction of the ideal state? The miraculous world which man's mind has been able to create—a world with infinite possibilities—seems to be irreconcilable with the finite, limited world of narrow human beings and the bounded territory of the earth.

> Un matin nous partons, le cerveau plein de flamme,
> Le coeur gros de rancune et de désirs amers,
> Et nous allons, suivant le rythme de la lame,
> Berçant notre infini sur le fini des mers.[1]

How can we purify ourselves of the rancor and bitterness of which Baudelaire speaks? How can we enlarge the finite world of land and ocean in the direction of the infinite world that, as Baudelaire tells us in his opening lines, a little child is sometimes given to see in a flash in his growing mind.

> Pour l'enfant, amoureux de cartes et d'estampes,
> L'univers est égal à son vaste appétit.

Like many poets before him, Baudelaire saw no solution on this earth for the overwhelming problem of reconciling man's vision with the actuality. What could be done toward its solution cannot be done quickly. Men can make suggestions; they cannot bring forward confidently bills that must be enacted. Any specific proposals that are put forward should be put forward tentatively, with great humility. If better schemes are

[1] Charles Baudelaire, "Le Voyage," *Les Fleurs du mal,* ed. Camille Vergniol (Paris, n.d.), p. 242.

offered, the earlier schemes should be withdrawn. It should not be our object to oppose all specific programs of reform suggested by persons who, in these days of intellectual and moral confusion, deny that there are general principles upon which men can agree or ought to agree. Men seek the good in different ways, and no man can feel certain that his own plans, if adopted, would actually bring about the results for which he hopes.

For none of the suggestions which follow is originality claimed. If one of them should prove helpful, the thought spent on them would be rewarded a thousandfold. The object of setting forth some rough "means of approach" is not so much to try to remake our institutions according to a fixed pattern as to suggest the overwhelming need for all men of good will, and particularly for persons who rise to places of influence or power, to live, to speak, to write, and to act in the light of two considerations. The first is that the United States, together with all other countries in the throes of industrialism, is at a turning point in history, where an emphasis on material objectives for their own sake is likely to drag us into an abyss. The second, which follows both from the first and from an examination of the past wisdom of the human race, is that the object of every proposal for improvement should be judged by the contribution it would make to truth, virtue, and beauty.

If we are to work toward these ultimate ends of civilized existence, it may be desirable to make over, bit by bit, the whole educational system of the United States, by strengthening and developing all the good elements which this system contains. But schools, colleges, and universities can never be independent of the society in which they grow up. To paraphrase Pascal:

A good society is formed by education; a good society is spoiled by education. Thus a good education will form, and a bad education will spoil, a good society. It is therefore essential to know how to choose in order to form and not to spoil a good society;

and one cannot make the right choice unless the good society is already formed and not spoiled. A vicious circle exists, and the society and education that can escape from it are fortunate indeed.[2]

The remaking of our education depends evidently upon the remaking of our society, just as the remaking of our society depends upon the remaking of our education. It is less the duty of education to train students to fit into the present environment than to show how the environment might be made fit for true education. Education should serve our people, but at the same time it should be recognized that the best way to serve them is to show them, through leadership, how they can serve humanity. So some of the members of educational institutions have a twofold obligation. They have the obligation to reform themselves and, if possible, their institutions in accordance with the ends of a good society, and they have the further obligation to show the persons engaged in economic, political, and social work the ways of reform that would lead toward the good society. The relation of the great majority of citizens, as well as teachers, to these reforms would consist in learning to distinguish good proposals from bad, and in rising above habit and prejudice when either obstructs the good.

It is the duty of education to inculcate in the young a love of those ends of civilization which raise mankind above the beasts. No one in this century has defined that objective more nobly than the late Sir Arthur Clutton-Brock. He wrote:

Education ought to teach us how to be in love always and what to be in love with. The great things of history have been done by the great lovers, by the saints and men of science and artists; and the problem of civilization is to give every man a chance of being a saint, a man of science, or an artist. But this problem cannot be attempted, much less solved, unless men desire to be saints, men of science, and artists, and if they are to desire that continuously and consciously, they must be taught what it means to be these things.[3]

2 "Pensées sur l'esprit," *Les Pensées*, ed. Adolphe Espiard (Paris, n.d.), I, 60.

3 *The Ultimate Belief* (New York, 1916), p. 123. As the position that I take in my book is in agreement with Clutton-Brock's, I should perhaps explain

The remaking of our educational system is the task not only of university faculties but of all persons who train the young. If the parents, the clergymen, the elementary-school teachers, and the teachers in the high schools and colleges fail to do their duty, there is little hope that the university professor can do his, because the number of persons who can be redeemed after the age at which they enter the university is exceedingly small. But the universities should define the nature of the duty. They should show the advantages of leadership by taking the lead. It is for them to break out from the circular course along which education and society, locked together, are rotating, in order to save industrial civilization from what might become a downward spiral.

1. *The Higher Learning*

After almost two centuries as a nation, the United States has not managed to establish any very firm artistic or intellectual tradition. That is partly the result of the failure of Americans as a people to husband and encourage such artistic and intellectual strength as they possess. When one reads the books and letters of earlier generations, one comes occasionally upon obscure persons whose thought on the basic matters of religion, moral philosophy, and art is in essential agreement with that of the wisest, the noblest, and the most artistically inspired men of the past. These persons form scattered specks on the landscape of American nineteenth-century history. Their judgment was instinctively good. Their writing had promise. Except in a few cases, their names are not found in books on American history. Few even got into those large volumes that purport to give brief biographies of everybody who is any-

---

that I came on his essay only after I had written mine! In its revision, I have been helped considerably by his. I have discussed in another place the contention that what is said by thinkers and teachers on behalf of these ultimate and abstract values does nothing to improve matters ("Philosophical Values and American Learning," *Review of Politics*, IV, No. 3 [1942], 257–70).

body. We meet them when we delve into the histories of families, where the public scale of values does not apply and where some fair thought has been rescued by fond relatives from the complete oblivion to which the American scene has consigned its authors. Yet, with a small number of exceptions, the thought and judgment of the Americans who have become what is called "prominent" are less elevated and discriminating, their style is less competent, than the thought and judgment and style of these obscure persons.

So also one occasionally meets today, here and there, men and women with views on religion, philosophy, and art which, if encouraged, might contribute to the formation of genuine intellectual and artistic traditions in the United States. As might be expected from the collapse of standards outside the sciences during the last seventy years, such persons get no more encouragement now than others like them got a century and a half ago when Americans were absorbed in conquering the western wilderness. So dispersed are these incipient thinkers and artists that they seldom know of each other's existence. When they do, the extreme localism in affairs of the mind that has prevailed on this continent hinders them from directing their impulses toward that measure of common understanding which would be to the advantage of civilized living.

They seldom find a way of making a livelihood by their activities without compromising their views or sacrificing their integrity. Even if they are financially independent, they are rarely made of stern enough stuff to face the disapproval which an uncompromising stand would involve. So they lose the confidence which the ideas they hold, if developed and enriched, would give them. As they are brought up by their companions, and usually by their parents and teachers, to suppose that nothing has value unless it can be sold or can obtain for its possessor publicity or a substantial post of some sort, they soon abandon their instincts for a more respectable career. If they have regrets, they take them out by grousing with their companions at lunch at the club, with their associates at a committee meeting, or amid the somewhat forced merriment that prevails at a cocktail party.

Is it undemocratic to give such persons an opportunity to husband what belongs less to them personally than to humanity? If we say that it is, then we exclude from democracy the very elements which alone are capable of ennobling man. Surely it was not the object of the founding fathers, of Thomas Jefferson, to have democracy lower the stature of man.

"The practice of science" is now more widespread than ever before in history. According to Professor Bronowski, it compels the practitioner "to form for himself a fundamental set of universal values."[4] Among them, one assumes, are a scrupulous honesty in the handling of evidence relating to all matters subject to material proof and the rigorously accurate statement of theories for which proofs are sought. Science has a profound educational value to humanity. It upholds the method of doubt, the salutary fear of error, the firm resolution to avoid it. The progress of the modern sciences and technologies, along with the progress of careful accounting and measurement in connection with every kind of commercial transaction, the spread of computers whose accuracy in recording is not subject to question, the insistence upon reliability in business and banking practices, have contributed much to integrity, at any rate in those public and private relationships which are subject to judicial control.

Yet, as Bronowski recognizes, the practice of science does not generate what he calls "the values of tenderness, of kindliness, of human intimacy and love." May not the want of these values have something to do with the weakness of science

[4] J. Bronowski, *Science and Human Values* (2d ed.; New York, 1965), p. xiii.

when it comes to those *moral standards* which, it has been suggested,[5] are among the foundations of civilization? May not the want of these values help to account for the disappointment which even scientists feel in their achievements which are now so widely acclaimed? "Although man has attained a power over nature such as he never before possessed," wrote the great physicist Maurice de Broglie, in 1954, "it is hardly possible to claim that moral standards have improved or even that they have not weakened. Has fanaticism diminished? Are not respect for the human personality and the ideal of liberty more grievously menaced than ever?"[6]

If the gentler values of which Bronowski speaks contribute to the virtue which Broglie missed, an important step in the direction of the better society we seek might be taken by nourishing them. They are related to the search for the good and the beautiful more than to the search for new scientific truths and to the solution of technological problems. Conditions need to be created, therefore, where the instincts toward tenderness, kindliness, human intimacy, and love can be fostered. How could the higher learning, at least indirectly, help to bring such conditions?

Since this book was first published twenty-five years ago, various academic initiatives taken within and without the universities have provided possibilities for that remaking of society on the basis of firm values which is inseparable from the remaking of education. These and other serious efforts at reform should make the most of the constructive traditions that have been handed down by universities across centuries of history. Largely, perhaps, as a result of their special concern, since the scientific revolution, with the new sciences, the American universities possess to some slight extent two elements indispensable in the cultivation of the intellect. One is

[5] See above, chap. 7

[6] Duc de Broglie, "Un grand physicien, Henri Poincaré," *France-Amérique Magazine*, Nos. 4–6 (1954), p. 89.

the tradition of careful, impartial inquiry. The other, closely allied to this, is the tradition of freedom of thought and speech.

Neither tradition is very effective in the universities today. As Veblen suggested, the impulse of scholars to seek new truth for its own sake has been more and more submerged by the adoption within the universities of the methods and outlook associated with business enterprise. "The training given by these two lines of endeavour—science and business—is wholly divergent. . . ." It follows from the encroachment of business practices on learning, he goes on to say, that "in many and devious ways . . . a university man may be able to serve the collective enterprise of his university to better effect than by an exclusive attention to the scholastic work on which alone he is ostensibly engaged." Yet, "in no field of human endeavour is competitive notoriety and a painstaking conformity to extraneous standards of living and of conduct so gratuitous a burden, since learning is in no degree a competitive enterprise; and all mandatory observance of the conventions—pecuniary or other—is necessarily a drag on the pursuit of knowledge."[7] Whatever the value of the business methods in their own sphere, they are, as Veblen says, a handicap to impartial inquiry and creative thought.

It is obvious, also, that in the universities and colleges the right to freedom of speech is sometimes abused. The justification for it is that it is essential to the cultivation of the intellect. Under the guise of defending freedom of speech, some university men waste time arguing about tenure and the rights of their members to indulge in propaganda that has no relation to the intellect. They have even been known to use freedom of speech as a cloak behind which "in many and devious ways" to carry on enterprises that have little or no scholarly purpose.

Nevertheless these two traditions, which are in the keeping

[7] Thorstein Veblen, *The Higher Learning in America* (New York, 1918), pp. 77, 165, 233.

first and foremost of the universities, are of great value. The problem is to make them count in relation to the whole life of our time, in a world that has been drawn into a material unity by the applications of the modern sciences without that merging of nations and races, which Chateaubriand thought possible, which has now quite possibly become a condition of human survival.[8]

From the Renaissance until the French Revolution, on the Continent of Europe, artists and writers depended for their livelihood mainly upon the patronage of kings, princes, and nobles. The great centers of art and creative life were the courts. The most brilliant and important in the seventeenth and eighteenth centuries was, of course, the famous French court of Versailles. Rich men, who owed their fortunes to finance, commerce, and industry, sometimes purchased works of art. But, until the nineteenth century, it was mainly in England and Holland that the middle class provided artists and writers with their livelihood and played a conspicuous part in the formation of taste. As Stendhal explained in the early nineteenth century, tremendous interrelated social and intellectual changes took place in France between 1785 and 1824. It became necessary for the writer to please an audience composed no longer mainly of courtiers and nobles but of bourgeois families living mostly in Paris, each with an income of from 10,000 to 100,000 francs a year.[9] In terms of our money this means roughly from $20,000 to $200,000. Rich burgesses in the provincial towns, like M. Bruyas of Montpellier, who patronized Courbet and Delacroix, also began to influence art.

With the growth of mass production and advertising, conditions changed again. Writers and artists, especially in the United States, have been placed at a far greater remove from

[8] See above, chap. 4 (IV). See also Nef (ed.), *Bridges of Human Understanding* (New York, 1964).

[9] Stendhal, *Racine et Shakespeare* (Edouard Champion ed.; Paris, 1925), I, 91; II, 168.

the public than they were in nineteenth-century Europe. The public which is expected to buy books and patronize art has less discernment and judgment of its own. Between the artist and his public, many kinds of middlemen have intervened. There are, for instance, dealers in art, publicity men, publishers, magazine editors, reviewers, members of museum staffs, etc. Such persons exercise a considerable influence in determining what the public shall see, hear, and read. But the decisions taken by many of these persons have little relation to either artistic or philosophical values, as these have been understood by past sages. Some of the critics are not much better equipped to judge values than the public. Even when they are, they nearly always have so much administrative work and talking to do that they cannot give their best attention to discrimination, which requires time for meditation. The publishing houses care less and less for true values. One of my older colleagues had been reading books on theology and religion for the same publishing house for half a century. He had been struck by the very great decline in the interest that his employers took in his judgment of the intrinsic merits of the works they submitted to him. Thus critics fall back, or are forced back, on other considerations than intellectual or artistic power. They consider, for example, in the case of a book or article, whether the subject has been recently treated, without seriously considering the value of the treatment in objective terms. They do not know that great art consists less in saying something for the first time than in saying something important better than it has ever been said before. They find it enough to ask such questions as these: Does the work contain sensational predictions, particularly concerning our economic future? Does it retail sensational stories concerning current events or contemporary persons made prominent by the newspaper, the radio, or television? The critics often find there is no place for some valuable article, in spite of its important message. They think the message well expressed, fundamental-

ly right. It is one of which Americans are in need. Such an
article could be published only in a serious magazine, they
remark, and there are virtually no serious magazines left.
There are, of course, the learned journals. But these are devoted exclusively to the results of research or to syntheses dealing with narrow fields. Even if a learned journal would take
the article, it is obviously intended for a general audience,
rather than for their small special groups of subscribers. The
persons capable of artistic and philosophical judgments are unable, for one reason or another, to exercise them, or, if they do,
they are denied by circumstances the opportunity to make
them count.

What is necessary to encourage art and creative thought and
to give them some influence in this country is freedom of inquiry for the artist and thinker, and an independence of sales,
an independence of most of the paraphernalia that has been
built up during the past fifty years for marketing books, pictures, musical compositions, and concerts. This paraphernalia
may well have a place in connection with entertainment. Entertainment is desirable in the well-ordered state, provided it is
not, as at present, confused and combined with art, to the
damage of art, and provided it is not, as at present, given time
and importance disproportionate to its value. The present confusion of art and thought with entertainment is submerging
both. It does not even contribute to wit!

It will now be apparent why the universities have an opportunity to cultivate art and thought. A few of them retain the
tradition of freedom of inquiry and at least remnants of the
equally important principle that there is no necessary connection between the value of new ideas or new works of art and
the publicity they obtain or the prices for which they are sold.
But universities and colleges have become so numerous, have
grown so big, have set up so many new specialized programs
of graduate study, are so expensive to operate and so entangled
in inconsequential and irrelevant, but time-consuming, affairs

of their localities, that the faculty and the students, under-graduates as well as graduates, fail to make the most of the traditions which are in their keeping. The unceasing fund-raising campaigns and the "development departments" which deal with fund-raising do little to help. They even give the impression that the importance of a university depends on the size of its budget.

It is hoped, therefore, that the experiments in the higher learning, started during the last generation, will do much to make the principles of free inquiry and of independence more effective, above all in the realms of thought and art. It is to be hoped that they will help to give body to "the values of tenderness, of kindliness, of human intimacy and love," in a world where the indulgence of motives of jealousy, enmity, and hatred on an international scale are luxuries that mankind can no longer afford.

II. *Experiments in Leadership*

Since the period surrounding the Second World War, the growing size and complexity of the university structure in all countries, and most of all in the United States, seemed to make the existing universities less and less promising settings for seminal thought and research. As a consequence, a considerable number of independent or semi-independent units of divers kinds have been formed to facilitate thought and research.

Paris and Oxford are historically perhaps the most celebrated university cities in the Western world, and the chief models for these new ventures in the higher learning seem to have been the Collège de France in Paris and All Souls College at Oxford. The first was founded more than four hundred years ago, in the reign of Francis I, as an institution separate from the University of Paris. The second, founded even earlier (in 1437), has always been part of the loose federation of col-

leges which forms Oxford University. During recent times the
raison d'être of both is to provide, in the interest of intellectual
discoveries, a limited number of exceptionally gifted persons
with freedom from the teaching, the administrative, and the
other routine obligations associated with universities. Neither
of the two institutions requires of its members any formal instruction, apart from the lectures all professors in the Collège
de France are expected to deliver each year, lectures open to
the general public. Neither confers degrees.

The influence of both can be discerned in the formation of
the new institutes, beginning in the United States with the
establishment late in the nineteen-thirties of the Institute for
Advanced Study at Princeton. It derived its original fame from
the secure retreat it provided for Einstein, obliged by the Nazi
tyranny to quit his native Germany. More recently other somewhat similar asylums have been founded for thinkers. In the
United States notable examples are the Center for the Study of
Democratic Institutions at Santa Barbara, California; the Center for Advanced Study in Behavioral Sciences at Palo Alto;
and the Center for Advanced Studies in the Liberal Arts at
Middletown, Connecticut, established on the margin of Wes-
leyan University.

A few distinguished and learned persons, some famous, have
been attached to these institutes permanently. A rather larger
number have been provided with a temporary retreat, charac-
teristically of a year's duration. During their sojourn, whether
it be long or short, they are relieved from the cares of earning
a living.

A remark attributed to the late Abraham Flexner, the chief
force in the formation of the Princeton Institute, may be apocryphal. It is nevertheless suggestive of an atmosphere which
pervades these centers. Flexner was asked by one of the scholars who had been invited to join the Institute for Advanced
Study what his principal responsibilities would be. "You have
none," came the ready answer. "You have only opportunities."

Freedom can be a great blessing. A substantial measure of freedom is indispensable for the flowering of a creative mind, as for all creative work and all creative love. But, given the human condition, absolute freedom is a mirage. Every person is a slave to something. To be a slave to freedom can become one of the worst forms of slavery, because it leaves one with nothing to serve.[10] The best freedom anyone can hope for is freedom to choose the right slavery and the most appropriate means of serving it.

The revolutionary changes of recent times have uprooted the great majority of people all over the world from old habits and conventions. The majority, the great majority of the younger generation, have been left without any sense of direction. Their great needs are for guidance in finding the right slavery and, in the interest of a more cosmopolitan outlook, for guidance in penetrating the barriers between subjects and peoples erected as a result of the ever more minute specialization and the increasing nationalism which have accompanied the conquest of the material world. Are these needs adequately met by institutes which offer only opportunities and which deny participation and partnership to the oncoming generation of students? Ought there not be a place also for institutes where freedom of inquiry is provided for persons with exceptional creative gifts who are seeking to transcend specialties through communion with other specialists and in company with exceptionally gifted students who are searching for the right slavery? Ought there not be a place where such students help reveal to all the world, in community with their older colleagues, the forms of freedom and restraint which are most promising for the future of humanity?

It was on the assumption that there *is* a place for centers of this kind that one was formed twenty-five years ago within the University of Chicago. The Committee on Social Thought is now a going concern. By its efforts, and by the example it

10 Cf. above, pp. 194–97.

provides for the establishment of other groups dedicated to similar purposes, it can offer leadership for the remaking of education and the remaking of society.

The Committee on Social Thought seems to be the first completely interdisciplinary department in any university. It offers its faculty and students exceptional facilities to pursue creative work cutting across the specialties and extending into the domain of the arts. It has no set curriculum and no course requirements. Both faculty and students are encouraged to work on their own as members of a group which will form, it is hoped, a community of scholars, exchanging ideas and knowledge derived from the various interests that they find compelling. While all students work under the guidance and general supervision of the committee's faculty, many of them have been farmed out for a portion of their studies and researches to special departments of the University of Chicago or to professors in other universities in the United States and also in foreign countries. There is, as a consequence, no line of inquiry—be it humanistic or scientific in its implications—from which the students or the faculty are excluded, provided they have the gifts and can acquire the knowledge necessary to treat their chosen assignment seriously and constructively. Opportunity indeed extends beyond scholarship to art—for the committee has had attached to it for short visits men of letters and artists such as Eliot, Bourbon Busset, Chagall, Schoenberg, and Schnabel. All of them carried on their creative work during their sojourns with the group. The principle behind instruction is that creative efforts in scholarship and the arts are contagious, that example is the best teacher for those dedicated to learning and to beauty. This connection with the arts now extends to the permanent faculty, which has included for some years Saul Bellow, whose contributions to letters have not diminished since his association with this institute.

One of the considerations which led to the formation of the Committee on Social Thought was the need to transcend the specialization which had become so minute in connection with the higher learning, and often so sterilizing, and to overcome it by more individualistic opportunities than those fostered by group inquiries in which a number of specialists are assigned separate parts like players on a baseball team. Specialization is of course inevitable. Without it no important results in works of the mind and heart are possible. Michelangelo was a specialist, a specialist in beauty. So was Plato, a specialist in ideas. But what ideas! So was Socrates. Though he denied it he specialized in wisdom. But wisdom is no specialty in the modern sense of that word. Therefore specialization cannot properly be, as it has become so pervasively in modern life as well as in modern research, an end in itself. The proper purpose of a center such as the Committee on Social Thought is to offer both the young and the old opportunities to acquire a universal, a cosmopolitan, outlook in which the human being is seen as a whole and each human being is seen as a part of humanity. For such a purpose the opportunities offered to the students and the faculty to work on their own, though of great importance, are not enough. It is necessary to kindle in those who have the inclination for independent work a purpose bigger than the self.

The attempt to do this revolves around small seminars, in which faculty and students alike participate. For the sake of communication, not only within the group, but potentially with an intelligent public all over this planet, it is necessary to cultivate a common language of concepts and propositions, transcending specialties and relating not only to the sciences but to the humanities and the creative arts, from architecture to literature, and to economics, political, and social relations. In the search for such a language, a central core of studies was established by the Committee on Social Thought more than twenty years ago. It is called "the fundamentals." Each student selects, with the approval of the faculty as a whole, a small number of major works representative of philosophy (including political philosophy), of history, and of literature or some other art. These are mastered with the help of discussions over which presides a member of the faculty familiar with the work considered. All students have to pass an examination on the fundamentals.

The thesis or essay which a student must offer in order to obtain a degree is representative of his interest. Its subject need not, indeed should not, be determined by the interests of the various members of the faculty. Scholars judged competent to pass on its merits are selected by the faculty of this institute. One at least is almost always chosen from outside. He is often from some other university, not infrequently from a foreign university. The objective is to elicit independent work of the highest quality which, when possible, breaks new ground in a zone where the interrelations between existing specialties are the object of examination.

The value of institutes of such a kind obviously depends on the example set by members of the faculty in their creative labor and by the works of others which are read and pondered. Borrowing plays an inevitable and an important part in training for the creative life. Discipleship and slavish imitation do not. It is worth remembering that Matisse gave up instruction in painting because his students imitated him to his and their detriment. The hope that a young person will steer clear of both discipleship and imitation rests on the visions he obtains of new truths, new realities, new beauties, that are to be discovered at the unexplored interstices of knowledge and of art.

The training provided by the fundamentals—which encompasses the disciplines of history, philosophy, and letters—can help in these discoveries. But the main thing is that the fundamentals should be studied in conjunction with the opportunities such an institute offers (through the independent creative work that is undertaken by each student as well as each member of the faculty) to break new ground through the study of subjects of their own choosing.

Let us take as an example of such exploration the subject of interrelations between specialties in the study of history. With the pursuit of historical research during the past hundred and fifty years, this study has been fragmented into a very large number of separate subjects as well as separate periods and separate areas. Attempts have been made, with considerable success, to synthesize certain special historical subjects, for instance, the history of political thought or of painting, or the philosophy of history (which provides, it would seem, one aspect of the history of thought). But what of history as a whole—what of the interrelations between events (such as disputes within a nation, wars and treaties between nations), the changes in human conditions and institutions, the courses taken by the many lines of thought and of art? Apart from the cycle historians, whose work (it has been suggested[11]) has been mainly destructive in its implications, very little has been accomplished. Yet nothing in the realm of scholarly effort is perhaps more important for the future of human understanding than knowledge of the connections between all the major aspects of man's endeavors and of the material circumstances which these endeavors, combined with conditions of the physical and animal environment, have imposed, and now impose, on humanity.

It is not that the historian can have access, by means of his calling, to what ought to be.[12] But it is open to him to reveal, more illuminatingly than ever before, by means of a new outlook, what has been. This is because, during the last two centuries, specialization (which *has* had very important merits) has led to the opening of a great many new areas of history. Historical knowledge has been pushed back to ancient Egypt, ancient Crete, ancient Greece, ancient China and India. New kinds of historical exploration—such as the evolution of painting, music, economic conditions, science, technology—have been opened. The materials now available are not only vastly more abundant than in Thucydides' time or even Voltaire's.

[11] See above, chap. 4 (IV).   [12] See above, p. 1.

They are much more all embracing of human experience. For the first time integral history, toward which both Voltaire and Gibbon looked in the eighteenth century (and ibn-Khaldun in the fourteenth), could be written, not as a joint enterprise (which has become the fashion in more recent times), but as the product of a single mind. A European or an American or a Russian historian can now bring China and India and the Arab countries into his studies to advantage, just as a Chinese, an Indian, or an Arab historian can bring Europe, America, or Russia into his. The opportunities for comparisons which lead to historical explanations are immensely enriched. The historian of interrelations has vastly greater choice in utilizing the documentary evidence according to what, philosophically considered, needs to be told.

In short, the more comprehensive picture of the past that insight concerning historical interrelations makes possible opens windows to truths about the past which might help in the search for the universal civilization that some eminent men of the eighteenth and early nineteenth centuries believed to be attainable. To such a search all parts of the planet could now contribute.

The study of interrelations is open not only to historians but to other scholars: It is up to creative original minds wherever they appear to help a few exceptional students learn—through exposure to interrelations—both the possibilities and the limitations of action in the practical realm. It is up to such leaders to consider these possibilities and limitations in their relations to the ends of civilization.

The difficulties imposed by the recent forms of academic specialization in the way of the general understanding, which some learned men now seek, are most disconcerting. This was illustrated some years ago by an account of discussions among participants in the "Rencontres" held in Geneva, Switzerland, with the aim of contributing to a common point of view among scholars and writers from many countries and disciplines.

"Nearly every speaker," it was discovered, "uses his own personal terminology. Even if we talk about literature one speaker talks with a sociological bias, one as a philosopher, one as though '*l'art pour l'art*' were still the doctrine. Philosophical terminology is specially varied. And the everlasting criticism in which the Western mind indulges gives a curious impression of negativeness. One wondered whether a stable basis for civilization can be found in reason, or whether, instead, there must be faith; and if so, what faith; and whether, beyond a certain point, reasoning itself somehow depends on faith."[13]

The multiplying divisions between subjects of inquiry in graduate study have now come to stand mainly in the way of the kinds of training and self-training that could help men to meet the new conditions facing mankind. It should be a major task of a few institutes in different parts of the world (for which the Committee on Social Thought might provide one model) to transcend all divisions in the interest of that more unified vision which is so greatly needed to make the most of those opportunities which the modern sciences, and the technologies derived from them, offer mankind.

Small and inconspicuous efforts can have a considerable impact on education, provided they catch the imagination of creative individuals. This is shown by the extent to which, according to the late Gaston Berger, the reforms he introduced into French teaching and research as director of the higher learning in France, were derived from his acquaintance with the particular initiative represented by the Committee on Social Thought. This is shown also by the influence which that institute is said to have had upon recent legislation for the improvement of education in the United States.

The training and research to which such institutes ought to be dedicated would be suited to only a tiny fraction of the persons engaged in higher education. Yet the *influence* of the new

[13] Bernard Wall, "Reflections on the Geneva 'Rencontres,'" *The Twentieth Century*, CL, No. 897 (November, 1951), 419.

institutes could to advantage extend to the entire area of education, including secondary and elementary education. For, as has been suggested, the major function of these institutes is to provide leadership.

In the case of the United States all sorts of new area studies have been organized in connection with the universities, the Peace Corps, and other agencies. They help many students to become acquainted with particular foreign countries and the ways people live in them. Such knowledge is essential for intelligent action. But in order to choose between different courses of action, there must be goals to serve, not only bigger than the self, but bigger than the service of any particular nation or particular cause.

So it is also with the existing special departments of graduate study and the professional schools of universities everywhere. They teach—often most effectively—how to undertake specific work of various kinds, from branches of medicine and surgery to the practice of law and the rendering of judicial decisions. But those who are being trained, often well, need to know for what ultimate purposes they undertake their work. Through the influence of the new institutes, if these prove equal to their responsibilities, specialists can acquire *principles* for choosing between alternatives.

Moreover, while the tendencies in postgraduate training have been toward increasing specialization, there has been in the American colleges during the past twenty-five years a reversal of this trend, a move in the direction of more general studies. The teachers who staff the colleges are trained almost always as specialists. They find themselves ill prepared for the instruction they are asked to give, and ill at ease over their futures, which they have been taught lie with particular and often minute areas of graduate research and teaching. By the broader kinds of graduate research the new institutes would offer, they could help promising teachers to reconcile the undergraduate instruction they are asked to give with their research careers. In every truly important area of specialization, a serious effort to understand the whole is indispensable if the scholar is to make the most of the particular.

The introduction into a few leading universities of interdisciplinary institutes should not cause increasing expense. Trends toward bigger undertakings are sapping the vitality of the higher learning. Quality rather than quantity is the great need. There are too many universities and too many students today. The multiplication of universities and of students gets in the way of progress. Reversing existing trends toward bigness could help to reveal the triviality of much that is now carried on in the name of graduate training and research. In that way it could help explode the prevalent notion that colleges and even universities are desirable for everyone. It would be of value in achieving the ends of civilization to clear away as much as possible of the deadwood that has accumulated during recent decades in connection with universities, as a result of the drives for size and for the multiplication of study programs.[14]

One possible way of giving a new importance to quality would be to build in a few leading universities all over the world small units similar in form and purpose to the Committee on Social Thought and to give these units a different status than that accorded specialized departments. This could be done by awarding their graduates a new kind of degree which would differentiate their titles from those awarded by hundreds of universities today. The so-called Ph.D. degrees are now so numerous that they have little more significance than a trade union card which admits its holder to an enormous teaching guild. In many cases the tasks for which that degree is awarded seem designed to narrow the outlook of the holders. The distinguished faculty of the Committee on Social Thought was built largely with scholars who did not have it!

[14] Cf. Eric Ashby, "Educating Prometheus," *Research* VIII (November, 1955), 419–22.

A few new institutes similar to the Committee on Social Thought could to advantage be made extraterritorial both in relation to the universities which they would serve and in relation to the countries in which these universities are situated. The word "university" is derived, obviously enough, from the concept of universality. When, in the twelfth and thirteenth centuries, the ancestors of modern universities were created—at Oxford, Paris, and in other cities—an early medieval European view of the world (derived partly from Christ's offer to *all* humans to follow Him and love one another) was not unrelated to the outlook upon universities.[15] They were conceived of as universal. For the Christian there could be properly only one learning, just as there could be only one faith.

However unreal and even dangerous this view may seem to a majority of men and women today as they look back on some ten centuries of European history, with its divisions and its innumerable wars, or because of their commitment to some other faith than the Christian or to no faith at all, time has played a trick by bringing all peoples into one community insofar as the sciences and technologies, now accepted everywhere, are concerned.

If the higher learning is to make the most of the opportunities which this material unification of mankind has produced, it is desirable to form small interdisciplinary groups modeled on the Committee on Social Thought, but sufficiently independent to make possible the diversity without which spiritual unification would be sterile. It is necessary also to establish ties between each of them and a world "Center for Human Understanding."

During the past decade a small model for such a center has been provided by a group of friends. They were drawn originally from France and the United States, not simply from the

15 Nef, "The Universities and World Community," in *Trois aspects du développement de l'université aujourd'hui* (Bureau International des Universités, UNESCO, Paris, 1953). See also Nef, *A Search for Unity* (Chicago, 1946), and Nef, "In Quest of Man," *Diogenes,* No. 1 (1953), pp. 71–82.

academic profession, but from business, law, letters, the visual arts—callings in which there are sometimes persons more universal in their outlook than is at all common among academics.[16] Humanity is too precious to entrust its destinies to any existing national institutions. A new kind of international institution needs to be founded, with members who are able to doff their nationalism and clothe themselves in a world point of view.

Its primary concern should center round what ought to be rather than what, in the light of present trends, is likely to be. Several groups have been formed in recent years to provide blueprints of what the world will be like twenty or fifty years hence.[17] Among the first of these was the one called *Prospectives*, formed in Paris through the initiative of the late Gaston Berger when he was Director of Higher Education in France. He agreed, on an important occasion when *Prospectives* was about to start, that it was essential at the same time to have a group to consider what the world *ought* to be like. That, he saw, should be the task of the proposed Center for Human Understanding. For, unless there is some merging of the nations and the peoples of the earth, toward which the present trends in international relations are hardly leading, there might easily be, in spite of all the prognostications that are becoming so fashionable, no future to prognosticate!

III. *Reforms in Universities and Colleges*

What are the changes in the higher learning generally which these new institutes, united in a world Center for Human Un-

---

16 Cf. *Bridges of Human Understanding*. A precedent for this development was set by a symposium held in 1946 at the University of Chicago, under the auspices of the Committee on Social Thought (*The Works of the Mind*, ed. Robert Heywood [Chicago: Phoenix edition, 1966]).

17 We should be wary of assuming that it is possible to plot the future of human conditions scientifically, with a precision at all comparable to that achieved by astronomers in predicting the appearance of a comet. In the nineteen-twenties and -thirties learned demographers were in general agreement that, as a well-known economist told me at the time, "all indications point definitely to a decline in world population"!

derstanding, could foster? What are the changes needed if living is to be given a purpose that it has largely lost since the struggle for existence has been mitigated and since the population, particularly the children and adolescents, have found themselves in possession of a vast amount of spare time that they have not been taught to improve?

On the eve of the First World War the late Geoffrey Scott described the condition of architecture in words that might be written today about almost every art or profession or intellectual discipline. "We subsist," he wrote,

on a number of architectural habits, on scraps of tradition, on caprices and prejudices, and above all on this mass of more or less specious axioms, on half-truths, unrelated, uncriticized and often contradictory, by means of which there is no building so bad that it cannot with a little ingenuity be justified, or so good that it cannot plausibly be condemned.[18]

The only difference between conditions when Scott wrote, in 1914, and now is that traditions are scrappier than they were, that propaganda plays a larger part in discussion than it used to, that caprice and prejudice are less restrained, and that it has become so common to justify the bad and belittle the good that the words "good" and "bad," "honor" and "dishonor," "truth" and "falsehood," together with nearly all words that once had a significance in connection with the arts, have lost most of their meaning for persons who influence opinion.

For this state of uncertainty and gullibility, for this trifling with meaningful words, for this impoverishment of the language, our education is partly to blame. The tendency among teachers and scholars for several decades has been to assume that if men follow their inclinations and selfish interests in whatever directions they lead, if they speak and write without hesitating long enough to think, the ends of teaching and research will take care of themselves. The belief, common not only in the Middle Ages but during most of the nineteenth

---

[18] *The Architecture of Humanism* (London, 1914), p. viii.

century, in the existence of general principles applicable to learning and to conduct, has been weakened and almost destroyed. Discredit has also been thrown on the view commonly held by the learned in our grandparents' time that there is a limited number of great and permanent books and that no man can call himself educated without a knowledge of some of them.

Attempts to remedy this ignorance have been made in the United States, especially during the last twenty-five years, by what may be called "the Great Books Movement." Beginning at the University of Chicago, an effort foreshadowed at Columbia and Swarthmore[19] to reintroduce, by means of translations, the classics of the Western world as an essential part of the curriculum in the colleges has made some headway. Close on the heels of this effort came the organization beyond the universities of small adult classes for reading such classics. That was followed by the publication and wide dissemination of a series of selected Western classics. Even more helpful perhaps was the inauguration, during the past quarter century, especially in the United States, of a new venture in publication —the paperback. The low prices at which these books are sold has led to a vast dissemination of the best works of recent and contemporary literature and scholarship, as well as of the ancient classics. The new accessibility of masterpieces not only of thought and literature but (through radio and television and cheap transport) of the visual arts, of music, and of the theatre has provided materials out of which could be born an epoch of universality and human brotherhood such as the world has never known before. What is lacking (as the words of Henry Miller which provide a text for Part Three of this book suggest) is the *desire* to achieve such a world.

The methods sometimes followed for propagandizing these

19 Cf. Nef, "Higher Education and Leadership in Human Understanding" (unpublished paper of the Center for Human Understanding, Washington, D.C., 1962), pp. 7–8.

recent efforts have frequently lent themselves to criticism and lampoon. The discernment evoked through independent reading by a few persons desirous of probing for themselves the great ideas, and still more of tasting the beauty represented in works of literature, has been too often sacrificed on the altar of mass sales. The manner of teaching in connection with college and adult classes has been sometimes lacking in the finer shades of discrimination, for it is extremely difficult not to sully the greatest works of art when they are subjected to interpretations by persons who fall short in genius and in wit of the authors, who spent their lives in making the books.

Nevertheless, the level of discussion in many realms has been already considerably raised. The numbers of serious persons who turn to important works of art for refreshment, for delight, and for inspiration have been much increased.

Through experiments carried on by the Committee on Social Thought, better methods of teaching the Greek and Roman classics in translation, in the perspective of a sensitive knowledge of Greek and Roman history, have been suggested. Through initiative in the same quarter, this growing acquaintance with classics is being extended to the great works of Islamic society, with a similar perspective.[20] If such a unifying purpose and discipline in teaching can be farther extended to enduring works of the Chinese and Indian societies, a basis could be laid for a cosmopolitan view of humanity and its problems, such as seems, during the late seventeenth and eighteenth centuries, to have been intimately related to progress in both the arts and the sciences of Europe.[21] If the efforts of

[20] For a discussion of the methods of introducing students to classical and Islamic works of genius, the reader is referred to two papers, David Grene, "The Classics in Translation: Their Place in a Modern Education," and Marshall Hodgson, "Two Pre-Modern Muslim Historians: Pitfalls and Opportunities in Presenting Them to Moderns." Both papers are to be published in the proceedings of the last plenary meeting of the Center for Human Understanding under the title *Towards World Community*.

[21] Cf. above, chap. 2 (IV).

Westerners to understand other peoples through their culture is reciprocated by Asians, Africans, and Latin Americans in an effort to understand Europe, the United States, and the British Commonwealth,[22] better conditions can be provided for that fusion of peoples and nations in a universal humanity which Chateaubriand envisioned more than a hundred years ago.[23]

Alas, conditions in the higher learning as at present carried on in the West fall far short of providing a basis for unifying principles, notwithstanding the development in the United States of those so-called area studies, dealing with conditions in every section of the earth. Such principles as are still taught in the colleges and universities are concerned not with learning in general but with some particular branch of it, such as qualitative analysis, money and banking, bibliography, map-making, or historical criticism. As the number of subjects taught has multiplied more rapidly during the last seventy years than during the whole of previous Western history, such principles are the possessions of small groups of specialists, who have woven them into esoteric codes. They seldom make these codes more accessible to the general public, or even to their colleagues in other departments, than the ritual of a Greek letter fraternity or a Masonic lodge. The codes are modified so frequently that they become obsolete in a few decades, if not in a few years.

At the same time, there has been an increasing disposition on the part of the teachers to belittle both the great works of the past and the serious works of the present, by debunking their authors and denying that there are such things as superior knowledge and wisdom among human beings. Of course great men of letters and other great artists have always been subject to abusive and irrelevant attacks. But now that everyone feels it necessary to be an author and assert his ego, now that the chief business of the "thinker" is supposed to be the "scien-

[22] Cf. *Bridges of Human Understanding* (pp. 67–112).

[23] See above, p. 104.

tific" one of rendering obsolete the labor of his predecessors, abuse has got mixed up with instruction as well as with what passes for criticism. Many of the teachers in the universities are writers. Instead of attempting, in their teaching, the difficult task of transmitting to their students the accumulated wisdom of the human race, some bring their puerile controversies into the classroom and handle great works of art and thought (on the rare occasions when they mention them) as if they were on the same level with the tens of thousands of cheap books and articles that pour every year from the printing presses. So, instead of learning to judge all men with the help of the wisdom of great men, the student learns to belittle great men armed with all the weaknesses and jealousies of small men. The student learns to conform where he ought to question and to question where he ought to conform. He does not learn self-criticism or independent judgment. The difference between mediocrity and distinction for a considerable number of persons lies precisely in the attempt they are able and willing to make to outdo themselves. It is to Marivaux, a man sometimes charged with affectation, that we owe what is perhaps the best statement of this truth. Like Beaumarchais, Marivaux belonged to that movement in French eighteenth-century literature which has been often misunderstood because it had a lightness of touch. There is nothing frivolous about his remark in *La Vie de Marianne*, ". . . il faut se redresser pour être grand: il n'a qu'à rester comme on est pour être petit."[24]

Yet from the cradle to the advanced age which it is now thought men and women must attain before they can venture into life, Americans are encouraged to do as they like, to remain what they are. Students are justified in concluding that there is not much value in education if men who are called educated have nothing better to offer by way of advice than to tell them to do what they please. Even when modern educa-

[24] "One must be better than one is in order to be great; to be small one has only to remain as one is" (*La Vie de Marianne* [1731–41], Pt. II).

tion does not make a positive contribution to vicious habits, it seldom provides students with any armor against their own weaknesses. In her remarkable book, *The House of Mirth*, Mrs. Wharton has a sentence about the heroine, Lily Bart, which provides a key to the whole work. "She could not breathe long on the heights; there had been nothing in her *training* to develop any continuity of moral strength; what she craved, and really felt herself entitled to, was a situation in which the noblest attitude should also be the easiest."[25] American education in homes, schools, and churches does little or nothing to fortify those aspirations toward virtue which material advantages have made more abundant in the United States than in any other nation.

A large majority of the graduates of the most sought after colleges now leave them without a rigorous training in any discipline. They have frequently gone, or have been sent, to college because statistics show that holders of college degrees, as adults, attain higher earned incomes than their less fortunate fellows. They frequently select the college, or their parents select it, not for the course of study and discipline it offers, but because of the social advantages it is reputed to provide for young men and women in search of "success."

With what should the universities concern themselves if they are to lead the United States and the world out of the intellectual chaos and the moral confusion which have undermined the confidence of men? Two principles which might be applied to the teaching and the study of all subjects, both in the graduate schools and in the colleges, may be suggested. In the first place, the universities might concentrate on the relations between the various branches of scholarship. While no professor can hope to know as much about the technique of banking as a good banker, he can know more than the banker about the relations between banking and ethics or between

[25] Edith Wharton, *The House of Mirth*, Bk. II, chap. 8 (my italics).

banking and politics. The study of these relationships might well become the special province of the most intelligent and enterprising university professors.

The university professor alone is in a position to examine these relationships disinterestedly, because he is not a banker or a statesman or a politician. The student should not be allowed, as he is now, to study special subjects without relation to the rest of knowledge. He should devote an important part of his time to questions such as these: How does government influence religion and how does religion influence government? What influence has philosophy upon poetry and poetry upon philosophy? In order to answer such questions professors as well as students would have to become acquainted with other subjects besides the ones they now teach. They would not be able to take refuge in the esoteric jargon of their special fields, for they would have to speak in a simple, common language intelligible to every intelligent person.

To discuss the relations between the various branches of knowledge will provide a way of discovering the relative importance of each branch. This leads to the second principle which might guide university instruction. It is to teach the student at every stage of his work that a hierarchy of values exists in relation to knowledge and wisdom, a hierarchy that has stood the test of time, in the sense that very wise men have been able to agree, in a rough and general way, upon the nature and order of the values, during some fifty centuries. It is frequently suggested today in American universities that there is nothing approaching agreement among ancient sages in this matter of values. Much is made of the different interpretations to which past works of the mind have been subject. To contend that distinctions make impossible rough and general agreement is to reveal a warped view of learning, a misunderstanding of the meaning of philosophical truth. As St. Augustine points out in the thirty-first chapter of the twelfth book of his *Confessions*, a general truth, by its nature, comprehends a number of different truths. When the interpretations to which it is legitimately subject are not entirely inconsistent with one another, they do not destroy the general truth, they reveal its fruitfulness. The greatest thinkers and the greatest poets are those who have known how to give each subject they treat a significance proportionate to its importance, according to a common view of the ends of man. Some arrangement is indispensable in carrying out research, and an arrangement directed toward important ends would give more meaning to the teaching and the written work of our universities than they now have.

Another purpose of teaching true values would be to enable each student to learn what aspect of his special studies deserves the most attention. The scholar and the advanced student who are devoting themselves mainly to economics or to political science should be taught what are the most important questions in connection with these subjects as determined by moral philosophy. All questions with which the discipline deals should be arranged according to their relative importance for the good life of society and of the individuals who make it up. The student should learn at first hand who have been the great economists and the great political scientists and why. The students of poetry, music, or history should steep themselves in the work of the great poets, the great musicians, and the great historians. They should make use of encyclopedias, handbooks, and monographs on special subjects, even if they are of no philosophical importance, but only for the sake of accurate information. They should be taught that no pains can be spared in the effort to achieve accuracy, when they make written and even spoken statements. But they should not assume that works which give reliable information are in the same class with those whose structure and content are determined by genius, and in which reliable information is introduced not simply for its own sake but as a part of creative thought or art.

At the same time, students might be taught that not all subjects within the university curriculum are equally important for the good life. They should be helped to learn that the study of the basic principles of moral philosophy, as set forth by ancient wise men of China, India, and Islam as well as of the West, is more important for constructive innovations than the study of public-utility administration, of ward political machinery, of labor injunctions, of sewage disposal, and other current conditions. The former study helps men to face every situation they meet in life, the latter only particular situations which have frequently ceased to exist by the time they are studied. Current problems would not be slighted by such a change of emphasis in the higher learning. If the arguments of great moral thinkers of the past were treated not, as at present, as "dead," if their relevance for our own age were sought, many present-day problems would be made more intelligible than they are with only the methods of studying them now in vogue. A firmer basis than now exists would be laid for wise political action.

Students should be helped to appreciate that a knowledge of philosophy, in the ancient sense of the basic principles of justice, virtue, and wisdom, is even more important than a knowledge of political science, which may be properly treated as the most fruitful branch of it. They should be encouraged to ask themselves whether the study of economic laws, which has engaged the attention of thinkers for hardly more than two or three centuries, is likely to be as fundamental a matter for human welfare as the study of the ends of the state, which comprehend the economic welfare of its members—a study that has engaged the attention of some of the greatest thinkers since the times of Plato and Confucius.

The philosophical attitude toward knowledge, in the ancient Platonic and Aristotelian sense, has a bearing on both the teaching and the writing to be done in the universities in the future. How might the present treatment of subjects be altered to help in establishing the unity of all knowledge and in showing the proper relationship of one branch to others?

Let us take the subject of economics as an example. The tendency in the work of Wicksteed, Pigou, Knight, and some others is to recognize the importance for general welfare of moral, intellectual, and artistic needs which can be satisfied only in ways that cannot be brought readily into direct or indirect relation with the measuring rod of money. It is even denied that any human activity can be treated as separate from economics. Insofar as these tendencies in economic thought emphasize the unity of knowledge and of human experience, they are to be welcomed. The danger would seem to lie, not in breaking down the largely artificial barriers which scholars have erected between different kinds of human endeavors and activities, but in the assumption that ultimate judgments concerning their value can be properly made in economic terms and purely on the basis of economic reasoning rather than in terms of a comprehensive philosophy.

There seem to be essentially two ways in which the autonomy of economics is conceived at present, and neither helps much in preserving Western culture. One is the conception of economics as a science, like mathematics, divorced from life and pursued for the sake of the elegant demonstrations that are possible. The other is the conception of economics as a body of doctrines which, if only applied by businessmen, statesmen, farmers, wage earners, lawyers, professors, and even artists, would solve all the important problems of existence. The holders of this second conception would be inclined to substitute economics for philosophy in a manner similar to that in which Gilson has shown us Descartes tried to substitute mathematics for philosophy, Kant to substitute physics for philosophy, and Comte to substitute sociology for philosophy.[26]

If the economist adopts the first conception, he washes his

[26] Cf. Étienne Gilson, *The Unity of Philosophical Experience* (New York, 1937).

hands of the difficult and dangerous world of which he is a part. He limits himself to the form of reasoning which Pascal calls mathematical. The result of reasoning solely as a mathematician is described by Pascal in the following words:

Mathematicians . . . who are merely mathematicians have sound minds, but they need to have everything carefully explained to them through definitions and axioms, otherwise they are unsound and insupportable, for they are only right when the principles are clearly set before them.[27]

If the economist adopts the second conception, he proposes to solve all the problems of the world by measures designed to increase the production and improve the distribution of commodities and services, without regard to the philosophical value of the wants which determine the nature of the commodities and services. The preoccupation with material values seems to be one of the chief sources of weakness in American education and in American life today. If, therefore, economics is to help in building a world culture, it should not set itself up as a substitute for philosophy. As has been suggested in the chapter on virtue, economics should try to find its place in relation to philosophy. It should reveal the best roads to the satisfaction of wants which moral philosophy indicates are worth satisfying. If the economist is to contribute to the good life, if he is to help in defending democracy and diminishing the likelihood of total war, he should be concerned with the production and distribution of wealth that will contribute most to righteousness, wisdom, and beauty.

When it comes to research and written work in connection with social and humanistic studies generally, such a philosophical approach might enable universities to make a more helpful

[27] H. F. Stewart, *Pascal's Pensées* (New York, 1950), pp. 498–99. Stewart devoted much of his life to understanding and translating Pascal. He gives what seem good reasons for translating "*géomètres*" as "mathematicians." In Pascal's time in France, geometrical inquiry covered substantially the whole realm of mathematics, as the French understood it. (Cf. Nef, *The Conquest of the Material World* [Chicago, 1964], pp. 308–9.)

contribution to the welfare of mankind than they are making at present. It should be recognized that creative thought and art, to be fostered by the new experiments in higher learning, are, at their best, in a higher category than purely analytical studies can ever be.

Let us again take the subject of history as an example. As Jacques Maritain has said, we must both insure the permanence of the purely analytical historical studies of the nineteenth century and go beyond them to the writing of creative, philosophical history which deals with the larger problems of human existence and which aims, like the histories of Herodotus and Thucydides and some other historical works, to help future generations of men in dealing with the recurring problems of existence. We must deal with these problems in the more comprehensive manner that, as we have seen, the recent extensions of our historical knowledge have made possible. It is only by going beyond the purely analytical studies in all subjects of inquiry, by incorporating some of the valuable information they contain in works of literature and human understanding, that the painstaking labor of the recent armies of fact-finders could be preserved for posterity.

If great writers and thinkers are to recover the place in education to which their genius entitles them, students must be discouraged from reading commentaries upon them which contribute nothing but simply summarize, often very badly, what the great men have said so much better. After the greatest works of an author have been read, it may often be desirable to become acquainted also with his lesser works and with the publications of some of his followers. But the reading should be done directly rather than through intermediaries. Unless students are sent to the sources, to the vineyards themselves, to drink the great wines of past ages, learning will sink to the position it occupied during the centuries of decaying Roman civilization. Then, if men read at all, they read commentaries on commentaries which were themselves commentaries on the works of great writers.

This leads to another important means which the universities have at their disposal of helping to cultivate the judgment, the discrimination, and the accuracy of their pupils. One thing that has raised the standards of American law schools above those of most graduate schools is the active attention paid by groups of students in analyzing cases to the weighing of evidence. Historical problems which involve the weighing of evidence should be treated by groups of graduate students in common, for the drill and discipline which such treatment can afford. The impartial study of evidence ought to be given a prominent place in the higher learning. It is closely related to the reading of great books, since one of the main objects in weighing evidence is to learn how far to trust authority. Students should be taught always to inquire into the source of any information or theory. Is the authority honest and objective? Is the information that he gives the information that is most relevant in answering the question that he is attempting to answer? What are his means of obtaining reliable information? Was he equipped to make the best possible use of his information and did he take pains to do so? All these are questions that the student should be taught to answer for himself, under the guidance of teachers who recognize their importance and insist on a conscientious and honest attempt to grapple with them. Such questions may help the student to understand that he cannot properly express an opinion about a book he has not read, or a speech he has not heard, and that he must not make use of a passage in a book without studying it, and without reading it a second and a third time, any more than a properly trained nurse will administer medicine to a patient until she has thrice examined the label on the bottle.

If the university student learns how to weigh evidence, he will be in a far better position than he is today to judge the world about him. The study of evidence will help him to retain and to enrich his common sense, and the lack of common sense among grown-up Americans today, the lack of wariness, is an important cause for their inability as parents to train their children in good moral and intellectual habits. Americans are prone to believe whatever they are told, though experience should teach them that most of the information circulating in the modern world is unreliable or irrelevant to the arguments it is used to support. When they are constantly allowing themselves to be fooled by the wrong persons, they are not in a position to be convinced by the right ones. It is partly because persons feel completely free to talk about subjects they have not studied or books they have not read or events they have not witnessed, that the public is so confused today about learning that it cannot distinguish the authentic from the false. The sense of the meaning of knowledge, particularly outside the natural sciences, is so warped that we find members of university faculties saying they are free to talk about a subject only when they know nothing about it. Again we hear people saying that they want to hear the other side of the question when they are unwilling to take the trouble to learn about either side.

The universities should ask the student to play a much more active part in his own schooling, by writing and speaking on the subjects that he is studying and in relation to the principles to which we have referred. Less time should be spent at lectures and conferences—many of which partake of the worst elements of textbooks—and more at hard work. The number of lectures a student is expected to attend as an undergraduate, and especially as a graduate, should be greatly reduced. Lectures should be much more formal and finished than at present. Their repetition beyond a limited number of times should be discouraged. They should be made to command the attention of the students by the importance of the subject matter. William James had some trenchant things to say about the flabby nature of the mind which spends a portion of its time every day at entertainments. Many college and university students think it is the main function of their teachers in lecturing to entertain them and to provide information which, if partly memorized, will enable them to pass examinations. They have apparently never heard of the old adage of John Dewey about the value of learning by doing.

The proportion of graduate students in American universities today who can write even tolerable English is deplorably small. The only way to learn to write is to write. The student should be required to write simply, clearly, and effectively about every subject that he studies. The principles of composition should always be in his mind rather than remain a separate part of the curriculum that he is free to forget when he has passed a perfunctory examination in English. If it is true that a man can write straight only when he can think straight, it is also true that writing straight helps a man to think straight —that his thought grows as he writes. Writing is not an easy task or one in which short cuts are possible. The student should spend a large portion of his time writing and re-writing—and then in re-examining what he has written in the light of his sources and authorities. This kind of work cannot be done in a hurry, late at night after an exhausting day. It requires a great deal of study and patience; it demands the best strength a man can give. By writing and speaking, if possible to a critical audience, the student will be helped to learn that the great lessons of education are the product, not of passive attendance and hasty summarizing, but of active exertion, of the elaboration and development of thought contained in the serious sources he is brought to consult.

The spirit of the new institutes,[28] set up by one, or two, or a few universities for the purpose of cultivating creative thought and art, should permeate to graduate study. Persons throughout the country who showed genuine promise for the

[28] Cf. above, pp. 279–88.

creative life would come naturally under the direct aegis of these institutes, if they wished to form a university connection. They would not necessarily have to reside at the universities in order to draw on the new intellectual resources.

In what directions might the new institutes and the new university spirit alter graduate study for the doctor's and the master's degrees throughout the world? To begin with, all course requirements and all course examinations would be abolished. The training of graduate students would not consist, as it often does at present, in committing to memory a large number of facts or theories relating to fields and courses within the department and based on the special interests of the particular professors in charge of the fields and courses. The training would be such as to enable the student to master the facts and theories relating to any field, if and when the need arose. Teachers might be expected to play a more active part than they generally do at present as advisers, counselors, and older colleagues for the better graduate students.

A candidate for the Ph.D. would be expected to understand ideas and to acquire a sufficient knowledge of research to present material on important subjects in an intelligent and attractive way, as he will have to do if he is to teach effectively without textbooks. Graduate schools would continue to train their students for teaching and research, but they would require of the candidates for the higher degree, not simply a mastery of special subjects, as at present, but, in addition, two other masteries. One would be a mastery of one of the great cultural traditions, as brought out in the works of past thought and literature and in the history of the society which bred them.[29] The other would be a mastery of philosophy, in the ancient Platonic and Aristotelian sense, in its relation to the candidates' special subjects of study. Candidates would be partly prepared for these two kinds of mastery by the training they would get in the secondary and elementary schools, to which we

[29] Cf. above, p. 292, n. 20.

are now about to turn. These last two requirements would be given as much importance in determining the candidates' qualifications for the degree as the present requirements.

The candidate would be expected to demonstrate his knowledge of these subjects, as well as his knowledge of the discipline in which he specializes, by his performance in several general examinations. He would be expected, also, to submit a considerable amount of well-composed written work and to give frequent oral discourses in seminars attended by his fellow students and his teachers. He would be encouraged to dig thoroughly into a special subject, not simply for the sake of fresh information, but in order to understand the relation of his particular discipline to the whole of knowledge. There would be no place in graduate writing for studies whose sole object is to dissect those elements in works of art which were not intended to be dissected or for studies without significance for knowledge as a whole.

In the writing of theses, the candidate would be taught to think and to make an intelligent use of his materials as well as to gather them. The late Graham Wallas used to tell the story of an American graduate student in one of our leading universities, which is typical of the procedure of many. He had been at work for more than a year on his dissertation when he sent an account of his progress to a friend who had gone to England. "I have now filled five drawers of my desk with carefully filed cards," he wrote. "Tomorrow I shall begin to write and two weeks hence my thesis will be in the hands of my committee." The process of creative writing is rather different. The creative writer is more likely to spend two weeks gathering materials and a year in composition and in adding to his materials as the need for new matter is revealed to him. What is needed in American universities are fewer theses and better theses. While all prospective teachers should have training in research and should be helped to acquire the habit of fresh exploration, without which teaching is bound to become dry and sterile, not every prospective teacher should be required to submit a full-length dissertation. The colleges seeking instructors should learn to content themselves with fewer doctors of philosophy. They should strive to obtain more "masters of creative teaching" who are not subject to the now pervasive academic dogma of "publish or perish."

The student's written work and his oral discourses, as well as his record in the examinations, would be taken into account in deciding whether he is entitled to the doctor's degree and on what terms. In order to give the most promising candidates the recognition which might stimulate them to outdo themselves, the old practice of granting the degree, the degree with honors, with high honors, or with highest honors would be revived. The results would be published.

Such a program would not involve the elimination of the principal subjects now taught in American universities. All these subjects would be subordinated to the fundamental aims of education, the love of knowledge, art, and righteousness for their own sake.

For many generations the trend in science and education has been toward the foundation of new, independent disciplines. The great need in education almost everywhere today is less for novelty than for agreement and unity. In the future the aim should be to reduce the number of disciplines by encouraging coalitions between departments and between "fields" within departments, by insisting that all departments should speak in a language that the others can understand and by acknowledging that all departments have a common objective in the pursuit of truth. If university professors try to see their subjects in relation to other subjects and to the moral and intellectual virtues, they will stop evading the question of what ought to be by taking shelter in minute descriptions of what is, especially of what is unimportant. If a description is to have any value it must be about a subject worth describing.

IV. *The Elementary and Secondary Schools*

A reformation of secondary and elementary schooling would obviously form an essential part of any plan for an improvement in the higher learning. The changes might be begun in the schools, if the teachers were prepared for them. But without standards—moral, intellectual, and artistic—teachers, parents, and clergymen are in no position to guide the worldly lives of the children and young people who are placed in their charge.

"Must I do what I want to," a child is represented recently as pleading with his teacher in one of our progressive schools. Children not only need guidance; a recent statistical inquiry suggests that the overwhelming majority of them want it, at least in the home. This inquiry also suggests that the great majority of teachers, parents, and clergymen do not attempt to give it.[30] Even when they have the best will in the world, they seldom have any idea what is sound, objective advice on moral, intellectual, and artistic questions. Most of them know that it is unsafe to let children play in the street, because automobiles are likely to run over them. Many know that it is desirable to put children to bed when they have a temperature, in order to lessen the risk of serious disease. But very few have any way of choosing, apart from their own predilections, which books would be best for the children to read, what subjects of study are most desirable for them, what works of art they should be taught to love, what statesmen and saints to admire, what moral habits to acquire. Whence are impartial standards on these great issues to come if not from the higher learning? The task of forming such standards rests partly with the universities. If carried out successfully, the work involved in such a task would draw the universities beyond their self-contained walls into touch with the life of

[30] Doris Drucker, "Authority for Our Children," *Harper's Magazine*, CLXXXII, No. 1089 (February, 1941), 277–80.

the country. This would give learning a meaning, a vitality, and a humanity that are possible only when thought, science, and art are rooted in the life of an age.

How should the course of schooling be altered to embody standards relating to the ultimate ends of civilization, to give the children best fitted to serve the good society the opportunities to develop in the fullest measure their impulses toward truth, virtue, and beauty? A profound change in the methods of education in the schools, the homes, and the churches is an indispensable part of any program which aims to nourish an enduring civilization.

American education will have to bear a direct relation to the economic and political order toward which it is suggested in the next chapters the United States should aim. Such an order could be adequately served only by persons trained in a variety of ways. There would be a need for persons trained primarily in the use of their minds, to serve as scientists, engineers, physicians, surgeons, journalists, lawyers, political and business administrators, teachers, ministers, professors, men of letters, and so on. There would be a need for others trained primarily in the fine arts, in music, and also in artistic manual labor, if there is to be, as it is suggested there could be to advantage, a revival of handicrafts. There would be a need for persons trained to perform office work, to staff warehouses, shops, and department stores, and a need for others deft in housekeeping. The need for trained soldiers and sailors and even for fighting airmen would diminish, it is hoped, if there were progress toward the establishment of world community and a world rule of law transcending nationalism. With the spread of computers and automata, the number of laborers required to staff the mining and manufacturing industries, as well as commercial and financial houses, would presumably diminish too, as the need for laborers to cultivate the soil has already diminished.

The preparation for the various types of work would differ

both in nature and in length. But there would be some kinds of instruction that all would need and that could best be given in common. Except for military training, such instruction ought to be given in the earliest stages of schooling.

The years of elementary school, in which all would have the same training, might well begin when the child is four or five. They might well continue until ten, eleven, or twelve. These early years are of crucial importance in the lives of most of us. Habits are formed which are never altogether outgrown. Consequently the greatest need in elementary schooling is for dedicated teachers, concerned with the character of their pupils because of the unequalled opportunity they are offered to form dedicated citizens for the new world created by the triumph of industrialism. This has to be done indirectly, by example. As Thoreau suggested, whatever good is done "must be aside from my main path, and for the most part wholly unintended. Men say, practically, . . . go about doing good. If I were to preach at all in this strain, I should rather say, 'Set about being good.' "[31] It is the fervor of the teacher over the subjects he communicates that alone can help him to form dedicated pupils. Teaching of the highest quality can never be adequately compensated in terms of cash. Basically teaching is an art, and the teacher, like the artist, who teaches simply for the livelihood will be a failure. Therefore it is less important to raise the standard pay for teachers than to create conditions where the best teachers and the best pupils are given opportunities to "set about being good."

In such subjects as spelling, arithmetic, geometry, grammar, English composition, reading, and music, as well as in elementary history and geography, it should be possible to give the child between ten and twelve a better foundation than children now have when they leave high school. At the same time, it should be possible to provide the child with a great deal of training that has been almost entirely neglected in

[31] Thoreau, *Walden* and *Civil Disobedience* (Boston, 1960), p. 50.

recent years. Education in good moral and intellectual habits can be combined to advantage. Such an education could be focused around the careful, methodical reading aloud of books that have permanent value. While only a small proportion of children would be capable of getting anything out of the most advanced books, all children should be encouraged to make the attempt to understand three types of books—works of devotional literature, fables and works of fancy, and general histories.

Reading classics of devout literature could serve as the basis of the training in moral conduct both in the home and in the school. As with all reading, the children should not be excused from the study of these books just because they do not take to them readily. Most of the things that are worth while in life are in many ways distasteful at first. A love for them comes only after difficult labor and partly as a result of it. Mature people ought to have learned this truth; they ought to be able to act upon their knowledge, though children in their early years cannot be expected to have any idea of it. The extreme modern view that it is the business of children, as a lively American columnist has written, to bring up and discipline their parents, is not likely to educate the children or even the parents, who are often too old to learn the discipline so many of them have missed. It is not necessary to be harsh in order to adopt the more normal view of education, according to which it is the duty of the older and more experienced human beings to supply the counsel and guidance. Violence in the home or the school, which is always regrettable, is even more likely to arise from a lack of leadership and example, from a lack of discipline, than from the existence of responsible authority. No mother and grandmother who has left a written record perhaps ever loved her progeny more, or treated them more tenderly, than Mme de Sévigné. Yet, on this very question of the reading of Christian literature, we find her advising her daughter, in connection with the upbringing of her tiny granddaughter, as follows: "Pour les beaux livres de dévotion, si elle ne les aime pas, tant pis pour elle; car nous ne savons que trop *que même sans dévotion*, on les trouve charmants."[32]

Fables and works of fancy arouse the sensitive child's imagination. They form a gateway to thought, to charm, to wit, and to art. Just as the training in good moral habits could be appropriately built around the reading of devotional books of enduring value, the training in spelling, in grammar, in delight, and in composition could be appropriately built around the reading of works of fancy of enduring value, some of them written primarily for children. For the English speaking child *Alice in Wonderland, Aesop's Fables, Robinson Crusoe, Gulliver's Travels, Huckleberry Finn, Tom Sawyer*, and perhaps specially prepared versions of the *Iliad* and *Odyssey*, of some of the *Arabian Nights*, together with selected plays of Shakespeare, provide the kind of literature likely to kindle fervor in the young. They should also be introduced in their tender years to stimulating contemporary literature and made aware of what the mechanized world they are entering is like. There has been during the last two decades a noteworthy improvement in the quality of children's books. The range of choice for children's reading has been widened. There is now plenty of good reading for children. It is much less important to have children read many books than to have them read and re-read a few good books and so become accustomed to seeing and hearing the language of great writers.

A school child in 1939 had to read fifteen times more matter than the average pupil of 1913, an "educator" told the American Optometric Association, according to the report in a Chicago paper. This report does not explain whether the conference regarded the increase as evidence of progress. For the

[32] "As for fine devotional works, if she doesn't like them, so much the worse for her; because we know only too well that *even if one is not devout*, one finds them charming" (*Lettres de Madame de Sévigné*, ed. M. Monmerqué [Paris, 1862], IX, 413, letter of January 15, 1690 [my italics]).

impartial statistician there can be little doubt on that point. As the time children give to reading has certainly not increased since 1913 (many experienced schoolteachers think that it has decreased),[33] the children must obviously be allowed to skip and skim even more than fifty years ago. There was far too much skipping and skimming then. So the report can be regarded only as evidence of retrogression. There is faint, but deceptive, consolation in the reflection that the quality of the reading matter submitted to children has possibly deteriorated so greatly that more of it is better skimmed and skipped than in the past! The report helps us to understand why fewer and fewer persons read intelligently or take joy in reading; why there is so little good literary judgment. The formation of a reading public, capable of providing the true artist with stimulus and valuable criticism, depends to a considerable extent on the acquaintance children make early in their lives with a few good books to which they will return later on. The number of children who can retain everything is limited. Therefore, the most important matter is to help them to learn to retain what they both need and find fascinating. Here the old adage about leading a horse to water is most applicable. Even though children are too young to grasp much of the meaning of good books, association with them at an early age often makes an indelible impression and thus prepares the ground for a true understanding. It is by the rediscovery of great books, as of great pictures and great works of music, at different ages in life that a love for art is acquired. Every rereading reveals treasures that once were hidden.

An elementary knowledge of history and geography could best be acquired by the reading of a few historical works. History provides the child with some conception of how the world has grown to be as he will find it, rather than as the works of devotion lead him to understand that it ought to be.

[33] See the views of Lloyd Triplett Holden, as reported in the *Baltimore Sun* of September 29, 1939.

Supplemented by the examination of maps and photographs, good films and television programs, it can also provide him with some conception of the nature of different lands and peoples. Historical works suitable for the child are rather more difficult to select than fables and works of fancy, partly because history is a particularly difficult subject to treat artistically. But the proper principle of selection would seem to be clear. What is wanted are books which treat in a comprehensive and easily understandable way the essentials of some important phase of history and which are at the same time works of art. The histories that are read should be chosen primarily for their enduring qualities as literature. It is not important that they should embody the latest results of historical research, for a knowledge of these results can be acquired later, if and when the need arises. It is not important that they should cover the *whole* history of Russia, Greece, Rome, Islam, modern Europe, the United States, ancient Egypt or India or China. It *is* important that they should introduce the child to the entire world, which is now part of everyone's responsibility, if possible by means of firsthand acquaintance with original source materials.[34] For example there is no better way of becoming acquainted with certain aspects of the classical world than by reading Herodotus, Polybius, or Tacitus, whether in full or in extracts from their accounts. Such reading should be accompanied by visual images of the areas under examination, which can now be so readily and often so engagingly supplied.

In addition to this reading program and the studies built about it, elementary education would include arithmetic and geometry. It would include music and poetry, which go well

[34] A series of books, now in process of publication, aims to provide such an introduction. It offers an account of every portion of the globe as given by the explorers who discovered it (The Great Explorers Series, edited by Evelyn Stefansson Nef (New York, 1966——). The first volume on the classical world, prepared by Rhys Carpenter, has already appeared (*Beyond the Pillars of Heracles*).

together because of the importance of song and rhythm in both. It might also fruitfully include training in appreciation of the visual arts. Some tests made in England suggest that young children gain considerably in discernment by *sound* teaching. Many examples of great works of art, mostly paintings, were paired with counterfeit art, and various school children of different ages were asked to choose the better of each pair. Only one of the groups of children had had the advantage of instruction from an art mistress of discrimination. Between the ages of twelve and fourteen, after several years of learning, the children in this group made the right choice three times as often as those in any of six other groups.[35] The excellent reproductions now made of great drawings and even of great paintings should facilitate training in the appreciation of art, if care were taken to explain to the children the inferiority of the finest reproductions to the originals. Poetry and music can be introduced directly by records and by broadcast concerts. Whenever the child shows a disposition for more active participation, the means for satisfying this inclination should, if possible, be supplied.

Even more important during childhood than wise education in the school is wise training in the home. The formation of virtuous character depends upon an intelligent and happy domestic life, possible only when the family circle has a spirit of its own independent of the school. But family life cannot to advantage be at cross purposes with that of the schools. The community of the future that we hope for will be well served if the level of both is raised, if their ultimate objectives are similar, and if the means employed by the one complements those of the other. Work in the elementary schools might well be combined with work in the home under the guidance of the parents. Manual tasks, designed to contribute

[35] Margaret H. Bulley, *Art and Counterfeit* (London, 1925), pp. 85–88.

to the order, cleanliness, and aesthetic appearance of the house and its surroundings, should be made part of a daily routine. Their performance would supplement regular periods of reading, visual and aural enjoyment, and physical exercise. Moral, aesthetic, and manual education could helpfully be begun in the home as soon as the child could walk and before it entered school.

The response of children to the various kinds of elementary instruction would differ. It would be partly on the basis of these differences that the child's parents and his schoolteachers would decide on the kind of education that the boy or girl could most suitably embark upon at the age of ten, eleven, or twelve. Children who showed an enthusiasm for, or a genuine interest in, books and other intellectual study would go on with instruction intended primarily to train the mind. Those who showed an inclination for music or the fine arts, and especially those who exhibited a genuine talent for them, would go on with instruction devoted primarily to the arts and the handicrafts. Those whose response was poor or mediocre to every variety of work calling for an exercise of the mind and imagination would presumably be better fitted to enter routine work of some kind. If these children showed an aptitude for using their hands it would be reasonable to assume they were especially adapted to manual work. If they showed an aptitude for calculating or for management, they might embark on an education designed primarily to fit them for work in offices, shops, and department stores and designed also, especially in the case of the girls, to prepare them to take care of homes.

There would be essentially four varieties of schooling for young people between the ages of ten or twelve and eighteen or twenty. They would not necessarily be carried on in separate schools. It should be made readily possible to transfer from one of the four courses of schooling to another, when it became apparent that a mistake had been made concerning a child's special aptitude.

The first course would be the shortest. It would be primarily, but by no means exclusively, for young men. Its object would be to train them for labor as farmers, industrial workers, and mechanics. It would consist, as the years went by, more and more in practical work. Apart from the training given in handling machines and in tilling the soil, there would be three additional kinds of instruction. As in each of the four kinds of education, religious instruction and training in good moral conduct, begun in the elementary schools, would be continued and developed. It would be combined with courses in literature, history, and economic and social conditions. There would be regular training of the body and of disciplined habits of cleanliness and order. There would be instruction in the elementary technical and scientific matters that would be of help in driving and repairing machines.

The second type of schooling would prepare young people for office and store work of various kinds and for the administration and care of the home. It would be primarily, but by no means exclusively, for young women. Just as the students taking the first type of schooling would get practical training, especially during summer vacations on farms and in factories, so the students under the second type would get practical training in stores and offices. There would be courses in arithmetic, typewriting, elementary accounting, cooking, mending, care of children, and other domestic occupations. As under the first type of schooling, there would be courses in literature, history, and economic and social conditions, and there would be instruction in religion and moral conduct.

The third type of schooling would be for those children who showed gifts for creative work with their hands or with musical instruments. Such schooling would be designed for painters, sculptors, and musicians, as well as for the persons who seemed fitted to engage in the artistic handicrafts. While the various arts and crafts are distinct, they have much in common. Young men and women who are receiving special training in one can usually profit by close association with those who are receiving special training in another. Courses in general culture, offered in different forms under all four types of schooling, would receive a special emphasis designed to help in the arts and crafts.

The fourth type of schooling would prepare young men and women for the universities and the professional schools. It would consist of an eight-year course, covering roughly the years now spent in the final grades of elementary school, in the high school, in the junior college, and in the Freshman and Sophomore years of college. The training now offered at these stages of American education would be altered considerably. At the outset all the children, with the possible exception of those bent on careers in the physical or the biological sciences, would have from two to four years devoted primarily to the study of foreign languages. They would be expected to learn thoroughly two or three languages. They would devote at least a whole year, preferably two, to each language. They would be expected to carry on all their educational work in the language. Their reading would be exclusively in it. They would be expected almost from the outset to converse in it, outside as well as inside the classroom. All their classes would be in company with other boys and girls engaged in learning it. When practicable, and in cases where it did not interfere with the home circle, the young people might live in a house where all the conversation was in the language they were learning. Language would occupy the pupils between the ages of roughly ten or eleven and fourteen or fifteen. The knowledge of literary classics, of grammar, and of composition would be obtained through the foreign tongue. The advantages of such training would come both from the discipline provided by the close study of a foreign tongue and from the unrivaled opportunities which the study of a great classical or a great modern language affords for an acquaintance with literature and with the perennial problems of man's relation to man as these are discussed by great writers. The advantages would also come from the information such training would provide for meeting and understanding people from other countries. In order to get the most out of such training, the books read should be treated not (as is the usual practice at present) as curiosities, but as guides to life. It has been wisely said that, with a second language, we can acquire a new soul. That can be true only when our knowledge of the new language is intimate and profound.

At the age of fourteen or fifteen the students who had been devoting themselves to the mastery of foreign tongues would be prepared for a college course of approximately four years in general education. In this course active participation would be continually expected from the student, particularly in the presentation of written exercises of all kinds. Lecture courses in history, in the physical and biological sciences, and in the study of man would be offered. But great emphasis would be placed (particularly in the case of students who planned to devote themselves either to social and humanistic studies or to the law) upon the reading and discussion of the great books of classical and Western history and on the handling of evidence. In addition there would be some preliminary training in research, readily combined with the study of evidence— in experimental research for students planning to devote their lives to science, medicine, or engineering; in historical research for students planning to devote their lives to social and humanistic studies, to business administration, and to the law.

For as long a time as military training should prove to be necessary, the young men who emerged from the colleges and the other schools, at ages of from eighteen to twenty or so, could receive it at this time. Those whom it was found desirable to call up would remain in the service as long as proved indispensable for purposes of defense.

After they returned from military service they would enter

the universities and professional schools or embark on their life work. But the development of general education in the United States would not be dependent upon military training. If the world should become saner, less ferocious, if it should be possible for the nations to understand each other better and to establish conditions of international order, general military training would be dropped. Conscription can be justified only as a means of self-preservation, and with the coming of nuclear weapons, self-preservation, for the first time in history, depends less on war than on peace.[36] It should be a primary object of foreign policy both to prevent the use, and eventually the accumulation, of nuclear and other total weapons and to abolish conscription by mutual agreement between all the national powers, small as well as great. On this newly industrialized planet, what is of fundamental importance in elementary and secondary, as in higher education, is training in understanding and in world community where all persons, whatever their race or color, are provided not with ways to assert any special claims, but with equal opportunities to fulfill their potentialities as fellow members of the human race.

v. *Family and Church*

The success of any educational program which aims to offer all people some training in true moral, intellectual, and artistic values, and, at the same time, to maintain the high standard of living established during the late nineteenth and twentieth centuries, depends upon the co-operation of the churches, the families, and the schools. Unless they agree on some ultimate objectives in training the young, family life or Sunday-school instruction is likely to undo the work of the schools and colleges or even to make it impossible to embark on that work. Again, a school with different objectives, or with no objectives at all, can undo the work of the most intelligent family,

[36] See below, chap. 12.

which has brought up its children in a love of righteousness, wisdom, and beauty. Some decades ago the late Graham Wallas, author of *The Great Society* and *The Art of Thought*, asked a gathering of well-to-do American parents in New York whether, if they could choose, they would have a child acquire a long but curable disease which forced him to withdraw from school at the age of eight or ten or go on in health with the kind of education offered most children. The majority of the parents voted for the disease. Similar answers to Wallas' question are not infrequently given by contemporary parents.

It is not enough for American children to have wise parents, or to have wise priests and clergymen, if the schools undermine their work. It is not enough to have wise teachers and professors unless the parents, together with the priests and clergymen, support the teachers and the professors in their wisdom. What help can we expect from the family and the church in working toward the ends of civilization sketched in Part Two?

The history of American churches and American families during the past fifty years can perhaps be summed up in the word "liberalization." Liberty is an excellent thing—as a means toward the good life. It has been advocated on the ground that it would do away with cant, secrecy, and hypocrisy. "Secrecy and hypocrisy," writes Frank Lloyd Wright, America's great architect, "both do something to the character never to be repaired. . . . Aren't the *pretended* lives the rotten threads in the social fabric?"[37]

Hypocrisy is a blot on any character and on any society. When it comes to secrecy, a good deal depends on the definition of the word. It is obviously no more helpful for the strength of the individual or of society to have a man empty all his private affairs into the ears of everyone he meets than it is helpful for the strength of a written work to have the

[37] *Autobiography* (New York, 1932), p. 202 (his italics).

author empty his notebooks onto its pages. But if secrecy is another name for cant and hypocrisy, if it means concealing from someone, with design, a matter he has a right to know, if it means preaching and teaching one thing and doing the opposite—living a lie—then Wright is justified in condemning it.

Insofar as the liberalization of manners and customs relating to family life has done away with artificiality, it is a blessing. There is no conspicuous benefit to humanity in high silk hats, tight-fitting corsets, or cumbersome bathing suits. There is no reason to regret the opportunity which women now have to escape from the barbaric brutality of monstrous husbands or fathers, who used to keep them in chains and spend their fortunes. But the new freedom would be more inspiring if it had positive achievements to its credit. Each of the steps that have been taken to break down the older social standards of the Anglo-Saxon world has been defended on the ground that it would result in a more honest, forthright way of living. Better for a man to divorce his wife openly than to visit a mistress secretly. Better to abandon all training in the moral virtues, better to stop maintaining a fear of hell, if teachers and clergymen indulge clandestinely in the very vices they pretend to abhor.

If such arguments were to carry weight, it was vital that the result of the absence of old conventions should be a greater honesty in the conduct of human affairs generally, more creative relationships between husband and wife, parent and child, colleague and colleague, employer and employee, governor and governed, nation and nation. It is hardly possible to claim that the breakdown of the older conventions during the twentieth century has been accompanied by a notable improvement in conduct or by a growing humanitarianism, a growing spirit of comradeship between the peoples of the world. It is hardly possible to claim that modern family life has improved the moral and intellectual training of children in the home.

Much evidence points in the other direction. Our courage, our sense of duty, our devotion to ideals and to each other, even our candor, all seem to have been as often weakened as strengthened. The "bright young people," with all their freedom to marry and divorce as they please, have seldom set an example capable of arousing much enthusiasm in an intelligent mind or an honest heart. The new conventions have not justified the hopes that were put in them. They have not contributed conspicuously to the dignity of man or to the happiness of mankind by cultivating the values of tenderness, of human intimacy and love, which are needed to fortify men and women to meet their responsibilities without anger and with grace.

No one in his senses would argue that on that account society should return, even if it could, to high hats and tightly laced corsets. The question that needs to be asked is why this experiment in freedom has proved barren. Our wisest leaders in education have already supplied a sound answer. Together with most other peoples in the modern world, Americans have sought freedom for its own sake, not for the sake of the good life. People have assumed that such virtues as kindness, courtesy, fortitude, tenderness, or fidelity are of the same texture as corsets, high hats, and cumbersome bathing suits. They are to be worn only if it is convenient. What society has failed to recognize is that kindness, courtesy, fortitude, tenderness, and fidelity are good things in themselves, and are to be respected and loved *for their own sake*. There is no reason for wearing a heavy suit in summer if it makes a person uncomfortable, but there are reasons for becoming and remaining loyal and faithful even when this is both troublesome and annoying, even though the reasons are not susceptible to scientific proof. Comfort may legitimately take precedence over fashion—it cannot legitimately take precedence over virtue. If that were recognized, family life would be strengthened; parents would assume a responsibility toward their children and toward each other that is now lacking. Recognizing virtue as a good thing in itself would help parents and their children to recognize that knowledge and beauty are good things in themselves. If the higher learning can give standards a new meaning and a new reality, so that parents see their value and take them on faith, then the parents will be in a position to co-operate with the teachers by giving training in the homes that will assist a wise program of education.

It may be questioned whether the liberalizing influences in recent American history have done more for faith than they have done for the family. The main problem that Protestant clergymen early in this century had to face was that of the empty church and the deserted Sunday school. Very often the test of a successful minister has not been the content of the sermons that he preaches, the nature of his religious beliefs, or even his character and intelligence; the test became the number of persons he was able to bring into his church. When a leading pastor dies, the American newspapers almost never ask what were his views on loving one's enemies or being the good Samaritan. The papers do not ask whether the pastor embodied the virtues Christ personified; they do not ask whether he said and did things to strengthen the faith or the compassion of the community in which he lived and preached. His obituary notices tell us that after he took over a small church in Iowa he boosted the list of members from 21 to 209 in less than a year. As the crowning feature of his successful career, he raised the annual income of one of the most important churches in the Middle West from $120,000 to $500,-000. Recently a friend of mine listened to the dean of a frequented divinity school talking with much enthusiasm about one of his pupils. My friend had happened to meet this pupil, who had been given charge of an imposing church in one of the principal cities in the South. He asked the dean in what the young clergyman excelled. "Why," said the dean, without a moment's hesitation, "he's got a church with an endowment of more than four million dollars."

Accounts of religious affairs that we read or hear seldom explain how all the new members are gathered, how the formidable endowments are obtained. When money becomes the measure of all things, the need for probing deeper disappears. If curiosity persists, candor forces the outsider to the conclusion that these miracles are not always produced by instilling in the local population a deep religious faith, by persuading doubters of the truth of the gospel, and by persuading them of the importance of trying to live in accordance with Christian ethics. In some cases, at any rate, success has been achieved by founding church golf clubs, by drawing attention to the opportunities offered by church socials for young women in pursuit of husbands, and by providing various kinds of entertainment designed to make churchgoing an occasional substitute for visiting the motion pictures or watching television. In extreme cases, everyone seems to applaud if the minister obtains his results partly with the help of alluring motion-picture actresses, who pose with him as hosts to some visiting celebrity. One is reminded of the remark in a recent French novel, "en Amérique la nobilité est remplacée par la publicité."

There is nothing precisely vicious in such practices. But it may be doubted whether, by themselves, they are any more likely to bring about a growth of faith or a renewal of respect for Christian ethics than the discarding of high hats, long bathing suits, and corsets. If the churches are to help in a movement to restore true values in the United States, they cannot do it by making themselves substitutes for dance halls and motion-picture palaces, any more than universities and colleges can improve education, as Robert Hutchins once remarked, by making campuses substitutes for country clubs. The way the churches can help is by concentrating on virtue and compassion and on the development and appreciation of the liturgical arts. The way they can help is by giving men and women a sense of the ultimate ends of life, which can hardly be obtained from entertainments. Such objectives may possibly reduce the attendance. But in England and the United States during the past forty years adult attendance has been better maintained at Roman Catholic than at Protestant churches, although the Protestants for the most part have made more concessions to the world than the Catholics. Worldly wants change so fast that it is difficult to keep church diversions up to date. Spiritual needs have a greater permanence. It is doubtful, therefore, whether the repeated liberalization of dogma (encouraged by the harsh rigidity prominent in Calvinism) and the attempt to make church life fit in with the worldly interests of the churchgoers have helped to achieve for the Protestant sects generally the objective for which they were instituted by individual pastors. In any case, whatever the consequences, it is better that a church should go down striving as a religious institution than that it should attempt a metamorphosis. If established churches are to contribute to the restoration of religious, moral, and aesthetic training in the elementary and secondary schools and in the colleges, they cannot begin by abandoning most of such training in connection with their own work.

VI. *Education and Life*

It is frequently said that the task of all persons and institutions concerned with instruction is to prepare children and youths to meet life. Everyone can agree on this objective. But we make a fundamental mistake when we assume that it can be achieved by turning the schools and colleges, the churches and universities, into replicas of the practical worlds of business, of entertainment, or of politics, which exist about us. Put to such purposes, these institutions do not teach their charges to meet life, they simply leave them to drown in life.

The kind of training that we have so imperfectly sketched, and that can doubtless not only be elaborated but greatly improved upon in its main lines, is what men need if they are to resist the domination of facts and events of which Emerson spoke in a striking passage. He wrote:

What is our life but an endless flight of winged facts or events? In splendid variety these changes come, all putting questions to the human spirit. Those men who cannot answer by a superior wisdom these facts or questions of time, serve them. Facts encumber them, tyrannize over them, and make the men of routine the men of *sense*, in whom a literal obedience to facts has extinguished every spark of that light by which man is truly man. But if the man is true to his better instincts or sentiments, and refuses the dominion of facts, as one that comes of a higher race, remains fast by the soul and sees the principle, then the facts fall aptly and supple into their places; they know their master, and the meanest of them glorifies him.[38]

Is it not proper for education to help men to cultivate their best instincts and sentiments? The goal of the higher learning is to make man the master of his materials; the true goal of all education is to make man the master of himself. Few Americans today suffer from lack of contact with the world about them. Most of them suffer from too many of the wrong kinds of contacts, from the lack of principles that would help them to give meaning to their experiences and that would help them to form enriching friendships. They suffer from a lack of moral fortitude, which many of our pioneering ancestors had to have and which is indispensable if they are to face the disappointments and the unhappiness that life always brings.

The student does not learn to meet life by being tossed from experience to experience, and from subject to subject, without the opportunity to digest his experiences and to reflect upon the subjects to which he is introduced. If men are to

[38] Ralph Waldo Emerson "History," *Essays* (1st ser.; Boston: The Riverside Library, 1883), p. 36.

keep their heads above water in the sea of noise, excitement, competitive scramble, and sensational rush that the modern world has become, the schools and universities will have to inspire in them the *desire* to follow the good life.

The view has become prevalent that every kind of work is an evil. A friend of mine, whose habits of labor resemble those of Trollope in regularity if not in fruitfulness, remarked to his luncheon partner that, while he did not work to excess, he found time for a long stretch of hard work every day. Over the quantity of labor my friend had been doing his partner had been showing the polite concern he did not expect to have taken seriously, a polite concern characteristic of such conversations. "Just as some people are steady drinkers," my friend said, "I am a steady worker." His partner hesitated. Then, as he thought he had caught my friend's meaning, he felt called upon to renew his pretended sympathy. My friend's lot, he remarked, was harder than that of the steady drinker, for the drinker at least "gets some fun out of it."

The urgency of the case and the weakness of American education make it indispensable that university professors, together with all those who train the young, should face their great task immediately. They should bury their petty jealousies, their private ambitions, and their quarrels in a consciousness of their great mission. If the universities are to succeed, no obstacles should be regarded as insurmountable; the professors should renounce their desire for quick results; the virtues of patience, courage, and self-discipline should be restored to the position from which they were dethroned by the American passion for getting ahead. Even if the difficulties seem insuperable, the task cannot be evaded. We shall do well to remember a motto sometimes attributed to William the Silent: "It is neither necessary to hope in order to undertake nor to succeed in order to persevere."

10 The Economic Structure of Society

In no other country has all enterprise been conducted so generally as in the United States on the principle that free competition is the mainspring behind material progress. As that has come to be regarded as the key to all progress, as economic relations have come to be treated not only as the ordinary but as the only important business of life, Americans have been entrenched in the opinion that the more it is possible to carry on every transaction by the give-and-take of the market place, without government intervention, the more a country is bound to prosper, and the happier its citizens will be.

1. *Origin and Strength of Laissez Faire*

Unlike other great nations of the world, the United States was born and reared in the tradition of laissez faire. Throughout its history this tradition has remained the accepted ideal in economic matters. Although American history is not venerable, it is already considerable. In setting about to build for the future, no country can afford to forget its history.

When the United States became a nation, in the last half of the eighteenth century, the two European countries most powerful politically and most influential intellectually were England and France. Next to the experience of the American colonies, it was to the contemporary thought and experience of England and France that the founding fathers turned for guidance in economic and political matters when they established the Republic and wrote the Constitution. On a question that was to be of crucial importance in American history, the question of the appropriate relations between government and economic enterprise, American, English, and French experience seemed to teach similar lessons.

Before the end of the seventeenth century, England had become the foremost country in Europe in mining and heavy manufacturing. The material standard of living was higher than in any continental nation. It happens that in 1696 Gregory King made an estimate of the national dividend of England and Wales. That was before the chief purpose in writing books was to sell them or to make an impression on one's associates by their publication. A modest man, King never published his. But it was resurrected nearly a century after his death.[1] It has proved a remarkably reliable work. It enabled Mr. Colin Clark to extend his comparisons of the national income produced per head of occupied population back to the revolution of 1688. According to Clark's calculations, the Englishman at that time had, on the average, a somewhat larger command of economic goods to console him for life than the Italian, the Japanese, or the Russian had in the interval between the two world wars, after more than two centuries of unparalleled economic progress.[2]

In the early eighteenth century, all the continental nations had begun to look to England for leadership in industrial technology, in manufacturing and mining alike. "Our artisans," wrote one of Gregory King's contemporaries, a certain James Puckle, "[are] universally allow'd the best upon Earth for Improvements."[3] That was in 1697. During the next fifty years almost every visitor to England who considered the matter came to agree with him. The continental peoples, the French in particular, sent technical experts to study the English methods of manufacturing. They brought back designs and draw-

[1] George Chalmers, *An Estimate of the Comparative Strength of Great Britain* (London, 1801). Some extracts had been published earlier by Charles Davenant.

[2] *The Conditions of Economic Progress* (London, 1940), pp. 41, 83.

[3] *A New Dialogue between a Burgermaster and an English Gentleman* (London, 1697), p. 20.

ings of the curious new machinery and furnaces. One of these experts, who had come over from France in 1738, wrote:

I explored the shires between Monmouth and Warwick, filled as they are with iron and copper manufactures, in the company of my [English] friend. [He] was well content to show me the wealth of the workers in this district. I observed with surprise the skill of these artisans and the comforts they enjoy. Their villages seemed to me as well built as the finest towns in Flanders and I think they are richer. The prodigious consumption of provisions brought into the markets astonished me greatly. . . . I noticed . . . a large number of processes which are unknown to our workers, notes of which I will show you in Paris.[4]

How had England done it? This was a question that eighteenth-century mechanics, tradesmen, and financiers, economists, scientists, and even men of letters were asking themselves with increasing frequency and increasing interest. For Frenchmen the question took on a compelling importance after the death, in 1715, of Louis XIV. They were beginning to care less for the qualities cultivated, in spite of much corruption, in the age of the great monarch—good form, finish, and delight in the fine arts and in the art of living, reason and moderation in thought, high *standards* of conduct, combined with a belief in the Church and the divine right of kings. They were beginning to care more for wealth, health, freedom of economic enterprise, and the discovery of the secrets of the material world. These were objectives upon which many Englishmen had begun to focus their attention during the previous century and a half.

As time went on, English artisans and consumers were more and more inclined to combine these objectives with a skill in artisanry and a love for the products of artistic craftsmanship, in which the French and the Dutch were their mentors.[5]

[4] Report of M. Ticquet, Archives nationales, Paris, O¹1293.

[5] This subject is treated further in essays of mine on "Delight and Commodity" and "Beauty in the Conquest of the Material World," which are to form a part of a general history of the coming of industrial civilization.

Means of Approach

Growing concern with beauty joined, in England, with growing efficiency to create a zest, characteristic of eighteenth-century English life and letters, for the rising laissez faire economy, in which the values of delight, as expressed in the baroque arts and crafts, could for a time happily coexist with the values of mechanical improvement.

The increasing value placed in France during the eighteenth century on quantity production was reflected in the changing attitude of the governing authorities toward mechanical inventors. Shortly after he came to power in 1622, Richelieu had one of them locked up as a madman in the asylum at Bicêtre, just outside Paris, for pestering him about the force contained in a jet of steam.[6] A hundred and thirty years later an expert technician, who was in fact a little mad but who had a special gift for directing a textile factory, was put in charge of a government cloth enterprise in central France, in spite of his infirmity. The local officials arranged the routine at the factory to help him to control the aberration which led him to imagine that the workmen were deriding him whenever they coughed or sneezed, even in the depth of winter. The officials considered his mechanical knowledge too valuable to dispense with.[7]

It was natural to seek for explanations of England's material prosperity during early modern times in the special features of English public policy which differentiated it from that of France and most other continental states. The attempts made by Queen Elizabeth and her two Stuart successors to establish an economic despotism on the Continental pattern had failed.[8] While there were plenty of English statutes and proclamations regulating domestic industry, commerce, and agriculture, they were seldom enforced. Their administration became particu-

[6] J. P. Muirhead, *The Life of James Watt* (London, 1859), p. 99.

[7] Nef, *Western Civilization since the Renaissance* (New York, 1963), pp. 280–81.

[8] Nef, *Industry and Government in France and England, 1540–1640* (Ithaca, N.Y., 1957), esp. pp. 25–27, 88–120. Cf. Nef, *The Conquest of the Material World* (Chicago, 1964), pp. 101–10.

332

larly lax after the civil war, which broke out in 1642, and still more after the revolution of 1688. Almost all efforts to set up government-owned or -controlled enterprises, resembling the French royal manufactures, were abandoned before the eighteenth century. Direct taxes, of the sort levied by the French crown, were not successfully established in England. There the man of wealth was freer than in France from levies on his income. He was also freer from the danger that the value of his money would depreciate as a result of governmental tinkering with the coinage.[9]

So economic thinkers in Europe and America were disposed to attribute English commercial and industrial leadership to freedom from government interference and to the absence of tolls on domestic trade. Adam Smith spoke of their absence as "perhaps one of the principal causes of the prosperity of Great Britain." Every great country is necessarily, he added, "the best and most extensive market for the greater part of the productions of its own industry."[10]

These views of economic thinkers concerning the most appropriate relation of political authority to agriculture, industry, and trade were strengthened by French history during the half-century from about 1735 to about 1785. For the first time since the Reformation the rate of industrial and commercial progress—the rate of growth in the volume of production—rivaled that in England. This progress was accompanied by modifications in the economic policies of the French government. There was a disposition on the part of public officials to disregard old regulations. Greater freedom was allowed to private individuals and companies to establish mines and factories outside the system of royal manufactures. The burdens imposed by the financial policies of the crown upon the private merchant were somewhat lightened.[11]

As the Revolution approached, progressive-minded French-

[9] Nef, *The Conquest of the Material World*, pp. 37–38.

[10] *Wealth of Nations*, Bk. V, chap. 2, Pt. II, Art. 4 (Rogers ed., II, 499).

[11] Nef, *The Conquest of the Material World*, pp. 342–45.

men were seldom, if ever, satisfied with the material advance their country had made. England was still setting the pace in mining and heavy manufacturing. Many Frenchmen felt that if France was to overtake England, she would have to copy English economic policies in almost every respect.

Such was the state of dominant opinion in Europe in 1787, when the American delegates assembled in Philadelphia to frame the Constitution. Whether they consulted recent American or European experience, it seemed to justify the very policies which were favorable, as Beard once showed,[12] to their private material interests and those of the classes they represented. They were in the happy position of believing that by serving themselves they were also serving the public. The Constitutional Convention found in recent history support for one of the most important innovations of modern English thought, that by seeking one's own financial advantage in the market place one increased the general welfare—that self-love and social interest are identical.

It is no wonder that this belief found expression in the Constitution. It is no wonder that, with an undeveloped continent before the American people and with no other tradition as a nation concerning the proper relations of government to economic life behind them, this belief should have become a more influential guide to private and public conduct in the United States than in any other country.

II. *Economic Freedom and Economic Progress*

In view of these constitutional traditions and of the laissez faire history of the United States during the nineteenth century, it is disconcerting to find that the role played by government in economic life has swelled almost continually since the Spanish-American War and especially since the entry of the country

[12] C. A. Beard, *An Economic Interpretation of the Constitution* (New York, 1913), esp. pp. 40–42 and chaps. 2 and 5 generally.

334

into the world wars and the cold war. This expansion of governmental activities is glaringly reflected in the mounting size of the federal budget from year to year and the scarcely less startling growth in the budgets of the states and the large municipalities. For what is becoming a long period, extending back to the second decade following the First World War, in the stretch of years between 1929 and 1965, the proportion of the national income appropriated in taxes has mounted at a much more rapid rate than the national income itself. During that period the rate of growth in the gross national product was much slower than that of the budget receipts taken by the federal government. One is reminded by analogy, of a prediction made facetiously in 1682 by William Petty, the early English statistician. If the population of London and that of England and Wales continued to grow at the rates which had prevailed during his lifetime, he suggested, by 1840 London would have swallowed almost all the inhabitants of the kingdom![13] In somewhat the same spirit, one is prompted now to ask whether Americans can look forward with equanimity to a time when no one has anything to spend unless he is an employee of the government.

Some seventy years ago, at the juncture of the nineteenth and twentieth centuries, a brilliant American congressional leader who was a Republican, Thomas B. Reed of Maine, the Speaker of the House of Representatives, stood out as best he could against a fundamental change in the foreign policy of the United States, which began about 1890 with pressure for expansion. To Reed this was "a policy no Republican ought to excuse much less adopt." He saw with dismay that a shift was occurring, with the Spanish-American War, from non-intervention outside the boundaries of the United States toward

[13] Petty, "Another Essay in Political Arithmetick" (1682), in *The Economic Writings of Sir William Petty*, ed. C. H. Hull (Cambridge, 1899), II, 464.

increasing participation in the affairs of foreign lands.[14] That fresh trend in foreign policy has augmented ever since, especially since the nineteen-thirties.

Politicians in the United States have not been as nimble as they might have been to see how closely this shift in foreign policy is related to the transition from relative freedom to extensive interference in the evolution of industry, trade, and finance. They have failed to recognize the extent to which the two spheres of policy—domestic and foreign—are interdependent. In view of the difficult problems in both spheres that confront the country in the latter part of the twentieth century, it is desirable to consider the relation of freedom of economic enterprise to the general welfare, in the light of wider historical knowledge than was available to those Americans who took part in the Constitutional Convention in 1787.[15] It is desirable also to consider to what extent involvements in the affairs of foreign countries are compatible with the domestic liberty necessary to the welfare of the United States. It is desirable finally to consider, in connection with the international relations of the newly interdependent world of the twentieth century, what foreign policies will encourage a renewal of the search for civilization that concerned Americans as well as Europeans in the times of Montesquieu, Adam Smith, and Jefferson.

The future of economic enterprise, the subject of this chapter, and the future of democratic government, the subject of the next, are as closely intertwined with future foreign policy as the future of education is intertwined with the future of society. For the United States, as well as for the rest of the world, civilization has come to depend upon a complete reform in international relations. The nature of that reform is dis-

14 Barbara Tuchman, *The Proud Tower* (New York, 1966), chap. 3, esp. pp. 142, 151, 162–63.

15 Nef, *The Conquest of the Material World*, chap. 8.

cussed in the last chapter.[16] It is on the assumption that it can be at least partly carried out during the next decades that the future of free enterprise and of democratic government are considered. For unless international relations are guided as never before by a concern with universal justice and peace, there may be no future for either. Or for education.

Like all liberty, economic liberty, philosophically considered, is a means, not an end. As the greatest Greek philosophers might have said, the amount of such liberty desirable for happiness varies. As all economists know, there never has been and never can be complete freedom from government interference in economic affairs. Even in the thought of the Constitutional Convention and the practice of United States policy for the first hundred and fifty years, the principle of freedom was never extended to cover international trade. There never can be, on the other hand, state control over every detail of economic affairs. The problem for the moral philosopher, and for the philosophically minded economist as well, should be to find the right emphasis. That is not the same at all times and places. As seekers after what ought to be, Americans should husband what is good in the tradition of free enterprise and discard what is harmful, either in itself or because changed conditions have made it obsolete.

For a historian, the first matters to consider in a rough and general way are the actual historical relations between economic liberty and economic welfare. Though the light which history might throw on this problem is perhaps less important than that which could be obtained from philosophical economic analysis, historical knowledge is essential to such an analysis. What has history to teach concerning the relation of freedom from government interference to material prosperity, to the increase in the production of goods and services "that can be brought directly or indirectly into relation with the measuring rod of money," and to the widespread dissemination

[16] See below, chap. 12.

of such goods and services among the population? Insofar as our present knowledge goes, periods of rapidly increasing prosperity have been, generally, periods of relatively great freedom from government interference in business. While this suggests that such freedom is favorable to prosperity, a close study of history warns us against regarding it as the only or even the primary cause.[17]

There have been periods of increasing prosperity during which government interference was relatively great. Such was notably the case in the late fifteenth and early sixteenth centuries, at the time of the rediscovery of America and the passage around the Cape of Good Hope. Industrial and commercial development was striking in many parts of Continental Europe—nowhere more so than in the disintegrating Holy Roman Empire, where Germans played the leading part in enterprise.[18] German historians have studied the economic progress of the Renaissance with an intensity and an interest comparable to that taken by English and American historians in the industrial revolution of the late eighteenth and early nineteenth centuries. Economic thought in Germany never went quite so far as that in other continental countries in accepting the position of the English classical economists concerning the advantages for national welfare of freedom from government interference. But if there was one period when in theory, and also to some extent in practice, the Germans adopted liberal economic principles, it was in the late nineteenth century. This was also a period when the German state brought little or no pressure to bear on scholarly writers to reach conclusions that would be in accord with the dominant political authority. It is the time, therefore, when we should expect German historians to be most likely to question the benefits of political interference with private enterprise. Yet several of them attributed the increased industrial efficiency

[17] Cf. above, chap. 4 (IV), pp. 102 ff.

[18] Cf. above, chap. 2, pp. 14–19.

and the reduction in costs made in central Europe at the time of the Renaissance to the increase in government control over mining, metallurgy, and salt-making. The most learned of all German economic historians, Gustav Schmoller, showed, for instance, that in some cases the consolidation of salt-making enterprises in the hands of the princes was accompanied by a halving of the labor costs.[19] To collaboration between merchants and princes, the late Jacob Strieder attributed much of the prosperity in mining and metallurgy.[20] Both probably exaggerate the economic advantages of Renaissance paternalism.[21] But it would be folly to suggest that government interference and even government ownership and management are always incompatible with improvements in technique and a rapid increase in production.

Government interference has undoubtedly a tendency to impose a handicap on the growth of output and of prosperity. But a trend toward greater freedom or toward greater political control in economic affairs, historically considered, is only one of many factors which influence the material welfare of a people. Such trends cannot properly be considered by themselves, if we are seeking for general truth; they have to be considered in relation to all the circumstances which influence prosperity. When an attempt is made to do this, it is seen to be doubtful whether the growth of economic freedom has been in the course of history the most important cause of economic progress. It has been contingent upon other circumstances, prominent among them liberty to devote the resources of the country to peaceful pursuits. If we probe the matter further, we discover that these other circumstances have on their own account, and independently of the economic freedom they

[19] "Die geschichtliche Entwickelung der Unternehmung," *Jahrbuch für Gesetzgebung, Verwaltung und Volkswirtschaft*, XV (1891), 660.

[20] *Studien zur Geschichte kapitalistischer Organisationsformen* (Munich, 1925), *passim*.

[21] Nef, *The Conquest of the Material World*, p. 108.

promote, much to do with the prosperity. They have possibly even more to do with it than economic freedom. Yet peace, like free enterprise, while undoubtedly favorable to economic growth, is not a necessary cause for it.

Space does not permit us to bring forward here much evidence in support of these general propositions.[22] A short demonstration of their reasonableness can nevertheless be made.

In classical times the government of the ancient Roman state became, under the empire, and especially under the later empire, after the second century of the Christian era, increasingly despotic. With his unrivaled knowledge of the social and economic history of the classical world, the late Professor Rostovtzeff showed how the emperors imposed heavy new burdens on the landowning and financial classes, until they snuffed out most of the incentive for private initiative. They regulated enterprises more and more minutely. They took many ventures, such as mines and metallurgical plants, into their own hands and confided the management to their fiscal administration. This growing paternalism was accompanied in the late third century and afterward by a notable shrinkage in the output of mines and manufactures in most parts of the Roman Empire and by the abandonment of land previously cultivated. There is a temptation to attribute the economic decline in large measure to the increased government interference. There is a temptation to attribute the prosperity during the first and early second centuries, in large measure, to the greater freedom which existed at that time.[23]

It is possible to argue that the rise of economic despotism was unfavorable to prosperity in late classical times, without making it the basic cause of the decay of commerce and manu-

[22] I hope to discuss the subject in more detail in the general history of industrial civilization which I have in hand.

[23] Cf. M. Rostovtzeff, "The Decay of the Ancient World and Its Economic Explanations," *Economic History Review*, II, No. 2 (1930), 197–214.

facturing. Can paternalism be considered, in any case, as the principal explanation for the failure of the classical peoples to develop a mechanized industrial civilization of the sort created by the Western peoples during the last four hundred years, particularly since the American and French revolutions?

Without a special knowledge of classical history it would be presumptuous to do more than offer an opinion, in the hope that it may be tested by careful research. In its early stages modern industrialism was based on the widespread substitution of power-driven machinery for hand labor and upon the use of steam, oil, gas, or hydroelectric power in place of the force of man, beast, wind, or stream.

No comparable substitution had occurred in Roman times. "In the second century of the Christian era," as Gibbon wrote, "the empire of Rome comprehended the fairest part of the earth, and the most civilized portion of mankind." Yet in that rich and highly sophisticated world, mines and quarries, together no doubt with industrial cities, "formed merely small islands in a sea of fields and meadows."[24] To understand why there was nothing remotely resembling what was found at the beginning of the twentieth century in the Ruhr district, the Black Country in the English midlands, or the Pittsburgh neighborhood, is it not necessary to discover what was missing in classical times to stimulate labor-saving inventions and the widespread use of mechanical energy? Why was there so little development of new mechanical principles, why was little or no attempt made to use steam for power, during the preceding hundred and fifty years or so of economic liberalism, when the imperial government protected private property and encouraged private initiative? The extension of the liberal economic system of Rome to the provinces created a market, with free trade, comparable in extent to that of modern America. Under the early empire, the entrepreneurs of classical times had a far

[24] Rostovtzeff, *The Social and Economic History of the Roman Empire* (Oxford, 1926), p. 296.

341

larger unified area in which to exploit the natural resources of the soil and the subsoil than the English adventurers had in a period of comparable length, between the late sixteenth and late eighteenth centuries. What conditions were lacking to make it possible for the classical peoples to set up steam engines, to discover cheap methods of smelting iron ore, and to work out most of the technical principles upon which the triumph of industrialism among the Western peoples has been based?

No final answer to that question is, perhaps, possible. But would any answer be adequate unless it took account of the lack of coal resources in the lands surrounding the Mediterranean, where the chief centers of classical industry and commerce were found?[25] Would it be adequate unless it took account of the special bent which the peoples of the north of Europe, and the British in particular, have shown for scientific inquiry and a philosophy of material improvement?[26] Would it be adequate unless it took account of the relatively great security afforded the British people by their island?[27] Their isolation made unnecessary the development of a military force, such as influenced the Roman emperors in embarking upon their policy of all-embracing paternalism.[28]

If Professor Toynbee is right, classical society was already doomed before the Romans dealt the other peoples of the Mediterranean area knockout blows and established the empire. Viewed in the light of his position, the commercial and industrial collapse was a symptom of a deeper malady. It cannot be treated as a primary result of economic despotism. In

[25] For the influence of coal see Nef, *Rise of the British Coal Industry* (reprinted London, 1966).

[26] Nef, *The Conquest of the Material World*, chap. 7.

[27] Nef, *Western Civilization since the Renaissance*, p. 88 and chap. 4 generally.

[28] Rostovtzeff, "The Decay of the Ancient World and its Economic Explanations," in *The Social and Economic History of the Roman Empire*, pp. 207–9.

any case, the collapse was accompanied by other circumstances, besides increasing paternalism, which were discouraging to agrarian, industrial, and commercial enterprise. There was the prolonged civil strife of the third century. There was the increasing cost of metal and of manufactured articles, brought about by the rise in the price of fuel and building materials, as the forests were thinned out and timber of every kind became scarce and dear. There was, finally and perhaps most important of all, the lack of any development during the late republic and early empire of a school of natural science such as arose in Europe—and especially in Great Britain—in the sixteenth, seventeenth, and eighteenth centuries. The Latin mind has never had, to the same extent as the British, the capacity to reopen the deal with fate; it has not the same longing to strive after low economic costs. The special aptitude of the English mind for natural science and material improvement appears even in the Middle Ages with Roger Bacon and William of Occam. In Roman times we have no philosophers quite comparable to them. We certainly have no one who took a philosophical line comparable to that taken later by Francis Bacon, Boyle, or even Descartes. All three looked forward to the conquest of nature and of disease on such a scale as no classical philosopher had ever contemplated. They looked forward confidently to a time when these conquests would greatly lighten man's labor, enormously increase production, and prolong human life. For many decades the Roman Empire had peace and a large measure of free trade. But peace and free trade were insufficient for the triumph of industrialism without the driving force of an intense belief in the possibility and desirability of material improvement. It is altogether improbable that the "new philosophy" (the name first attached to modern science), bound up as it was with the origins of industrialism in Europe, would have developed in the later centuries of the Roman Empire, even if the relatively greater economic freedom of earlier times had persisted.

From the historical point of view, it is hardly less one-sided to attribute the great prosperity of the Western peoples in modern times entirely to the skill and enthusiasm of private businessmen, stimulated by the profit motive, than to deny to them any share whatever in bringing it about. In their enthusiasm for the business adventurer, some champions of free enterprise minimize, or forget altogether, a number of other factors. They minimize the part played in the material prosperity of Western civilization by natural resources (especially coal and other mineral wealth), by the growing area of free trade, by orderly manual labor, by invention, by the natural science behind invention, and by the philosophy of improvement behind both science and invention.[29] They also ignore the role of artistic craftsmanship and tender manners in encouraging the hope that the better sides of human nature could limit the power of evil.[30] They forget especially the part played by peace in the material prosperity of Great Britain and America. Except for the civil war of the seventeenth century, there has been no serious and prolonged fighting on British soil since the Reformation. Except for the War of Secession of the nineteenth century, there has been no serious and prolonged fighting on North American soil since the United States became a nation. Neither of these wars lasted long enough to interfere profoundly with economic progress. Protected by the sea and united within the unrivaled frontiers which the sea had hitherto provided, Great Britain and the United States enjoyed opportunities to occupy their energies, without the threat of destruction, with the industrial exploitation of natural resources to a degree that had never been possible on the continents of Europe or of Asia. There the various nations have been continually subject to the ravages of war, to the fear

[29] These matters are discussed in Nef, *La Naissance de la civilisation industrielle* (Paris, 1954), Pt. I.

[30] See above, chap. 2 (IV).

of invasion, and to frequent shifts in the frontiers which have provided barriers to trade.[31]

In Western history, war has been a factor working to increase the scale of enterprise, as the late Werner Sombart has emphasized in his studies of the rise of capitalism. With the use of gunpowder, with the use of metal for building defenses and for hurling at the enemy, larger and larger munitions plants, arsenals, and shipyards were required to provide for victory. So there is a sense in which war contributed to the triumph of industrialism, by promoting the assembly of great blocks of capital. But the waging of war on a large scale, when accompanied by invasion and serious material destruction within the national boundaries, was generally unfavorable both to the growth in the output of consumable commodities and to the freedom of business activity.[32] One factor that promoted the rise of economic despotism in the states and principalities of Continental Europe on the eve of the Reformation was a change in the nature of the weapons of warfare. This change was hardly less sweeping than that which took place between the two world wars of the twentieth century, with the introduction of airplanes, tanks, and motorized troops. On the eve of the Reformation gunpowder, cannon and other firearms were being introduced extensively for the first time. It seemed to some contemporaries that the technique of warfare changed overnight. The nature of the new weapons led the political authorities to declare their production state monopolies. This was done in one country of Continental Europe after another, in connection with the manufacture of saltpeter and gunpowder as well as of ordnance of all kinds.[33] The administration of the armament industries by the government encouraged

---

[31] The subject is discussed at length in Nef, *Western Civilization since the Renaissance, passim.*

[32] *Ibid,* pp. 65–66 and *passim.*

[33] Cf. Nef, *Industry and Government in France and England, 1540–1640,* pp. 59–68, 88–98.

state interference with and control over all kinds of enterprises in industry and commerce.

The security provided by geographical conditions both for Great Britain and for the United States has helped the two countries to exploit their great natural resources and to raise their standard of living. At the same time, this security has been an important element in reducing the desire for government regulation and control over industry and commerce. Insofar as the general industrial system of a country has to be harnessed for war purposes, a degree of unified control is indispensable. This can be supplied effectively only by the central government. It is supplied at the expense of a considerable measure of economic freedom. When an adequate defense or offense in war depends on a quick response, it is necessary to maintain a greater control over private enterprise, even in times of nominal peace, than when the danger of foreign attack and invasion is remote. So in Great Britain and the United States we owe both our prosperity and our freedom of enterprise in a measure to the security provided by our natural frontiers. In considering the services which free enterprise has rendered to material prosperity, it is important that we should not include, as is frequently done, those which prosperity owes to geographical advantages. Without these geographical advantages we should not have had anything like the measure of liberty in economic life that we have possessed.

With the coming of jet planes and the creation of atomic and hydrogen bombs and other devastating and insidious weapons, these natural geographic advantages have evaporated. In warfare the world has entered a totally new period. The new conditions have involved the assembling of armaments on a vastly larger scale than in the past. The United States, which considers itself threatened by possible sudden and almost total destruction, has prepared, as a means of forestalling this threat, to wage every kind of warfare, in the air, on the seas, and overseas. So has Russia, which has felt no less threatened than the

United States. Other nations seem disposed to follow suit according to their capacities for production, because no nation is free from fear, least of all perhaps China, which has been invaded in the past as often as Russia.

Unless more peaceful relations can be established among all the nations of the world, and especially among the most industrialized nations, the change in the nature and scale of warfare will bring with it, even in the United States, as it has already begun to bring, mounting governmental interference in economic enterprise. Statesmen cannot have it both ways. They cannot prepare to wage war, especially in the nuclear age, and at the same time nourish that freedom of economic enterprise and those conditions of individual liberty and tolerance in the hope of which the North American colonies and the United States itself were founded and have grown.

Laissez faire may well be, then, more a symptom than the cause of the general well-being of a nation and its people. But to recognize this should not lead anyone to minimize the importance for well-being of free enterprise, individual liberty, and tolerance. They have always been precious as means of seeking the ends of civilization.

They have become more precious for all peoples of the world in the nuclear age than they were ever before, at the very time when the United States is threatened as never before with their loss. That is because, as has been indicated, they thrive on peace and languish in war. The more total the war the more complete their eclipse. As war has been made potentially almost infinitely more destructive by the discovery of nuclear fission and other scientific advances, and their application to armament, the dangers of war for liberty have multiplied manyfold during the last two decades. A diminution of violence in settling disputes among nations has become a necessity for the future of civilization and perhaps for the existence of the human race.

III. *Economic Freedom and General Welfare*

The liberty to be sought in the interest of civilization, and of the humanity without which there can be no civilization, is integral liberty. Economic freedom is a part of it.

With the exaggerated emphasis today in most countries on the economic sides of life, materialism threatens to become its own worst enemy.[34] Now that economic welfare has come to be dependent upon an improvement in the moral, intellectual, and artistic life of mankind, upon a greater measure of common faith than exists today, it is no longer helpful to concentrate our minds and our efforts on economic welfare.

Up to a point, increases in the national dividend of material goods and services, in the gross national product—and particularly a rise in the standard of living of the poor, who are the most populous—together with reductions in the manual labor required to produce a given quantity of physical wealth, do contribute to the love of virtue, knowledge, and beauty. But it is not true that by focusing all the attention of a people upon the production of physical goods and entertainment, upon methods of producing them at a lower cost in manual labor, and upon the transportation, the advertising, the sale, and the consumption of goods in the largest possible quantities we shall approach as close as possible either to happiness, in Aristotle's sense, or to justice, in Plato's. Justice, as Plato might have said, is brought about by the most harmonious possible balance between all the needs of men, their desire for physical goods and entertainment, their yearning for faith, and their love of righteousness, wisdom, and art. Such a balance in any state—certainly in a vast state like the United States, with its two hundred million people sprawled over a continent and extending west to Hawaii and north to Alaska—can be produced only with the help of wise advice, good government, and many independent units, each capable of performing economic or non-

[34] See above, chap. 4, secs. I and III.

economic functions which contribute to the common welfare.

What seems to have come about with the triumph of industrialism, and with the moral and intellectual crisis of our time, is this: The disproportionate emphasis laid by our institutions and our social and economic life upon material values is depriving the American people of the opportunity to cultivate for their own sake the needs of the mind and spirit. The mechanized nature of physical work in mines and factories and the almost equally mechanical mental chores performed in most large stores, shops, and offices which sell and advertise the products of industry give the people who labor in them very little room, while working, to exercise their reason. The work of housewives, as well as of men, has been lightened. But many of the synthetic objects produced and sold by the new methods clutter up the increased leisure hours—at home, on the way to and from work, and in vacation time—in ways that provide little more scope for the quiet mind and heart than does the labor of making and selling the new products.

As the opportunity to seek righteousness for its own sake disappears, selfishness blots out the altruism and the sense of responsibility that existed to some extent during the great age of laissez faire—the age of Hume, Voltaire, Adam Smith, Franklin, and Jefferson—an age which lasted until the early twentieth century. As the opportunity to seek knowledge for its own sake disappears, there is a steady decline in the zest for work that was fairly widespread during that age. As the opportunity to seek beauty for its own sake disappears, disorder and untidiness obliterate the delight that persisted among the middle class and among the craftsmen during that age.

Responsibility, orderliness, and pleasure in steady and even hard work are all necessary—not only to create a good society but to maintain a wealthy one. Insofar as economic liberty raises the standard of living, it provides comfort and leisure which help men to cultivate the goods of the mind and spirit. But by the ways in which it has worked to raise the standard of living in recent decades, it has often deprived men of the training and experience which are indispensable if they are to cultivate these higher goods. In a country where there are few private institutions which effectively stand for goods of life other than material wealth or publicity, it is doubtful whether a full return (hardly practicable in any case) to the economic liberty which prevailed in the United States in the late nineteenth century would contribute as much to happiness as it would destroy.

Happiness seems to have become contingent upon a growing love for the higher goods of life and upon increasing opportunities to participate in enjoyment of these goods. The initiative that would nourish such love and provide such opportunities can hardly come from an *extension* of the practices of advertising and publicity that are associated with private business today. But such initiative is perhaps even less likely to come from an *extension* of government authority. Disinterested individuals alone could provide it, individuals who are free to cultivate, and to encourage others to cultivate, the best heritage of the arts and crafts and by virtue of this liberty to open new, more creative areas to private enterprise. It would be almost certainly in the interest of such initiative to halt the continuous rise in the national and the state budgets, and eventually to diminish government and increase private spending, as a demand is nourished for goods of quality and for living conditions of greater charm and delight than are generated by mass production and automation.

The more we consider either history or philosophy, the more apparent becomes the danger of regarding *material* well-being and freedom for private business as ends in themselves. As a nation the United States has given both places of special importance. From the point of view of national welfare the emphasis upon both, especially in the early decades of the Republic, did much to husband the energy and promote the prosperity of the country, though throughout American history the disproportionate attention paid to them has interfered with the cultivation of thought and art. Since the Civil War, and especially during the two world wars, American policy has discarded most of the other values embodied in the religion and the general culture that had been derived from Europe and from classical antiquity.

The United States is at a parting of the ways. Even if the country is able to survive in a world of dangerous neighbors without a fundamental change in its scale of values, it will not succeed in offering light for other people without such a change. The hope of building a great American civilization lies in the contributions the United States can make to world civilization by an emphasis on the needs of the mind and heart. Such a change in emphasis might be brought about by providing institutions independent of both the private businessman and the politician, devoted to the cultivation of righteousness, knowledge, and beauty for the sake of mankind.

The trouble is not that most citizens have too many material goods. It is doubtful whether a reduction in the supply would be a tonic of the kind that is so greatly needed. A reduction in the standard of living, like a further extension of government control, would be fraught with serious dangers for the freedom of thought and speech, the kindly physical treatment of human beings, and the rough equality of opportunity that still command the outward support of this nation. As means to the good life, these values need to be saved. Machinery, automation, and cheap power make it feasible to produce plenty of economic goods for the entire population without the continuous labor of a large portion of it. If it is possible to bring about a change in values, so that work for non-material purposes is treated as no less respectable than labor which increases the volume of goods and services already supplied in abundance, this should help to provide fresh markets if a reduction in the defense budget should become feasible.

If the peoples of the world are to make the most of the new

powers of production which the applications of the sciences have conferred upon them, there will have to be a great increase in the confidence they feel in the peaceful settlement of international disputes. There will have to be, as a result of this confidence, a great reduction in armament, and in the military and intelligence establishments maintained by the nations.

The notion that expenditures for armament and for military establishments are indispensable as stimuli to economic progress is ill founded. It was not war but limitations on the power of waging war and on the desire to wage it that laid the foundations for the civilization of which some eighteenth-century Europeans and Americans were conscious.[35] The rapid industrialization that followed was encouraged by the confidence inspired by the eighteenth-century Enlightenment, and still felt during much of the nineteenth century in Europe and North America, that the world was being gradually delivered from "barbarism" and that it was safe consequently to put new knowledge in the natural sciences freely at the disposal of all mankind.[36] In most progressive countries during the nineteenth century, expenditures on armament increased more slowly than the national income. This was the very period when, among many countries of the West, an economy of abundance replaced for the first time in history the age-old economies of scarcity.[37] Neither the technological developments, nor the new scientific discoveries which prepared the way for still more astonishing technological developments, can be attributed mainly to problems raised by warlike preparations. The basic scientific revelations of Einstein and Rutherford, for example, were in no way a result of war work.

In more recent times of greater wars and greater preparations for wars the impression has spread, in no small measure as a result of the discovery of nuclear weapons, that war pro-

[35] Nef, *Western Civilization since the Renaissance*, Pts. I and II.

[36] See above, pp. 33–37.

[37] Nef, *Western Civilization since the Renaissance*, p. 357.

vides an enormous stimulus not only for the application of the sciences to practical economic problems but for basic advances in the pure sciences. This has been questioned recently by an eminent American authority.[38] What the expansion of armament during the mid-twentieth century has certainly done is to stimulate the lavish endowments by governments of scientific inquiries to enhance national prestige and power. This has contributed to three tendencies, none of them in the interest of the creative scientific tradition as it had developed from Galileo and Newton to Einstein and Rutherford. One is the tendency to draw on scientific resources for specific technological purposes. The second is the tendency toward group inquiries at the expense of individual scientific genius, which flourished during the earlier decades of the twentieth century. The third, closely related to the first two, is the diversion of promising scientists to work for the government and to become dependent on government grants. This tends to narrow the scope of their inquiries and diminishes their value, when it comes to independent advice, even for statesmen. A former Secretary of the Air Force, James H. Douglas, recently told an academic audience that "during the years [he] served the Air Force and Defense Department [he] found great comfort in consulting scientific advisors who were representatives of no service or agency and committed to no particular program."[39] This suggests that, even from the point of view of defense, we need the freedom of thought which work for the government tends to frustrate.

So, in various ways, modern war preparations and government subsidizing of research are becoming a threat to the independence of the individual and even to the most imaginative and constructive sides of scientific adventure.

[38] Report of the President of the Carnegie Institution (Caryl P. Haskins), reprinted from *Carnegie Institution Year Book 65 for the Year 1965–66* (December, 1966), p. 12 and *passim*.

[39] James H. Douglas, manuscript of address at a dinner of the trustees of the University of Chicago for the faculty, January 11, 1967.

Even if, as seems possible, these preparations have recently contributed heavily to the rapid progress of practical inventions, their contribution to economic welfare will obviously be short-lived if full use is ever made of the stocks of weapons accumulated by the nations. Moreover, the great problem today in connection with peaceful technological progress in Europe and the United States is not so much how to find new means of tearing down and building up afresh, as how to assimilate recent scientific discoveries and their practical applications to the needs human beings have to live whole and wholesome lives.[40] Hasn't the time come to make haste more slowly? The advantage of supersonic jets which can go from New York to Paris in the time it often takes to get to and from the airports at each end is somewhat dubious. Human dignity and fervor are contingent upon an assimilation of the technological progress already made, and the diminution in the propensity of human beings to misunderstand and to destroy their fellows, more than upon additional doses of speed and efficiency.[41]

iv. *The Endowment of Creative Institutions*

In the light of these inquiries, can a balanced view be reached concerning the extent of government interference with free enterprise appropriate to the ends of civilization? The sphere within which business enterprise, conducted for private profit, came to dominate until the end of the nineteenth century was perhaps wider than is desirable for the happiness of the people of the United States in the twentieth. At the same time, the increase in government-sponsored enterprise since the end of the nineteenth century constitutes an even greater threat to their happiness. It would be wise to confine more and more the

[40] Cf. Haskins, Report of the President of the Carnegie Corporation, pp. 14, 18–29.

[41] *Ibid.*, p. 30.

role of the government to providing conditions under which constructive liberty can thrive.

A considerable part of the legislative, judicial, and executive regulation of business and financial practices that has been introduced and extended during the past seventy-five years has been in the interest of business honesty and integrity and of healthy sanitary conditions, clean foods and safe water supplies. In the sphere in which economic freedom is most appropriate—the extractive industries, heavy manufacturing, the provision of food and clothing, the ever widening transport—government interference has not as yet shackled that freedom to the point where the imaginative, adventurous entrepreneur and business executive have no scope to develop their creative ideas. And this is good, for, in spite of strictures against business, there has been no dearth in recent times of gifted industrial leaders. In the sphere of commerce, in salesmanship, in communications, there are abundant opportunities for innovations. But it is questionable whether, in this sphere particularly, private initiative is generally working in the interest of individual welfare. Nowhere perhaps more than in connection with communications are the consequences of the astounding technical progress of very recent times so disproportionately great as compared with the progress of human understanding. The late Harold Innis, who devoted the last years of his life to a detailed study of communications, reached alarming conclusions. He suggested that, with the incredible material improvements in communications (effected by speedy distribution of news by telegraph, and by increasingly cheap and easy telephone facilities), actual communication among human beings has broken down. According to Innis' researches, advances in the technical means of communication have impoverished communication. These researches have been recently given a wider audience by Marshall McLuhan, but the sweeping reforms which Innis' apocalyptical conclusions render desirable have been hardly considered.

Communications provide perhaps only one example of the way in which economic enterprise no longer serves the human needs for dignity as well as it did during the eighteenth and early nineteenth centuries, when the materials for building and the commodities for furnishing that were traded were fashioned by skilled craftsmen[42] whose delight in workmanship contributed to the delight of their clients.

Whatever exaggerations the views of Innis contain concerning the deterioration of quality, it would seem that people generally today (whether or not they are aware of it) are beginning to have a surfeit of some of the commodities produced, and of some of the facilities provided, under private competition and pushed onto the public by advertising, installment selling, and other high pressure methods, initiated not infrequently by public relations firms. Most of these methods are new. Far from providing nourishment for the eager students who leave college with a background in the intellectual and imaginative delights provided by stimulating thought and art, the kinds of work and entertainment which are provided by the existing economy dull the faculties of those young men and women who are seeking for full, enriching lives. Few escape boredom. Some despair. The present economic structure of society fails to provide adequately for those among the youth who are potentially most gifted and for whom affluence is not enough.

During the past seventy-five years there has been an overwhelming increase in printed matter and in a host of other cheap products, for which there was no real equivalent in the eighteenth or even during the nineteenth century. Moreover, industrialism has now spread to the entire world. It is necessary to consider, therefore, whether freedom of economic enterprise, which served Europe and North America well in the eighteenth and nineteenth centuries and which served the English people well ever since the Elizabethan age, is advanc-

42 Cf. above, pp. 45–47.

ing those human values and nourishing those human resources that were sought by the founding fathers when they wrote the Constitution of the United States. It is necessary to ask whether free enterprise, as a cure-all, can help to build the nobler civilization that will be so needed in the late twentieth and twenty-first centuries. Already in the early nineteenth century Sismondi foresaw the dangers for the further progress of civilization that abundance might hold. "The nation in which no one suffers," he wrote, "but where no one enjoys enough leisure or ease to feel fervently or to think deeply, is only half civilized, even though it has conquered poverty."[43] As Marya Mannes has recently expressed it, "what is good for business is not necessarily good for the human being."[44]

If, as seems evident, economic freedom by itself is not a *guarantee* of the liberty that makes for civilization, is it not even less likely that a nobler civilization can be created by government fiat? Would it actually help the United States to extend the sphere of government interference, to continue the decade-long trend toward increased public spending and larger federal and state budgets? What the national government seems inclined toward is vast expenditures and vast undertakings—enterprise on an even more massive scale than those of the largest private business combines. If we are seeking civilization, the great needs seem to lie in the other direction—not away from but toward the dignity and fulfillment of the individual person for which small-scale efforts are often of vital importance.

Governments with their massive programs for improvement do even less than large corporations for such persons. Their freedom is the most precious freedom for the human future. As Maritain has just written:

[43] Sismondi, *Nouveaux principes d'économie politique* (3d ed.; Paris, 1951), I, 34 (my translation).

[44] Mannes, "Other Poisons in the Air," *New York Times,* December 10, 1966.

It is invariably tiny groups and small flocks that accomplish the great things. Our epoch seems to call for them more than any other, because under the impact of technology it is an epoch of massiveness. . . . It is only tiny groups and small flocks that can join together around this thing that escapes technology and mass production: the love of wisdom and intelligence and the confidence in the power of this love to radiate. Its invisible rays carry far. Their diffusion in the realm of the spirit resembles that of the fission of the atom and the miracles of micro-physics in the realm of matter.[45]

What is the use of trying to settle the moon and other planets, with massive government funds, if humans are unable to provide reasonably peaceful conditions among the age-old settlers of their own planet? The great need is for more opportunities to strengthen the ties that bind one individual to another in tiny groups and small flocks. Government spending and organization almost never provide those opportunities. They are inclined to move people massively toward the big and the impersonal, at the expense of those inner adventures of the spirit which illuminate life not just for oneself but also for those close friends who, as Saint-Exupéry's fantasy suggests, can be acquired only by domesticating one's neighbor!

The remedy for one extreme is never to rush to the other. It is well to remember that one extreme is as bad as another and that justice in the state consists in cultivating the greatest possible harmony between all the needs and all the inevitable desires of human beings.

Among the legitimate wants are the desires for private property and for freedom to pursue business for the sake of profit. If it ever came in the United States, communism might be even worse than in Stalin's Russia. All but the most blind in all countries are beginning to realize how bad that was. Laissez faire is part of the American heritage. The danger that its complete abandonment would constitute to political and moral

[45] Jacques Maritain, *Le Paysan de la Garonne* (Paris, 1966), pp. 249, 251–52 (my translation).

stability is increased by the disposition of Americans to magnify their disagreements and to neglect opportunities for agreement when they present themselves. What is important for the United States is the recognition that private property and economic individualism are means rather than ends and that, as with all means, it is possible to have more of both than is desirable, not only for the general welfare but for the welfare of the few creative individuals upon whom the general welfare ultimately depends.

In the interest of civilization, the need would seem to be to find means of encouraging, beside the mass production that must be maintained for peaceful consumption, an ever increasing sphere of workmanship and exchange devoted to the satisfaction of individual desires for delight, for the love of wisdom and intelligence, and for the *love* which can bind two for life. Equality of opportunity, freedom of thought and speech, the humane physical treatment of fellow men and women and children everywhere, could then be combined with an effort to build, in company with all the peoples of the earth, a society nobler and more enduring than any the historian or the archeologist has discovered.

If the United States is to move toward such a society, Americans should strive to avoid the further concentration of wealth or power either in the central or local governments, or in the hands of private businessmen, or in the hands of labor-union leaders. The central government will have to exercise, as it already does, greater economic authority than it exercised in the United States during the nineteenth century, but it should exercise this authority with restraint on behalf of the highest ends of civilization and not in order to make the state dominant in the life of the nation. An important step in the direction of this goal would be a redistribution of the economic resources of the country in the interest of a better society, devoting its energy less exclusively to the present major economic objectives.

If the expenditures on war and armament can be greatly reduced, and taxes continually cut, it should be left to individual
initiative, through the private foundations, to subsidize the arts
and crafts. A movement in this direction has already begun.
Such foundations have been increasing in number and in financial resources. Public policy should encourage their further increase, especially the increase of small foundations. They must
be left free to expend their money as their officers see fit. The
hope that they would want to move in the direction of the arts
and crafts must be confided to the efforts in education, which
might result from the reforms suggested in the previous chapter. If the foundations did in fact subsidize more and more those
forms of workmanship and creative performance which have
been neglected in the recent conquest of the material world,
this could be trusted to draw private economic enterprise into
the sphere where it is most possible to nourish the values which
constitute the ends of civilization.

The arts and crafts would then be free to develop independently of the current demands of the market place for
cheap machine-made products and for all synthetic works
which are made, not according to the requirements of beauty
as they develop in the inner life of the artist, but according to
the requirements of persons with little or no creative fervor and
little or no aesthetic knowledge, who depend for their livelihood upon sales. Such a policy undertaken by the private
foundations could contribute to the renewal of artistic styles
which the most creative of modern artists have managed to
achieve in spite of the formidable obstacles.[46] With such styles,
cities and villages could be gradually rebuilt on aesthetic principles and made fitter to live in than they have now become. If
these results were achieved or even approached, the sovereign
people of the United States would have no reason to feel that
their investment in the arts and crafts had been wasted.

There would remain an immense sphere within which pri-

[46] See above, pp. 61–68.

vate business, as now constituted, would be free to operate. The demand for food, heat, conveyances, and materials of all kinds would hardly diminish if an increasing proportion of the population were employed in creative tasks, though the nature of the demand might change. Business could extend its scope into new areas by adapting itself to the new developments connected with the arts and crafts. Time and energy would no longer be so much wasted in private drives designed to raise money for worthy causes. The life of the community would no longer be dominated as completely as it is today by the business or the labor-union view of life. Industry, trade, and finance would exist to serve man, not man to serve industry, trade, and finance.

11 The Future of Constitutional Government

O repos! O tranquillité!
O d'un parfait bonheur assurance éternelle,
Quand la suprême Autorité
Dans ses Conseils a toûjours auprès d'elle,
La Justice, & la Vérité!

Racine, ESTHER, III, iii

"We must prepare ourselves," writes Walter Lippmann, "for political inventions which are as radical as the technological revolution in which we are living."[1] The overwhelmingly rapid changes in material conditions all over the world during the past century and a half, and especially during the past three decades, call for unprecedented inventiveness not only in the economic but in the political sphere.

Changes in one sphere of human development have repercussions in all spheres. One of the great tasks of thought is to understand better the interrelations between developments in different spheres, in order to help those who want to build constructively in any sphere to recognize the possible reverberations of what they advocate or do. It is not enough, moreover, to *foresee* such repercussions, unless the builders have invariably before them the objective of serving the whole human being as an individual who desires a future for civilization, in a world where there are no longer any natural boundaries to the power to destroy.

So constructive thought in connection with politics (as in other realms) demands more from the mind and heart than it ever has before. Political liberty requires greater protection.

[1] *The Washington Post,* December 6, 1966.

To nourish fruitful results in the practical realm from fresh political thought, society will have to go far in wagering on the responsibility and integrity of the individual thinker.

Already, a generation ago, one of the most creative students of political thought wrote,

. . . perhaps never in its long history has the principle of constitutionalism been so questioned as it is questioned today. The world is trembling in the balance between the orderly procedure of law and the procedures of force which seem to be so much more quick and effective. We must make our choice between the two, and it must be made in the very near future.[2]

That choice has not yet been made. The problem is still essentially the same; the urgency of choosing is at least as great as when Professor McIlwain wrote those words about thirty years ago, when the Second World War was breaking out in Europe. He never concealed his preference for constitutionalism. On several occasions he brought his almost unrivaled knowledge of constitutional history to bear on the twentieth-century crisis of government. A principal cause of the crisis, he said, "is the feebleness of government. It must be strengthened. The present danger is despotism. It must be prevented and by legal limitations on government. . . . We must preserve and strengthen those laws beyond which no free government ought ever to go, and make them the limits beyond which no government whatever can legally go."

With the ending of the Second World War in 1945, a new element was imposed upon the problem of constitutionalism: the problem of achieving world order as a necessary basis for liberty within any nation. McIlwain had not considered this element before the war, but it engaged him actively afterward through his membership in the Committee to Frame a World Constitution from 1945 to 1950. He saw that the future of constitutionalism was coming to depend upon limitations on

[2] C. H. McIlwain, *Constitutionalism, Ancient and Modern* (Ithaca, 1940), p. 3.

wars. He saw that limitations on wars were bound up with a new movement among all states gradually to diminish the sphere of national sovereignty, in the interest of a rule of law under a supranational authority representative of all the nations of the world. The world in the twentieth century may be compared to North America in the eighteenth. Its future at that time (like the future of all nations today) depended upon the willingness of the individual states to hand over part of their executive, legislative, and judicial powers to a federal government, the United States.

Constitutionalism as an objective for the United States today rests, then, upon political inventions aimed in three directions. It depends upon a narrowing of the sphere in which government intervention is legitimate. First, within the country the liberty of the citizen needs to be protected, both by diminishing the scope of government activity at the expense of free enterprise and by erecting bulwarks against every form of tyranny, including personal abuse. Second, in international affairs, the protection of United States citizens, in company with the protection of all the world's peoples in the nuclear age, calls for the steady strengthening of world authority until that authority is able to settle disputes between independent states without resort to war. In the third place, the national authority, limited in those two directions, needs to be made less wasteful, less subject to private corruption, less expensive and complicated, and more effective in those spheres where it can properly operate.

It is impossible to suggest in which of these three directions political inventions are most needed. An advance in any of the three directions is dependent upon advances in the other two. Advances in all three directions are dependent ultimately on the attainment of a greater measure of international peace and understanding—the subject of the next and final chapter of this book. Perhaps the greatest need today of all nations, including the United States, is to design a new independent but more altruistic nationalism within the framework of effective world federalism.

These three objectives of politics transcend all, and comprehend most of, the smaller issues that today habitually engage the political scientist and statesman. They provide keys to a fresh conception of democratic government which may enable Americans to decide, as McIlwain so ardently hoped, for the orderly procedure of law rather than for the disorderly procedures of force. Such a conception would place constitutionalism on a more permanent basis than it has ever occupied in history. If Americans can prove inventive in developing, under inspiring leadership, a strong new constitutionalism, the value of which would be apparent throughout the world, similar innovations might be gradually adopted by other countries of their own free will, as the British conception of government was adopted in its essentials to a considerable extent at the end of the eighteenth and during the nineteenth centuries.

1. *Democracy and Totalitarianism*

"No one can foresee the future," wrote James Harvey Robinson in 1921, "but . . . the future has so far proved different from the past and will continue to do so."[3] This truth is widely ignored today, at a time when there is perhaps a greater need than there has ever been for men to accept it. The political inventiveness that is called for cannot be bound by past experience; particularly it should not be bound by the experience of despotism, totalitarianism, and tyranny in all the forms that have recently compromised the hopes inherited from the eighteenth and nineteenth centuries for the dignity and responsibility of the individual.

The history of the past, including the experience our age has had with dictatorships, both communist and anticommunist, provides much instructive material for new political thinking.

[3] *The Mind in the Making* (New York, 1950 ed.), p. 229.

Frequently this experience has lent itself to misleading interpretations. What is expedient in the interest of power is sometimes mistaken for what is good and just. What is good and just is sometimes mistaken for the pursuit of power. The meaning of recent tyrannies ought to be seen more truly and less emotionally. The ultimate defeat of tyranny can no longer be realized on the battlefield, as it *could* be to some extent until 1945. It can be realized only if leaders throughout the world recognize that totalitarianism in all its forms, whether declared or masked by some milder word, is alien to the spirit of those political systems which were part of the civilization that helped make possible the conquest of the material world.[4]

The representative form of government, as Western societies in modern times know it, grew up during the eighteenth and nineteenth centuries under the aegis of what is best in the humanist and the Christian traditions, as those were expressed in the *culture* of the baroque age. Persons who, like Hume and J. S. Mill, rejected formal religious creeds were champions of the ethics associated with Christ, though they were far from assimilating perfectly the humility and love He personified.

This is not to say that the humanist and the Christian traditions account for modern constitutionalism. Its history in Holland and in Stuart Britain, as explained by historians, is complex. Rapid economic progress was one of a large number of factors which contributed to its establishment in the north of Europe. Rapid economic progress helped to strengthen the political power of the private merchants and to put them in a position to resist effectively the exercise of absolute authority by a monarch. The early English "industrial revolution" strengthened the House of Commons.[5] It does not follow that modern constitutionalism can be explained adequately by economic causes. Still less does it follow that the collapse of moral

[4] Cf. above, chap. 2 (IV).

[5] Cf. Nef, *Industry and Government in France and England, 1540–1640* (Ithaca, N.Y., 1957).

and intellectual standards during the twentieth century is a source of strength to constitutionalism, as some of those scholars who regard as totalitarian every attempt to establish the authority of human wisdom sometimes almost seem to suppose.

The moral and intellectual foundations of modern constitutionalism are more fundamental than the economic ones. Constitutionalism takes for granted the dignity of the individual. It assumes that every individual has within him an element of goodness. In spite of the prevalence of evil, which may submerge this element in some people all of the time and in all people some of the time, constitutionalism assumes that mankind will be best served when men and women have a considerable measure of freedom to cultivate the good. Therefore, true freedom is possible only when there is a knowledge of good and evil, independent of individual preferences. Since the world about us is made up of individuals, it follows that impersonal knowledge of good and evil depends upon the embodiment in customs and traditions of the wisdom and saintliness of the past. Christianity in its Catholic form has stood for such customs and traditions, with an institution to cultivate and to enforce them. Humanism, as developed by the greatest classical philosophers and as revived in the Middle Ages and early modern times, has stood for essentially the same customs and traditions, without an institution to enforce them. Modern constitutionalism rests partly on the assumption, as Professor McIlwain has done much to emphasize, that these customs and traditions have an existence, not only independent of individuals but also independent of all organized authority, whether political or religious. According to a conception which is essentially modern, and which cannot, perhaps, be traced in Western history back farther than Bodin, these customs and traditions impose effective limits on the power of any ruler, whether it be a monarch or an assembly, as over against the individuals within the state. Medieval constitutionalism embodied a tradition of natural law,[6] but, as McIlwain has said, "the fundamental weakness of all medieval constitutionalism lay in its failure to enforce any penalty, except the threat or the exercise of revolutionary force, against a prince who actually trampled under foot those rights of his subjects which undoubtedly lay beyond the scope of his legitimate authority." In the late sixteenth and seventeenth centuries, after the rise of Renaissance despotism, political thinkers attempted, with success in England and some other countries, to secure for these rights embodied in natural law a sanction short of force.[7] Upon such a limitation of political authority rest the rights to freedom of speech and freedom of assembly. Obviously such rights can exist only if the individuals themselves assume obligations to accept the same customs and traditions that should be binding on the state.

Without the existence of unwritten and uninstitutionalized, but nevertheless accepted, authority in moral and intellectual matters, there is no check on the authority of political or religious rulers. Unless men, when it comes to a showdown, care more for virtue and honor than they care for themselves or for any individual no matter how powerful, they are bound in the end, paradoxically enough, to lose their rights as individuals. And what appears still stranger in a world which has lost its standards, these customs and traditions which are so essential to our liberties have to be created by, and based upon, that fragile and imperfect instrument, man's reason. They have to be taken on faith. They have to be written in the heart. Their validity is not susceptible of scientific proof, in the natural scientist's sense, to the same degree as are propositions in physics or chemistry.

Scientific methods are excellent things in their proper places.

[6] Cf. above, pp. 84–85.

[7] C. H. McIlwain, *Constitutionalism, Ancient and Modern*, p. 95 and *passim*. Cf. Felix Gilbert, "Political Thought of the Renaissance and Reformation," *Huntington Library Quarterly*, IV, No. 4 (1941), 462–63.

They have done much for mankind. But when scientific methods are regarded as the only appropriate methods for dealing with man's relation to man and even to art, or when individualism becomes solely a right and is divorced from the responsibilities for good which alone can justify it, constitutionalism and democracy are endangered. The human will and the human mind demand expression in some other forms besides those of laboratory experiments, equations, and factual reports. Democracy's chief claim to glory was not that it made men rich, but that it contributed to the dignity of all men. Neither the natural sciences, with their handmaiden technologies, nor individualism, could have contributed to man's dignity without the conceptions of righteousness and love which both Christianity and humanism at their best helped to establish and which are basically the same as the conceptions of righteousness and love which arouse the conscience of humans everywhere whatever their religions or philosophies.

At a time when standards have broken down, attempts to re-establish wise authority in matters of the mind are to be welcomed. Far from leading us toward totalitarianism, they may well offer us the only means of overcoming it. The one thing which a man who aspires to become a successful totalitarian leader must not have, it has been suggested, is a definite program in which he *believes*. Least of all must he *believe* in general principles of good and evil and in the dignity of man. What a successful dictator has to have is an overwhelming belief in himself, and an overwhelming desire for power.[8] Far from being allies, political absolutism and the authority of independent minds embodied in natural law are uncompromising opponents.

In a world of independent nations, in any world made up of human beings, neither the physical nor the human sciences, nor realistic studies of facts, will be left for long to work out the salvation of the race without interference. If these forms of

8 Cf. *The New Statesman and Nation*, February 4, 1939.

inquiry are not controlled by faith and reason, if the heart and mind are not invoked in issues that science does not settle, they are likely to be controlled by might. The recent history of the establishment of totalitarianism in western Europe, and especially in Germany, shows how easy it is for people belonging to the West to lose their liberties when they cease to value the principles of righteousness, justice, and compassion.

It is true that, insofar as the West is concerned, totalitarianism triumphed first in Italy, central Europe, and Spain, in countries which had a relatively short experience with the forms of constitutional government created in modern times in Great Britain, France, and the United States. It is true that, insofar as the West is concerned, totalitarianism triumphed first in the countries to which it is most congenial, the countries which fostered a rather similar conception of government and sovereign authority, on a much smaller scale, in the age of the Renaissance. Who would expect totalitarianism to win out first where fundamentally different governing traditions were strongest? We can derive some comfort from these traditions, but we cannot afford to think that of themselves, and without positive effort on our part, they will preserve human freedom during the centuries that lie ahead.

It is also true that material want has facilitated the triumph of despotism. Hungry men have no time to think. If they are faced with the choice of starving in liberty or being fed by a despot, they will make the easy choice, unless they are inspired by reason and the faith needed to sustain it.

Yet neither hunger nor the lack of democratic traditions accounts satisfactorily for the rise in the West of dictatorship in the twentieth century. The most important cause would seem to be the weakness of natural law. The collapse of traditional standards in the fifteenth and sixteenth centuries gave the Renaissance despot his opportunity. The collapse of traditional standards in our own time gave the modern despot his opportunity. What enabled men successfully to combat despotism in Europe after the age of the Renaissance was not the rejection of past customs and traditions. It was their recovery, development, and incorporation in new forms. It would seem to follow that the way to meet the latest wave of despotism is not by the destruction of natural law, but by its recovery, development, and incorporation in new forms. The only ultimate fortress against absolute government consists in strong disinterested objectives, of whose value people in responsible political positions become so convinced that they are willing in the end to risk everything, even their wealth and comfort and their lives, to maintain them.

If the United States is to be saved from totalitarianism and barbarism, it is even more important that Americans should discover these principles than that they should improve or even maintain their material standard of life. Let us hope they can do both. But let us reflect they are not likely to do either unless they put first things first.

It is difficult for any powerful nation to resist pressure toward dictatorship in times of crisis unless the tradition of the citizens' liberty within the state is strong, and is combined with a strong belief in the validity of the natural law. A book which appeared soon after the Second World War bore some such title as "The Hitler in Ourselves." No doubt evil and lust for power are to be found everywhere, but the recent German experience with dictatorship and conquest was partly the result of the particular history of the Germanic peoples. We make a mistake in assuming that all countries are equally subject to the expansionist mentality which was embodied in national socialism. We make a mistake in presuming that, now that this Germanic threat has subsided, constitutionalism in the United States is threatened mainly by alien dogma.

It is not difficult to form a conception of the position which the pan-German movement, with its contempt for natural law, would have taken if Germany had conquered the world, as it set out to do under Hitler. Yet to suppose that all totalitarian peoples are like the Germans in their passion for conquest is to misread history.

Recent historical inquiry has thrown doubt upon the old nineteenth-century view, fostered by German and to some extent by English historians (like Freeman and Maitland), that the conception of freedom in Western society is derived primarily from the medieval Germans. In mining, for example, it used to be supposed that freedom, the right of the finder of ore to share possession of it with the royalty owner, was of German origin. It now seems that a similar arrangement was common in the Roman Empire in the second century after Christ and even earlier. The medieval miner owed his free status partly to ancient custom, which had been handed down in certain regions where the digging of ore had never been long abandoned, and partly to new conditions related to the rapid economic and social and intellectual development of Europe in the twelfth and thirteenth centuries. These conditions were common to all the Western peoples and not peculiar to the Germans.[9]

In the wider matter of the general relation of the political subject to his ruler, Professor McIlwain's work has made it more difficult than it once was to accept the thesis that Western civilization owes its conception of liberty to the German tribes. According to the theory behind the Roman constitution, "the people alone are the source of all law." McIlwain has brought out the resemblance between the development of individual liberty in Roman and in English history. He has suggested that the influence of Roman law, before the Italian Renaissance, was exercised even through the legal compilation of Justinian on behalf not of absolutism but of constitutionalism. If McIlwain's tentative conclusions are justified, we have to thank early Rome more than has been supposed, and medi-

[9] Nef, *The Conquest of the Material World* (Chicago, 1964), pp. 24–29.

eval Germany less, for the political liberties that we rightly hold so precious.[10]

In the light of this recent historical research, as well as of the showing of the German government from 1933 to 1945, it becomes very difficult to hope for a recognition of the dignity of man, independent of his power to plow, organize efficiently, and conquer, in order to plow and organize efficiently further afield, in the pure Germanic conception of life and civilization. That view of life has its grandeur, but it is not Christian. It is more likely to arouse the enthusiasm of those who participate in it than of those who are rendered subordinate by it. The code of morality which is associated with Christ's example and the view that the independent mind should play a part in the establishment of justice and beauty, a view which we associate with the greatest Greek philosophers, are alien to this Germanic conception. They were handed down to us from classical times by the Latins. It is not accidental that the English language (as well as the French and all the other Romance languages) derives much more from Latin than does German. It will be even more difficult to prove, to persons for whom words still retain precise meanings, that it was the intention of the pan-Germans to help the meek inherit the earth than it was to prove, as some American writers once tried to do, that Christ was preeminently a man of business.

History, then, partly accounts for the peculiarly expansionist and the peculiarly efficient character of German totalitarianism. As believers in the value of liberty and a stronger constitutionalism, Americans need to probe the conditions within a country which lead to dictatorship. What made totalitarianism more powerful than it otherwise would have been in Germany (and also in Italy and Spain), as well as beyond the West in Russia and China, has been the lack of an alternative

10 McIlwain, *Constitutionalism, Ancient and Modern*, pp. 43-44, 48, 53-56, 59, 64-65, 68.

system that men are capable of practicing, a system that embodies the eternal values inherent in the conception of humanity set forth in Part Two of this book. These values were undermined in Europe by the increasingly popular view that there are no such things as firm principles, that there is no such thing as right, that there is no such thing as wrong. If principles are denied, the only test of an idea becomes its success.

II. *The Challenge of Totalitarianism*

The Second World War only partly demonstrated the *success* of constitutionalism. It resulted in the total military defeat of the forces assembled under Hitler in the cause of pan-Germanism (forces which included Italy and Japan and many smaller states which Germany had reduced to vassalage). That victory was an immense material achievement, and no such material triumph would have been possible without a widespread sense of the iniquities against which the Western allies were fighting. But the indignation and horror aroused by the liquidation, under Nazi Germany's direction, of millions of innocent noncombatants, was not accompanied by a positive moral and spiritual awakening, on the part of the Americans or the British, such as the cause of democracy might have merited. Little inventiveness emerged from the war in the realm of constitutional government.

Such inventiveness as there was came years afterward from France, a country which had suffered a defeat in the war. It is in all probability impossible for wars to produce a spiritual awakening among the victors lasting beyond the defeat of the enemy. But that reflection does not diminish the overwhelming need the peoples of the world have for such an awakening and for its embodiment in a fresh constitutionalism. For this awakening the British and Americans have looked mainly in vain during the last twenty years since 1945. In Great Britain no moral leadership in peace arose to match Churchill's leadership in war. In the United States the hopes aroused in some by Kennedy's administration were shattered by the bullets which tore his flesh apart before there was time to discover whether those hopes (which were shared by people all over the world) were well founded.

The excuse for the lack of creative politics among the victors since the war has been that all the energies of the winning nations, and above all of the United States, had to be spent in the containment of communism. Such an excuse ignores the fact that in the end no effective answer to communism can come from armed might, when the ultimate consequences of armed might have been irretrievably revolutionized by the progress of the sciences and their practical application. An effective answer could now come only from a better and more inspiring creed than can be supplied by any form of communism or anticommunism. That creed would have to be embodied in a new constitutionalism, to which peoples all over the world might respond because they could find within it a way of bettering their human condition without conquest.

If we are to decide as reasonable men between despotism and constitutionalism, our decision should depend upon a comparison of their ends. The end of despotism is power. In the despotic state of the present time every other objective is pursued only insofar as it promotes the power of the leader and of the nation he leads. Thus the interests of the people—their art, their virtue, their religion, their philosophy, their economics, the most private aspects of their family relationships, and even sometimes their science—are subordinated to the strengthening of the leader. If it is felt necessary to destroy art or religion in order to strengthen the leader, then art and religion must be destroyed or so modified that they lose the independence essential to both. Hitler is reported to have said, "The art of a national socialist era can be only national socialist." We are told that during the Nazi period some of the works of Rembrandt—regarded by many excellent painters and critics for

generations as perhaps the greatest Western painter—were
taken from the German museums whose walls they had ornamented.

Are the ends of constitutionalism any better? During the
years preceding the Second World War the fascists and national socialists used to taunt the democracies by telling them
that they cared for only one thing, material wealth—that their
statesmen were willing to sacrifice everything so long as they
could increase or retain their dividends and their salaries and
those of the supporters who kept them in office. The taunts of
the communists were of a somewhat different nature. They
suggested that all would be well if only the wealthy were dis-
appropriated so that the poor could pursue material ends un-
impeded by the rich.

Since the Second World War the communists, both in Russia and in China, and all other totalitarian states, have continued this line, but have made in their economies concessions
to private initiative. They have adopted much the same objective with which the totalitarians reproached the democracies
in the years before 1939, namely, an ever greater national dividend. Everywhere, as we have seen, progress is measured mainly in terms of economic growth, reckoned by quantity.

It is open to the states of what is called "the free world" to
demonstrate their liberty by establishing a nobler hierarchy of
values, which might eventually recommend the new constitutionalism that should be associated with these values to
countries in process of industrial development, in eastern
Europe, in the Near East, in Africa, in Asia, and in Latin
America. The purposes of constitutionalism would in this way
become superior to those of totalitarianism in the eyes of all
wise impartial observers. May their tribe increase.

III. *Toward Strong Constitutional Democracy*

The survival of constitutional government in the United
States, in Europe, and in the British Commonwealth, like its

revival or discovery in other countries, seems to depend, above all, upon the assignment of economic objectives to a less predominant place in the hierarchy of values, to a reaffirmation of the ancient belief that there are principles of right conduct which remain always essentially the same. It is only by acknowledging the existence of these principles and striving to live by them that men can fulfill their highest purpose. If it is to survive, democracy will have to appeal to men as an opportunity for service, as an opportunity for cultivating those values in art and religion, philosophy and science, which transcend material advance and material advantage. So long as men believe that ethical and aesthetic problems will take care of themselves if the death rate is reduced and the national dividend increased, the constitutional state will be unable to take its stand on the principles that alone can provide it with a firm foundation. No government which, like that of a democracy, does not coerce its subjects into supporting it can hope to maintain itself unless it finds among the governed a belief that there are general truths independent of circumstances and private interests which they are free to embrace and to hold. As long as men believe that each problem is unique and set out to solve it without the help of principles, they can fall easy victims to the coercion of dictators. How are men to gain convictions if they suppose that all truth and all conduct must bend to circumstances?

The future of constitutional government rests, therefore, not so exclusively in the hands of statesmen, generals, and admirals, scientists and economists, as is frequently assumed. It rests also in the hands of the persons who determine the curriculums of our schools and colleges, the nature of religious instruction, and the ideals of family life. It is up to these people to re-establish the permanent, unifying, non-material values in education, in religion, and in the family, which the last three generations undermined in an excessive zeal for freedom without responsibility and self-discipline.

The first step in defense of constitutionalism should be to

persuade our political leaders to stop making their main appeal to the voters by promises of material prosperity. It is not necessary or desirable that government should cease to be concerned with increasing wealth and with keeping up the standard of living, but questions of wealth should be made subordinate to questions of justice, of true liberty, and of beauty. When candidates for the Presidency, the Senate, or the House of Representatives ask the electors to judge them in terms of their success in reducing crime, in reducing waste both within the government and outside it, in diminishing the influence of propagandists and other self-seekers, when they ask the electors to judge them for their skill in fostering a love of beauty, of craftsmanship, in providing better opportunities for the virtuous, the intelligent, the deserving, and the honorable, whatever their race or status, they will perform an important service for constitutional government.

Statesmen should make plain to the people that the material prosperity of the state, like that of the individual, may suffer through no fault of the men in control. They should ask their constituents to face the fact that a sacrifice of material goods may sometimes be necessary in the interest of justice and intelligent understanding or of the beauty of the surroundings in which they live.

A statesman must not neglect, of course, to deal with the difficult problems of the needy and the unemployed. But it is certain that the proportion of the people who die from actual want is smaller in the United States than in any other country at this time or at any other. If material quantity made for political contentment, the people of the United States, ever since the depression of 1929–33, ought to be more contented with their form of government than any people who ever lived. The fact that discontent is sometimes widespread, especially among the young, indicates that the remedy of material improvement is inadequate.

In the economic sphere it is right, of course, for statesmen to promote prosperity, to provide for old persons, for cripples who are destitute, as also for the able-bodied unemployed when they cannot find work. But these should not be a statesman's only objectives, nor should they invariably be given precedence over others. He must also encourage social stability, reduce taxes, foster through private foundations interesting and useful work of new kinds connected with the arts and crafts, and encourage the widespread private ownership of property, in order to give the common man a stake in the economy of the country similar to that of wealthy businessmen with large holdings in industry, commerce, and finance. Harrington's statement concerning the relations between the form of government and the distribution of property has never been seriously refuted. "If the whole People," he wrote, "be Landlords, or hold the Lands so divided among them, that no one Man or number of Men . . . overbalance them, the Empire (without the interposition of force) is a Commonwealth."[11] Land is not the only form of property that needs to be considered. Since in the United States, and in all extensively industrialized countries, small-scale farming by small landholders has ceased to have the importance it had before the twentieth century, the endowment by private foundations of creative craftsmanship would help to produce the balance of wealth that is needed for the future of democracy. The maintenance of our form of government depends not upon the indiscriminate granting to the needy and the non-needy of income without work, as was once suggested by the numerous share-the-wealth schemes, but upon the granting to as many men as possible of the property and the conditions necessary for absorbing, useful work and creative leisure. The maintenance of our form of government depends less upon granting people facilities for moving from one part of the country to another than upon encouraging them to make the most of the opportunities

11 *The Oceana of James Harrington and His Other Works,* ed. John Tolland (London, 1700), p. 40.

provided within the region where they have already settled. A growing stability, a growing attachment of men to the particular region where they live and in which they are made to feel they have, through local institutions and private ownership, a stake of their own, would help to create those common bonds that have been lost in our age of specialized work and constant migration. It would help to divert men's minds from the fleeting to the permanent.

What would be the nature of the righteous government that we are seeking? There are three aspects of government in the United States that call for re-examination. There is, first, the form of government. This is determined by the manner in which the rulers obtain their authority. There is, second, the effectiveness of their power to act (within the sphere where they may legitimately exercise authority) and to carry through programs of reform in the interest of justice and the common good, programs involving changes in connection with education and with economic and social life. There is, third, the reinforcement of certain old limits on the powers of rulers and the creation of new limits, to insure righteousness and legality and to protect the individual from arbitrary arrest and from persecution of the kind that grew to such monstrous proportions in Russia, Italy, and Germany and that threatens since the Second World War to spread to the entire world.

In the discussion of the possible means to the attainment of civilization, attention was drawn to Pascal's vicious circle. It was suggested that a higher conception of education depends upon a higher conception of society.[12] It is equally true that a higher conception of government depends upon improvements in education and in the social order. These improvements can be made only if there is a recognition by the people that too much emphasis has been laid upon the function of man as voter, and above all as talker, and too little upon his function as a person. What government at its best has to do is to provide

[12] See above, pp. 267–68.

protection for what is noblest in the human being, to encourage men and women to shoulder their responsibilities as citizens in the spheres where they have special capacities for assuming such responsibilities—in their families, their occupations, and their social life.

All the reforms that are needed could be carried out within the framework of our government as it is at present constituted. Their initiation and their successful evolution would depend upon a change of heart among the governed and their governors. The power of the executive during the term for which it is elected must not be so hedged in that it cannot successfully take vigorous initiative. In all probability the electoral college has outlived its usefulness and Presidents should be chosen by direct vote. The test of the desirability of a statesman's action under the constitutional form of government must always be the free vote of the people when he stands for re-election. During the interval the President, the other executive officers, the members of the Senate and the House, in their appropriate spheres, should be expected to lead public opinion on current issues rather than follow it. They have an opportunity, now that the two political parties seem to be losing some of their glamor as patronage organizations, to curb wasteful expenditures, to reduce the sphere in which government activity replaces private initiative. In order to do so, they should set about strengthening the conditions, above all in the realm of foreign policy, which would make it possible to limit and eventually greatly to reduce the costs of armament throughout the world.

If the persons elected to, or chosen to serve in, political office are intelligent, they will nearly always be in a better position to make decisions than equally intelligent outsiders, but they should consult experts and competent persons on every technical matter. Moreover, as time goes on and a body of fresh opinion on the deeper general issues of human survival and dignity is formed with the help of interdisciplinary research and discussion, wise and disinterested counsel on basic policies, now lacking, should become available. Such counsel could be of the greatest moment to the persons occupying the highest offices in the state. They should read and listen to it.

The basic philosophical position behind the decisions and acts of statesmen, legislators, and judges cannot properly depend upon prejudices that they have picked up here and there in the course of their lives. They should turn to moral philosophy, in the Platonic and Aristotelian sense, as interpreted and augmented by the wisdom which it is hoped may emerge from the leading universities and institutes. Statesmen, legislators, and judges should be encouraged to make decisions based on a high sense of justice and intelligence and in accordance with a conscience schooled in the natural law. If they do this, they will always be in a stronger position to appeal to their constituents than if they bend with every wind set in motion by the bellows of propaganda and of special private interests.

The inability of government in the democratic states to deal with instability and moral disorder, or even to formulate the problems which instability and moral disorder have created, will bring constitutionalism into disrepute, unless statesmen are able to surmount these weaknesses. If they are to overcome them, they should not have to justify every small act, for it is possible to arouse against almost any act a chorus of propaganda that is the result not of intelligence and conviction but of chicanery, sometimes of a most sinister kind.

The crisis which has followed the Second World War has led inevitably to an increase in the powers of government. The future of constitutionalism depends in a great measure upon how our rulers resolve that crisis. It depends on whether they are able increasingly to co-operate with foreign powers and to strengthen the authority of international law to a point where it is possible to reverse the trend toward increasing government interference and expenditure at home. It depends also on whether our rulers are able to use the larger powers they have obtained, in such ways as to create confidence in democratic leadership independent of the old economic principle of laissez faire. Such confidence could be strengthened partly by improvements in the administration of public funds in the direction of greater efficiency and thrift. The American people are in much need of examples of both. Such confidence depends partly upon a limitation of military and naval tasks to objectives which are consistent with the cultivation of a righteous state in this country. Such confidence depends mainly upon the creation of a nobler conception of citizenship among Americans, such as will give their ancient right to liberty a meaning that has been lost now that freedom has come to be confused with license.

The program of educational and economic reform, set out in the two preceding chapters, should go forward now, insofar as this is consistent with the national defense. In any case, that program should go forward if and when the present military crisis is surmounted. The success of the reforms hinges upon a self-denying government, acting not in the interest of power as such but in the interest of the welfare of the citizens.

A redistribution of property, such as would be involved in the endowment of the arts and handicrafts,[13] would not destroy private business enterprise. It would leave private business enterprise a large measure of freedom but would limit the sphere in which it dominates to the kinds of work to which it is best suited. It would create a sphere devoted to training in good moral and intellectual habits, to art, craftsmanship, religion, science, moral philosophy, and studies relevant to moral philosophy. All the persons engaged in work independent of the ordinary give-and-take of the market place would be subjects of the nation, just like workmen, managers, technicians, employers, and investors in existing enterprise. Like private businessmen, they would have rights and functions of their own independent of the government. Moreover it is to be

13 See above, chap. 10 (IV).

hoped that business enterprise would find advantages in entering fresh areas of craftsmanship, art, and even education, and
in adopting new practices suited to those areas.

Economic and political conditions in the twentieth century
make any return to the kind of economic freedom that existed
in the United States in the nineteenth century out of the question. The choice is not between a nineteenth-century kind of
economic freedom and dictatorship, as we have been frequently told. The choice is between a fresh form of democracy and
dictatorship. The choice is between an unrighteous state and
some approximation to that righteous state envisaged by the
wisest philosophers of the past—a state in which mass industries
have an important but not a predominant place, a state which
aims to increase the wealth of the citizens, but only insofar as
this is consistent with the cultivation of faith, virtue, and
beauty. "Remove righteousness," wrote St. Augustine, "and
what are kingdoms but great bands of brigands?"[14] In this
world righteousness will always wither unless it is nourished.
The command obtained by the Western peoples over the
material world provides them with an opportunity unique in
history to guide mankind toward the ultimate ends of civilized
existence.

The rulers in the state, chosen by vote, should be imbued
more and more as time goes on with the importance of service,
with the importance of emphasizing now the sphere of private
business, now that of the endowed institutions, now that of
national defense, in accordance with the needs of the whole
people. The check upon the rulers would be the freedom to
reject them at the polls, together with the growth of principles
based on natural law and administered by the courts.

There is no use in having an executive power unless it is
given authority. If the function of the executive is merely to
be ornamental, then he should be dressed up in a costume and

[14] *The City of God* iv. 4. I have used Professor Ernest Barker's translation
of this passage.

treated as a master of ceremonies. No ship can be efficiently governed by a crew. No ship of state can be effectively governed by the people as a whole. But a ship of state is obviously a bundle of infinitely more complicated rights and obligations than a ship, and the executive in a state is the servant of the people in a comprehensive sense in which the captain of a ship, with his obligations to the passengers and to the company which employs him, can never be of the crew. Therefore, a need for limitations upon the powers of the executive arises. It is plain enough what some of these limitations should be. No change should be permitted in the system of elections or in the right of free speech and of every citizen to a legal trial. No change should be permitted in our form of government except through constitutional channels. In case laws are passed which do in fact alter the form of government or the system of free elections or which do abridge the right of free speech or interfere with the rights of all citizens to a fair trial in the courts, then the Supreme Court should annul these laws.

The rights of groups within the state—the rights, for example, of the schools and colleges, of the churches, of the family, of endowed institutions of all kinds, of new arts and crafts which it is to be hoped foundations will create—to an independent existence should be affirmed. It is no more desirable for the state than for private donors to determine the nature of the curriculum in the schools and colleges or to influence their administration. It is no more justifiable for the state than for wealthy parishioners to determine the content of sermons and the ways in which the churches shall spend their money. It is no more justifiable for the state than for the neighbors to determine the nature of instruction within the home—to decide what books the children should be encouraged to read or what political doctrines they should be taught. It is not justifiable for the state or even the foundations to determine the directions the new arts and crafts shall follow. That should be the responsibility of those who participate in them. Thus the school, the university, the church, the family, and the new arts and crafts would all have independent functions to perform in the defense of democracy and civilization. The future of constitutionalism depends upon making these institutions aware of their obligations in the hope that they will rise to their opportunities.

Finally, it is plain that the properly elected government of the United States, faced with the threat of despotism, should possess the strength to deal with the enemies of constitutional government within the United States and to meet the threat of aggression from without. Come what may, the Bill of Rights must be maintained. But there are in this country laws against spying. There are in this country laws against advocating the overthrow of our government by force. If Americans set out to advocate a revolution in this country which would replace our present constitutional government by a government under which the people would be denied the right to free elections, free speech, and a fair trial in the law courts, they are in effect advocating the use of force to undermine our principles of government. People cannot be denied the right of free speech or fair trial without the exercise of force. Herr Goebbels is reported to have said in 1935: "We, national socialists, have never stated we were democrats. On the contrary, we publicly stated that we only used democratic means to win power but after the seizure of power we would ruthlessly deny our opponents the facilities that were granted us when we were in opposition." Could the danger that confronts the constitutional government which tolerates the advocates of despotism be put more plainly?

The laws against the overthrow of our form of government by force should be extended to cover the activities of persons, whether citizens or not, who scheme to deprive us of our liberty. In addition, libel laws similar to those in England should be enacted, making it possible to punish by fine in the

courts persons who spread lies in print or on the public plat-
form concerning our statesmen or any of our citizens. With
despotism knocking at the door, constitutional government
has the right to defend itself.

The price of retaining the constitutional form of government is the recognition that nothing worth while has ever been
obtained by a people except through collective effort. The
price is the establishment of a democracy in which the standards of justice, honor, truth, and art are much higher than at
present, of a democracy in which the people place justice,
honor, art, and truth above material advantage. If we cannot
discipline ourselves, powerful men whose objectives are not
those of the better civilization we seek will discipline us. The
defense of constitutional government is in the hands of every
American. It is dependent upon fresh developments in the
realms of education and economic life. Still more, and above
all, it is dependent upon fresh and constructive developments
in foreign policy.

12 The Future of International Relations

O douce paix!
O lumiere éternelle!
Beauté toûjours nouvelle!
O douce paix!
Heureux le coeur qui ne te perd jamais!

Racine, ESTHER, II, viii

I. *A Revolution in World Politics*

Almost fifty years ago, in 1921, the distinguished American historian, James Harvey Robinson, set forth a proposition that seems fundamental to the future of the United States and of civilization. "There can be no secure peace now," he wrote, "but a common peace of the whole world; no prosperity but a general prosperity, and this for the simple reason that we are all now brought so near together and are so pathetically and intricately interdependent, that the old notions of noble isolation and national sovereignty are magnificently criminal."[1]

The astounding technological revolution of the past fifty years has brought all parts of the world and all peoples still closer together. The pathetic and intricate interdependence of which Robinson spoke has been rendered total by the applications of the sciences, of nuclear physics in particular, to technological development. For the first time in history a common peace and a general prosperity are within the range of possibility. If Robinson's proposition seemed true to a few already in 1921, how can any rational being evade its truth today?

Yet the countries of the world have scarcely harkened to the proposition. Even the United States, the most redoubtable

[1] *The Mind in the Making* (New York, 1950 ed.), pp. 228–29.

power among them, has not. Here noble isolation, in the material sense, has indeed been abandoned, in the financial sphere with a largesse without precedent in international relations. But in the spiritual and human senses, isolation and the bellows which fans isolation—ungenerous hatred—have been propelled as never before by a rising tide of nationalism, masked from many citizens by an enormous increase in the number and size of organizations which concern themselves with various forms of international co-operation.

Vilhjalmur Stefansson once remarked that "man finds it easier to change the face of nature than to change his own mind."[2] Now that men have changed the face of nature more suddenly and radically than during the whole of their history, the new face seems to confront them with the choice of changing their minds or perishing.

Nowhere is man's inability to think afresh more painfully evident than in the realm where fresh thinking is most vital, the realm of diplomacy and foreign relations. It was plain enough to the sensitive intelligence of such a great astronomer as the late Edwin Hubble, who had served as an American soldier in the First World War and as a leading protagonist and scientific adviser in the second, that the conditions behind diplomacy had been revolutionized by the weapons which began to be forged as the Second World War was ending. In the past, he said in a lecture delivered in Los Angeles in 1946,

[wars] have been tragic, ugly episodes; but with fortitude they have been bearable.

But now, in this age of technology, war is suicide. . . . Warfare with the new weapons will be the ruin of civilization as we know it. If you accept this thesis, and are interested in survival, you must accept the conclusion, namely, the absolute necessity of eliminating warfare.[3]

[2] Evelyn Stefansson Nef, Introduction to "The Great Explorers Series," in Rhys Carpenter, Beyond the Pillars of Heracles (New York, 1966), p. xvii.

[3] Edwin P. Hubble, "The War That Must Not Happen" (1946), in The Nature of Science and Other Lectures (San Marino, California, 1954), pp. 75–76.

Nothing in the twenty years since Hubble spoke these words has diminished their import! Yet the statesmen of the world have still to accept the conclusion. And much of the public, increasingly subjected to novel shocks of every kind,[4] has grown callous to the warning.

The comparison not infrequently made today between the discovery of gunpowder and of nuclear fission produces a false sense of security. War cannot be *adapted*—without destroying civilization—to the ever more extensive use of nuclear weapons, as it was to the ever more extensive use of gunpowder from the fourteenth to the twentieth centuries.[5] The arms produced in the past two decades, by the application of the modern sciences to the technology of destruction, have actually changed the meaning of the "national interest," as another sensitive mind, of a different religious persuasion from Hubble's, has just emphasized. Jacques Maritain's words, "To place the national interest above everything is the sure means of losing everything,"[6] would not have been as valid as they now are before the technological revolution in armament which took place between 1945 and 1955. Yet statesmen in all countries go on thinking and acting, and are pressured by their constituents to think and act, not in terms of what has become, but in terms of what used to be, the national interest.

Nor do political leaders, in handling international negotiations, usually recognize another closely allied truth. Unlike the first, this truth is not new, but it has been made even more difficult to grasp than it once was because of growing specialization and multiplication of data. These add enormously to the seeming complexity of the world in which foreign service officers operate. They are often literally drowned in red tape: procedure, protocol and security regulations, details of policy

4 Cf. above, pp. 48–49, 52–54, 57–59.

5 My *Western Civilization since the Renaissance* (New York, 1963; originally entitled *War and Human Progress*) attempts to sketch the history of that adaptation.

6 Jacques Maritain, *Le Paysan de la Garonne* (Paris, 1966), p. 105.

administration and of office management, information storage and retrieval fostered by constant admonitions to record everything, never to throw away anything, and to keep and file all the increasingly complicated forms in triplicate. With this exhausting routine of small matters, officials are deprived of the time and the energy needed to think about large ones, for example, how to invent new ways of dealing with foreign affairs in order to meet the revolutionary challenge of nuclear weapons. The pressure is all in the direction of taking refuge in those grooves of professional competence which Whitehead describes[7] or, when even professional competence is lacking, as it not infrequently is, of falling back on outworn clichés concerning the ways the most aggressively nationalistic powers have behaved in the past.

Such uncreative preoccupations also make it more difficult to recognize a condition frequently touched on in these pages: *All sides of historical change are interrelated.* Therefore any political policy needs to be considered in the light of its consequences, *not only in the sphere with which it is immediately concerned, but in other spheres!* Now that mistakes in foreign policy can prove fatal to an extent never before true, the reforms which this book outlines—in education, in economic, social, cultural, and constitutional life—are all contingent upon a reasonable solution of the problem of peace on earth.

Influential opinion in the United States today is governed widely by the assumption that the present conditions of foreign politics are almost identical with those which prevailed more than a quarter century ago. Then the great danger to liberty and so to civilization, was totalitarianism, especially as it was evolving among the Germans under the leadership of Hitler and his Nazis, with their expansionist outlook bred of the successful German war of 1870–71 and the bigger war of 1914–18, in which the Germans never acknowledged defeat.[8]

The defense of freedom is no less vital now than it was in

[7] Cf. above, p. 108.

[8] See Nef, *Western Civilization since the Renaissance*, Pt. III.

the nineteen-thirties,[9] but the means of defending it have changed. Then it was necessary, under Churchill's leadership, in the cause of liberty to take the risk of total war against Germany (along with her numerous European vassals and her conquering Japanese ally). It was necessary to resist with all the resources the free world could muster and not to refuse the extensive additional resources in men and materials provided, as a military ally, by a totalitarian Russia, equally threatened by Germany and then governed by an unscrupulous tyrant. The United States eventually threw all its material resources successfully into the titanic struggle, on the side of Great Britain and Free France and, however reluctantly, on the side of Russia, whose resistance contributed substantially to the defeat of Germany.

In was in the hour of victory over Japan, as well as over Germany and Italy, that the conditions of war and peace alike were profoundly altered, mainly as a result of efforts in the practical realm by scientists, many of European origin, working in the United States. As a result humanity was presented with weapons and powers which would be safe only in the hands of God.[10] The price of using these powers to resume the progress toward civilization that some of our noblest ancestors felt was being made (during the seventeenth and eighteenth centuries in Europe as well as in America) will be new policies in international relations directed toward peace and a world rule of law. The hope for Atlantic community lies in world community.[11]

In reiterating his maxim that the future has always proved different from the past,[12] Robinson foresaw in 1921 that "the future is tending to become *more and more widely* different

[9] Nef, "In Defense of Democracy," *General Magazine and Historical Chronicle* (University of Pennsylvania), October, 1939.

[10] Nef, *Western Civilization since the Renaissance*, p. 416.

[11] Nef, "L'Avenir de la communauté atlantique," in *Mélanges à la Mémoire de Jean Sarrailh* (Paris, 1966), II, 193–204.

[12] See above, p. 365.

from the past."[13] Yet, a half-century later, when this prediction seems to have proved transparently accurate, international policies continue to be framed and carried out as if the factors were essentially the same as in the nineteen-thirties, except that "the enemy" has changed. Policies are improvised and implemented on the assumption that the United States should deal with Russia or China, or both, as it is now believed this country, together with Great Britain and France, should have dealt before 1939 with the Germany of Hitler, the Italy of Mussolini, and the Japan presided over by Hirohito. The United States seems bent on fighting over again, with hindsight but with different enemies and a different strategy, the conflict in which Fascist Italy and Nazi Germany ranged themselves from 1933 to 1939 against the two leading west European countries with whom the United States was eventually allied. The United States also seems bent on fighting over again, with hindsight but with a different enemy and a different strategy, the war in which Japan added to her resources by conquering much of China and attacking Pearl Harbor.

In the past it has been common enough for nations to prepare for a previous war when faced with the prospect of another. That is what France did before 1914 and again before 1940. But the dangers in such a misreading of history have multiplied overwhelmingly since 1945. Total war no longer offers a road to a peaceful armistice as it did in the early twentieth century. As Hubble and many other wise men have warned, total war has become the road to annihilation. The road to peace is now the only road to freedom.

The difficulties in the way of building society and civilization in the United States would be great if the country were completely isolated from the rest of the world or if it were in a world by itself. The difficulties are tremendously increased

13 Robinson, *The Mind in the Making*, p. 229 (my italics).

by the fact that it is part of a world which contains many countries and peoples. The information available to Americans concerning other nations comes largely from foreign correspondents, radio commentators, diplomats, and other professors of current events, whose knowledge is seldom profound. When the information comes from scholars, it comes from specialists who not infrequently make a virtue of avoiding the attempt to see the world as a whole or of examining the meaning of what they find in relation to a world philosophy. As a result even the responsible political leaders understand far too little that is of importance in dealing with foreign nations. Americans know almost nothing of the essential nature of foreign countries. They are bombarded with a host of ill-assorted, ill-digested facts, many inaccurately presented, about events past and current. If these facts are interpreted for us, or if we try to interpret them for ourselves, the interpretation is generally made without any real understanding of the history and traditions of foreign nations, which would give the facts a meaning different from the one they now have for us. Many Americans in responsible positions, together with most of those who speak on matters of foreign policy, are in a worse case than if they were simply ignorant. They have mistaken their ignorance for knowledge.

In the nineteenth century this ignorance of Americans was in many ways greater than today. But then ignorance about the rest of the world did not matter much. However inaccurate were American opinions about the other world powers, however much Americans misunderstood the intellectual and cultural forces of history, their misunderstanding was not a serious danger when the prospect of a mortal conflict with any of these powers was remote. The only powerful nation with an important foothold on this continent was Great Britain. No other country had a conception of the objectives of civilization so much like our own. To a greater degree even than the British, we regarded economic growth, commercial and industrial prosperity, as the chief purposes of existence. Both in Great Britain and in this country the cultivation of growth and prosperity was proving consistent with increasing physical gentleness in the relations between man and man. It was proving consistent with constitutional government and with an extension of the suffrage. The two countries were in essential agreement on the position in military matters adopted by the English ever since the late sixteenth and seventeenth centuries. The British conquests, like those of the United States, had been carried on mainly at the expense of what are now called underdeveloped countries rather than at the expense of the nations of western European stock. After the loss of Calais in 1558, England never attempted to acquire sovereign authority over a substantial block of territory in Continental Europe. She intervened in Continental wars only for the purpose of preventing any single power from gaining absolute political control over the Continent. As Great Britain and the rapidly growing United States regarded each other as on the whole civilized, in spite of the strictures at the expense of Americans by writers like Mrs. Trollope and Dickens and in spite of the traditional antipathy of Americans toward the patronizing "mother country," it was not difficult to reach peaceful accommodations when issues arose between them. No love was lost; but both countries abandoned in practice the view that the best way to settle private or public differences was to fight. Since the battles of 1812–15, notwithstanding some serious friction, the two countries have never been at war with each other.

It is in the interest of civilization that these conditions of recent Anglo-American relations should now be extended to the foreign relations of all countries.

II. *Commerce as an Instrument of Peace*

As long as the conceptions of civilization and government, developed in the north of Europe and above all by the British and Americans, were accepted by the other great states, as long as no other state with fundamentally different conceptions grew strong enough to challenge Great Britain or this country, both nations remained secure from any serious threat to their existence from abroad. In the seventeenth and eighteenth centuries, the cultivation of industrial and commercial prosperity by the British came to be regarded as a sign of as great a virility and enterprise as the military qualities of some other European peoples. The old Germanic conception, expressed by Georgius Agricola in his authoritative sixteenth-century treatise on mining and metallurgy, that the calling of the soldier and even the calling of the miner were superior to that of "the merchant trading for lucre,"[14] lost strength even on the Continent. In eighteenth-century England, men had begun to put the soldier and the merchant on a par. Soldiering was becoming a *profession* in all the Western countries. During most of the eighteenth century, wars threatened the lives of great nations hardly more than duels in France in the early twentieth century threatened the lives of the participants. According to Dean Tucker, writing about British social standards in 1751, "the Profession of a Merchant is esteemed full as honourable as that of an Officer."[15] Even earlier, Defoe had claimed that "the descendants of tradesmen here [in England], for gallantry of spirit and greatness of soul, are not inferior to the descendants of the best families."[16]

During the fifty years preceding the Second World War the mercantile conception of the end of life was placed on the defensive for a variety of reasons. It was challenged in all countries by the workmen and their leaders. They claimed that the profits arising from free enterprise, and the interest

[14] *De re metallica* (1556), ed. H. C. and L. H. Hoover (London, 1912), p. 24.

[15] Josiah Tucker, *A Brief Essay on the Advantages and Disadvantages Which Respectively Attend France and Great Britain with Regard to Trade* (2d ed.; London, 1750), p. 34.

[16] *The Complete English Tradesman* (London, 1745), chap. 25.

paid on capital, were received for little or no service rendered. At the same time businessmen were discredited especially in pacifist circles by the disposition to saddle them with responsibility for making war. Again, somewhat inconsistently, businessmen were scoffed at by the Fascists and the Nazis (with their German homage for the military calling) on the ground that the place accorded merchants in non-totalitarian countries was an expression of nations not virile enough to fight![17] As the British Empire and the United States had been the strongholds of the mercantile conception of life, the weakening in the prestige of this conception as a force in international politics tended to put the United States and more especially Great Britain (where the burdens of taxation and government interference have weighed more heavily on free enterprise) in defensive positions to which they had not been hitherto accustomed.

During the same period—the late nineteenth and early twentieth centuries—the development of the submarine, and then the airplane, deprived first Great Britain and then the United States of much of the protection they had possessed against the danger of foreign attack. The development of propaganda through the newspapers and magazines, the motion pictures, the radio, and through clubs devoted to the discussion of current affairs made it easier than in the past to sow discord within the borders of these states to the advantage of warlike despotisms. The new military despotisms of Italy, Germany, and Japan felt even fewer scruples than the British and Americans had felt about seizing territory by conquest and about preparing the way for war by propaganda. The greater physical protection which the United States possessed until 1945–50 by virtue of her geographical position, as compared with Great Britain, was partly offset by the gullibility of her people to more insidious forms of attack than those of overt warfare.

Much has been heard, especially in the United States since

[17] Nef, *Western Civilization since the Renaissance*, Pt. III.

the defeat of Italy, Germany, and Japan, to the effect that force is the only language *other* peoples understand. It is sobering to reflect that less has been done than might have been to convince the rising nations of Asia, Latin America, and even Africa of what one would like to think is a fact: that they have alternatives to force as a means of maintaining their independence and integrity when it is threatened from without.

Two total wars in the twentieth century between the Western peoples themselves have confirmed, among the "underdeveloped" (some of whom have the heritage of very sophisticated cultures of their own), an impression that they have little to learn in compassion and charity from the "civilization" of the West. That impression was originally derived from the record of cruelties—both mental and physical—in connection with "colonization" ever since the voyages of Columbus. Between 1914 and 1918 and 1939 and 1945 the impression was reinforced by evidence that the Europeans and Americans, among themselves, are no less brutal and barbaric than the "disadvantaged," as the Westerners sometimes call other peoples.

At the same time the two world wars have made Great Britain, the British dominions, and especially the United States feel threatened as never before. The result, particularly in the United States, has been to breed something of a totalitarian mentality. Bolsheviks and anti-Bolsheviks caused a stir after the First World War, to the accompaniment of some witchhunting by the Department of Justice. Later communism had a lure for a few young Americans, particularly as a result of the Depression of 1929–33. Like is inclined to beget like. In both Great Britain and the United States there were also movements to create Fascist and Nazi parties, modeled on those of Italy and Germany.

Happily the totalitarian mentality has not taken possession of either the United States or the British Commonwealth. Yet every move on the part of the United States government in the direction of total war, whether or not the principal blame for the move rests with others, is likely to give totalitarian movements of both right and left a stronger hold on opinion at home without ending totalitarianism abroad. Has not the time arrived to move in the other direction, away from total war, especially when victory in such war has been made virtually impossible?

Not the least promising means of moving toward peace is the extension of the role of the private businessman in world trade. The results of communism, in countries such as Russia and her satellites, where attempts were made to suppress private business initiative altogether, have increasingly disappointed the rulers as well as the ruled. A measure of free enterprise has been introduced even in the nations which adopted the communist form of government and which have used communism to strengthen their positions as world powers.[18] What is more encouraging still, countries all over the world, including those behind the so-called iron curtain, have shown an increasing disposition to enter into ever more extensive trading relationships with the so-called capitalist merchants of the Western powers. This increasing receptivity to trade has come at a time when some business executives, especially private men from the United States, have shown an imaginative mentality in dealing with foreign countries and their people which seems to be rare among the representatives of the government, as well as among those of labor and at times even of the Peace Corps. If, as is to be hoped, the years and decades ahead bring about a growing cultural diversification in the United States, including a great increase in the products of craftsmanship, American businessmen will have available for exchange an ever wider range of products which foreign countries will want to receive. Americans, in their turn, because of the development

[18] Nef (ed.), *Bridges of Human Understanding* (New York, 1964), pp. 39 ff

of the arts and crafts at home, will have an increasing need for materials and articles which other countries can offer.

Contrary to what used to be argued by critics of "capitalism" in the late nineteenth and early twentieth centuries, the influence of private business in the development of Europe since the seventeenth and eighteenth centuries was mainly in the interest of peace. Warfare was by no means eliminated during the seventeenth and eighteenth centuries, but wars became less ferocious and less total than they had been. In European history trade became increasingly a substitute for war, to a degree that was not true in the history of earlier societies. An English authority on the art of war, writing in 1677, praised the ancient Roman military administration. "But then," he added, "I must say, their Trade was war, and I thank God ours is not."[19] A generation later Daniel Defoe, a most persuasive champion of trade and tradesmen, summed up the military history of his age by remarking that wars now spent "less blood" and "more money."[20] Commerce in western European history developed as an important element in the civilization which Europeans in the eighteenth century felt was being created for the first time in history.[21]

Shortly before the word civilization appeared in print in 1757,[22] Montesquieu composed between 1728 and 1748 his great *De l'Esprit des Lois*. It is a *summa* not only of the spirit of the laws but of the spirit of early eighteenth-century universalism and of its historical origins. In Montesquieu's considered and extensive reading of history, the natural effect of "commerce" was to improve manners and to lead toward peace. "Wherever there is commerce there are gentle man-

[19] Earl of Orrery, *A Treatise of the Art of War* (London, 1677), p. 22.

[20] "An Essay upon Projects," in Henry Morley, *The Earlier Life and the Earlier Works of Daniel Defoe* (London, 1889), p. 135.

[21] On the whole subject, compare Nef, *Western Civilization since the Renaissance*, chaps. 8, 9, 12, 13.

[22] Cf. above, pp. 35–36.

ners," he suggested, "and wherever there are gentle manners there is commerce."[23] Commerce, then, with its unwritten but respected conventions and rules, helped during the baroque age, as did the arts and crafts,[24] to lay the foundations on which the spreading industrialism of the nineteenth century rested. Now, in the later twentieth century, after the defeat of the most dangerous form of totalitarianism, Western industrialism (under United States leadership) is bringing much that is wanted in the way of technological knowledge to parts of the world which are comparatively underdeveloped industrially. The old colonialism which discredited the West is passing, as Great Britain and France have liquidated their colonial empires. Therefore commerce might now play a role in the relations between all countries similar to the one it played in Europe during the seventeenth and eighteenth centuries, as a brake on violence.

At that time the persistence of an economy of scarcity, such as had prevailed hitherto in history, was also a factor in keeping warfare within bounds. In diminishing the will to fight, commercial and cultural evolution was helped by what were then for the civilized the prohibitively high expenses of waging total war.[25]

With the coming in more recent times of an affluent economy, the material barriers to total war were undermined.[26] As a result, the problem of restraining the warlike propensities of nations has been enormously complicated, at a time when few statesmen deny that the consequence of unleashing these propensities to the full could produce only total disaster. The spread of foreign commerce and of a love of beauty, as a universal value, could help the United States, in company with

[23] See Nef, *Western Civilization since the Renaissance*, pp. 260, 316, and chap. 9 generally.

[24] See above, p. 35.

[25] Nef, *Western Civilization since the Renaissance*, chaps. 9–13.

[26] *Ibid.*, chap. 18.

the rest of the world, to avoid that disaster. But more is needed to offset the effects of multiplying armament. More must be done to divert the will to fight from national confrontations. Nationalism has become a psychological luxury which the peoples of the earth can no longer afford. The human desire for violence will have to find other less dangerous outlets!

How could the United States meet this new situation?

iii. *The Enforcement of World Peace*

It is paradoxical that, in the early twentieth century, at the very time when movements to outlaw war became more numerous and vociferous than ever before in history, the Western peoples entered anew on a period of wars. When so large a portion of the population of the earth voiced their desire to live in peace, not only with their fellow countrymen but with foreigners, how has it come about that they should have been drawn, in spite of themselves, into battle?

Never before have there been so many peace societies as in the twentieth century. Never has the subject of international law been studied so widely in universities and colleges. Never has so much machinery been devised for settling disputes between nations without recourse to war. Why have all these movements and all this machinery come to so little?

One obvious explanation for the failure of the League of Nations after the First World War was its weakness, to which the United States contributed by its refusal to join. As there turned out to be no effective strength behind that international body formed to outlaw war, the very prevalence of the desire for peace among the peoples of the earth offered an unparalleled opportunity for conquest to martial nations prepared to use war as an instrument of policy. With the rise of despotism at the service of nationalism, such countries could send their agents to encourage the pacifist movements in other countries, while they prohibited all pacifist expressions of opinion and exterminated all pacifist movements in their own. By exploiting at once the fears, the martial ardor, and the sense of frustration of their own people, they were able, with the help of modern science and technology, to build striking forces of such tremendous power that they cowed their immediate neighbors. At the same time they felt able to risk war with any of the chief pacifistically inclined powers—a category which between the wars included the United States. Political leaders in the countries where constitutional government prevailed were always devising new schemes for keeping the peace between nations. The publicity given these schemes reassured their peoples that peace was likely to last and so further convinced the foreign leaders, who were prepared to risk war for the sake of conquest, that they stood to gain by taking chances. Totalitarian ideology proved a most effective tool for rising nationalist expansion.

These lessons of the nineteen-thirties were far from lost among the political leaders who framed and implemented American foreign policy after the Second World War. They were, if anything, learned too well. The United States, whose statesmen had worked mainly for disarmament between the two world wars, has armed since 1945 in preparation for war more intensively than any nation in history, with the possible exception of Germany from 1934 to 1939. Not only did the United States join the United Nations (as it had failed to join the League of Nations); the United States became the leading sponsor of this new international body. For some time American armament was used effectively as a deterrent to Russian ambitions, to the satisfaction on the whole of the nations of western Europe, which had been allied in the war with the United States and whose citizens felt in varying degrees that Russia, with her satellite states, threatened their independence. There was always, however, a considerable element among the western Europeans (independent of members of the communist parties) who regarded this newly manifested United States power as a danger likely to *provoke* total war, at a time when the inhabitants of France and Great Britain were coming to have a greater passion for peace than ever before in history. Their fears over the possible consequences of United States policy have been increased by the growing disposition of American statesmen to reach decisions in international relations independently of the United Nations. That body was originally designed at San Francisco in 1945 to represent all sovereign states, including China, which had been on our side in the Second World War and by no means against us in the first. The chief *raison d'être* of the United Nations is to settle disputes between nations without war. The need for that has assumed greater importance almost every year since 1945. But the universality of the United Nations and its authority to handle disputes has tended rather to diminish than to augment.

The fault lies with all the member states, not least with Russia. Yet the United States bears a share of the responsibility, and this share sometimes seems large in the eyes of its principal fellow members. The disposition of the United States to operate independently on matters vital to peace has been manifested repeatedly, most strikingly in the first instance by the formation of NATO, the North Atlantic Treaty Organization, as a defense primarily against Russia and its satellite states, all members of the United Nations. Much more recently, as the threat of Russian aggression has seemed to recede, this disposition of the United States to operate independently has not diminished. American statesmen, though diplomatic and often amiable in their discussions with the representatives of their former allies (and enemies) in the world wars, have been increasingly inclined to make the decisions on vital matters of policy, and then to assume, often in the teeth of tangible evidence, that "the free world agrees." They are inclined to regard foreign statesmen who hold and state views which do not accord with American policy as at best perverse. These moves of the United States on the international chessboard have bred in some quarters, especially abroad, the suspicion that this country might effectively, if unwittingly, replace the United Nations as the guardian of peace in this dangerous world. It might adopt the policy of deciding unilaterally (without any vote of the United Nations) when, in any hemisphere, there is a case of aggression. As a logical outcome of such a decision, the United States might serve as a self-appointed policeman to put an end to aggression by the force of its arms.

Whether that is in fact ever to become settled United States policy remains to be determined. There is a certain grandeur in the conception of a new universal role for America as the future guardian of world peace, coming after a period when the totalitarian government of Germany did in fact set out to conquer other nations under the Nazi battle scream of "tomorrow the world." Furthermore, it is easier to get a single country to pursue a policy of containment than to get a group of countries to agree and to pool their resources to make such a policy effective. But the success of a unilateral policy of containment by the United States is predicated on a number of assumptions about international affairs which most of the world today, including some of the least communist elements, is not likely altogether to share.

What are these assumptions? First, such a policy would assume that the leaders of the United States have a capacity for deciding where virtue lies in any dispute between nations denied to any other sovereign state and to that collectivity of sovereign states, the United Nations, which has its headquarters in New York. Secondly, such a policy assumes that every country which adopts what the United States decides is a communist government is the eternal enemy of world peace. Thirdly, the policy would involve the assumption that the United States, now a country of little more than two hundred million people on a planet with some three billions, has sufficient power and skill and restraint, in the means of fighting it employs, to enforce peace anywhere without either exhausting its own material resources or touching off the nuclear war which is the dread of every nation not bent on suicide.

If, as has been suggested, putting the national interest above everything has become the surest way of losing everything, these assumptions should be examined not only from the point of view of the United States but (insofar as this is possible) from that of humanity. From a world point of view, would these three assumptions be consistent with the ideals upon which this nation was reared? Would they be democratic, would they be constitutional, assumptions? In making them, would the United States dedicate itself "to the proposition that all men are created equal"?

Even if it were possible to answer those questions in the affirmative, two final interrelated questions remain. First, would such a policy be the most effective means of preventing what Hubble called "the war that must not happen"? Second, would the United States be able consistently and persistently to carry out such a policy without eventually making itself, in the eyes of other nations, the very enemy of world peace we had set about to hold in check?

1. Totalitarian ideologies in political rulership were used, before and during the Second World War, as means to support national aggressiveness and expansion to such a point that it has been widely forgotten that nationalism was the fundamental cause of that total war. As has happened so often in the affairs of mankind, means have been mistaken for ends. It was not so much to make the world Nazi as to make the world German, with the help of naziism, that Germany enlisted its citizens effectively on the colossal adventure of the nineteen-thirties and early forties. It was less because they were totalitarian and despotic than because they were nationalistically aggressive, that Germany and Japan set about to conquer

their neighbors. Conquest had become part of their traditions. Isn't that lesson being too often forgotten? Whatever may be their other iniquities, neither Russia nor China has in recent times a record of conquest comparable to Germany's or Japan's. Unlike Japan, and to an extent that is not true of Germany, both have been invaded on the initiative of other countries bent on conquest, especially since the era of Napoleon. In view of modern history, therefore, it is worth inquiring whether both Russia and China might not be persuaded to renounce a portion of their liberty to fight, and eventually a portion of their national sovereignty, in return for a guarantee that any attempt to invade *them* would be resisted by force. And would not such a guarantee be more likely to satisfy them if it were enforced internationally by a police force of the United Nations than simply by the armed might of the United States acting unilaterally?

And now for the second and closely interrelated question: Might not the pursuit of a unilateral policy of containment lead the rest of the world to regard the United States as aggressively disposed?

2. Of course the elements in the United States that are inclining America toward such a policy are generally convinced that all right-thinking people everywhere should share the first two assumptions that would justify it: that we are the best judges of what is right and that a "communistic" government is wrong for any country. They are convinced, therefore, that if American statesmen present their position in each case through the ordinary diplomatic channels and inform the assembly and council of the United Nations, the United States will always have the moral support of the best elements in foreign countries, whether or not those countries align themselves on the American side, whether or not they share the military burdens and expenses that the last assumption is not unlikely to impose.

Might not an impartial, uncommitted human being (if any

such exists) from some other planet find in the first two assumptions, a trace of arrogance? Does the United States, with its complicated mixture of races, religions, and opinions, constitute God's chosen people? Are we that perfect? If we are, as not a few of us would like to believe, will other groups, other nations share that belief? If we are about to commit our all to an adventure which may put us on trial before other nations, should we not attempt to see ourselves as others see us?

The United States has produced some very great men and women, whose strength shines through all the debunking assaults that have been so frequently made on them, not least by fellow Americans, especially in recent decades. Lincoln was such a man. Herbert Croly, in his *Promise of American Life*, published sixty years ago, singled Lincoln out as an example, not least because, in Croly's judgment, his character *contrasted sharply* with that of his countrymen. "As all commentators have noted," Croly wrote,

he was not only good natured, strong and innocent; he had made himself intellectually candid, concentrated, and disinterested, and morally humane, magnanimous, and *humble*. All these qualities, which were the very flower of his personal life, were not possessed *either by the average or the exceptional American of his day;* and not only were they not possessed, but *they were either wholly ignored or consciously under-valued.*[27]

However much these qualities may be valued now in the quiet of a few exceptional and intimate American relationships, Lincoln remains for foreigners who appreciate him, as Croly did, what Croly tells us he was a century ago, "more than an American." There have been a few other Americans of his stature before and since his time, not all of them prominent. Yet the face that the United States presents to the world seldom represents that combination "of high intelligence, humanity, magnanimity, and humility," which Croly suggested

[27] *The Promise of American Life* (1909) (New York, 1963), pp. 98–99 (my italics).

"Americans, in order to become better democrats, should add to their strength, their homogeneity, and their innocence." If, as some might suggest, they have lost some of their innocence since Croly's time and Lincoln's, it would be difficult to find many foreigners who would argue that they had acquired, in exchange, the humility Croly thought they lacked.

This may be an unjust portrait of us that others paint. But if, as is our profound hope, it is unjust, the first task of the United States is to develop its foreign policy in the light of the humanity, the magnanimity, and the humility that Croly wished we might acquire. In that light, it would hardly be an act of "high intelligence" for those who lead the United States in the last quarter of the twentieth century to adopt the policy of unilateral decision which some of our critics claim we are following already.

What are the alternatives?

So far as the United States is concerned, the hope lies in gradually lending the prestige of our great power on behalf of the formation of a world outlook transcending the national interests of particular states. Such a transformation as is needed, in ourselves and in other peoples, depends partly on an amplification and a strengthening of international institutions for settling disputes and for creating world opinion. It depends also, and at least as much, on the discovery by the peoples of the earth that they have in common those universal values in the possession of which, it has been suggested, civilization consists. The acquisition and pursuit of these values cannot be the work of institutions or of any kind of collectivity. All that world institutions or national institutions can contribute—and it would be an important contribution—is to help provide conditions, to create an atmosphere, favorable to the freedom and the integrity of individuals who seek to serve the true, the good, and the beautiful. This freedom is not something that any country could or should impose on others. In fact the meaning of freedom, and especially of free government, differs greatly in different parts of the world. It would be, moreover, a contradiction in terms to force another country to be free. Each nation, like each individual, needs to work out its own destiny. Out of a rich diversity, all peoples of the earth might contribute to a unified vision of the purpose of human existence: the vision of perfection against the knowledge of the universality of imperfection.

Since at least the early seventeenth century, the ideas of a world authority and a law of nations, binding on all states, have had some reality in the realm of thought. Such ideas were advocated and discussed by a number of distinguished Europeans during the period of the late seventeenth and eighteenth centuries. No actual international authority was then established, but this was in western Europe a period of limited warfare. The limits then imposed on organized violence were nourished by polite manners, unwritten conventions, and negotiations between the ministers of the sovereign princes who then governed most of Europe.[28]

Comparing what seems superficially the success of national statecraft and diplomacy, as means of restraining warfare, with the failure of the World Court at The Hague and of the League of Nations to block total wars twice in the twentieth century, there has been in recent years in some military and diplomatic circles, a growing belief that the best hope for keeping war within bounds in the future, rests not with strengthening world authority, but with duels and negotiations between responsibly appointed officials of sovereign nations, and with partial groupings of nations, to hold other nations back from total war by the specter of nuclear destruction. It is assumed

[28] These conditions are the subject of Part II of my *Western Civilization since the Renaissance,* to which the reader is referred.

that a policy of limited warfare might prevent such destruction by providing an alternative to total war. Negotiations through existing diplomatic channels are indispensable, and there is no doubt value in partial and temporary groupings of like-minded nations. But is traditional diplomacy enough to meet the new conditions of the contemporary world? Is it not a delusion to suppose that warfare can be limited in the future without world institutions to which separate states make binding commitments?

The comparisons on behalf of the old diplomacy drawn between conditions today and those in the late seventeenth and eighteenth centuries seem unrealistic. What made for limited warfare two hundred and more years ago was not so much fear as the spread of civilization,[29] the deep sense of cosmopolitan community which the common search for civilization then implied for influential European thought. These conditions diminished the will to push the fighting,[30] at a time when the material means for waging extensive warfare grew more costly so that the expense soon became prohibitive.[31]

In all these respects, conditions have changed mightily during the last hundred and especially the last twenty-five years. With the crisis in beauty, with the moral and intellectual crisis,[32] the sense of community among the Atlantic nations has weakened.[33] Peace among *them*, moreover, is no longer enough in the face of the growth of powerful states elsewhere. At the same time states have the economic means, which they lacked in the era of limited warfare, for waging total war. It has become incomparably easier to kill and destroy on a massive scale.[34]

[29] Cf. above, chap. 2 (IV).

[30] Cf. Nef, *Western Civilization since the Renaissance*, chap. 14.

[31] Above, p. 401. For a fuller description of the expenses of war, see Nef, *Western Civilization since the Renaissance*, chaps. 12 and 13.

[32] See above, chaps. 3 and 4.

[33] Nef, "L'Avenir de la communauté atlantique," *Mélanges à la mémoire de Jean Sarrailh* (Paris, 1966), II, 194–97.

[34] Nef, *Western Civilization since the Renaissance*, esp. chap. 18.

For the first time the entire planet has become potentially one battlefield.

With this almost incredible improvement in the means of obliterating life and property, the problems of keeping warfare within bounds are very different today from what they were in the eighteenth century. There is an imperative need for strong international institutions to formulate, and eventually as an expression of evolving world opinion to enforce, the law of nations on behalf of *all* states. There is also a crying need for a renewal of cosmopolitan civilization, as our noblest ancestors conceived it, and for a flowering of such a civilization on a world stage, which our ancestors were lamentably far from achieving.

In both directions the United States could provide leadership, which is likely to be denied this country if it should pursue increasingly a policy of making unilateral decisions concerning the merits of serious international disputes, to be enforced by its own armed might. Greatly strengthened international institutions, to which all nations relinquish part of their sovereignty, are indispensable for the limitation of war in the future. If these institutions can be devised and built up in such ways as to provide encouragement for the progress of world community, they might prepare the peoples of the earth for international peace and eventually for constitutional world government. Without both, the civilization envisaged in the eighteenth century, and hitherto not achieved, can hardly be realized. Without both, as Hubble foresaw twenty years ago, "we may not [even] have a tomorrow. . . . Mankind is forced to make a choice which could lead from brute violence to a nobler level of existence."[35]

How can the United States help mankind to make that choice? Fear and hatred are the most formidable obstacles to peace. There is much fear among Americans over the hatred that is supposedly generated for the United States abroad in

[35] Hubble, "The War That Must Not Happen," pp. 81, 83.

countries with various kinds of communist governments, especially in recent years by communist governments in Asia, China's government first among them. Might it not be helpful to recognize that a similar fear exists, in China and some other parts of Asia, for the United States, many of whose citizens formerly liked to regard their country as a special friend of China? The Asians' fear of us is in part an inheritance from the period of Western colonization. As far back as the sixteenth century, the European settlement of Asia was accompanied on occasions by most ruthless and violent treatment of Asians, who were the heirs of ancient sophisticated societies that rivaled in culture the Egyptian, the Cretan, and the classical Greek and Roman societies of the Mediterranean basin.

The Asian fear of the Americans as imperialists is partly a carryover from an earlier Western outlook on colonization which the United States does not share. Yet the fear is not altogether unfounded. Is it not reasonable to suppose that the enmity for the United States in communist countries is generated at least partly by the hatred for *them* which some Americans have not hesitated to express, especially since the Russian Revolution of 1917? The fever which the anticommunists have generated among themselves (since 1945 even more in the United States than in Europe) partakes, like communism itself, of the nature of a religion.[36] The fever is fanned no doubt, like the fever of hatred in some communist states, by fear of the spread of an hostile ideology. Hatred and fear are like unhappy bedfellows who arouse together unending nightmares in place of dreams. Anticommunism, as well as communism, is charged with an emotionalism that makes rational discussion difficult.

As the years pass and increasing splits occur, rising in some cases to a high pitch of mutual distrust between nations belonging to the so-called communist bloc, the irrational nature of extreme anticommunism becomes ever more patent. Am-

[36] See above, pp. 101–2, 109.

bassador George F. Kennan, perhaps the foremost authority in the United States on the actual history of communism, recently told American senators that "the unity of the Communist bloc is a matter of the past; and it will not be restored. This Humpty Dumpty will not and cannot be reassembled."[37] The evolution which is taking place on both sides of the contemporary ideological struggle (so flimsily based on actual history)[38] reminds one of what occurred on a smaller stage, and with much smaller populations, during the religious wars that followed the Reformation during the first part of the sixteenth century.

After 1540, when, according to Ranke, it became definitely sure that the efforts at reformation of the Church of Rome had given life to several different forms of worship, it became to a considerable extent the purpose of both sides—of the Roman Catholics and Protestants alike—to destroy each other, on the ground that there was but one road to Heaven and that they had discovered it. The way to save mankind, therefore, seemed to some to root out altogether those Europeans who did not share their religion.

It was on that theory that the "Spanish fury" was undertaken in the Low Countries in the seventies of the sixteenth century and that the Armada, which so alarmed Napier,[39] was launched against Great Britain in the late eighties.

Religious hatred was by no means confined to the Spaniards or to the south Germans and Austrians who embarked later on the Thirty Years' War. Among almost innumerable examples of this extreme hatred, we have a pamphlet issued in 1590 in France by a group of Roman Catholics, who called themselves *English* Catholics. The pamphlet tells us there is only one sound reformation for the religious troubles which have beset Europe. That is the extermination of the other side. Protestantism is heresy. It must be strangled, it must be rooted

[37] As quoted in *The New York Times,* January 31, 1967, sec. C, p. 14.

[38] See above, pp. 103, 106–7.

[39] See above, p. 32.

out from every town, village, and hamlet by unstinted force. Extermination is the recipe not only for Europe, "of which France is the small eye"; extermination alone can provide the salvation "of all Christendom."[40]

As events turned out, wiser counsels eventually prevailed. After another half-century of fighting, especially in central Europe, the toleration and charity evoked by those counselors who saw war as an evil in itself, "the mother of all the vices,"[41] won over the peoples of Christendom so far as religious differences were concerned. Protestantism split into many sects and even Catholicism was no longer held together by virulent hatred of its rivals. The two sides in the ideological struggle tacitly agreed to disagree. Everyone was thenceforth at least nominally free to worship according to his conscience. Freedom in this respect has gone on increasing to this day.

It would be difficult to show that in numbers either side lost much by subsiding into a policy of non-violence. It is sobering to reflect that if the Europeans had possessed and unleashed nuclear weapons, the civilization of the late seventeenth and eighteenth centuries, on which the material triumphs of the Europeans and Americans are based, might never have existed.

Of all wars, ideological wars, which is another name for religious wars, are the least susceptible to settlement by violence. Changing circumstances have left this at least as true in 1967 as it was in 1590. Moreover, the nationalistic appeal for expansion by conquest, which has been at the root of the two world wars of the twentieth century, no longer has even the semblance of justification it once had as a way of finding "a place in the sun." The recent applications of science to technology make it readily possible for the countries of the world, including China, to nourish themselves, in reasonable affluence, if only sensible measures prevail during the next generations

[40] *Premier et Second Avertissement des Catholiques Anglois aux Francois Catholiques et a la Noblesse qui suit a present le Roy de Navarre* (Paris, 1590) (in the collection of Newberry Library, Chicago, C. 204), I, 2, II, 19.

[41] As cited in Nef, *Cultural Foundations of Industrial Civilization* (New York, 1960), p. 93.

for restricting the inordinately rapid growth of population. Never before have such opportunities existed for every country, small as well as large, to cultivate its own garden.

The objections to communism as a way of living, felt by Americans, are justified. Communism seems to us with reason to be counter to human nature as we know it. But we cannot eliminate it by force from the world any more than the communists can by force oblige the Americans to follow communist "ways of living." In discussing in 1587 the possibility of bringing Protestants back to what he professed to regard as the one true faith, a Frenchman[42] wrote:

War cannot be the means of establishing a single religious faith in our kingdom; it is rather the means of insuring that there shall be neither faith nor conscience. . . . The best means of restoring . . . one religion in France is by good example in conduct, . . . by patient instruction . . . and by the gradual amendment of the lives which Catholics lead. . . . All this will take time, it cannot be done immediately and with violence.[43]

So it is today with the single kingdom this planet has become. The true way of strengthening freedom is to demonstrate its virtues at home. In an age of enormously increased travel, the lessons will be most effective, if the pursuit of virtue is unconscious, so that foreigners can discover for themselves how a "free society" can nourish those values, and humility stands high among them, which guide individuals toward civilized lives.

IV. *Standards of Righteousness and World Peace*

So it is open to the peoples of the earth, if they restrain their instincts to become very much more numerous, to enjoy some-

[42] He was quite possibly Duplessis-Mornay (1549–1623), the chief Protestant adviser of the future French king, Henry of Navarre, but he masked himself in the guise of a Catholic.

[43] *Response a un Ligueur masque du nom de catholique anglois, par un vray Catholique bon Francois* (in the collection of Newberry Library, Chicago, F. 39193.636), pp. 5–7, 130–32 (my translation).

thing of that "general prosperity" of which Robinson wrote in 1921. It is open to them to live increasingly under world law and to build together the world government needed to limit wars among men.

The maintenance of peace through world government depends upon the power of the belief that the way to get peace is to enforce right, that the object in international relations is, in the words of Pascal, to make justice strong and force just. That can be done only when people everywhere are taught that righteousness and justice are something more than matters of opinion, that they are essentially the same for all humans, for peoples in all "stages of development."

During the past century the belief in the value and even the existence of such a thing as righteous conduct, independent of private advantage or personal idiosyncrasies, has waned again and again throughout the world. It is this more than anything else that has given the despot his power. The improved machinery for settling disputes provided by the United Nations is more than offset by the deterioration of any consensus of belief in the values we have attempted to restate in Part Two of this book. When the Western peoples cease to care for truth and virtue, when they even deny that truth and virtue exist independently of the whims of individuals, they pave the way for the triumph of evil. We shall do well to remember the words of one of the greatest English poets:

> . . . sometimes Nations will decline so low
> From vertue, which is reason, that no wrong,
> But Justice, and some fatal curse annext
> Deprives them of thir outward libertie,
> Thir inward lost. . . .

The lesson of *Paradise Lost* is a lesson that mankind had forgotten, which, let us hope, it has learned again amid a hail of bombs and steel in two world wars. We have freed ourselves from much of the hypocrisy for which our Victorian ancestors are famous, but along with it we have thrown away most of the residue of belief in the value of righteous conduct which they possessed.[44] We have made the error of assuming that it is better to deny the existence of truth and virtue than to affirm a belief in them when human nature makes their attainment, in forms invulnerable to criticism, impossible. It is shocking to find persons who talk of virtue straying away from it. But as long as there are persons who can be shocked by that, there is still hope of recovering a measure of virtue. Remove the belief in virtue, remove the capacity of men to be shocked by lapses from it, and there remain few obstacles to impede the advance of evil.

During a large part of the nineteenth century, the Western people had high ideals of righteousness, however far away from them they drifted in practice. The happy industrial and commercial developments which poured material riches into the lap of every Western nation gave their peoples an opportunity to develop a code of justice in international relations higher in many ways than had prevailed at any earlier time in Western history, unless it was to some extent in the reign of St. Louis in the thirteenth century. In the nineteenth century there were fewer pacifist societies than in the interval between the two recent world wars. There was no League of Nations. But there was more peace. What was the strongest factor working for the maintenance of peace? It seems to have been a common belief in righteousness, independent of the private ends either of the individual citizen or of the individual nation. This sense of righteousness created a bond between the great powers of the world. Fragile though the bond was, it was an important factor in preventing for a century a major international disaster. As long as this bond existed there were limits beyond which the political leaders of nations felt it unwise to go in trifling with their country's pledged word. There were also conventions of international decency which had to

[44] See above, pp. 71, 322–23.

be adhered to. There were bounds to the territorial aspirations of even the most warlike state. No European nation was free to step beyond these limits, conventions, and bounds. To do so, they knew, would arouse the general will to war among the rest of the European peoples. They knew they would encounter the spirit of resistance, expressed on the eve of the First World War by one of righteousness' great champions and one of the most powerful French poets of modern times. Charles Péguy died in the first battle of the Marne when he was forty-one, as he had shown himself willing to die in the lines he had written some years before.

> Heureux ceux qui sont morts pour la terre charnelle
> Mais pourvu que ce fut dans une juste guerre
>
> .   .   .   .
>
> Heureux ceux qui sont morts dans les grandes batailles
> Couché dessus le sol à la face de Dieu.[45]

These were lines such as were not to be written in the interval between the great war that cost Péguy his life and the great war that cost France her army.

As long as righteousness remained an ideal, it was impossible to outrage righteousness too far with impunity. The differences between the limited objectives of Bismarck, the far wider but still limited objectives of the Kaiser, and the almost limitless objectives of Adolf Hitler are a measure of the debasement of the conception of righteousness without which all treaties, pacifist societies, and leagues of nations are bound to be impotent. It is not accidental that Hitler felt free to declare openly his policy of conquest. In the nineteenth century such a declaration by the head of a state, even if he had made it before he came to power, would have put the other peoples of Europe on the alert instead of leaving them cringing in fear or averting their eyes from unpleasant dangers. It is not accidental that Hitler was able to tear up treaties and make several

---

[45] "Heureux ceux qui sont morts," *Souvenirs* (Paris, 1938), p. 124.

moves on the European chessboard before 1939, any one of which would have precipitated a general war in the nine-teenth century. A less serious move, the declaration of war by Austria on Serbia, did precipitate a general war in 1914.

Eight years after that war, a general strike was declared in Great Britain in 1926.[46] All employees (the overwhelming majority) who belonged to trade unions quit work, to show the solidarity of the entire labor class with the coal miners who had struck for better terms when their contracts with the mine owners had expired. The other wage earners went out while still under contract to work. As the British Labour party was behind the strike, it took on a sharp political mean-ing. An elderly Englishman, brought up with *Victorian* values, whose sympathies were supposed to lie with the Labour party, surprised his younger friends by expressing his firm opposition to the general strike. He explained that his posi-tion came from the shock he felt over the *breaking of con-tracts*. He suggested that the fabric of civilization rested upon respect for contracts and that the issue of honoring agree-ments, freely entered into, ought properly to take precedence over all matters of material disadvantage that were brought forward on behalf of the miners. The lightheartedness with which the Labour party overlooked that moral issue seemed to exemplify a threat to civilization.

So it was proving. At the time of the general strike in Great Britain, the League of Nations was still functioning at least partly according to the plan of its founders. It was still re-garded as an important arbiter in disputes between the various world powers. Yet for many diplomats who, like the Labour party leaders, were little concerned over the value of the pledged word, the League was already dead. They had buried it long before Hitler directed his representatives to secede

[46] A year that seems to have constituted a turning point in contemporary history, when efforts to retain standards in art, as well as in politics, were giv-ing way (see above, p. 65).

from it in 1933. What wonder was it, then, that the secession caused little more than a murmur among the great powers of Europe. In their hearts a growing proportion of the political leaders no longer recognized contracts as binding. Cynicism concerning international relations increased. It was a reflection of the decline in moral and intellectual standards that had taken place among the Western peoples everywhere since the mid-nineteenth century.

What good were pacifist societies when their aim was not to promote righteousness in international relations but to protect the bodies of the young men of their own nations? Apart from a few leaders, of whom the late Jane Addams was an outstanding example, the majority of persons who organized for peace were interested in peace less because it was righteous than because it was comfortable. War had proved horrible beyond measure, especially to men and women brought up to suppose that the infliction of intense physical cruelty was a thing of the past. Meanwhile, the sense of moral obligation to one's fellow men, which had played a great part in the decline of cruelty, was being lost. Responsibility to others was giving way to license to do whatever one pleased for one's self. It is of little help to dwell upon the destruction that war brings to property and life and to the physical fitness of the young, it is even of little help to show that war may mean the end of the human race, unless something is done to strengthen the standards of morality among the peoples of the earth. Of what good are property and long life and physical fitness if men do not use them to improve the better sides of their natures? Man can be, as Aristotle says in his *Politics*, "the noblest of all animals." But, Aristotle goes on to say,

apart from law and justice [man] is the vilest of all. For injustice is always most formidable when it is armed; and Nature has endowed Man with arms which are intended to subserve the purposes of prudence and virtue but are capable of being wholly turned to contrary ends. Hence if Man be devoid of virtue, no animal is so unscrupulous or savage, none so sensual, none so gluttonous.[47]

This is still true. It is partly the moral weaknesses so prevalent during the past century that make it possible for men to contemplate war now when total war has become suicide. It will not be enough to emphasize, as has been emphasized in this book, that war threatens to bring civilization to an end once and for all, unless something positive is done to renew the civilized values on which industrialism was built. With the world now become more of a unit than ever before in history, habits of wickedness and, let us hope, standards of righteousness spread from one country to another almost as rapidly as mechanical inventions. If there is truth in the view of Aristotle and other great sages concerning the importance of justice in the state, then a lack of harmony, such as mankind can no longer afford, is created when righteousness is not given its proper place above riches in the hierarchy of values.

If there is to be a world state in which the American people play a leading part, it can be brought into being only by a long process of building. It can be brought into being only if Americans work toward the highest goals set forth by the wisest and noblest persons of the past. The nature of these goals and possible means of approaching them have been the subject of two of the three parts of this essay. A recapitulation of the main argument should therefore point the way toward a better international order, such as could be constructed only in peace.

v. *Conclusion*

For good or ill, the United States emerged out of the civilization it originally shared with western Europe, whence came most of the ancestors of those persons who now populate it.

[47] Book I, chap. iii.

There was a time when Americans thought of themselves as a new people, free from the trials and strains of the Old World, free to ignore European experience. These were not views which most of the founding fathers shared. They were developed as part and parcel of the pioneering movement to the West, into largely unpeopled country, full of fabulous natural resources. They were views developed as part of that spirit of the frontier which influenced every aspect of American life during the nineteenth century, as F. J. Turner showed.[48]

The influence of the frontier has become so much a commonplace among Americans that a country which has not been profoundly interested in ideas, and which has found it hard to remember its dead, has almost forgotten how much of a debt it owes to Turner. When we read him now we find that (making all allowances for the differences in creative stature) Turner is, like Shakespeare, full of quotations.

If the country is in danger of forgetting the author of the theory of the frontier, it is, paradoxically enough, also in danger of failing to recognize that the conditions which created the frontier spirit among Americans no longer exist. The last frontier was crossed almost a century ago. Since then the United States has brought itself, and has been brought, within fighting range of the nations to the east and west as well as to the north and south. America, one of our poets has told us, "is neither a land nor a people."[49] That is a great danger now when we no longer have the freedom to work out our destiny by ourselves, as a race of men armed with gunpowder could have done if they had peopled the whole country and remained united at the time when Columbus visited it with his fragile little wooden sailing vessels.

From the point of view of traditions and intelligence, from the point of view of creative art, the United States is not the

48 F. J. Turner, *The Frontier in American History* (New York, 1921).

49 Archibald MacLeish, "American Letter," *New Found Land* (Paris, 1930)

best prepared nation to deal constructively with the problems of the new epoch which all peoples have entered in the twentieth century. She is probably less well prepared than France. But circumstances, and her own initiative in mass production, have placed her in a position of power where her role in determining whether or not there shall be civilization may well prove decisive.

If the country is to use its influence on behalf of the values with which this book has been concerned, we should have the faith to discard two preconceptions of our time, though the discarding of either appears superficially to add to the difficulty of discarding the other. One is the view that immediate worldly success is a test of the merit of a work of thought or art. The other is the view that whatever a man does with his mind is without influence for good or ill upon the course of history. That view has always been held by some people, but it has become especially prevalent in recent decades. The best answer to it was given almost a century and a half ago by Tocqueville. In ending his great book on *Democracy in America*, he wrote:

I am aware that many of my contemporaries maintain that nations are never their own masters here below, and that they necessarily obey some insurmountable and unintelligent power, arising from anterior events, from their race, or from the soil and climate of their country. Such principles are false and cowardly; such principles can never produce aught but feeble men and pusillanimous nations. Providence has not created mankind entirely independent or entirely free. It is true that around every man a fatal circle is traced, beyond which he cannot pass; but within the wide verge of that circle he is powerful and free; as it is with man, so with communities. The nations of our time cannot prevent the conditions of men from becoming equal; but it depends upon themselves whether the principle of equality is to lead them to servitude or freedom, to knowledge or barbarism, to prosperity or wretchedness.

The task of churchmen, scholars, teachers, artists, businessmen, lawyers, and future craftsmen is to hold out to man the vision of a better world, here on earth as well as in the hereafter. Their task is to provide mankind, with the help of reason, of compassion and love, of the sciences and the arts, with a pattern of that better world. Their task is to re-create a belief in truth, righteousness, and beauty, as the ends of civilization, in spite of the impossibility for mere man to attain to a complete and perfect knowledge of these values. These tasks are not community tasks. They must be initiated by individuals of genius. But every man and woman, insofar as any trace of humanity exists within them, can do something to facilitate the accomplishment of these tasks in a simple, common-sense way.

Here a lesson could be learned from the recent past. We have left the world of the nineteenth century, where an attempt, however imperfect, was made to see that honor was rewarded, where men were able to say with a semblance of truth that honesty was the best policy. There is little attempt now to see that honor is rewarded or even to admit that honor exists. Honesty, in the deeper sense, is the best policy less frequently than in the nineteenth century. Therefore, if men are to work for honor, truth, and beauty, they must be willing to lose by the work. In the nineteenth century, especially in England and the United States, for almost the first time in Western history some supposed that in this world the good were rewarded. They began to forget that behind many actions, even in the realm of scholarship and learning, lay ulterior and even sinister motives. Many reasonably honorable men of the older generation persist today in the idea that there is some connection between worldly rewards and virtue, when this is less true than it was a century ago. In the meantime the bad men and the evil elements in man have taken advantage of the persistence of this nineteenth-century idea. As things have turned out, to play the game in that old nineteenth-century way is to play the game for the destruction of what is best in man.

Is it not at just this point that it might be possible to break away from the vicious circle of Pascal, according to which a weak society encourages a weak system of education, and a weak system of education, a weak society? If it is possible, then all honorable men should work ceaselessly to find the good in the world that lies about them, much as the placer miners scour the streams for gravel containing gold. Faith, righteousness, and beauty are scarce. Truth is difficult to distinguish from falsehood. Good is difficult to distinguish from evil. Love is less publicized than hatred. The efforts to domesticate which make for friendship require time and humility, when hurry and self-advertisement have become the currency of the accepted active life.

Therefore, it is more now than ever before by efforts to steer an independent course that humans can serve what is best in themselves, and in others who are close to them, in ways which will encourage what is best in humanity. Some lines of John Donne's suggest the difficult and steep ascent that is required of those who seek the goals of civilization:

> And the right; aske thy father which is shee,
> Let him aske his; though truth and falshood bee
> Neere twins, yet truth a little elder is;
> Be busie to seeke her, beleeve mee this,
> Hee's not of none, nor worst, that seekes the best.
> To adore, or scorne an image, or protest,
> May all be bad; doubt wisely; in strange way
> To stand inquiring right, is not to stray;
> To sleepe, or runne wrong, is. On a huge hill,
> Cragged, and steep, Truth stands, and hee that will
> Reech her, about must, and about must goe;
> And what the hills suddennes resists, winne so;
> Yet strive so, that before age, deaths twilight,
> Thy Soule rest, for none can worke in that night.[50]

It is not by popular appeals that Americans can best help to build the world order upon which the future of the United

[50] "Satyre III," *The Poems of John Donne*, ed. Herbert J. C. Grierson (Oxford, 1912), I, 157.

States and the American pursuit of happiness depend. Americans need to rewrite two famous and enormously influential passages in Rousseau and Marx. In their original form these passages have been leading several generations all over the world away from truth. If they were rewritten they could help to lead mankind away from the destruction which would involve the annihilation of truth in the century that lies head. Let these passages then read:

"Wisdom, virtue, and beauty were born free, but everywhere they are in chains. Truth-loving, virtue-loving, beauty-loving individuals of the world unite. You have nothing material to gain. You have the opportunity of serving humanity. You have the opportunity of bringing about a rebirth of the mind and heart; of instilling the fervor of the love the best of you feel, for those who are closest to you, among people everywhere who are starving for it."

Index